Mingus:
A Critical Biography

Mingus:
A Critical Biography

Brian Priestley

A Da Capo Paperback

To Amei,
who gave me
the strength and the typewriter
and without whom
a lot of things
would have been
harder to understand

Library of Congress Cataloging in Publication Data

Priestley, Brian, 1946–
  Mingus, a critical biography.

  (A Da Capo paperback)
  Discography: p.
  Includes bibliographical references and index.
  1. Mingus, Charles, 1922–   . 2. Violinists, violoncellists, etc.—United
States—Biography. 3. Jazz musicians—United States—Biography. I. Title.
[ML418.M45P7   1984   785.42′092′4 [B]   83-26155
ISBN 0-306-80217-1 (pbk.)

This Da Capo Press paperback edition of *Mingus: A Critical Biography*
is an unabridged republication of the first edition published in
New York in 1983. It is reprinted by arrangement with Quartet Books, Inc.

Published by Da Capo Press, Inc.
A Subsidiary of Plenum Publishing Corporation
233 Spring Street, New York, N.Y. 10013

Manufactured in the United States of America

Contents

Illustrations

Acknowledgements

Without the following, this book could not exist in its present form. I am deeply indebted to Susan Graham Mingus for her encouragement and co-operation, and likewise to Celia Zaentz; to Roger Rowland for his enormous file of Mingus documentation and much other assistance, and to Charles Fox for access to his general reference library; to Nat Hentoff, who has written more on Mingus and set down more of Mingus's own words than any other commentator; and to two musicians who gave so freely of their time to point me in the right direction, Jimmy Knepper and Dannie Richmond.

The copyright owners of the illustrations, pictorial and musical, are mentioned elsewhere, but I am also beholden to all those writers and interviewees whose previously published comments are listed under 'References', as I am to those whose conversations with me have been quoted. For further help of various kinds, my gratitude goes to: the BBC and especially David Perry; Hugh Attwooll (CBS); Debbie Balsley (California Dept. of Health Services); Bill Banbury; Alam Bates; Joachim Berendt; Johs Bergh; Ran Blake; Alfonso Bravo (Arizona Dept. of Health Services); Roy Burchell (*Melody Maker*); Chris Burn; Philippe Carles (*Jazz Magazine*); Ian Carr; John Chilton; Alan Cohen; Howard Colson (BMI); Michael Cuscuna; Stanley Dance; Ed Dipple; Mike Doyle; Frank Driggs; Jim Fishel (CBS); Sebastian Freudenberg; Dave Green; Jasper Hampton; James 'Potts' Jackson; Lee Jeske; Art Lange and Jack Maher (*Down Beat*); Joe McEwen (CBS); David Meeker (BFI); Tony Middleton; Ilhan Mimaroglu (Atlantic); Dan Morgenstern

(Rutgers University Institute of Jazz Studies); T. Neeswinter (National Personnel Records Center); Howard Riley; Tony Russell; K.C. Sulkin; J.R. Taylor (Smithsonian Institution); Patricia Willard; and Bob Yates.

Finally, my thanks to Janet Law, Clare Walters, Richard Williams and Chris Parker of Quartet, and to Karin Ziemann for her secretarial assistance.

Musical Examples

Introduction

As a representative of a racial and cultural minority of the society into which he was born, Charles Mingus took some beating. At least in part, this was because – whatever the therapeutic potential of his musical endeavours – he reacted to his own situation in a manner that was often self-defeating, and certainly revealing to the outside observer. This in turn was symptomatic of the generation which came to maturity during and immediately after World War II, and which was no longer content to adopt either the seeming sub-servience of a Louis Armstrong or the sophisticated scorn of a Duke Ellington.

For black Americans, the hopes and fears of that decade of indecision, 1945–55, were expressed in markedly different ways. The two artistic archetypes of their generation, Charlie Parker and Dizzy Gillespie, reflected a deep polarization of attitudes: the alienated yet hypercreative Parker sacrificed himself, fully conscious, on the rocks of prejudice and cultural ignorance; while Gillespie, heeding that awful warning, waited until he reached the shores of economic and creative security before even obliquely criticizing American society. Mingus (five years younger than Dizzy, less than two years younger than Bird) was temperamentally drawn to follow both these directions. In both, he nearly succeeded, and he constantly lived out the tension between such mutually exclusive approaches. It is small wonder, then, that his artistic development did not follow a smooth graph of continuously evolving achievement and – if this is not being too cynical – small wonder that his tragic death came just as he was entering the Dizzy Gillespie 'elder statesman' class.

Unlike primitive cultures which feed and clothe their musicians, and venerate them almost in the same way as religious leaders, Western societies now leave them to fend for themselves within the market system. It is this system which encourages the increased fame of an artist immediately after his decease, and it is the Western criteria for posthumous evaluation which emphasize such factors as innovation and influence on others. Measured against these criteria, Mingus comes out extremely well. His redefinition of collective improvisation in jazz and his introduction of episodic structures were as important historically as his incorporation of modal materials and other exotica such as repeating bass-figures. Similarly, his insistence on featuring his own compositions from the mid-1950s onwards set an example for other musicians, as did his tenacity in running the longest-lived of the early attempts at creating a specialist record company owned by musicians themselves. As well as seeking to alter the mechanics of reaching the jazz audience, Mingus also wished to improve the musicians' relationship with the audience and, although by no means the first jazzman to be interested in painting and literature, his attempts to co-opt the descriptive virtues of these arts were only part of a wider (and, for the time, untypical) concern to force otherwise passive listeners into an involvement with the very act of creating music.

Compared to innovation and influence, Western society has less enthusiasm these days for the continuity of tradition which was the hallmark of pre-technological cultures; and it has not yet understood the concept of asserting individuality as an expression of that tradition – doing your own thing in order to be human just like the rest of us – which is essentially an Afro-American concept. Nevertheless, it is by this standard that Mingus's music will eventually be assessed. Its utter uniqueness of tone and accent (even when stylistically derivative) is what will guarantee his place in the jazz pantheon, rather than innovations which have already been absorbed, in some cases unconsciously. For, unlike the enormous influence of Mingus's bass-playing, directly traceable although often overlooked except by other bassists, the influence of anyone who succeeds as the 'composer' of a music which nevertheless remains 'improvised' is difficult to grasp, for practitioners as well as observers. In fact, Mingus's efforts to involve his audience in what was going down on the bandstand can also be seen as an attempt to dramatize the role of the composer in jazz. Duke Ellington in his best work had set such an impossibly high standard of cannibalizing his musicians' very souls, as if by some beneficent form of osmosis, that only a handful of bandleaders have ever tried to emulate him (as opposed to copying his stylistic features). No one, until Mingus, had taken what Ellington achieved with New Orleans and swing-style musicians and tried to apply it to the more rigid and complex language of bebop, and to the more insistent virtuosity of its players. That Mingus often made it work should not blind us to the enormity of his self-imposed task.

Of Mingus's extramusical efforts to dramatize his own personality, some mention must also be made here. If these are largely subordinated in the following pages to the description and assessment of his musical career, this is partly because of the existence of his autobiographical work *Beneath the Underdog*. One of the subsidiary aims of my initial research was to provide a context and a counterweight for Mingus's book, and it is hoped that, whether the reader is baffled, infuriated or impressed by *Beneath the Underdog*, the present book will render it somewhat more tangible. Although the events Mingus covers are almost exclusively confined to the first three decades of his life, and therefore to my first two chapters, they all contain at least a symbolic truth. Careful verification can also relate many of them to objective reality, but their purpose as narrated by Mingus is clearly to explain to his audience the pressures on a sensitive and self-aware artist in his position. And Mingus was nothing if not self-aware. Before his final illness was correctly diagnosed, he offered his own tongue-in-cheek diagnosis: 'I think I have an extremely aggravated case of paranoia.'

But his book is also symbolic in another way. For, although Mingus was self-*aware*, he also (like many creative artists) had a self-*image* which was slightly removed from reality. His musical companion for so many years, Dannie Richmond, makes the comment: 'I still feel that a lot of Mingus's writing was fantasy, [not only in *Beneath the Underdog* but] throughout his life.' If this applies to his writing of words, how much more true must it have been of his composing? And, however liberating this free-flowing fantasy was for the act of composition, how problematic must it be to conceive music which – whether actually notated on paper or (as Mingus later found preferable) not written down at all – can after all only be brought into being through the sympathetic collaboration of others? Put another way, is it better to be a composer who makes impossible demands on his collaborators, or one who writes what musicians can easily play in their sleep and whose music is then played by musicians who actually *are* asleep?

Some of the musical details included in the following book, which show exactly why musicians could not afford to sleep while playing with Mingus, may possibly have the opposite effect on readers. And sadly, because of the relative perfection of the technological approach to music in the West, it is easier to be specific about structural and to some extent metrical complexities than it is to describe the rhythmic subtlety within a single bar of jazz, let alone the enormous flexibility of tonal expressivity which even players not especially noted for this gift demonstrate. So far, we do not possess the vocabulary to discuss these particular factors, which are so significant in the impact of jazz and related Afro-American music. If there are gaps then in describing the minutiae of a specific piece, there are equally gaps in our ability to quantify the patterns of tension and release which determine the effectiveness of a whole performance, or its emotional ambiguities, so that the writer is reduced to encouraging the reader to listen for him- or herself.

As to the musical data which can be quantified, the responsibility of a biographer, especially the author of the first biography of a major artist, is surely to get it all down – just as much as the names and the places, and the inevitably conflicting opinions. Naturally, there is still an element of selection and emphasis involved here, as in any 'impartial' documentary film, but my aim has been to present as much material as possible for the would-be 'interpreters' of Mingus to pick over at their leisure. Clearly, though, anyone who seeks a simple, one-sided interpretation of such a complex figure is asking for trouble. So it can hardly be surprising that there are few conclusions here, but rather an expression of the conviction that Charles Mingus was one of the most important musicians to have transcended his origin in the America of the twentieth century.

Brian Priestley
March 1982

1

Bass-ically Speaking

Perhaps the baby was born under a bad sign: unlike the self-styled Black Bull, Stevie Wonder (13 May), and unlike the Suave Bull, Duke Ellington (29 April), Charles Mingus Jr was born under Taurus with Taurus rising – otherwise known as the Bull in a China Shop. Probably it was lucky that he was born at all, for when he emerged into the world on 22 April 1922 (9.30 p.m., Pacific Standard Time), his mother had only twenty-three weeks to live. Certainly the Texas-born Harriett Sophia Mingus was already so ill with chronic myocarditis, an inflammation of the heart muscles often associated with alcohol consumption, that on 31 August her husband was honourably retired from his post of Staff Sergeant with the Quartermaster Corps on an army base in Arizona – to be precise, in Nogales ('walnut-trees' in Spanish), which is right on the Mexican border.

Sergeant Mingus had joined the army in 1915 at the age of thirty-eight after a frustrating career in the post office, but, when he moved the family back to 1545 East 52nd Street, Los Angeles, it was to obtain medical attention for Harriett, who nevertheless died on 3 October, aged thirty-four. Intriguingly, her death certificate shows that, although her own mother was of Chinese descent, her father was born in England. (Unfortunately, with the whole of England to choose from, and with a common name like John Philips, there seems little hope of tracing the lineage further.) Sergeant Mingus, born in 1877 in North Carolina, was the offspring of a liaison between a black farm-hand and a Swedish lady in the 'big

1

house', who was claimed to be a cousin of the late President Lincoln. In Mingus's autobiography, *Beneath the Underdog*, it is also suggested that the Sergeant's own father was not only an African chieftain but retained an African name. This may, however, be artistic licence, especially since 'Mingus' is so close to one of the old spellings and to the still surviving pronunciation of the Scottish name Menzies.

Nevertheless Sergeant Mingus, whom Charles Jr grew to resemble in many ways, was sufficiently light-skinned and blue-eyed to accept the prevailing view of that time that, in the words of Bill Broonzy, 'If you're white, you're alright/And if you're brown, stick around/But if you're black, oh brother, get back.'[1] The extent to which this attitude was adopted by blacks themselves was noted by bassist Pops Foster, who spoke of 'a coloured church . . . that had seating by colour. The lightest ones down in front and darker and darker as you went back.'[2] And, when Charles Jr was asked fifty years later whether his father was ashamed of his ancestry, he replied:

He never gave us any pride in being black. I don't think he was *ashamed*, I don't think he knew anything about it, about the fact that there was anything to be proud about. And I think he put his hopes in the strength of the fact that he passed for white. And I guess that meant security to him. That's what it means still, isn't it, in the way that whites are employed without thinking about it, automatically?

While this may have given him some financial security, the deep emotional insecurity of having passed for white and the consequent fear of being found out made its mark, even before the darker complexions of his children put paid to this idea. The fact that he took out some of his frustrations on these children can hardly have been a coincidence:

He was almost impossible to like, anyway, 'cause he was a soldier, you know, an ex-soldier. So the quick way to get you to do something was with his fist. Or a belt held tight by the fist, and you could feel the fist in the belt. I would say, looking back, I'm kinda glad he whipped me for some things, but I think he kinda overdid it, a little cruel . . . I know that he would fight anybody. You know, if that point came, he would fight even a white man . . . My father took a rifle – he was a very good shot, everybody knew that – he let that be known by shooting sparrows flying, you know. But something happened one day, and we walked down to these people's house that he called 'the blacks', and he told me to stay away from them, 'they were no good' . . . I guess that my father scared me, he made blacks sound very unbeatable. Something that you would have to be careful if you were going to fight one, because you could get cut.[3]

The social pressures which aggravated such attitudes must have been considerable for, while the importance and size of greater Los Angeles was growing rapidly during the 1920s, its coloured population increased by 150 per cent within the decade. And, as this rate of increase was maintained in the 1930s, the small suburb of Watts three miles south-east of the centre of Los Angeles changed from a racially mixed poor quarter to a classic example of the overcrowded black ghetto.

Nevertheless, in his childhood Charles Jr may have been partly insulated from the worst side-effects of this situation, and indeed he described himself as overprotected. The white saxophonist Art Pepper, who also spent his early years in Watts and later worked alongside Mingus in the early 1940s, categorized the bassist's parents as essentially 'middle-class'. Certainly, when Sergeant Mingus remarried and moved into 1621 East 108th Street (where Charles Jr lived until the start of 1944), the personality of his stepmother became a crucial factor in Mingus's upbringing, and not only by indulging his taste for ice-cream. Born in South Carolina and resident in California since 1920, the half-Indian Mamie Carson (née Newton) clearly had aspirations which accorded well with Sergeant Mingus's notions of superiority. And, most importantly, she approved of the value of European classical music for, although the ageing head of the family was fairly remote from his children's concerns, Mamie's own son (who now became Odell Carson Mingus) had already been encouraged to take an interest in music; he eventually took up the Spanish guitar, presumably playing folk music since this was the main use of the guitar at the time. But, for Mingus's older sisters Grace and Vivian, the instruments deemed most suitable were those most strongly identified with the European classical tradition, namely the violin and the piano.

Apart from the sound of his sisters practising, however, the only music allowed in the home (via the radio, or later, the victrola) was devotional music but, ironically, it was the religious leanings of Mingus's stepmother which were responsible for his earliest contact

3

with Afro-American music. Officially the Mingus family attended the African Methodist Episcopal Chapel, which was relatively staid in its worship, the term 'African' merely designating a black break-away branch of a basically Anglo-Saxon tradition – indeed, Mingus's later attempts 'to trust, to give, to flagellate himself emotionally to be "better" and more understanding of others',[4] in the words of Nat Hentoff, must have derived directly from this Protestant background. But, whereas his father's more earthy side surfaced regularly in his overbearing nature and unbridled temper, his stepmother was only able to abandon her strict deportment in a religious context; hence her preference for going to the local Holiness Church, home of the Holy Rollers. 'My father didn't dig my mother going there,' Mingus said. 'People went into trances and the congregation's response was wilder and more uninhibited than in the Methodist church. The blues was in the Holiness churches – moaning and riffs and that sort of thing between the audience and the preacher.'[5]

So, while Grace and Vivian accompanied their father to the A.M.E. Chapel, young Mingus was at least sometimes taken along to the Holiness Church, which turned out to be a musical as well as a spiritual experience. Not only was the singing of both choir and congregation filled with a wild emotionalism which expressed itself in uncontrollable vibrato and melismatic improvisation, but according to Pops Foster: 'The Holiness Church was the only one that didn't consider music sinful.'[6] As a result, the use in their services of those instruments sanctified by mentions in the Bible, such as cymbals and sackbuts (trombones), made the singing sound even more like a precursor of big-band jazz than most other early gospel music. And it was here too that Mingus learned, subconsciously at the time, the crucial importance of an underlying beat sufficiently tight to allow all kinds of rhythmic flexibility on top. 'If you go to a white church, they clap their hands like this, right together. You go to a black church, prrrrwopp! 'Cause black people would never get together, they prove it in church. They're on the upbeat every time, but it's freer. Their hands are so free they fall sloppily on the upbeat . . . The white people like it stiff, the black people like it loose. Different strokes for every folks!'[7]

Mingus's first tentative steps towards the world of music were most easily taken by lifting the lid of the piano, and vocally, and in both of these ways he quickly demonstrated a responsive and increasingly accurate ear for pitch. But it was not until he was at least six and possibly older that his father, bowing to the inevitable,

4

agreed to order an instrument from Sears Roebuck for Christmas. The trombone, which Mingus selected because he had seen it used in the Holiness Church to provide a Dixieland-style bass-part (as in the recordings of Reverend A.M. Kelsey), was a revealing but ill-advised choice: even though beginning to be big for his age, he would have had difficulty extending the slide fully. However, the question proved to be somewhat academic, since the choirmaster, whose offer of lessons was readily accepted, seems to have had some holes in his own musical education. Thus Mingus was soon left with a little encouragement from his sisters and a lot of playing solely by ear, a much more hit-and-miss process with the brass family than it is with saxophones, woodwinds, strings or keyboards, where there are visual clues to the location of different notes. But, although Mingus finally gave up, the fact that he became the only post-Ellington composer to display a real affinity for the instrument can be linked to this early love affair with the trombone.

Sadly, the story of Mingus's music lessons was repeated in his schooling, and one of his constant themes in later life was the way in which he (and so many others) had been disadvantaged. As an articulate and sensitive adult, he felt strongly that he had missed out, and that he was misjudged by others as a direct result. 'People may not underestimate my intelligence, but they overestimate my education,'[8] was one of his more concise expositions of this grievance. Apparently his apathy in elementary school and onwards was caused by an early encounter with a racist teacher who referred to him in front of the other children as a 'yellow nigger'. 'If you called *each other* "nigger", that was an insult,' said Mingus, but this was doubly traumatic since at home he had been told a light complexion made him superior to blacks. The teacher's reaction may well have been a follow-up to the playground incident mentioned in *Beneath the Underdog* and subtly embellished in a later interview: 'I was looking at a white girl one day a little closer – more than looking – and her brothers pointed out to me. . . With slaps they pointed it out, that I too was black.'[9]

Colour aside, this activity of Mingus's resulted in the school's decision to transfer him to an establishment for problem children called Boyle Heights, a decision communicated to Mingus's parents in the headmaster's office. For once, Sergeant Mingus's temper and pride told in the boy's favour, and he kicked up an almighty fuss: 'I remember the principal, a fairly conscientious man, didn't want to make a hasty decision. While we were all there, he checked by telephone to find out what my IQ tests had shown. It turned out, as

5

my father later explained to me, that "even by a white man's standards, you're supposed to be a genius".[10] So Mingus remained at the 103rd Street grade school and became a yellow nigger, in other words not even a minority of a minority, but an outcast, a freak: 'I just found myself with the Japanese, the Greeks, the Italians, and Mexicans, and a few more guys like me.'[11]

Apart from his childish curiosity about little girls, the one thing Mingus was becoming emotionally dependent on was music – the music played by his sisters, the music in the Holiness Church, and the music he himself tried to wrest from the trombone. The moment when these influences came together, by being combined in something far greater, was the moment which changed his life. At the age of eight or nine, he was playing around with his father's crystal set late one night and came across the sound of Duke Ellington's band, playing his theme song *East St Louis Toodle-oo*. He was thrilled to the core by this performance (not necessarily a record, as these were not much used in the early days of radio, but quite possibly a remote broadcast from Ellington's first West Coast trip during the summer of 1930), but obviously it did not mean as much in detail to the young Mingus as it would in later years. It is not even clear what immediate effect it had on Mingus's attitude to music, except that he definitely did not see it as a separate category from what he had heard up until then – it was just *more* music, and he wanted to hear more of it. He searched the radio waves as often as he could for similar sounds and, impressed by the mobile trombone of Tricky Sam Nanton, spent many fruitless hours trying to convert inspiration into the reality of his own playing.

He was also impressed with his own dedication to the instrument and, after making at least some headway, he approached another young trombonist Britt Woodman, who was two years older and just starting high school. With the misplaced confidence of the self-taught, Mingus 'went to where I knew he was playing because I wanted to cut him'.[12] But Woodman came from a highly musical family, with a trombonist father who had already worked with pioneer West Coast bandleader Sonny Clay back in 1922, recorded with him in 1925–6 and was in the pit orchestra of the Los Angeles Folies Theatre throughout the 1930s; William B. Woodman Sr re-emerged in the 1950s with Teddy Buckner's Dixieland band. So Britt, well on his way to becoming a master of the instrument, would have found it easy to show up the deficiencies in Mingus's playing and even to shame him into giving up altogether. Instead, he reacted favourably to this younger kid's enthusiasm for music in

6

general and for learning how to do what Woodman could do, and a lifetime friendship was born.

Britt noted that Mingus did not fully grasp the principles of reading music, despite the informal hints he had had from his sisters, and set about relating this to his ear knowledge. In the process, he discovered that Mingus really had an excellent pitch sense and indeed, if his reading had been able to develop simultaneously and given him an early familiarity with the names of the notes, he would already have been able to claim 'perfect' pitch. Woodman helped to expand on this by playing him chords and encouraging him to identify the constituent parts, which Mingus did with ease as well as adding other notes; Britt's reaction was, 'Sounds weird but it sounds good – like Duke.' And, now that the subject of Ellington had come up, Britt offered Mingus the supreme gift and sought his parents' permission to take the youngster to a live show featuring the Ellington band. 'I never heard no music like that in church. I nearly jumped out of the bleachers. Britt had to hold me. Some place, something he did, I screamed.'[13] Most significantly of all for Mingus's future career, Britt pointed out tactfully that, despite Mingus's progress which was considerable, given his lack of technical knowledge, he was perhaps not really cut out for the trombone anyway. Britt suggested instead the stringed instrument closest in range to the trombone, namely the cello.

Part of the idea was that on the cello Mingus would be able to express better the romantic, rather lush sounds he seemed drawn to, both in the European music he and Britt had discussed and in the work of Ellington's new 1932 recruit from the West Coast, Lawrence Brown, who impressed both of them and who, incidentally, had played cello as a child. It was also part of the idea that Mingus would gain inspiration and assistance from his sister Grace, who was now a more than adequate violinist; and that, having finally become acquainted through Britt with the bass clef, he would have no further problem with his reading. This hope proved vain, since Britt's studies with his father had not prepared him for the natural preference for ear-playing of one who had still not conquered the hard graft of deciphering the dots fluently; nor had they prepared him for the approach of the door-to-door salesman who gave Mingus cello lessons. 'He took advantage of my ear and never taught me the fingerboard positions. He'd give me the first note and I'd be gone. My mother thought I was good because I was playing the tunes.'[14] Nevertheless, the change of instrument forced Mingus to tackle 'classical' trifles which began to open up the world of

European music more fully for him, and prompted some early compositional experimentation: 'when I laid my cello down with my sisters Vivian and Grace to figure out on piano why my sister's violin clashed with my cello on certain notes'.[15] (The later Mingus's tendency to exaggerate for effect is demonstrated by his claim to have been five years old at the time.) But his combination of bravado and talent not only enabled him to play as an equal with his sisters in a trio that became good enough to give concerts at the Methodist Chapel, but it got him into the cello section of the Los Angeles Junior Philharmonic. However, when he went on to Jordan High School and joined the school's Senior Symphony Orchestra, a smaller ensemble in which Grace was already playing violin, he discovered that his basic musicality could not make up for his slow reading. 'They were waiting for a cello player and knew about me. When I got there I couldn't make it.'[16]

Interestingly, a similar situation obtained with Mingus's intellectual growth. Although he turned in some terrible grades at school because of his disaffection, he felt creatively involved with words and recalled with pride even in 1960 how he had written an appeal for the Community Chest, which he called *Give and Let Live*. His vocabulary in fact became enviably wide, although occasionally off-target during his frequent moments of excitement, and the range of subjects of which he had some knowledge even wider. Indeed, he may have seemed to many to have a butterfly mind, incapable of pursuing one line of thought logically for more than a moment, but it is perhaps truer to say he had the instinct of a magpie, constantly searching for new information to absorb and sometimes to digest. In the manner of the neighbourhood encyclopaedia-owner whom Mingus described in his autobiography as telling him about Amerigo Vespucci, Julius Caesar and Buffalo Bill, he began to educate himself as a teenager by reading Freud, H.G. Wells and works on hypnosis, theosophy and oriental religion. Looked at in this light, it is less surprising that the underprivileged and unwilling school pupil gave his musical compositions titles which related to extrasensory perception, reincarnation, Gregorian chant or, in the case of *Pithecanthropus Erectus*, palaeontology.*

Already in his teenage years, he was preparing himself to become the garrulous and opinionated individual who, in the words of his

---

*In 1964, Mingus's bookshelves were found to contain works by Wells, Sartre, Churchill, D.H. Lawrence and Rilke, among others.

widow Susan, 'was capable of talking for four hours straight with twenty other people in the room'. But initially this development was purely an internal one, for Mingus's verbosity only came to the fore after one or two adolescent problems had been sorted out. His insecurity about his physical strength and ability to defend himself had been fostered at an early age, especially by the bullying of one of his fellow 'outcasts' called Coustie (whose name is changed to 'Feisty' in *Beneath the Underdog*). And this was gradually overcome by the judo lessons from two other outcasts Noba and Maso (or Mosa) Oke, and by the encouragement of Britt Woodman in taking up boxing and weightlifting. Following on from this, the Bull acquired an ability to treat sex as a sport, for which he credited the father of another high-school friend Buddy Collette, which probably solved some physical problems also, while leaving unassuaged Mingus's yearning for Love-with-a-capital-L. However, one of the most revealing moments in the whole of Mingus's book (and no doubt intentionally revealing, even rationalizing) is the remark that, in the act of sex, 'For the first time Charles felt completely accepted by a black Negro.'[17] In fact the final problem for Mingus at this period was having to decide to be black rather than yellow: if being born black in a white-dominated society is a cross to bear, then choosing wholeheartedly to join the crucified is more painful still. And what evidence there is suggests that it was a conscious choice to be an underdog instead of an outcast, and that, having made an intellectual decision to relinquish his father's delusions of superiority, he felt compelled to expose the similar delusions of white society.

Not surprisingly, perhaps, these same teenage years saw Mingus's musical life start to take on a positive shape. In high school he was exposed to records of some heavyweight European music which took his interest several stages further, without disrupting his overall view that good music is one indivisible spectrum, and he at least browsed enviously in the record stores. In those Depression years, 'They had a few hillbilly and a few records they called rhythm and blues. But it wasn't a big market then. The record stores were mainly for white people. They had classical music. I remember Richard Strauss, Debussy, Ravel, Bach, Beethoven.'[18] Mingus's particular favourites at the time seem to have been the advanced but pre-atonal works of the first three, and he mentioned specifically Strauss's *Death and Transfiguration* on more than one occasion. But the influence of his contemporary Buddy Collette, who, only eight months older than Mingus, played clarinet both in the school symphony orchestra and the school jazz band, inspired the cellist to try and express his feeling for jazz once again. A distant impression of his somewhat mixed success at using his cello in the school jazz group may be gained from the rather feeble efforts of cellists George Koutzen and Jackson Wiley on Mingus's 1952–4 record sessions. According to his book, Mingus's next change of instrument was suggested by Collette, but Mingus later said that the idea had been planted in his mind some time before it became a musical necessity:

> In church, I was carrying the cello from a concert my sisters and I had just done . . . and a very good violin player, who was much better than my sister and probably should have been in the symphony then, said to my father, 'Why don't you get him a bass? Because at least a black man can get employment with a bass, because he can play *our* music.' . . . Later on, though, when he found I was serious, he did get a bass.[19]

But it was Buddy Collette who provided the specific reason for the change, by pointing out that what the school band needed was not a cellist but a bass player, and for this he earned Mingus's undying gratitude.

On bass his first role model was Joe Comfort, who later worked with both the Lionel Hampton band and the Nat King Cole trio, but whose family were such close neighbours they attended the same Methodist church. Being nearly three years older than Mingus, Comfort was already doing paid gigs with the Woodman Brothers family band, in which Britt was joined by pianist Coney Woodman and William Jr on tenor. But the biggest boost to Mingus's enthusiasm for his new instrument came when Collette introduced him to Red Callender. This was in 1938, when Mingus was sixteen and Callender (who has usually been described, uncomplainingly, as a 'veteran' at the time) was just twenty. True, Red already had an extensive reputation, having arrived from the East Coast a year earlier and then having briefly replaced the great Pops Foster in the Louis Armstrong band, but he confirms Mingus's own feeling that the two of them got on like a house on fire: 'All students should be as apt as Charles was. Our relationship was more on a friendship basis, rather than teacher/pupil.' But the cement of the relationship was clearly Mingus's respect for his best-equipped teacher so far, and it is noticeable that the full yet piercing tone which Mingus favoured on bass is something he picked up directly from Callender;

10

although the recorded evidence is after the fact on both sides (and none too well recorded, a problem which bedevils all comparisons of bassists on disc), Red agrees with this assessment: 'I would have to say that he was into my sound because I had or have a way of playing that gets the most out of the instrument soundwise – this was before the event of the amplified string bass.'

Mingus in fact was now becoming deeply immersed both in learning to play effectively and in trying out his first, rather sketchy arrangements for the school jazz group. And it may be safely assumed that he was starting to copy the simpler sounding charts from popular records to add to the stock arrangements Collette acquired, and was studying them to see how they worked and how they could be successfully amended. But by far the greatest influence on Mingus's ambitions as a writer came when he began seriously studying the piano, of which he even said: 'I never really understood the bass until I started working out harmonies and other things on the piano. Then I came to regard the fingerboard of the bass like a piano keyboard.'[20] His teacher, a multi-talented musician then probably in his mid-thirties, was Lloyd Reese, who had played trumpet for Les Hite on and off since 1929 and recorded on this instrument at Art Tatum's first-ever non-solo session (with a small group from the Hite band). He also played alto saxophone and clarinet in the 1929–30 band of Paul Howard, which included Lawrence Brown and Lionel Hampton. Another of his students, Dexter Gordon, says of Reese: 'All of the top bands wanted him – Lunceford, Duke – but he wouldn't leave Los Angeles . . . He taught us like we were going to be professionals, not like some kid just learning to play an instrument in the school band and marching band. Another concept – 'cause, I mean, he taught me about Art Tatum, and about listening to the film music when you go to the movies. You know, a much broader scope.' So that what may have started as piano lessons soon became theory lessons, and Mingus himself has given a striking example of how this was applied to aspiring composers:

I remember one day when I came to Lloyd's house, he said 'What is this?' and he played a record. I didn't know the title at the time, but he said 'What do you think is going on in this particular movement right there?' And I said 'I don't know, man, but there's a whole lotta shit going on. There's too much to figure out.' The timpani was playing and the basses were playing and the piano was playing a percussional sound with the bass – you

11

could hardly hear the piano – and the flutes were playing synco-pated chop rhythms, the trumpets were playing cock valves, and this cat said 'Well, here it is,' and he took a C7th chord – I remember it started on the 3rd, and he played E, G, B flat, and D natural, and he said 'This is what the clarinets are doing,' and he began to decipher down what was going on. He said 'Here's the french-horn part,' and it came in on G, B flat, D, F an octave down and ended A natural, which clashed against the B flat the clarinets were playing in the E, G, B flat, D natural line, and it made a beautiful sound. I said 'Whaaa? What is that?'[21]

Whether or not Reese actually set written exercises of this nature for Mingus to work out, he certainly gave him to believe that any combination of sounds produced by however many musicians can be notated and, conversely, that a series of sounds in one indi-vidual's head can be written in such a way as to be reproduced by other musicians. For Mingus, this was often easier said than done but, at this stage of his career, he composed without bothering whether his music would be performed or not. ('That was when I was energetic and wrote all the time. Music was my life.')[22] It was enough of a thrill just to work out a piece at the piano, get it down on paper, and imagine it being played by a large ensemble.

The musical ideals with which Reese had fired him remained as a constant thread throughout Mingus's life. Because he often longed to recapture the pristine self-confidence of his late adolescence, there are a couple of relics from this early period, namely *The Chill of Death* (finally recorded in 1971) and *Half-Mast Inhibition* (the one piece on the 1960 album *Pre-Bird* which justified the album title by pre-dating Charlie Parker's influence). The fact that the first is also a literary work shows just how limitless Mingus's ambition was at this period, while its content demonstrates what a profound effect the Christian account of after-life had had on the young author:

The chill of Death, as she clutched my hand
I knew she was coming, so I stood like a man
She drew up closer, close enough for me to look into her face
And then I began to wonder, 'Hadn't I seen her some other
    place?'
She beckoned for me to come closer, as if to pay an old debt
I knew what she wanted; it wasn't quite time yet

She threw her arms about me, as so many women had done
    before

I heard her whisper, 'You'll never cheat me, never any more'
Darkness and nothingness clouded my mind
I began to realize Death was nothing to fear, but something
    sweet and kind
I pinched to see if I was dreaming, but failed to find bodily form
I then began to realize Death *had* worked her charm

Taking my self of nothingness I chose a road to walk
I noticed Death's pleasantness, with no one to stop me to talk
I remembered stories of Heaven, as I visioned the glory ahead
Two roads lay waiting for me to choose one, now that I was dead
One road was dark; I could not see clearly such a long stretched
    highway
The other road was golden and glowing and shining as bright as
    day
I then remembered stories of pearly gates, golden streets – or
    however those stories were told
I knew I'd reach Heaven on *this* highway; if not, I'd have the gold

I took one footstep, feeling safe and acting bold
Suddenly I realized my mistake; my chosen road turned black
    bittery and white cold
No longer was it golden glory, nor Heaven at its end
White hot flames were blazing; I saw the Devil with his grin
I had taken but one footstep, so I turned to hurry back
But there a sound wall waited, and not a door nor a crack
Finally, coming to my senses, I walked on to my Hell
For long before Death had called me, my end was planned –
    planned but well.[23]

Because like Duke Ellington Mingus was rarely content to resurrect earlier pieces without updating them in some way, this work as presented on the album *Let My Children Hear Music* is heard in two consecutive versions, one which may be described as pre-Bird (accompanying Mingus's narration of the poem) immediately followed by the same performance repeated with post-Bird comments by the alto saxophone of Charles McPherson. And it is necessary to hear the second version in order to feel the full force which the written score should have had behind the narration, were it not so far back in the mix. What is immediately evident is that this is an episodic composition and, while intended to be capable of standing alone as a piece of programmatic music, it is more closely tied to the story of the poem than in most of Mingus's later experiments involving words. Indeed, Dexter Gordon's reference to film soundtracks strikes the right chord here, for not only is the written piece as such utterly remote from the feeling of jazz, stylistically it resembles strongly the 1930s underscores of Max Steiner and Dimitri Tiomkin and their melodramatic borrowings from Wagner and Mahler. (The latter is recalled particularly in Mingus's use of the clarinets, although Ellington could conceivably have been an influence here also, but in any case it is by no means certain how closely the 1971 orchestration represents the original concept.)

There is, incidentally, no great similarity to *Death and Transfiguration*, but the choice of subject-matter is certainly cause for speculation. It may well be, now that 'music was his life', that Mingus was aware of the danger of becoming a totally one-sided personality. 'I didn't think I dug life the way other people did. I didn't have any lust or love for life. It was just living and breathing.' When in the summer of 1939 Mingus had taken off for San Francisco he had met another lifelong-friend-to-be, painter Farwell Taylor, and stayed with him and his wife in Mill Valley, across the Golden Gate Bridge into Marin County; Taylor encouraged him to follow his inclination and become a composer, and also introduced him to the practice of Karma Yoga. 'I learned through meditation the will to control and actually feel calmness. I found a thing that made me think I could die if I wanted to.' And a year or so after this, Mingus was feeling sufficiently disturbed that he decided to end it all by sheer force of will, pausing only to complete the composition he had been working on.

'While I was laying there, I got to such a point that it scared me and I decided I wasn't ready. And ever since, actually, I've been running because I saw something I didn't want to see. I felt I was too young to reach this point.' It would be tempting to think that the piece Mingus had just written was *The Chill of Death* but apparently it was *Half-Mast Inhibition*, a title which suggests that what was troubling him was merely a bout of youthful impotence. Mingus said of the piece in question, 'I had a little thing in there like "Jingle bells, jingle bells" – not funny style, but because it represented Christmas and Christ,'[24] and this does in fact occur five minutes after the start of *Inhibition*. Although twice as long, the composition is as episodic as *Chill* and incorporates a prominent bowed cello solo; occasional details foreshadow later Mingus pieces, such as a fast waltz passage and one moment which suggests the opening of *The Black Saint and the Sinner Lady*, but the only jazz feeling in the 1960 recording comes from the interpretation of a couple of trumpet soloists, and opinions of the work have varied wildly. According to Sy Johnson, a subsequent collaborator of Mingus, it is 'a great piece',[25] while for Mingus commentator Jack Cooke it 'comes off as a hotchpotch of rather undigested influences, steering a rather unsteady course'.[26]

Although on balance it is reasonable to accept Mingus's dating of these two compositions as belonging to the period 1939–40, they differ markedly from his other known activities at the time, and indicate depths of his personality already hidden from all but his closest friends. Even Buddy Collette would perhaps have been surprised at the discrepancy between the inner Mingus and the image he was creating for himself; Collette has said:

> I knew what Mingus was like even before I met him; he was doing a lot of crazy stuff even then – shaving his head in the middle . . . [wearing] different clothes . . . We never got into a fight; we had a special relationship . . . In fact, sometimes when Mingus was getting into trouble and just about to go off on someone, they might say, 'We're going to call Buddy', and he would say, 'No, no, don't do that'.[27]

The Bullish exterior was certainly what impressed Dexter Gordon, nearly a year younger than Mingus – 'which at that age makes a difference' – who first got to know him in early 1940 and found him 'the same – just the same' as the Mingus of later years. The cause of their meeting was that Lloyd Reese had formed a Sunday morning rehearsal band of his students, which met at the segregated union branch (Local 767 of the American Federation of Musicians): 'Nat Cole wrote a couple of charts for us, and a few other guys, you know. Maybe Ming did too, I just can't remember.' As well as rehearsing in this big-band context, Mingus and Buddy Collette, the two stars of the Jordan High group, now in their last year at school, also became involved in the Al Adams band alongside pupils from the slightly more mid-town Jefferson High School, including Gordon, Chico Hamilton, Jack Kelso and Ernie Royal (who, though only the same age as Collette, had already been working professionally, as had a recent arrival in Los Angeles and occasional member of this band, Illinois Jacquet). Chico Hamilton has said, 'Basie, Lunceford, Chick Webb . . . we played the same arrangements they played. We copied them down, you know,'[28] and, even if not for Lloyd Reese, Dexter says that 'Mingus was already

15

writing, taking things off the records . . . and he was always a Duke aficionado, and Jimmy Blanton . . . That was his bailiwick.' One can well imagine the boost to Mingus's bass studies provided by the sudden appearance of the first Ellington sides with Blanton, all recorded (and particularly well for the period) during the autumn and winter of 1939–40. Even if Red Callender had been thinking along similar lines, the startlingly melodic and horn-like work of Jimmy Blanton showed all the bassists the way of the future, and set the standard for many years to come.

Two other figures made a profound, if less obvious, impact on Mingus at this period for, until entering the circle of young musicians intent on making a career in jazz, he had had little contact (outside of the church and some Ellington pieces) with the gutsier side of black music; even Buddy Collette preferred the clean, ethereal sound of 'Pres' (Lester Young). But when, late in 1939, the band for whom Britt Woodman was now playing (led by altoist Floyd Turnham) suddenly became *en bloc* the new Les Hite band, Mingus was made aware of their added attraction, the electric guitarist and vocalist T-Bone Walker, who until then had been working in obscure clubs. Had it not been for this then-novel combination of a big swing band and a blues artist, and the resultant 1940 hit record *T-Bone Blues* arranged by Gil Fuller, the power of gospel music's secular counterpart might have eluded Mingus for quite a while longer.

Another revealing experience in the same year came when the young Los Angeles group played with Roy Eldridge and, according to Mingus's original account, 'One of the guys in the band . . .[had] written a little thing for Roy to play, and Roy preferred not to.'[29] In a later description of the same incident, as it were an improvisation on the theme of the first version, Mingus himself was the culprit:

I was real snobbish about anybody who didn't study with Lloyd Reese or go to a conservatory or couldn't answer some of the questions we learned, like 'What's the supertonic chord of B flat?' 'What's the relative minor of A?' We had a gig at Jefferson High School to play with Roy Eldridge and a couple of older guys. And I remember I used to think Roy Eldridge had a cocky attitude. Well, I walked in to him and said, 'What's the relative minor of B flat?' He looked me over. 'I'm gonna tell you something, nigger. You young punks out here, I'm running into you every time I turn around. You don't know nothing about me, you don't know about your own people's music. I bet you never heard of Coleman Hawkins, I bet you never listened to him, I bet you can't sing one of his solos. You come in here and ask me if I know what the relative minor of B flat is. How do you know I don't know the supertonic chord?' I said, 'What?' I wasn't that far yet.[30]

As with his other musical experiences, including his first hearings of Ellington, the effect on Mingus of this dressing-down was not immediate, at least in terms of his own output. But one way of looking at his subsequent career is as a constant struggle between his love and respect for the tradition of 'our' music, and his continuing belief that its future lay in being fully integrated into something much wider. And, although the internal struggle was real enough sometimes, he felt also that he should reserve the right to be inconsistent and to take different approaches on different occasions. In 1972 he told me:

When I was young I saw a prospective [*sic*] of Gauguin, you know, in a museum . . . From one painting . . . the next one was like another human being had done it. It was not just another nude woman or another group of women pouring water. Yet I knew he did it, the same genius was there, you know. I knew it was Gauguin, but it was *another* painting, man!

As it happens, Mingus was to have his closest contact with the traditional virtues of black music during the next decade, in between experiments of his own, but the chronology of his activities after leaving school is extremely hard to tie down. It seems that it was touch-and-go for a while whether Mingus would become a post-office employee ('That's what my father wanted me to do . . . I thought about it and said "But I don't want to do this, I'd rather shine shoes first" . . . So I walked away, and told my father I took the test and failed'.)[31] Having decided that music would be his sole livelihood, his first 'professional' gigs may have been extremely lowly, and it appears unlikely that he worked regularly with drummer Lee Young at this period, especially as the 1941 sextet Young co-led with his brother Lester (the front line being completed by Bumps Myers and trumpeter Red Mack Morris) normally had Red Callender on bass. On the other hand, from the late 1930s onwards Lee Young had close connections with the major film studios, often doing speciality numbers on soundtrack and sometimes appearing on screen; he may therefore have assisted during the autumn of 1940 in finding the black 'extras' for *The Road to Zanzibar*, who, in the cases of Mingus and Buddy Collette, were left on the cutting-room floor. And, while it may well be true that Mingus played at this period with Art Tatum, the collaboration might not have gone very far, since Mingus once said 'I tried to sit in with him, but he'd laugh at me.'[32] Although he may have tried out some of his early small-group compositions with a line-up including Collette and Britt Woodman, it is equally unlikely that they worked together in public at this stage, for Woodman was now touring nationally with Les Hite, as was his brother Coney until, early in 1942, they both enlisted for World War II. By the middle of 1942, as Hite lost more men to the war effort, Buddy Collette had also become a member of the band before he too enlisted in the service.

Mingus was filled with similar conflicting emotions about the war as he had been about the post office, veering from a genuine abhorrence (especially when Japanese residents of the US started being interned) to the burst of patriotism that led to a preliminary medical, which he failed. Thus he was in the right place at the right time when two unique New Orleans musicians came, independently, to Los Angeles, and a third who had lived there for more than a decade came out of his nine-year retirement. The reappearance of trombonist Kid Ory, in fact, was occasioned by the decision of the great Ellington clarinet soloist Barney Bigard to leave Duke's band in August 1942 in favour of a gig at Los Angeles's Trouville Club – as Mingus explained to John Litweiler, 'Bigard brought Kid Ory up out of the mothballs, and then Kid Ory got a band *after* that . . . I was never in Kid Ory's band.'[33] Unlike this later Revivalist endeavour, Bigard had assembled a swing-orientated group which also played a couple of New Orleans numbers and, according to *Down Beat*, he opened on 20 August with Red Mack Morris, Ory, Jack Calso [*sic*] on alto and clarinet, pianist Garland Finney, drummer Henry Tucker and Charlie Engels on bass![34] In retrospect, it seems somehow typical of Mingus's chequered career that the first printed mention of his name, presumably transcribed from someone's handwriting, makes him a member of another persecuted minority. But it helps to date his association with Louis Armstrong, which, according to the same interview, was 'after John Simmons and Sid Catlett left',[35] in other words during a period when Louis could not only have met Bigard and Ory again but even perhaps sat in with them at the Trouville.

Armstrong had returned to Los Angeles in August 1942, having appeared there with great success earlier in the year, as well as

18

recording and making a couple of short 'soundie' films, but this time he went into rehearsal for filming the all-black musical *Cabin in the Sky*. It is possible that his big band continued to draw their salaries or even fulfilled a few engagements with Louis between studio calls, but Catlett decided that this period of relative inactivity was the time to leave for New York, and bassist Simmons did likewise. So, when his work on the film was over, Armstrong's band needed a new bass player and Mingus – the New Orleans veteran of the Bigard group – got the job. 'I was with him just a little while, about two or three months. We went north, to Port Angeles, Washington, then to Canada, across the river.' Sadly, although Mingus was full of admiration for Louis's instrumental creativity, he could not stomach his facial grimaces and apparent self-abasement before white audiences ('Mugging and Tomming', as it was termed in the black community). And, unlike other young bloods of the day who made similar accusations but subsequently mellowed towards Louis, Mingus was still describing him as an Uncle Tom in the mid-1970s. Came the crunch: 'It was on the ferry boat going to Canada that somebody said we were going to the South, and I gave them my views. I wasn't going to take any shit from anybody in the South. So Louis decided it was best that I leave the band.'[36] Of course, Mingus's knowledge of race relations in the South was second-hand, but it was being added to constantly; for instance, only the previous year a black congressman from Chicago (and there weren't many of them in 1941) was forced to move into the segregated compartment of a train as it crossed the border into Arkansas.

Later, Mingus came to believe that any black musician permitted to become a star, while working through the established channels of the music business, can be isolated from fellow blacks in order to preserve the 'system'. He commented in 1972 that:

> If Louis Armstrong could have got a pile of money, like he should have made – which he *did* make, but it went to some of the agencies . . . If that money went to *his* society, *his* people, there wouldn't have had to be the Watts riot. Because he could have set up schools to teach what he was doing to younger children, and it would have been a whole different feeling about our music . . .
>
> I'd rather go for a D harmonic and, if I miss, I admit it; I see it myself, and I try and make up for it. But I don't want to be searching, and have anybody say [that] *anything* I do is right. I

19

don't want me to be so deserving of being freed as a black man, for the white man to tell me [*patronizing tone*], 'Mingus, you can do anything you want to do, it's alright, man, be an idiot and stay drunk, lay in the gutter. You know, you're alright, man, it's a wrong note really, but a *black* man played it! White men can't do that, but black men do anything they want!' Come on, man, don't tell *my* children this crap!

Perhaps, then, it is not surprising that, when he returned to Los Angeles from Canada, he set about improving his double-bass technique with a renewed zeal. Red Callender, feeling that there was little he could add to what Mingus had already absorbed from his concept, suggested that for sheer technique Mingus should study with a symphonic player, namely Herman Rheinshagen. A former member of the New York Philharmonic now presumably engaged in the film studios, Rheinshagen was just the taskmaster Mingus needed at this point, covering the extreme high register near the bridge where the thumb and third finger of the left hand have to be brought into play, and Mingus responded by practising for hours each day.

Simultaneously he felt that there ought to be a parallel way for the jazz repertoire to develop away from its roots into an art music which would elude the pigeonhole set aside for it by the music industry. Inevitably at this stage, he thought in terms of jazz 'composition' as the answer, and he wrote later of how he was inspired around this period by attending a series of 'classical' music workshop concerts at Los Angeles City College. For, even during this period of unprecedented popularity for the big (mostly white) swing bands, the more informal and more creative (predominantly black) small groups were largely restricted to the less prestigious nightclubs and after-hours joints, whose number and significance was also temporarily boosted by the wartime economy. Dexter Gordon, just twenty when he returned from two and a half years' touring with Lionel Hampton, notes that 'They didn't have a black-out, they had what they called a brown-out in L.A., you know. So the regular clubs worked like from 8 to 12, and all these other joints that you're hearing about around Central Avenue, they were like from 1 to 5.' And the regular club where Dexter worked on his return was the famous Club Alabam, and the band in which he joined Mingus in 1943 was the Lee Young Sextet, which had been reviewed a few months earlier at Billy Berg's Swing Club by Leonard Feather; the personnel on Friday, 11 March was trumpeter

George Treadwell, Floyd Turnham, Bumps Myers, Irving Ashby, Charlie Davis on piano and Mingus, with arrangements by Gerald Wilson and Dudley Brooks, and among Feather's brief comments is: 'The pianist and bass are worth watching.'[37] But, although on Central Avenue rather than in Hollywood, the main function of the Club Alabam band was to play backing music for the nightly show, with the result that Dexter and Mingus also worked regularly at after-hours clubs such as the Ritz, where among the younger musicians coming to jam all night was Art Pepper. Before Mingus left, Pepper also joined the Lee Young Sextet, and told me of Mingus's playing then, 'He had a different style, completely his own . . . It wasn't like one of those things that just hits you right away . . . Unfortunately, when I was coming up, they didn't have these tape-decks and things like that. It would have been marvellous to have tapes from those days.'

Even studio recordings, of Mingus or anyone else, are non-existent from this period; because of the refusal of the three major record corporations to pay higher fees to A.F.M. union members, a ban on all new recording of instrumentalists had been in force since August 1942 and the first breakthrough did not come until first Decca and then the recently founded West Coast label Capitol agreed to the new rates in November 1943. Given that the only specialist jazz labels (Commodore and Blue Note) were back in action within days and several more were soon started in the East, it is surprising that there was no West Coast follow-up until well into 1944 when the Gilt Edge/4 Star group began operations. Being on the West Coast was clearly no way to build a national reputation in those days. By contrast, Oscar Pettiford, although a few months younger than Mingus, became the main contender for the succession following Jimmy Blanton's death in 1942, by settling in New York the next year. He immediately impressed both colleagues and fans (being voted a New Star in *Esquire*'s 1943 critics' poll) and, by the end of the year, had made no less than four influential record dates, all led by Coleman Hawkins, with many more to come during 1944 for Hawkins, Ben Webster, Billy Eckstine *et al*. But for the time being Mingus was wedded to the Coast, and had become more than somewhat involved with Canilla Jeanne Gross. The 'Barbara Jane Parks' of the autobiography, Canilla Jeanne was employed as a playground director, both when Mingus met her and when, just turned eighteen, she married him in Santa Ana on 3 January 1944. But, although she had initially provided a stabilizing influence on Mingus and inspired him musically ('I found something else, a little

21

girl named Jean[ne] who I fell in love with. I started to write again,')[38] the marriage seems to have been doomed to failure from the start. Jeanne's parents made it clear that she had married beneath herself, and she felt painfully neglected when Mingus was out every night on his regular gig. In all likelihood, he was by now playing a more commercial kind of music, since this was his only means of supporting her, but he was also still heavily involved in more advanced jazz and at least sometimes played again with Lloyd Reese's Sunday morning band – which was how he first met the young Eric Dolphy when the latter began studying the alto saxophone in 1944. ('He used to stand on the steps of the union hall, and listen.')[39]

The birth certificate of Charles Mingus III, who came along early in the morning of 12 September 1944 after a long and difficult delivery, confirms that Jeanne was not then living at the marital home (4260 Vermont Street, according to the autobiography) but at her parents' more salubrious East 48th Street address. It also confirms that Mingus's place of business was at 'Long Beach with Trio', the trio in question being the guitar/piano/bass combination christened Pick, Plank and Plunk in Mingus's book and which worked under the name the Strings And Keys. But the chief confirmation for this lies in an item in the December 1944–January 1945 edition of *Music Dial*, which actually carries a photograph of the group – probably the first published of Mingus – over the caption: 'The Strings And Keys trio, the current feature in the Venetian Room, Long Beach, California, moves to a Beverly Hills "swank" for the next engagement. Juan Panalie, piano; Louis Speigner, guitar; Charles Mingus, bass.'[40] This, of course, ties in directly with the reference in *Beneath the Underdog* (Chapter 19) to the trio's work at 'the Venice place' and to Mingus's relationship with the clubowner's wife, one of the first white women with whom he was involved. But the key item in this sudden rush of documentation ought to have been a recording done, around this same period of late 1944, or early 1945, under Mingus's own name for an unidentified label (possibly Excelsior).

The existence of this previously unknown session emerged from correspondence with the drummer Roy Porter, who gives the personnel as being himself, Mingus, Spaulding Givens (who had by then replaced Panalie in the Strings And Keys), Buddy Collette on alto and Britt Woodman. This would require the two front-line players to have been on leave simultaneously, which is of course not impossible, but there are two reasons why the date must be more or less correct. First, Porter had only recently moved to Los Angeles and this was his first-ever record session, which makes him likely to have placed it accurately; and, more significantly, he was the drummer on Mingus's first *issued* session under his own name from mid-1945, which must necessarily be preceded by the quintet recordings. These, unfortunately, were not from Mingus's commercial repertoire and, as Roy says, 'Charlie Mingus was so far ahead of his time that people didn't quite know how to cope with him as a person or his playing. As you know he was a genius and very introverted – but as I recall one of the most beautiful people in existence . . . The first record session I did was . . . never released. Misunderstood, dig?'

2

West Coast Ghost

Obviously, breaking through as a composing bandleader was not going to be as easy as getting a record date, which (to be fair) had probably been offered to Mingus on the basis of his work with the Strings And Keys. But, although he continued his night-club playing, he was certainly becoming known to both musicians and cognoscenti as a most promising bassist – and a keen one. Journalist Patricia Willard has written: 'He so loved his bass that he played it everywhere he went – friends' front porches, streetcars en route to a gig,'[1] while disc-jockey Jimmy Lyons once said, 'The first time I heard him was in an after-hours club playing *Body and Soul* for forty-five minutes, on top of a little table.'[2] As a result, Sergeant Lyons used Mingus on several of the Armed Forces Radio Service 'Jubilee' shows he produced. Mingus was undoubtedly also doing a certain amount of undocumented film 'extra' work, subsequent to his known appearance in the 1943 *Higher and Higher*, and quite likely more recording than can be accurately identified. For, as the mushroom growth of new independent record-labels finally took hold on the West Coast during the years 1945–6, Mingus began to be called for studio gigs with a wide variety of jazzmen and popular black artists, successfully competing in a field where the front-runners on bass were Red Callender, Joe Comfort and Billy Hadnott, with players such as Benny Booker and Shifty Henry not far behind. Although Mingus may have been idealizing the situation to some extent, he later said 'I was lucky, man . . . I was having all the studio jobs, Red Callender and myself, Lee Young, . . . Buddy

Collette. Lucky Thompson was even there. Miles Davis came [for] a little while, but Miles couldn't get any record dates.'[3]

Much of this casual work is seemingly lost forever since, although the new labels were not intentionally fly-by-night operations, very few of them had financial backing sound enough to survive the short-lived post-war boom. As it happens, Mingus's first sessions to gain wide distribution (on Apollo, which, thanks to the strength of its gospel catalogue, lasted into the mid-1950s) must have been some of the most satisfying musically, with a working band led by Illinois Jacquet who, after his arrival on the Coast, had made his name as a star soloist with the Lionel Hampton band. And on them Mingus gives some immediate indications of 'a different style, completely his own'. Given the functional role of a mini-Hampton rhythm section, most of the bass playing is straightforward for the period, though with an unhackneyed choice of notes and an easy fluency in the upper register, but the two-bar bass break which concludes *Merle's Mood* is something else: not only does Mingus play a series of double-stops (two strings sounding simultaneously), which was unheard-of except in Jimmy Blanton's work on *Jumpin' Punkins*, but he plays them with a viciously aggressive pizzicato which seems at least fifteen years ahead of its time. Instructive in a different way is Mingus's backing to the tenor solo on *Jacquet Mood*,* the first four bars of which are underpinned by a tonic pedal-point, alternating the mid-range E flat played on the A string with the high E flat on the G string; and these octave leaps are subsequently taken through different notes of the scale, with a technique which reached its culmination in the 1959 *E's Flat Ah's Flat Too*. And finally, on the ballad-tempo *Ghost of a Chance*, Mingus links the quarter-notes with eighth-note triplets in a manner which, if not originating with him, is more thoroughgoing than either Blanton (as on Ellington's *All Too Soon*) or Callender (on Lester Young's *Body and Soul*), and almost elevates a mere double-bass part into a countermelody dialoguing with the tenor lead (see Appendix A).

Each of these three approaches – the double-stops, the octave leaps, and the subdivision of the beat by means of passing-notes – were eventually to develop further in Mingus's playing, of course.

*Because of considerable confusion over the use of two titles for three different pieces, the item referred to is not that originally issued on 78 rpm as *Jacquet Mood* (Apollo 769). The recording in question was released on ten-inch LP as *Jacquet Mood* and on twelve-inch LP (Vogue CLDAP 858) as *Merle's Mood*, which is quite distinct from the 78/ten-inch LP *Merle's Mood* mentioned above!

But, equally, they were to influence many of his successors and, ultimately, not so much through Mingus's own example but through the combined weight of all the jazz bassists he had influenced by the 1960s, they had a marked effect on the style of bass-guitar players, first in the soul field and then in rock and pop music generally. But initially there was no consistent follow-through from Mingus himself, perhaps because he didn't yet see any organic relationship between his playing and his interest in composing, arranging and indeed songwriting. For, in spite of the strain which the rejection of his first recordings must have put on his belief in the oneness of music, he clearly had a genuine interest in the more popular forms such as blues and ballads. Not only had he been inspired in this direction by the need to support his wife and Charles III, but his poetic talents may have convinced him that success in the popular field could finance his other music. Mingus may also have been not unaware that this was in fact the case with his idol Duke Ellington. Like Duke's first records, many of Mingus's earliest issued sides, both under his own name and others', show him trying to establish his credentials as a songwriter. (Because of the more embryonic state of the music industry, Ellington did not make his first disc recordings until he was twenty-five, but the parallel is intriguing.) Thus the sessions with the young Dinah Washington, as well as bass playing which follows up the approach of *Ghost of a Chance*, include at least two numbers co-written by Mingus and Wilbert Baranco. One of these, *Pacific Coast Blues*, contains the less than idiomatic lines: 'I'm a fugitive from slumber, can't count one hour that I've slept/I'm just as blue as the Pacific, and I know my eyes are just as wet.'[4]

Baranco, seemingly some years older than Mingus, had been based in San Francisco before the war, and had chosen this moment to make his mark on the Los Angeles music scene; but, after using Mingus in his short-lived big band (whose records included a guest appearance by Dizzy Gillespie) he went on to form a Nat Cole-style trio and subsequently taught a jazz history course at Berkeley in the early 1950s. He therefore missed out on being another of Mingus's long-term mentors but, as well as encouraging his songwriting, he may have helped Mingus in assembling the all-star personnel for his second issued Excelsior session, which produced the only one of Mingus's early recordings to have been released in Europe. This, not surprisingly, was one of the solely instrumental tracks and, although there are numerous points of interest, it is as well to point out that these sessions are at the least rather uneven and eclectic.

The tone is set by the derivativeness of the vocalists, who sound like Betty Roche (*The Texas Hop*) or Cleanhead Vinson (*Ain't Jivin' Blues*) or a cross between Herb Jeffries and Al Hibbler on all three recordings of *Baby/Honey Take a Chance with Me*, and it is matched by fairly dreary arrangements. Nevertheless, the format of the latter is subtly different each time, with the written trumpet intro of the first attempt converted into a high-register Lawrence Brown-style trombone part, while the bass solo introduced on the later versions is backed by distinctly Ellingtonian clarinet-led chords. More important are the two different approaches to *Weird Nightmare/Pipe Dream*, the first with lyrics and the second a sort of concerto for pianist Lady Will Carr (a former member of the Al Adams band, who does a straight copy of the Erskine Hawkins hit *After Hours* on the reverse). Although harmonically similar to the 1941 pop tune *You Don't Know What Love Is*, this thirty-two bar theme in D minor is the first typically melancholy Mingus ballad, and was re-recorded on no less than four occasions, in 1953 as *Smooch*, again in 1958 and twice in 1960 (once under the title *Vassarlean*), and always with slight variations in the arrangement. Interestingly, despite changes in instrumentation, Mingus ignored the optimum range of different soloists (vocal or otherwise) and never altered the key-signature of a piece after he had once worked it out at the piano.

Of the instrumentals, *This Subdues My Passion* is a would-be Strayhornesque mood piece, but unlike Strayhorn's *Chelsea Bridge* which it resembles initially – and most interestingly in view of Mingus's later development (see Appendix B) – it avoids the standard A/A/B/A chorus format. Although the harmonic scheme might justify on paper the description intro/A/B/C/B^1/C^1/A, its continuous melodic invention (all composed, and allowing virtually no improvisation) makes it sound in practice to be intro/A/B/C/D/E/A. The actual performance is somewhat unfinished, the sustained high trombone lines presenting some difficulty, but this is the only work from this period to be mentioned, not without cause, in the autobiography. The most successful combination of conception and execution occurs in *Shuffle Bass Boogie*, whose theme is like a medium-tempo variant of *Jeep's Blues*, while the four-bar bridge after the bass solo seems to be another (Ellingtonian?) quotation which turned up again later in Duke Jordan's coda to *Scrapple from the Apple*. The piece takes its title from the ingenious imitation by bass and baritone sax of a pianist's left-hand boogie-woogie figure; but, unlike such figures which traditionally follow the blues chords by changing the root at the fifth bar, this figure remains anchored to the tonic throughout, demonstrating that Mingus's use of the pedal-point on *Jacquet Mood* was no accident.

Somewhere in the midst of these sessions, Mingus first heard Charlie Parker in the flesh, an event with considerable reper-cussions. It would be naive to expect an instantaneous reflection of this in Mingus's music, and certainly there is none. As opposed to the average instrumentalist, who may immediately start to practise any new approach worthy of imitation (as so many did with Parker and, before him, Armstrong), the aspiring jazz composer must be open to so many potential influences that the process of absorption is, as with Ellington, much more subconscious and protracted. For this reason, one can accept Mingus's statement that 'I didn't like [Parker] right away.'[5] In fact, despite the presence of the star-studded Billy Eckstine band in Los Angeles early in 1945, he may have had no contact with any bebop until later that year when playing a one-nighter in San Pedro with the legendary Dean Benedetti, a saxophonist then in his mid-twenties whose band included trumpeter Dale Snow and the eighteen-year-old Jimmy Knepper on trombone. Dean, the popular picture of whom is, according to Knepper, seriously inaccurate, was certainly an apostle of Parker, having learned tunes such as *Groovin' High* and *Hot House* from the first Gillespie/Parker records and turned his own band into the first white bebop band on the West Coast.

Says Knepper, 'Years later Mingus told me that it was the first white band he'd worked with . . . and that he hadn't paid much attention to Parker. But these guys were so enthusiastic, all they could listen to was Charlie Parker.' In fact, now that Parker was actually here as part of Dizzy Gillespie's Rebop Six and appearing at Billy Berg's Supper Club in Hollywood during December 1945 and January 1946, Mingus may not have been in a great hurry to hear him. Lengthy lists of young Los Angeles musicians who claim to have been present during his opening week – or played with him during his subsequent residency at the Finale – show Mingus's name conspicuous by its absence, perhaps because of his continued night-club work. But he certainly took the opportunity to check out the 'Bird' at private sessions and at the 'official' jam-sessions such as the one described in *Beneath the Underdog*, which clubs like Berg's ran on Sunday afternoons. But the evidence of Mingus's records would tend to confirm that Parker's sweeping innovations were just too fundamental, and his emotionalism too apparently disorganized, to be readily accepted by the composer of *This Subdues My Passion*.

It will be observed by anyone comparing notes that the chronology of the autobiography, generally not one of its stronger points, is especially confused around this period. Mingus wrote of playing with Parker in August, but the only August during Bird's fifteen months in California was spent in Camarillo State Hospital, while drummer Stan Levey (also mentioned in the jam-session sequence) returned to New York with Gillespie in February 1946. In addition, the order of Mingus's chapters appears to have been deliberately jumbled in the process of being edited for publication, and it makes more sense after Chapter 16 to read Chapters 19, 18, 24 and 17 in that order. Certainly the last two chapters just listed seem written to be read in this way.

At the time of Mingus's initial exposure to Bird, it seems rather as if he was more drawn to the relatively contained approaches of Lucky Thompson and the nineteen-year-old Miles Davis:

> Miles Davis once came to my house in California with Lucky Thompson, showing his idea of contrapuntal music which Gil Evans did most for him on records, credited to Gerry Mulligan. That was Miles's idea. Miles even named the instrumentation to Lucky and myself – french horn, tuba, etc., remember? This was in the mid-forties before he met Evans or Mulligan or even this bassist's extended form.[6]

But Davis did apparently encounter some of Mingus's music, for he wrote of Miles rehearsing on 'third trumpet' with him in what was presumably a big band on the lines of Lloyd Reese's Sunday sessions. On the other hand Thompson, only twenty-one but already a veteran of the Basie band (which he had left a few months earlier, to be replaced by Illinois Jacquet), actually worked with Mingus for six weeks in the spring at the Down Beat on Central Avenue, in a cooperative group called the Stars Of Swing. Formed when first Buddy Collette (in late 1945) and then Britt Woodman (January 1946) were demobilized, the group was completed by John Anderson on trumpet, Spaulding Givens and drummer Oscar Bradley, and was described by Woodman as growing out of the musicians' dissatisfaction with bandleaders:

> Each musician in it was leader conscious but at the same time maintained his feeling of individuality as a sideman. As a result, each idea that a musician put forward was treated with respect by the others and made use of. Charles Mingus, for instance,

revealed power and an unusual concept as a jazz composer which the others encouraged him to develop . . . Often [he] would introduce a composition requiring a different approach to jazz playing.[7]

As to what these pieces sound like, there are perhaps clues in the improvised ensembles of the 1954 recordings *Getting Together* and *Gregarian Chant*, which Mingus categorized as new material based on the kind of arrangements he had used with the Stars Of Swing. Other tracks from the same 1954 session suggest that the pre-planned counterpoint of playing, for instance, *Take the 'A' Train* and *Exactly Like You* simultaneously (as on the *Pre-Bird* album) may also stem from this period. At least some of this group's repertoire such as Buddy Collette's *Bedspread* was recorded by the Mingus octet on 4 Star, but it is especially intriguing to note that *What Love* (based on one of Mingus's favourite chord-sequences, *What Is This Thing Called Love*, and recorded twice during 1960) was said by the composer to have been written for Collette and to have been played by the Stars Of Swing at the Down Beat. Sadly, as Woodman recalled, 'During the six weeks different agents and club owners . . . seemed impressed, but kept asking if we had a floor show. Did any of us sing, or did any of us dance while we were playing? . . . Unfortunately, the only recording we did was for an audition. Later we tried to obtain the recordings, but the company had sold out and the masters were never found.'[8]

Although Mingus had given up the Strings And Keys in favour of this idealistic (and now unemployed) cooperative group, he was for a short while quite busy. There are mentions of him freelancing at places such as the Elks' Ballroom and the Last Word on Central Avenue and the Streets Of Paris in Hollywood, and playing a dance at which the band included Eric Dolphy on his first paid engagement. Later in 1946 – presumably after Woodman had been recommended by Lucky Thompson to the white bandleader Boyd Raeburn, who promptly 'discovered' him – Mingus landed a couple of nights under his own name at Billy Berg's, for which he used Dale Snow and Jimmy Knepper but apparently no original music: 'We came in and just played some bebop arrangements,' says Knepper. And, like a number of budding composer-arrangers, Mingus did his share of 'ghost-writing' for film scores:

> I used to ghost-write for Dimitri Tiomkin. It was a common practice. My teacher [Lloyd Reese] sent some of us over to see

him to write some things. He would give us an assignment like, 'Write this for eight bars; modulate to the key of C and I'll be back a little later.' Jimmy Knepper did that too. But Tiomkin got Maxwell Davis, who is very fast, so he fired all of us.[9]

It was in mid-1946 that the Ellington band returned to the West Coast for the first time since Oscar Pettiford had joined and, knowing the evenly matched abilities but unequal reputations of Mingus and Pettiford, bassist Vernon Alley (who had worked with singer-guitarist Saunders King in San Francisco and with Lionel Hampton's first big band) attempted to set up a cutting contest between the two players. In the event, Pettiford didn't turn up but, being on his mettle for the occasion, Mingus achieved a sudden breakthrough on his instrument: 'I began playing and didn't stop for a long time. It was suddenly *me*; it wasn't the bass any more. Now I'm not conscious of the instrument as an instrument when I play. And I don't dig any longer thinking in terms of whether one man is a "better" bassist than another.'[10]

Musically, then, Mingus's future at the age of twenty-four could hardly have been more promising, but, without any steady employment, his income was actually down. And the fact that some months earlier Jeanne had come back to live with him had led to her becoming pregnant again, which in turn led to Mingus's renewed involvement in more commercial music. At the birth of Eugene Mingus in September 1946, his father was working regularly with Floyd Ray, whose band earlier in the year included trumpeter Art Farmer; he confirms having known Mingus at this period and that Mingus was practising the cello again ('I was playing jazz cello before Pettiford ever played one. Art Farmer was a witness to this.')[11] Mingus is most unlikely to have done so on his actual gigs, however, for while Ray's big band of the late 1930s was, according to Dexter Gordon, 'a young band – very hip', nevertheless it sold itself (especially on records) through its strength in the vocal department. But the group that Ray fronted after the war did not last very long, and Mingus's association with him may have terminated abruptly as a result of Ray cutting down in size or disbanding altogether. The standard potted history of Mingus's activities, as given in his first *Down Beat* interview and quoted in the *Encyclopedia of Jazz* (Quartet) and by every other writer thereafter, claims that he worked around this period with Alvino Rey. Mingus also makes this claim in *Beneath the Underdog*, but a composite personnel of Rey's otherwise all-white 1946 band (established in Arne Astrup's discography of Zoot Sims) does not include him among the four bassists mentioned and it seems possible that Mingus confused him with Ray.

Not only was the night-club scene generally contracting and some of the small record companies beginning to go out of business, Mingus now found himself without a wife again. Having once more stayed at her mother's prior to her confinement, Jeanne this time decided to remain there permanently, and Mingus, very conscious of his own failures in making the marriage work, fell into a depression not unlike the one he had experienced when he was seventeen. His solution was once again to visit San Francisco and, feeling in his self-doubt that music was the cause of his problems, he did what he told his father he would not do and took a temporary job with the Post Office during the Christmas of 1946. However, apart from some unpaid sessions and sitting-in on other people's jobs, the employment scene in San Francisco was even bleaker than in Los Angeles. So, eager now to get back to regular playing and armed with further encouragement from Farwell Taylor to follow his compositional muse, Mingus returned to Los Angeles and started looking for gigs again.

It was probably at this period that he organized one if not two more recordings which were never issued. Jimmy Knepper recalls a big-band date with some rather complex music, for which he recruited some of the other trombonists: 'The date was kind of a mess. We played some of Mingus's original material . . . Whether it was released or not, we didn't get paid – there was no money involved – or whether he used it as a demonstration record for some job, I don't know.' But, in a way, the most ambitious attempt to capitalize on his writing was Mingus's effort to interest a major label in his words-and-music extravaganza *The Chill of Death:*

It was recorded then, in fact, in Columbia Studios with a Columbia conductor . . . Just to see if they would like it enough to put it out. I thought in those days they would even like it, in those days there was a lot of poetry going round. Not particularly with music, but I think Orson Welles had done one, from the Bible. And someone else, that *Manhattan Towers* gave me the idea, remember *Manhattan Towers?** . . . They thought it was too weird, they said, and not saleable.

*This unusual and unexpected best-seller, composed by Gordon Jenkins and combining music and the spoken word, had been released in 1946.

The large and prestigious orchestra, which no doubt Columbia Records paid for, sported a whole section of double-basses and included (perhaps surprisingly) some of the top black players in Los Angeles, alongside white sessionmen such as Art Shapiro, Artie Bernstein and Ted Nash; the latter, according to Sy Johnson, was said by Mingus to have helped with the orchestration,[12] thus becoming the first musician to assist Mingus in a role which Johnson himself and others were to fill later on. One of the consequences of this session was that Mingus received encouragement from no less than Charlie Parker, who was now out of hospital and working with Howard McGhee at the Hi-De-Ho prior to returning to New York. 'He heard it in the studio; they never released it. He said it was the sort of thing I should keep on doing, and that I shouldn't be discouraged . . . He never mentioned whether he thought my bass playing was good or bad, but he always thought I was a good writer.'[13]

Being around Parker when he was not strung out on heroin also reinforced Mingus's later determination not to become dependent on hard drugs, and when in 1950 he was turned on by a member of the medical profession, 'It seemed like, coming out of it, I was going to die. At least if I was going to die I wanted to die the way I came in – sober, and watching everything that happened – because I had an unwinding that I felt was a death.' He was, however, well acquainted with the other ways of the night-club world, the violence and the prostitution and the opportunities for musicians themselves to become involved; certainly, by the time of his twenty-fifth birthday, Mingus's charismatic self-absorption when playing – not to mention his 200-pound figure which seemed to dwarf the instrument rather than, as with most bassists, the other way round – guaranteed him the attentions of numerous women, some of whom were prostitutes. Of his own attraction to pimping as a way of life, Mingus said:

> Well, that's like being a President. Because, first of all, you'd be abnormal to not like a Cadillac or Rolls-Royce, in Watts . . . But I began to look at the human beings involved . . . If I send a girl into the streets and tell her I love her, I got to live with myself. So a pimp is something I could never be. I tried it, to say 'I'm as good as you are' or 'I can do what you can do.'[14]

And yet Mingus hung on to the idea of sex as a form of power throughout his life. In the 1966 documentary film *Mingus*, he is heard to say (referring to the person threatening to evict him at the time) 'I'll take his daughter and sell her back to him, if necessary.'[15]

An event also capable of drawing extravagant claims from Mingus was the death in August 1947 of his forty-six-year-old stepbrother Odell Carson, which a certain amount of poetic licence in the autobiography attributes to a loss of the will to live (and to a date some years earlier). The official cause of death was a 'probable carcinoma [cancer] of the stomach'. But, again in the 1960s, Mingus told a gullible interviewer that 'They lynched my stepbrother – he was twenty-three years old . . . The white people passed by and laughed about it.'[16] Despite Odell's death and Jeanne's divorce suit,* Mingus at this period had an overwhelming desire to play as much as possible. His new regular gig was with Cee Pee Johnson who, although chiefly an entertainer, was known like Cab Calloway for employing excellent musicians (including at different times Ernie and Marshall Royal, Karl George, William Woodman Jr and – in the edition just before the one Mingus worked with – Dexter Gordon, Gerald Wilson, Trummy Young and Red Callender). In addition, the Swing Club was nearby where, as pianist Joe Albany recalled, 'I was working with Stan Getz and a drummer named Jimmy Falcone – we didn't have a bass player – and I always was grateful for the fact that Mingus would come [and] sit in with us.'[17] This further example of taking every opportunity to play perhaps shows why Mingus was good and ready when in the summer and autumn of 1947 Lionel Hampton spent three months on the Coast touring, and as usual looking for new personnel. Hampton not only formed his 1940 big band on the Coast but frequently sought his replacements there too, hiring for instance Joe Comfort and Jack Kelso in 1946 and Britt Woodman in early 1947. Now that Comfort had decided to stay in Los Angeles at the end of Hamp's latest visit, he recommended Mingus in his place.

As in the Ellington band of the late 1930s, Hampton had for a couple of years carried two bass players, and the first chair, in terms of seniority and of being the one with the amplifier (small as they were in those days), belonged to the workmanlike Charlie Harris, who like Joe Comfort later played with the Nat King Cole Trio. But Hamp, who was always receptive to genuine new talent, decided to feature Mingus as a bass soloist, which made something of a change of pace compared to the rest of the band's repertoire. Most of the arrangements came from within the band, written by saxists Bobby

*Jeanne Page, as she later became, died of cancer on 9 September 1981.

Plater and Ben Kynard among others, and despite some imitation of the current Gillespie band (an influence also heard in Mingus's small-group contribution *Zoo-Baba-Da-Oo-Ee*) it continued the Hampton tradition of heavy brass and an even heavier but intensely swinging rhythm section. Mingus's score for *Body and Soul*, however, would have sounded out of place in anyone's book except possibly Stan Kenton's, and it uses clarinets and trombones as blocks of colour (rather in the manner of *Chill of Death* or of *Bemoanable Lady*, which belongs to this period), to back the arranger's partly bowed solo, and concludes with a screech from high-note trumpeter Leo 'The Whistler' Sheppard. *Mingus Fingers*, although closer to the Hampton norm, is inspired by the Oscar Pettiford (and subsequently Ray Brown) feature *For Bass Faces Only/One Bass Hit*, but with more adventurous scoring again incorporating woodwinds, and with a commanding bass solo (see Appendix A). Furthermore, the basic thirty-two bar chorus includes some whole eight-bar sections based entirely on pedal points, one of these sections being prolonged by extra bars, which represent the first recorded glimmerings of what Mingus was later to call 'extended form'.

The fact that the same arrangement (opened up to feature two tenors and all five trumpets) was re-recorded in 1960 as *Mingus Fingus No. 2*, which was then credited solely to Mingus instead of to Mingus-Hampton-Hamner, points up a business lesson Mingus had learned in 1947. 'I wrote a lot of arrangements for him, but I took them back when I left; he never paid me. That's why he's a millionaire. I had a copyright on *Mingus Fingers* myself, I copyrighted it in California, but his wife said they wouldn't record it unless I assigned it to their publishing firm. A lot of people do that.'[18] But the fact that his technically impressive bass feature had been recorded on a major label by a nationally touring band was clearly to Mingus's advantage, and in any case he was filled with reluctant admiration for Gladys Hampton. 'I remember when we recorded . . . *Mingus Fingers* . . . She bought them all, bought a truckload, man. I said, "Look here, you can't buy them at a regular store." "Don't worry, Mingus, I'll sell them five years later." And she did just that . . . And they'd sell them for three bucks in those days, she upped them to five dollars, sold them at theatres.'[19] Mingus claimed that such tactics enabled Hampton to leave 'the big system – the people who owned Louis Armstrong – he left it and he was able to make some money, he was the only one I know';[20] but, at the period in question, Hamp's band was handled by Joe Glaser's Associated

Booking Corporation. Indeed, this fact very nearly led to an early visit to France, for both *Down Beat* and *Melody Maker* announced that Hampton, along with the Armstrong, Bechet and Hawkins groups, was being considered for the Nice Jazz Festival of February 1948, and the idea may only have been abandoned when the very tradition-minded Hot-Club de France realized that the band was employing beboppers such as Mingus and Fats Navarro.

Navarro, the phenomenal trumpeter who was more consistent than Gillespie (if more predictable rhythmically), had joined the band on its return to the East Coast in the winter of 1947–8. Like Parker a noted heroin addict, he was to die of tuberculosis a couple of years later at the age of only twenty-six, and, for the few months he stayed before returning to New York and Tadd Dameron, he was the most creative soloist in the Hampton band, a fact which the leader recognized by featuring him with Mingus in small-group numbers such as Dameron's *Hot House* (also based on *What Is This Thing Called Love*). Mingus was also considered a suitable companion when Navarro went jamming after the band jobs, ('He knew all the places where they had jam-sessions. He used to go to some Puerto Rican places, some Cuban clubs, too, and sit in with the Cuban bands')[21] but Mingus seems to have been chiefly impressed by his vulnerability. Imitating – as others tend to, when recalling him – Navarro's high-pitched pleading voice, Mingus described a game of 'Follow the leader' which the two were playing dangerously close to a dam:

> He walked in the middle of this little beam, that a tightrope walker would think about, and turned around and said, 'Come on, will you follow the leader, Mingus? Follow me.' And he stopped and sat down, and says 'Are you afraid? Don't be afraid to die, Mingus. I ain't afraid to die' . . . Then he walked to the side, came back, you know. Lit a cigarette, looked down. And he discussed his death on the bus most of the time, and spit up blood. He knew he had TB.[22]

When Hampton began his series of Saturday afternoon broadcasts on the Mutual Network in April 1948, Mingus was also brought into contact with guest artists such as Billie Holiday, for whom he was inspired to write the song *Eclipse* (which he first recorded in 1953, although if she herself ever performed it she must have found it rather unsuited to her style). Even Benny Goodman is known to have appeared on the East Coast as guest soloist with the

Hampton rhythm section, at least for a few engagements, possibly including Hampton's Carnegie Hall concert on 10 April. And one of the few forward-looking members of the regular band, Wes Montgomery, had his first recorded solo preserved via one of the broadcasts, on the tune *Brant Inn Boogie*.

The young white baritonist Pepper Adams, who worked with the band for a few weeks at the tender age of sixteen, has said of this episode:. 'It was a disappointing experience, the band was *capable* of playing very well but it didn't play well.'[23] Although Adams became one of the white musicians he remained friendly with, the Hampton experience was ultimately disappointing for Mingus too, for he made an unmistakable reference to the leader's showmanship in his hopes for a time when 'it will no longer be necessary for a musician to jump up and down on a drum or to dance on a bandstand to receive recognition of his talent'.[24] But his association with Hampton not only brought Mingus to the attention of other musicians and fans (he was voted into joint nineteenth place in the *Metronome* poll at the end of 1948), it also took him for the first time to the southern states with dates in Washington's Howard Theatre and the Royal in Baltimore; Mingus only left, in fact, when after nearly a year the band arrived back on the Coast where Hampton was to work, with Benny Goodman among others, on the film *A Song Is Born*. (Shortly before Mingus's departure, Charlie Harris had been replaced by Roy Johnson who, four years later, while still a member of the Hampton band, became the first player to use a Fender bass regularly.) His timing of this move, however, was not ideal, as clubs and ballrooms were trying (and failing) to cope with increased federal taxes, while the record companies which had not already succumbed were sitting out another A.F.M. strike that lasted until November 1948. It may be that Mingus's decision could have been motivated by meeting a redheaded jazz fan named Celia in San Francisco. She says: 'Actually I wrote out his resignation from the band,' but this proved insufficient to detain him in Frisco, since she turned out to be on the point of marrying a childhood friend, trumpeter Jon Nielson.

So, for a couple of months, Mingus found himself back in Los Angeles, and working two regular gigs each night for the same owner (probably at a cut rate) in order to keep up his alimony payments. Both at the Down Beat and the after-hours Jack's Basket, he appeared with Lou Speigner and pianist Charlie Davis (Spaulding Givens having been co-opted by Oscar Pettiford's trio at the Streets Of Paris), backing the former Lunceford vocalist Dan

Grissom, apparently still trading on his 1946 solo hit *Diane*. Mingus's only musical stimulation came from a couple of rehearsals by the embryonic Roy Porter band, which was shortly to include Art Farmer, Eric Dolphy and Jimmy Knepper, and which may have inspired Mingus to think of an outlet for the big-band arrangements he had retrieved from Lionel Hampton. The situation was saved temporarily by Red Callender who, having gone to Hawaii with Cee Pee Johnson in 1947 and stayed on as a leader in his own right, came back to California for an engagement at the Beige Room of the Barbizon Hotel in San Francisco. Perhaps the name of the Beige Room inspired Red to conceive his Pastel Sextet including two basses, the second of whom was Mingus. Audience reaction, however, was a disappointment, causing the premature termination of the gig and the sadder-but-wiser comment of Callender to *Down Beat*: 'Got to play for the people.'[25] While Red returned to Los Angeles more or less simultaneously with the end of the recording ban, Mingus decided once again to remain in northern California and just before Christmas landed a residency at the Knotty Pine in San Francisco's black suburb of Oakland. For this he used a quartet comprising Herb Caro on tenor (who, incidentally, was to die the following autumn from a drug overdose), Buzz Wheeler on piano and drummer Kenny McDonald.

Clearly, in Oakland, playing for the people permitted a more hip style of music, as is shown by the single this group recorded for Harold Fenton's Fentone label. *Lyon's Roar*, which carries a joint credit to Caro and Mingus, is a hectic boppish blues dedicated to, and obviously intended to be played frequently by, KFRC's Jimmy Lyons, who has recalled that 'Mingus would come by my . . . radio show. Two in the morning, I'd find this huge figure of a man huddled up in a coat, with the wind blowing down Taylor Street.'[26] The reverse side, *Pennies from Heaven*, is the first instance on record of Mingus taking a popular standard and presenting it in a lugubrious arrangement which directly contradicts the optimistic lyrics. This attempt to make more explicit the ambiguity and even irony in solos by musicians like Lester Young, Billie Holiday and the earlier Louis Armstrong later led, in Mingus's case, to such notable performances as *A Foggy Day*, *Flamingo* and (more indirectly, perhaps) *Cocktails for Two*. But by far the most successful aspect of this particular stay in San Francisco was the rehearsal big band which Mingus formed and which also recorded for Fentone in early 1949. Significantly, the sides are important not so much because of the larger forces used – in the following decade, many small groups tried to emulate the punch of the big bands, while Mingus's ambition was always to use a large ensemble with the flexibility of a small group – but because of the ambitious ideas involved.

Granted that 'ambitious' is a rather ambivalent compliment, the song *He's Gone*, arranged but not composed by Mingus, begins with a long quasi-symphonic introduction featuring Mingus's only known recording on the cello, alongside a written flute part played by Dante Profumato of the San Francisco Symphony Orchestra. Ralph Gleason, who reported on the session itself, appeared to be echoing Mingus's own words when he wrote later: 'He has proven that there should be no segregation in music between classical and jazz. And that it is possible to make classical musicians swing by *writing* it correctly for them.'[27] This may also apply to the Mingus composition *God's Portrait*, the performance of which 'isn't all its composer had hoped it would be'[28] and which, despite a worldwide search by the Smithsonian Institution, has not come to light at the time of writing. We do, however, know a bit about it, for Nat Hentoff wrote that *God's Portrait* was later retitled *Self-Portrait* (an interesting progression!), then *Portrait* and finally *Old Portrait*: 'Mingus wrote the song shortly after the end of his first marriage. He was depressed at the loss of his family, and while on a train, he was led by the passing landscape to think about the kind of man who loves all aspects of nature but cannot love people. At the time, Mingus felt he fitted that description.'[29] The evidence of the revised title makes *God's Portrait* the first version of a piece which stayed in Mingus's performing repertoire longer than any other (till at least 1971) and also, since Mingus never revised the key-signatures assigned to his compositions, it is the first of a series of lyrical and often very personal ballads in the key of D flat. As well as being a tonality to which Mingus returned with increasing frequency as he grew older, D flat is the key invariably used for non-vocal versions of both *Body and Soul* and *Lush Life*, and a favourite Ellington key (*Don't Get Around Much Anymore*, *On a Turquoise Cloud*, *Things Ain't What They Used To Be* etc.).

The composition that stands out from all the rest of Mingus's 1940s output, however, is *The Story of Love*, which, in its two very similar big-band versions, looks forward to many aspects of the heady sounds Mingus eventually became known for. Although the ensemble theme statement is a conventional A/A/B/A thirty-two bar chorus, both the trumpet and trombone sections are sometimes used in unison as a vehicle for piling up simultaneous melodic lines over the same harmonic base (and, incidentally, the limitations of the recording make the result sound excitingly chaotic in the manner of, say, *Blues and Roots* which was done exactly ten years later). The use of a tambourine in the intro distinguishes the Latin vamp from similar passages by Gillespie and, unlike *Night in Tunisia* or *Manteca*, the two chords alternating throughout the A sections of the theme are E7 and Fmajor7; though the effect is weakened by the more conventional F major backing to the solos, the harmonic base for the ensemble choruses thus necessitates melodies on the same 'Spanish' scale heard in Mingus's 1957 *Tijuana Table Dance*. In fact, given the known autobiographical background of *God's Portrait*, it may not be too fanciful to relate the title of *The Story of Love* and its musical content to an earlier trip to Mexico, the one undertaken according to Mingus's book with his childhood sweetheart 'Lee-Marie'. Whether or not this was a factor in its success, *The Story of Love* lends the most weight to Mingus's statement that 'all his discoveries were made in the forties',[30] and illustrates best Buddy Collette's summation of this period: 'In a sense, Mingus was the most creative here. He had his own thing he was doing no matter what else was going on. He wasn't completely out of the bebop, and he wasn't completely in it.'[31] And, although the style is very different, this session on an unspecified date shortly before Mingus's twenty-seventh birthday may be compared, as a landmark, with the twenty-seven-year-old Duke Ellington beginning to find himself musically with his first recordings of *East St Louis Toodle-oo*.

Despite the hints of things to come, Mingus's music at this time is perhaps best seen as part of a trend, a bop-inspired experimental trend exemplified during 1949 by the first public appearances of the Dave Brubeck Octet, also in San Francisco, and Bill Russo's Chicago big band (including the Los Angeles trumpeter Hobart Dotson). However, Mingus's career was noticeably unsettled around this time, and his stay in San Francisco ended with what sounded like another important affiliation, when he was invited to join Billie Holiday. Actually, the gig was with the Red Norvo Sextet who, having backed Billie on an Armed Forces Radio Service recording in January, had undertaken a West Coast tour with her in March and, when in San Francisco, had lost the services of their bassist Iggy Shevack. But Billie, under pressure from a recent court appearance and what she felt to be morbid curiosity on the part of her audiences, left the tour prematurely and caused the cancellation of the remaining dates for the band also. Finding further work in the

San Francisco area proved impossible, so Mingus returned once more to Los Angeles and, with Red Callender as producer, recorded two sessions issued by the music store Dolphin's of Hollywood. One was another relatively commercial effort, featuring a Mingus song reminiscent of the vocal duets of the Gillespie band, *Boppin' n' Boston*, while the quartet session consists principally of two bass solos, *Mingus Fingers* (with Buddy Collette on clarinet) and *These Foolish Things*, on which Collette improvises backing phrases as behind another front-line horn, rather than a bass. But these sides and those recorded for Fentone – for which Harold Fenton had announced plans to lease to a national distributor, although nothing ever came of this – appeared towards the end of this particular outcropping of small labels and must have been some of the least well distributed records ever made. In addition, Mingus's 1946 Excelsior tracks had by now disappeared along with the company itself, while the 4 Star recordings, although technically still available, were already hard to find as a result of their minimal sales. Despite the beginnings of a national reputation, working with other people's bands had usually been a disappointment, one way or another, while his own music seemed destined to sink without trace.

Whether or not he paid a brief visit to New York, the one described in Chapters 30–32 of *Beneath the Underdog*, he was neither playing music regularly nor keeping up his union dues. By the spring of 1950, he was not listed in the A.F.M. directories of either the Los Angeles (segregated) locals or the San Francisco (segregated) locals. In fact he had used his previous temporary job with the post office as a lever to become a full-time mailman. Less romantic than music-making, it was at least providing a regular income and the sort of peace of mind that comes from undemanding work, and it was probably this creative limbo – as well as the McCarthyism referred to in the first line – which prompted Mingus's poem *Suite Freedom*:

> This mule ain't from Moscow; / This mule ain't from the south,
> But this mule's got some learning . . . / Mostly mouth-to-mouth.

> This mule could be called stubborn – and lazy
> But in a clever sort of way, / This mule's been waiting and
>   planning . . .
> And working . . . / In seclusion – / For a sacred kind of day.

41

The day that burning sticks – / Or crosses – / Is not mere child's
 play . . .
But a mad man / In his bloom
Whose loveless soul / Is imperfection / In its most lustrous
 bloom.

Stand still, old mule, / Soothe in contemplation
Thy burning whole / And aching thigh.
That your stubbornness / Is of the living,
And cruel anxiety / Has begun to die.

Stand fast, / Young old mule, / Stand fast.[32]

Soothing himself in contemplation, then, Mingus had completely
opted out of the scene when vibraphonist Red Norvo, returning to
Los Angeles for a residency at the Haig with his new trio, including
Tal Farlow, needed to replace bassist Red Kelly. It was pianist
Jimmy Rowles who suggested that Norvo seek out Mingus again,
and it was Buddy Collette who knew his whereabouts: 'Sure, he
works for the Post Office, delivering mail.'[33] Who it was who was
quoted by Nat Hentoff as saying to Mingus: 'Why do you go with
them and make those whites sound good? That combo wouldn't
swing at all if you weren't there,'[34] is not recorded.

On paper, Norvo's instrumentation was merely the popular
piano-guitar-bass trio (as used by Nat Cole, Art Tatum, the Strings
And Keys, Charles Brown etc.) carried on by other means, and that
there was a popular appeal in the group's sound is confirmed by
their adoption of the George Shearing arrangements of *September
in the Rain* and *East of the Sun*. But with only the guitar of Farlow
amplified, and that at a very low level so as not to overwhelm the
vibraphone, this quietly revolutionary group ushered in a half-
decade of 'cool' jazz which culminated in the emergence of the not
dissimilar Modern Jazz Quartet. And, historically, it represented
the first time that the double-bass had been treated as an equal voice
with other melody instruments; to be sure, there had been experimental precedents such as Ellington's duets with Blanton, Mingus's
own recent quartet session and doubtless Red Callender's Pastel
Sextet, but this was the first regularly organized group in which the
bassist was seen – and, more importantly, heard – as more than just
a rhythm instrument. According to Norvo, the recordings which
best illustrate the group's live balance were the Standard transcriptions since, on their other sessions, 'If we played soft, they

brought us up. If we played loud, they brought us down.'[35] However, because of the all-purpose nature of radio transcriptions, the performances are both shorter and less adventurous than those on the 78s and LPs done for the Discovery label. On these, there are not only hints of Mingus's later work, such as the repetitive introductory figures on *I've Got You Under My Skin* or on *Time and Tide* (the latter consisting of bowed double-stops in the rhythm of the famous 1932 *paso doble Spanish Gypsy Dance*), but also a general flexibility about instrumental roles which allows Mingus to play a high countermelody (again bowed) against vibes and guitar tremeloes on *Mood Indigo*, or Tal Farlow to use a walking bass line on guitar(!) under Mingus's solos on *Godchild*. Occasionally these collective head-arrangements veer towards the twee or the melodramatic but, taken overall, they are more creative than almost anything else that emerged from the West Coast in the early 1950s.

Norvo's original long-running residency at the Haig, during which Mingus had learned of the death of Fats Navarro, was followed by a trip as far as Chicago and a return to the Coast by Christmas 1950. In addition, the trio's first records had been issued in time for them to be voted in sixth place in the year-end *Down Beat* poll, with Mingus himself now becoming joint seventeenth in popularity on bass; Eddie Safranski (the bassist formerly with Kenton) was first, Ray Brown (with Ella Fitzgerald, then Oscar Peterson) was second, while Pettiford had earned third place. To put the icing on the cake, the group visited San Francisco's Black Hawk for four weeks from mid-March, bringing Mingus 'back as a star with the hottest thing in music at the moment',[36] in the words of Ralph Gleason. Mingus celebrated this particular visit in a number of ways, for instance by sitting in at the famous Bop City, where Roy Porter was now the house drummer, and by doing his first *Down Beat* interview with Gleason (interestingly, in view of his involvement in the written word, Mingus not only felt the initial interview session to be unsatisfactory but remedied this by expressing his thoughts in a long letter, which Gleason printed instead). And then on 2 April the lady who a couple of years earlier had become Celia Nielson became Celia Mingus. 'Actually,' she recalls, 'we wanted to be married on 1 April, which was the day that my divorce was final. But Red wouldn't let us, he said it was a bad omen.'

While still on the Coast, Mingus persuaded Richard Bock of Discovery to record a duo session with his colleague Spaulding Givens (including a bass feature on *Body and Soul*, plus many other favourite standards which Mingus was later to record with other

43

pianists). And he made his first two performing appearances on film with the trio, which then travelled across country via fortnights in Denver, Chicago and Toronto to make its successful New York debut at the Embers in mid-July. (In view of what was about to happen in New York, it is worth noting that the producers of the feature film *Texas Carnival* did not allow Mingus to appear on screen with the [white] vocalist and his fellow musicians. Interesting in a different way is the coincidence that the short subject *Eddie Peabody and Sonny Burke's Orchestra* not only features the trio in their 'Spanish' arrangement of *Time and Tide*, but this number is immediately preceded by an 'exotic' dancer who accompanies herself on the castanets.) It must have been around this time, certainly after the trio reached the East Coast, that Mingus took part in one of the famous jam-sessions at Christy's near Boston with, among others, Charlie Parker; the one track to have been issued from this date includes a three-chorus solo on *I'll Remember April* with several trademarks of the later Mingus, not least among them quotations from *All God's Children Got Rhythm* (played ironically right across the beat!) and from *God Bless America*. As well as being on top form musically during the Embers residency, Mingus got what seemed like another good break when in September the trio was signed to play on television, for a series of early colour transmissions five afternoons a week, with vocalist Mel Torme on WCBS. But suddenly the icing melted, and the whole cake went soggy. Thanks to a combination of A.F.M. officials and almost certainly other corporate pressures, the Red Norvo Trio first of all spent a couple of days in the studio completely idle, and then appeared on screen with a temporary (white) replacement. *Down Beat* reported unemotionally that 'Because bassist Charlie Mingus is not a member of Local 802, he was nixed out of the show at the last minute and Red used Clyde Lombardi instead.'[37]

Thinking to soften the blow, but in Mingus's eyes adding insult to injury, Norvo offered to continue using him at the Embers. But Mingus had been planning to stay in New York anyway and chose this moment to make the break, under at least a glimmer of publicity surrounding the WCBS incident. The very next week he went to work with Miles Davis at Birdland, and the week after that made his presence felt at Miles's first Prestige long-playing recording. 'Carrying his bass on his back,' according to sideman Jackie McLean, Mingus 'stood at the piano, running over the tunes'.[38] Doubtless he ran over a few of his own too, in a vain attempt to gain his own Prestige record date.

3
Bird Calls

So finally, at the age of twenty-nine, Mingus was gigging in New York. For the remainder of his life, he was to be an adopted New Yorker, with the necessary credentials of a love-hate relationship with the city he made his new home. Getting established there, and especially getting record dates under his own name, was another matter, but Mingus came with an enviable reputation as a bassist, and a less enviable one of being able to throw his weight around. With the exception of the television booking, he seems to have sidestepped any problems with the A.F.M. branch, who normally required six months' residence in New York before a potential member of Local 802 could undertake any except casual engagements. Because Celia was already working as a secretary Mingus could weather the lack of income from playing, but he was offered some casual engagements and, after appearing at Birdland with Miles Davis and Billy Taylor, he was free to travel to Boston for a fortnight with the Billy Taylor Trio. Taylor described the association as follows: 'I was influenced by Ellington, and so was he. I knew many Tatum voicings, and so did he. We learned a lot from each other. I taught him what a *montuna** was, and he taught me not to make the drums and bass subservient to the piano in a trio.'[1]

This particular fortnight at Storyville in Boston also brought him

---

*The section of a mambo performance which is based on a single chord (usually the dominant 7th) and which incorporates open-ended improvisation (on the mixolydian mode), for example, Bud Powell's *Un Poco Loco*. This may well be a distant influence on Mingus's later use of modal passages, and of 'extended forms'.

into contact with two figures not only important in their own right but of considerable significance in the Mingus story: namely George Wein, then owner/manager of the Storyville, later festival producer and frequent booker of Mingus's bands; and his counterpart and subsequent adversary Nat Hentoff, then jazz/folk/classical disc-jockey (and boxing commentator) for station WMEX and Boston correspondent of *Down Beat*, and later a noted political writer. Neither Mingus nor Wein ever recalled much of their early employee/employer relationship, but Mingus and Hentoff seem to have taken to each other right away. Mingus appeared on Hentoff's jazz programme and discussed the future of both jazz and European music, and started a long-running correspondence on these and other subjects, which meant so much to him that he quoted from Hentoff's letters both in *Beneath the Underdog* and in the sleeve-notes to one of his albums. Hentoff also produced the Roost album of the Taylor trio's live broadcast from the Storyville.

By the spring of 1952, when Mingus's Local 802 card came through, he and Celia had moved from the Maryland Hotel into an apartment at 89th and 3rd Street, where they stayed for two years before moving out to Long Island. Mingus had also received the sum of $500 claimed from Red Norvo in lieu of notice and, with the addition of a small donation from two of Celia's workmates, he put it to good use (and, incidentally, celebrated his thirtieth birthday) by recording the first session for his own record company, Debut. The new phase of independent labels, in which for the first time the musicians themselves took a major role in ownership and manage-ment, seems to have gathered momentum at the turn of the decade (of the shortlived 1940s companies, only Mezz Mezzrow's King Jazz and bassist Al Hall's Wax labels came into this category). With the major companies' interest in jazz at a new low after the second A.F.M. strike, first Dave Brubeck had helped start the Fantasy label in 1950, then in 1951 Dizzy Gillespie (Dee Gee) and Lennie Tristano (Jazz Records) had created their own outlets, as did Woody Herman (Mars) around the same time that Debut was founded. Also, despite still being contracted to Columbia, Duke Ellington had in 1950 formed the Mercer label to record small-group tracks which would not tempt the major companies, and he it was too who a decade earlier had set the precedent of an independ-ent publishing company (Tempo Music) for his less commercial compositions.

Musicians may have been slower to follow up this latter idea (although by 1951 Lucky Thompson had published his song *The*

Bluest Blues and had it recorded by Gillespie) but one of Mingus's chief purposes in forming the record-label was for his own music, so it made sense also to have his own publishing company. Its name Chazz-Mar Inc. is explained by the fact that the eventual third partner in both companies, along with Mingus and Celia, was the drummer and composer Max Roach, who was to be Mingus's soul brother for many years to come. Roach's playing, even more than Mingus's at this period, expressed powerful emotion with a controlled precision. His lively intellect, and the fact that he and Mingus saw eye to eye about the position of blacks and black music in American society clearly helped cement their friendship, but their initial admiration for each other was musical. Roach described being taken by Miles Davis, when both were still members of the Charlie Parker Quintet, to hear this 'new young voice from the West Coast'[2] with Lionel Hampton's band, while Mingus spoke of the impact of walking in on a Roach drum solo and recognizing the tune merely from Roach's solo construction: 'He wasn't playing the melody, but . . . he was able to let you know that he knew where he was. He wasn't lost in the environment of the tune, he wasn't just banging, like tom-toms from an African jungle.'[3]

As a bass-and-drums team Max and Mingus worked together well, if infrequently, and possibly the first occasion was a reunion between Parker and Gillespie, part of which was recorded by Leonard Feather for broadcast on the Voice Of America. The intermittent three-year association as Parker's bassist was what finally persuaded Mingus that many of the self-styled beboppers had been musical 'groupies', whereas Bird himself was one of a kind, just like Ellington. But it was not sufficient merely to put Parker on the same level as Duke; for Duke, in any case, was not then particularly fashionable – Mingus even wrote to *Down Beat* after an unfavourable review of the Ellington band to defend the 'great man who has done more for music and the betterment of his race than few [*sic*] other men have'[4] – and it appeared that black musicians in New York were far more fashion-conscious than those on the West Coast. Ironically, this was partly a reaction to the white West Coast jazz of the period (whose increasing popularity might have rubbed off on Mingus, had he not left the Coast just when it all started to take off), but once again Mingus had to make a symbolic choice and decide consciously to become a disciple of Parker:

> He put something else in there that had another kind of expression, . . . more than just, say, the blues or the pain that the black

people have been through. And in fact he brought hope in. As Max Roach was saying, we played like this, 'It's hopeless'; now it's like 'Everything gonna be alright.' . . . I knew I had an uplift to life from hearing his playing. In fact, I immediately gave up what I believed in, which came from classical and Duke, and I felt a whole change in my *soul* when I joined up and accepted that I liked Charlie Parker. 'Cause I didn't like him right away. I was almost pushed into it by my wife.[5]

'It's true,' adds Celia, 'I sort of bombarded Mingus with all my Bird records,' and, when he actually got to know Parker, Mingus recognized that he shared some of the same aspirations: 'For instance, Bird called me on the phone one day and said: "How does this sound?" and he was playing – ad-libbing – to the Berceuse, or Lullaby, section of Stravinsky's *Firebird Suite*! . . . I'd like to write a suite of three or four hours and have a solo in spots that is like Charlie Parker, with Bird in mind, playing ad lib.'[6]

So Mingus was after all a bona-fide 'modernist' but, as usual where fashion is concerned, many different styles were lumped under one heading. Being a modernist meant playing with Bird, it meant playing with Stan Getz (which Mingus did for part of the spring and summer of 1952, both in New York and Boston), and it meant playing with Lennie Tristano. In retrospect, it may seem odd that Mingus and Max Roach, virtually alone among black musicians, were for a short while quite enamoured of Tristano's approach to jazz, which restricted the rhythmic contribution of bass and drums (as opposed to the improvising soloists) quite severely. Mingus credited Fats Navarro with encouraging him to keep an open mind about Tristano ('Mingus, cats say Lennie's music is weird, what's weird Mingus? I got ears, Lennie can't play nothing I can't play 'cause I can hear him')[7] but both Mingus and Roach were attracted by the fact that Tristano was a thinker and teacher, just as Mingus was interested in the work of pianist-teacher-theorist John Mehegan. Tristano was trying to create a group of like-minded players, and clearly Mingus and Roach were pleased by the prospect of earning money by teaching students at Tristano's school; and, at least in theory, they approved of such consciously articulated developments as that of emasculating the rhythm section in order to free the front line. Mingus said at the time, 'Individuals can swing alone like Bird, and groups can swing collectively like Tristano's,'[8] revealing his lack of understanding that collective swing can barely exist unless each individual can swing alone, as several of the Tristano alumni did subsequently. However, the fact that Mingus never saw swinging as the be-all and end-all of music – indeed until the late 1950s he undervalued it – was what enabled him to test some of his innovations which only really fell into place later.

There are signs of this imbalance in Mingus's first Debut singles (most of which were pressed, incidentally, by RCA-Victor), and Mingus did use Lee Konitz to play a typically Tristanoesque line on *Extrasensory Perception*, an original based on the amended chord-sequence of *Idaho* with a new middle-eight. But the liaison between Tristano, blind and by all accounts a rather prickly personality, and the outspoken Mingus was an uneasy one. This is illustrated by a story which, until after Mingus's death, was always printed with the relevant names omitted:

> I was driving to work with Lennie Tristano and two black musicians. Lennie asked why we objected to being called 'niggers'. 'Hell,' he said, 'you use it among yourselves all the time.' The way he asked showed he was just bugging us . . . Now this was a guy I really loved, and especially at that time. But this was too much. I finally told him: 'You keep this up and when we get to the gig, I'm going to turn off all the lights and kick your ass.' Lennie laughed, kind of. Then he was silent for a while, and finally told us about something that had happened to him at Birdland a few nights before. Woody Herman, who's supposed to be a very nice guy and a funny one, came over to Lennie. He asked Tristano if he were *really* blind. 'Yes,' Lennie said, 'I can't see anything.' . . . 'Good,' said Woody. 'Good, you motherfucker, I'm glad you can't see!' The car got very still. The other guys were shocked at such wanton cruelty. But I knew Lennie; I knew how destructive he could be. And I asked him, 'But what did you do to get that guy so hurt and angry?'[9]

Although Tristano did exert a minor but undeniable influence on Mingus's thinking about group approaches to improvisation, it is perhaps not surprising that Mingus found more freedom as a bass player alongside the many other pianists he gigged with, including on several occasions in 1953 the bebop giant Bud Powell (for whom he created several introductory bass figures), and especially Billy Taylor.

But, apart from some work with Charlie Parker in New York, Mingus's freelance activities were scarce, to say the least. And, as the winter of 1952 came on, he decided rather than consider playing non-jazz music to turn again to the Post Office. He was thus employed for several weeks at least. 'But this security was taken from me by Charlie Parker, who called me up, reminded me of my aesthetic responsibilities, and made me give up my chance at a pension and Blue Cross.'[10] Celia says that, at the time, 'I don't think he would have done it for anyone else,' so for $150 a week Mingus travelled to Philadelphia for his first out-of-town job with Parker, although as soon as Parker didn't have a job to offer he sorely missed the Post Office salary. At least trips such as the one to Philadelphia enabled Mingus to act as debt-collector for Debut records. 'There's one guy owed us quite a bit of money,' recalls Celia, 'and just said he couldn't pay. So Mingus looked around the office and he picked up an adding machine, he says "What's this worth?" And the guy says "Oh, a couple of hundred dollars," so Mingus says "OK I'll take this, then!" So the guy says "Wait a minute!" and gave him a cheque.'

Ironically, indeed farcically as it turned out, the same problem which marred Mingus's relationship with Tristano also proved fatal when Duke Ellington's bassist Wendell Marshall, who had succeeded Pettiford, took leave of absence to get married in January 1953 and Mingus was asked to work with his original idol. Britt Woodman was already in the band, and Mingus might conceivably have settled down to a long stay, but for his ready tongue. When saxist/clarinettist Tony Scott replaced Paul Gonsalves some days after Mingus joined, the bassist berated him thus: 'Where are you going, Tony? Man, don't you know you're doing a Negro musician out of a job?'[11] Scott also mentioned in another interview:

> He says, 'You white people are always telling us how to talk.' I turned around and said, 'I'm darker than you are, Mingus.' Mingus is about my colour, I'm a Sicilian and he had a lotta white blood in there. He was trying to prove he was a black man, and I took his negritude away. He came up behind me . . . and strangled me, one hand around my throat and one over my eyes. Britt and Clark [Terry] pulled him off. Britt wouldn't look at him after that, and Mingus said, 'Man, I must've stepped on my dick. My best friend won't look at me.' I was there when Mingus had that big to-do with Juan Tizol . . . Juan with a machete, Mingus with a fire-axe. Duke had to fire him.[12]

According to Mingus's own account, this particular altercation which on 3 February ended his period with Duke began with a musical disagreement, aggravated by the fact that the extremely light-skinned Tizol characterized Mingus's musical ability as that of a 'nigger'. In the event, it was to be almost ten years before Ellington could employ Mingus's musicianship to the full and, although he could conceivably have found ways to incorporate Mingus's gifts in his compositions as he had done with Blanton and Pettiford, in the early 1950s Mingus was nearing the peak of his virtuoso period and might have chafed at the restrictions of regular big-band playing.

Mingus himself put it slightly differently when interviewed at this period by Nat Hentoff: 'I've come to the point, musically and personally, where I have to play the way I want to . . . Great artists like Bird, Pres, Dizzy, Max Roach, Blanton and Charlie Christian have worked and suffered to develop their own style. Then the copyists come, singing their praises while stealing their phrases.' And, while mentioning the related problem of inferior musicians with superior salesmanship, Mingus introduced the description 'clowns', a word which was highly significant in Mingus's vocabulary: 'The impresarios bill these circus artists as jazzmen because "jazz" has become a commodity to sell, like apples or, more accurately, corn.'[13]

An artistically successful association with three of the great artists Mingus described took place in the same month the interview was published, when the Toronto New Jazz Society held an all-star concert at Massey Hall on 15 May. Because in retrospect the event bulked large in the careers of all the participants, many words have been spent on it over the years, and there have even been differing accounts of who was supposed to take part. Bill Coss's notes to the record album which resulted noted that the Society 'decided to reunite as many of the early bop greats as they possibly could . . . Running into early trouble, the club finally contracted with bassist Charlie Mingus to bring such a group,'[14] but Max Roach has stated on a couple of recent occasions that he was responsible for suggesting Mingus as 'substitute for Oscar Pettiford who had broken his arm playing baseball'.[15] This only proves how fallible memory can be, for Pettiford's injury occurred in 1949, but it has to be admitted that Parker, Gillespie, Bud Powell and Roach himself were originators of New York bebop, and the choice of Pettiford would therefore have been logical. To complicate matters further, in 1968 writer Len Dobbin quoted one of the concert organizers as saying that 'the original intention was to have Lennie Tristano on piano',[16]

51

but this was doubtless before Mingus was asked to book the group. Concerning its all-star nature, Mingus recalled that 'Bud Powell was billed first . . . because Oscar Goodstein [Powell's manager and legal guardian at the time] had gotten Bud more money than Dizzy or Bird had asked for. And of course me and Max, just the supporters of the soloists, never thought we'd get as much as the horns.'[17]

The actual music performed at the concert, as well as a set by a specially organized local big band, comprised six quintet numbers, six piano trio numbers, a bass feature with piano and drums, and an unaccompanied drum solo, all of which (apart from the bass feature) was issued on Debut records. Mingus and Roach had planned the recording quite carefully, jointly purchasing several reels of green-backed tape, and Mingus later defended himself against charges of 'amateur' recording by saying, 'That concert was recorded on professional equipment . . . but we didn't have the best engineer.'[18] Nevertheless, while the slightly thin sound – seemingly taken from the P.A. system – allowed for a reasonable internal balance between the rhythm section, the addition of the front-line instruments left the bass lines barely audible except during Mingus's solo on *Hot House*. This number was not included in the initial release of two ten-inch albums, consisting respectively of half the quintet set and most of the trio set (plus a studio-recorded version of Mingus's *Bass-ically Speaking*, improvised on a D minor sequence similar to *Weird Nightmare*). But, having already re-recorded one number because of unsatisfactory balance, Mingus decided for the final ten-inch album of the remaining quintet items to overdub new bass parts, with the production assistance of Max Roach, and then did the same for the previously released tracks when these were reissued in the twelve-inch format in 1956. The practice of over-dubbing new accompaniments went back to the mid-1930s when early acoustic discs of Enrico Caruso were reissued with newly recorded backing, while multi-tracking to create a 'one-man band' (as in Sidney Bechet's 1941 session) had more recently been popularized by Les Paul's recordings such as *How High the Moon* and used in Lennie Tristano's session released on his own Jazz label (*Ju-Ju* and *Pastome*). The only point at which Mingus's original Massey Hall performance is heard clearly is during his *Hot House* solo, which was left to stand, whereas the solo on *All the Things You Are* (immediately after Powell's chorus), being partially obscured by the front line, *was* overdubbed and therefore gives the listener an opportunity to hear Mingus duetting with himself.

As the last occasion on which the other four musicians played together, this concert has been seen as signifying the end of an era, but for Mingus, who 'wasn't completely in it', it symbolized his acceptance by the New York beboppers. One week afterwards, Mingus and Roach recorded with Parker for Norman Granz on the aborted Bird-with-woodwinds session arranged by Gil Evans (this was doubtless the point at which the three protagonists attempted to sell Granz the Massey Hall tapes) and the following week Parker and Gillespie appeared at Birdland as soloists with a Bud Powell trio which included Mingus. Possibly it was at this period, rather than (as in one of Mingus's accounts) immediately before Parker's death, that the two of them had a discussion between sets about reincarnation:

> We were having a conversation with probably Bud and Monk at a table, . . . and I made a view on it and he said, 'Mingus, that's something to think about. I'll give my views, let's discuss it on the bandstand.' When I got to the bandstand, man, what he played – it totalled up everything we was talking about! . . . And we discussed it *off* the bandstand, and we heard the same things, everybody involved heard the same things . . . I'm saying *Bird* started this, I never heard it in Duke. I heard Duke's emotions and feelings, but I never heard him communicate a definite A-B-C-D-E-F thought, or words.

Just four days after the Canadian concert, Mingus attended the first New York recording of one of his tunes by another artist. His piano appearance on Miles Davis's Prestige session (unscheduled and almost certainly unpaid) was probably prompted by misgivings about the pianist on the date, John Lewis. It has recently been said – in a slightly different context – that Mingus 'would not have trusted someone like John Lewis whom he considered a little "too white" for his purposes', and certainly the pianist who came close to ruining *Parker's Mood* would have made *Smooch* (a retitling of *Weird Nightmare*) less sombre than Mingus's own Powellish voicings.

It was only after his death that most musicians other than those who worked with him would begin to value Mingus's compositions, but at this point in his life he was gaining quite a reputation as a bass teacher. Percy Heath, who had been on the *Smooch* session, says 'In the beginning of the formation of the Modern Jazz Quartet, I needed some more technical information that I didn't have. And I took a few lessons with Mingus, and he gave me an exercise that straightened me out considerably on a lot of things.' And, as an indication of the sort of exercise Mingus might give to an advanced student such as Heath, Joe Albany recalled: 'A bass player told me he had studied with Mingus, and one of the things that Mingus required him to do was the introduction I did for Pres on *She's Funny That Way.*'[19] By this time, indeed, as well as being voted New Star bassist in *Down Beat*'s first Critics' Poll in the summer of 1953, Mingus had advanced beyond the Blanton/Pettiford concept of melodic solos which nevertheless fell easily under the fingers. His ambitions for the bass as a solo instrument were clearly influenced not only by pianists but by Parker, especially in the matter of anticipating or delaying chord-changes in the solo line; on occasion, this sounded strained or unnatural, and certainly harder to 'hear' on the bass than most of what his contemporaries produced. As well as his left-hand facility in all the positions over a range of three octaves, Mingus was greatly aided by the guitar-picking style of his right hand, for, according to Percy Heath, 'Mingus was the first person *I* saw who used different [right-hand] fingers to play successive notes in a phrase.' In short, it was Mingus's solo work of the early and middle 1950s which chiefly led to the further advances of bassists such as Scott LaFaro and Richard Davis in the next few years, while Paul Chambers's extension of the Ray Brown walking style owed at least something to Mingus's avoidance of the obvious when playing 'time' (that is, four notes to the bar).

But Mingus was chiefly busy capitalizing on his role of record company producer, and organizer of the Massey Hall group, and in the summer of 1953 he and Roach ran a series of small concerts at the Putnam Central Club in Brooklyn. Max recalls, 'Mingus also was a person who would just go to a place and see a bar that has a piano in it – any place – he'd go and talk to the owner and say "Listen, I'm going to work in here, don't worry about the money, whatever percentage we get," and he would go into his work-shops.'[20] At about the same time, he took part in at least one of the Sunday afternoon sessions at the Open Door, playing in a quartet with Parker, Roy Haynes and Thelonious Monk, while his own Friday night Jazz Workshops (later to become a generic name for Mingus groups) featured such as Monk, Art Blakey, probably Miles and, of course, Max. The concert which provided material for the next Debut album, however, was a jam-session with four trombonists, J.J. Johnson, Kai Winding, Bennie Green and former Tristano student Willie Dennis. As well as blowing vehicles and solo features (*Stardust* by Green and *Yesterdays* led off by Johnson),

Mingus wrote some special material, such as the autobiographically titled *Chazzanova*, which has a harmonically wayward sequence disguising its thirty-two bar structure, and allows and encourages the trombonists, even when playing backing parts, to interpret them freely. However, if it had also been Mingus's intention to release the other Brooklyn concerts on Debut, this was thwarted either by indifferent performance or, more likely, by contractual difficulties with other companies whose artists were involved. Nevertheless, the Massey Hall issues not only put Debut on the map as a company specializing in quality East Coast jazz, ready to rival Blue Note and Prestige, but brought about distribution and leasing deals with European companies, including the independent Danish Debut label. The money thus earned engendered quite a flurry of studio activity in the winter of 1953–4, including the first albums under their own names by Kenny Dorham, Paul Bley, Sam Most, John LaPorta and Teo Macero.

Mingus did not, of course, play on all these sessions. He did appear, however, in the album featuring Oscar Pettiford on the cello, which Mingus himself by now seems to have dropped again while retaining his interest in it as a composer (for example, its prominent part on his 1953 recording of *Eclipse*, featuring Jimmy Cleveland's wife Janet Thurlow singing the lyrics written for Billie Holiday). By this stage too, Mingus and Pettiford had developed something of a mutual admiration society, and aspiring bassist Buell Neidlinger (who later played with Cecil Taylor) has recalled sessions at Pettiford's apartment when such as Percy Heath, Paul Chambers, Mingus and others 'would come around and pay tribute, you know, just play and talk'.[21] Mingus had also become recognized and respected by a somewhat older generation of players including Gene Ramey, with whom he had alternated at Birdland during 1952 and whom he still knew in the 1970s when Ramey was a bank employee, and Milt Hinton, who appeared on Sam Most's Debut album and on Mingus's two big-band concerts at Town Hall (1962) and Philharmonic Hall (1972).

One further instance of the high-level acceptance accorded to Mingus was also the fulfilment of an ambition harboured for fifteen years, when at the start of 1954, he flew to Miami Beach to do four weeks at the local Birdland with another idol, Art Tatum. The inclusion of a guitar (Everett Barksdale at this period) actually forced Tatum to stick to relatively fixed arrangements, but Mingus still had a lot of listening to do in order to keep up: 'Tatum taught me a lesson. The hippies were so proud of themselves, making minor 9ths and going through a circle of 4ths on a song like *I Can't Get Started*. Tatum had been doing it all the time, sometimes so fast you weren't even conscious of it.'[22] Mingus also spoke of Tatum's attention being caught by hearing Bud Powell on a juke-box ('Who's that? We better go back and find out who's on that record'),[23] and made the following perceptive comparison between the pianists: 'Tatum knew every tune written, including the classics, and I think it got in the way of his composition, because he wasn't a Bud Powell. He wasn't as melodically inventive as Bud . . . Bud and Bird to me should go down as composers.'[24]

The continuity of the Debut operation was hardly jeopardized during Mingus's absence, even though Max Roach was simultaneously in California for several months, for the capable Celia was in charge of the paperwork and of promotional activity. But one could also speculate about the effect on Mingus's marital fidelity of the stay in Miami, and conclude that the Bull was still freelancing, in more ways than one. Any minimally serious astrological guide will describe the typical Taurean as having outsize physical appetites, whether sexual or gastronomical; what is perhaps even more relevant to Mingus is the ability to treat extramarital liaisons (like the ice-cream of which he was so fond) as a dessert complementing, but in no way threatening, any long-established relationship. On the other hand, the long-standing relationship is likely to be regarded with a possessiveness bordering on violence. Perhaps this explains why Mingus was unhappy during this separation from Celia. Fellow bassist George Duvivier, who found himself staying in the same hotel in Miami, has said, 'We ended up talking for about three hours. He seemed to need someone to talk to, and he just poured his whole heart and soul out to me.'[25]

What is certain is that, in order to work with Tatum, Mingus had had to back out of the first concert at Carnegie Recital Hall on 31 January by the two-month-old Jazz Composers' Workshop. Prominent in this loose grouping were saxophonists John LaPorta and Teo Macero and vibraphonist Teddy Charles who in November had been responsible for getting Mingus one of his first brief gigs as a leader, replacing Charles's quartet for a week at Ciro's where Mingus used Macero, Ed Shaughnessy and Spaulding Givens. (The Givens/Mingus duo session, recently purchased from the now-defunct Discovery, had just been issued as part of the first batch of Debut long-player albums.) Other members of the nine-piece group which played the concert were Shaughnessy and such later Mingus associates as Eddie Bert and Don Butterfield. Despite his absence in Miami, the group performed three mid-1940s Mingus compositions that were found by reviewer Barry Ulanov to be 'all swinging, quite modern and wonderfully individual'.[26] That the quality of swing was worth remarking on shows that, although this group was partly an outgrowth of Mingus's workshops the previous summer and partly an outgrowth of the Tristano school (LaPorta was a former student of his, while Macero, who had studied composition at Juilliard, played like an enervated Warne Marsh), their music was by and large far more aridly experimental. Certainly all the leading lights were committed to the idea of making 'musicians swing by writing it correctly', but conclusions must be somewhat tentative since the full JCW ensemble never recorded, and mere hints as to its sound are the most that can be gleaned from the Debut albums of Macero and LaPorta, Teddy Charles's albums on Atlantic and New Jazz, and Mingus's own late 1954 recordings.

It was in fact rumoured that the second concert, on 5 May at the Museum of Modern Art, was to be recorded – by whom it is not clear, and a comparative lull in the activities of Debut (the only sessions done in the first half of 1954 were the John LaPorta LP and a small-group 'Jazz Workshop' featuring LaPorta and vocalist Ada Moore) may mean that the company was short of funds. But this concert too was reviewed, this time by George T. Simon, who noted that the augmented ensemble (now including such as Sam Most, Louis Mucci and pianists Givens and Wally Cirillo) featured a number of Mingus solos, as well as his *Background for Thought*, 'an involved bit of writing, far too confusing to be digested at one hearing, and even intricate enough to call for a halt by Mingus and then a fresh start'.[27] But an indication that Mingus felt improvisation to be underemphasized by the JCW, despite his obvious interest in their general aims, is found in the enthusiasm generated by his sitting in with trumpeter Thad Jones in Detroit (probably earlier in the year, and possibly with Teddy Charles's quartet):

I just heard the greatest trumpet player that I've heard in this life. He uses all the classical [compositional] techniques, and is the first man to make them swing . . . He does . . . the things Diz heard Bird do, and Fats made us think were possible. Yet we wait and wait and a Clifford Brown comes along and reminds us today that this is the way Fats would play those things if we had heard him a week later, when or if he practised instead of junked. Here is a man who practised while Fats goofed and thought while Brownie copied . . . His brother [Elvin] is about as great a

57

prophet. I never swung so much or, rather, lived so much in my life.[28]

Thus, when Mingus began recording again, it was not to document the full JCW but to set up two sessions featuring Thad Jones, one with a quintet (probably the first album to list the bassist's name as 'Charles Mingus' instead of 'Charlie' – always a sore point, the familiar form of his name once provoked Mingus to say, 'Don't call me Charlie; that's not a man's name, that's a name for a horse,')[29] – and one with an ensemble which Mingus once claimed was 'the Chesterfield [radio show] string section and the N.Y. Philharmonic string section combined'.[30] At this session, for economic reasons which were becoming standard in the industry when large groups were used, the strings directed by Mingus and Alonzo Levister were recorded first and the soloists dubbed in afterwards.

That Mingus's own albums were now on labels other than Debut was doubtless a tribute to his increasing fame, and indirectly a by-product of his appearance on the first ten-inch LP by J.J. Johnson and Kai Winding. Perhaps repaying the compliment of being featured on Mingus's four-trombone workshop and album, they used Mingus on bass and requested an original composition from him. *Reflections* turned out to be unlike anything else the popular trombone duo recorded: a miniature suite in six sections, almost entirely written and with a doom-laden atmosphere. It includes one repeated section with the trombones in parallel 4ths and high-register bowed bass adding a third parallel line, which shows a freedom in orchestration derived not only from the innovations of the Norvo Trio but doubtless also of the Jazz Composers' Workshop. The session may have included some fast talking too, for producer Ozzie Cadena (whose second-ever date it was) managed to sign both Mingus and Wally Cirillo to do an album each for Savoy. Three of the items on Mingus's album are based on standard chord-sequences but are particularly interesting for their contrapuntal ensembles: in two instances, these are rather stilted since they consist of different songs played on different instruments at the same time (*Tea for Two* alternates with *Perdido* and has *Body and Soul* as a countermelody, while the version of *Body and Soul* itself also involves *They Can't Take That Away from Me* as an accompanying line). *Getting Together*, based on the chords of *All the Things You Are*, is different in that the three reeds do not play written lines but improvise together in a logical and occasionally semi-atonal manner, and, although the piece's title is copyrighted by Mingus, he freely admitted in the sleeve-notes that 'Teo, John, George, Rudy and Mal, of course, are just as responsible as I am for the final construction here.'[31]

In similar fashion, Mingus's original *Purple Heart* (which he claimed was written for Miles Davis, without however saying when) finds LaPorta and Macero improvising countermelodies behind each other's solo choruses – and this at a time when collective improvisation was considered the exclusive preserve of Dixieland ensembles. Even more extraordinary for the period is *Gregarian Chant*, whose title describes the first recorded attempt since Lennie Tristano's in 1949 to create a totally unplanned group improvisation (Mal Waldron has quoted Mingus as saying at the session, 'When we play this tune, we're not going to play any changes, we're just going to play moods. Just follow me, and put your moods in, and we'll build something beautiful')[32] and in the event Mingus's bowed introduction clearly leads the others into a D minor passage similar to *Bass-ically Speaking*. The remaining item from this session, the equally mournful *Eulogy for Rudy Williams*, is less apparently revolutionary but perhaps more significant in terms of Mingus's development. Inspired by the pre-bop saxophonist's death in a swimming accident the previous month, it contains hints of the famous *Pithecanthropus Erectus* in the work of the saxophones and in a repeated four-bar turnaround (Im|bVImaj7|IIm7b5|V7). It is also the first tribute to a fellow musician, and the immediacy of the subject-matter suggests that Mingus was motivated by more than mere emulation of Ellington, who also wrote many portraits of fellow artists.

The group on this recording, with Mal Waldron and drummer Rudy Nichols (who also recorded with Cleanhead Vinson), but minus George Barrow, also gave a concert at Carnegie Recital Hall on 5 December under the title 'Developments in Modern Jazz', which was described as having evolved from the Jazz Composers' Workshop. As reported by *Down Beat*, 'Audience participation in the form of questions after each number . . . led to lively debates between not only the composer-musicians and members of the audience but between the musicians on the stand themselves,'[33] but in performance the Savoy line-up proved more unified than that which in the same month recorded two albums of *Jazzical Moods* for Period (produced by Leonard Feather) with Thad Jones on trumpet, cellist Jackson Wiley and one Clem DeRosa on drums. The latter, possibly chosen for his ability to wield a tambourine, proves far less effective than Rudy Nichols especially on the three numbers where Mingus takes to the keyboard. Attempting to play more than a pure accompanimental role (such as on *Smooch*), Mingus manages to add four beats to his solo at bars 11–12 of *Trilogy Pogo*, one of two items on which Wiley provides arhythmic plopping noises in lieu of a walking bass line; while on *Four Hands* he loses his place just before the tenor solo, and his overdubbed bass part (hence the title) has to fall into line later. It should be said that Wiley's bowed cello work is excellently carried off – directly foreshadowing the instrument's use in the mid-1955 quintet of Mingus's contemporary Chico Hamilton (with Buddy Collette on tenor and clarinet), as does the interplay of baritone and clarinet on parts of *Purple Heart*. However, the lack of solidity, not to mention dynamism, in the rhythm section combines with the saxophones' lack of expressivity (rather well shown up by Thad Jones's presence) to detract from material which is again interesting in itself. Of the five Mingus originals (*Abstractions* is by Macero, while LaPorta arranged *Stormy Weather*), three are based on standard material: *Spur of the Moment* derives from *'S Wonderful*, and *Four Hands* from the *Extrasensory* conception of *Idaho* (but with a new middle-eight harmonically closer to that of the original song), while *Trilogy Pogo* is really *What Is This Thing Called Love* played in counterpoint with not only *Hot House* but *Woody'n You*. The quartet track *Thrice upon a Theme* is very close in feel and in detail to *Eulogy*, with LaPorta hinting at the opening of *Pithecanthropus*. And finally the ten-minute *Minor Intrusion*, a third F minor piece to look forward to *Pithecanthropus* (for instance, in the second eight bars of the trumpet solo), is not only based on the *Chelsea Bridge* figure but, even more so than *This Subdues My Passion*, develops into a large and complex structure; omitting the piano solo, all the material leading up to the trumpet solo (see Appendix B) is repeated before the tenor solo, but the forty-four bar section preceding this repeat consists largely of five-bar phrases and, as well as recalling (*God's*) *Portrait*, has elements which recur in the 1971 *I of Hurricane Sue* and even the 1977 *Farwell Farewell*.

Mingus's continuing studio activity as a sideman included the Savoy album by Wally Cirillo (whose *Trans-Season* was claimed as the first twelve-tone jazz composition), but one indication that Mingus's journeyman period was due for termination occurred at Birdland five weeks later, when Bird himself was booked for a reunion with Kenny Dorham, Bud Powell, Art Blakey and Mingus. The personal sufferings of Parker (a suicide attempt only six months behind him) and of Powell (whose 1951–2 hospitalization had included electro-convulsive treatment) manifested themselves on this occasion in a complete inability to work together. The tension finally became unbearable after Powell had been helped from the stand, totally incapable, and Parker had stood at the microphone, slowly calling out 'Bud Powell! Bud Powell!' some thirty or forty times. Mingus, whether from compassion or self-vindication, stepped forward and said, 'Ladies and gentlemen, please don't associate me with any of this. This is not jazz. These are sick people.' Later that night, as Mingus added in 1978, 'Thelonious Monk went over to Bird and to Bud and said, "I told you guys to act crazy, but I didn't tell you to fall in love with the act. You're really crazy now." . . . They just stood there, limp. There was truth to what Monk was saying, you know. Some musicians were putting on an act in those years to get attention.'[34] A week later, Parker was dead at the age of thirty-four, and his common-law wife Chan Richardson began planning a service at which Mingus and Lennie Tristano were to have played. When his last legal wife Doris regained control, there was a much more elaborate ceremony at Harlem's Abyssinian Baptist Church with Reverend Adam Clayton Powell officiating, and other arrangements in the care of a committee including Mary Lou Williams, Clayton Powell's wife Hazel Scott, William Dufty, Tristano and Mingus. As Mingus's own widow Susan has said, 'He had a great distaste for the kind of fanfare and hassles that often accompany jazzmen's funerals. Like Bird's, with people fighting over who was to play.'[35] Nevertheless, he took part in the all-star tribute held on 3 April at Carnegie Hall (also the location of a recent Duke Ellington concert Mingus and Teddy Charles had attended on 16 March, not on the night of Parker's death, as Mingus once claimed). But it is likely that his feelings about Parker were best expressed in the following *Poem to Bird*:

A feather drifts and falls / Drifts and falls as it is / Blown and
    carried
By the winds of over a billion / Years ago . . .
Frees itself / And drifts toward our earth
Its beauties of knowledge / Here / And of the past
Ring out / In melodic reveal
Tired / And weary of its long drifting travel
It lay down at our feet / To rest / Awhile
To rest / For peace has come
And set it free on its last / Final journey . . .

Careful as we go / Our ways
So as not to trample the feathers / Of the love
And / The knowledge / Left to us
Who / Have yet to journey / Far . . .[36]

Having worked, however briefly, under Armstrong, Ellington, Tatum and Parker, there was little more for Mingus to learn about jazz history, and at the age of nearly thirty-three he knew that he had still to find his own identity. But bassists, like drummers, were in most people's minds 'just the supporters of the soloists' and, if drummer-bandleaders were so far thin on the ground, bassist-leaders were almost non-existent. With the Debut label enjoying an excellent critical reputation, Mingus may have felt that he could accomplish his destiny through the records he produced. However, the theory that Debut's sales figures were not spectacular, with the sole exception of the Massey Hall albums, may be supported by the taping in early 1955 of a session by an artist who might have been expected to appeal to a wider audience than many Debut records, namely Hazel Scott. Co-directors Mingus and Roach who accompanied 'never took any money and left ours in the company',[37] as Mingus noted later. However, by the time this was recorded, ten-inch albums (while not yet going out of style) were being overtaken in prestige and saleability by the twelve-inch format, and Debut's last ten-inch issue was recorded a few weeks later by the only musician apart from Mingus and Roach to lead more than one session for the label, Thad Jones. (While the co-directors, perhaps wisely, never refused invitations to record for other labels, Mingus thought sufficiently highly of Jones to sign him to an exclusive one-year contract; hence, Thad's appearance on the Mingus albums for Period under the pseudonym 'Oliver King'.)

On Jones's second Debut LP, Mingus's interest in turning the task of supporting the soloist into a dialogue, which had taken a further step forward in the Savoy session, comes on in leaps and bounds; indeed the entire opening chorus and closing half-chorus of *I Can't Get Started* (the second A section of which features Mingus's reharmonization incorporated in all his later versions of the tune) are played as an unaccompanied duet between Thad and Mingus. This may be partly because he considered Jones his protégé, but often it is also a response to the stimulating rhythmic variety of the trumpeter's style and, as well as occasional direct imitation, there are many instances of new rhythmic ideas fed to Jones by Mingus and vice versa. Not only does the session abound in Mingus's ebullient octave leaps, but the start of the second chorus of Jones's improvisation on the other standard song, *Get out of Town*, finds him inspiring the bassist to play an eighth-note-triplet figure which later became part of the second version of *Haitian Fight Song* (in the same key). Incidentally, *Get out of Town* is a particularly interesting choice of material, since like some of Mingus's original compositions recorded in the preceding months it has a single chord (G minor) for the whole eight bars of the A section, and therefore requires non-harmonic (modal) improvisation. Since Mingus frequently described such lack of harmonic movement as a 'pedal point', it should be pointed out that, strictly speaking, this refers to the retention of a single bass-note under *changing* harmonies (as in *Shuffle Bass Boogie* or the intro to Ellington's *Ko-Ko*), whereas what Mingus was now moving towards with the *Eulogy/Thrice upon a Theme/Minor Intrusion* series and *Gregarian Chant* was the continuation of a single chord and a single scale throughout an entire section, often 'extended' for an indefinite number of bars.

What is also noticeable from now on is Mingus's growing attention, in solo and in accompaniment, to variety of tone and articulation in order to make his lines more alive and more horn-like, as well as a number of special effects which he introduced to the bass vocabulary. Classical bassist Bertram Turetsky has pointed out how sometimes Mingus's bending of a note's pitch was achieved by the left hand not only stopping the string but stretching it out of true *across* the fingerboard (in the manner probably pioneered in the blues-guitar field by T-Bone Walker).[38] Similarly, the willingness to bend pitches is combined in the second chorus of Mingus's *Get out of Town* solo with the playing of the same pitch (almost) on another string to simulate Lester Young's 'alternate fingering' of a single note. Mingus uses the same effect on *Machajo*, one of the rare trio tracks recorded the same day with the obscure Philadelphia pianist John Dennis (who, like Max Roach's regular pianist, Richie Powell, seems to have inflenced McCoy Tyner), as he does the wide-spaced double-stops using the open A and D strings as successive chord roots (bars A 15–16 of *Get out of Town*, see Appendix A). This later became something of a cliché with other bassists, but the equally wide-spaced double-stops in bars 3–4 of *I Can't Get Started* are impossible to obtain in this manner. However, as casually demonstrated in the documentary film *Mingus* (immediately before the cut to *Take the 'A' Train*, where the introduction is achieved with the same open-string double-stops mentioned above), he both stops and plucks one string with the same hand, while simultaneously stopping and plucking another string with the other hand!

For all his technical prowess and his unchallenged position as the leading innovator on his instrument, the nearest Mingus had come to having his own band was to be billed as co-leader of Teddy Charles's quartet (with J.R. Monterose and Rudy Nichols) on a couple of follow-up gigs to Charles's recording on New Jazz. The fact that one of these engagements in the spring of 1955 was at Café Society, which had just reverted to its jazz policy, and that new venues were just beginning to present jazz, such as the Café Bohemia in Greenwich Village where Oscar Pettiford led the house band, signalled something of an upsurge of interest in live music. Another sign was the start of the festival fashion, and the success of the first Newport Festival produced in 1954 by George Wein led to a repeat the following year which, perhaps in an effort to dignify the whole process of playing such 'night-club music' out of doors, included an afternoon seminar at which Mingus and Teddy Charles played with a nine-piece group. Although not billed as such, this was one of the last performances of the Jazz Composers' Workshop personnel (only Britt Woodman, currently in New York with Ellington, and Elvin Jones, who had now replaced Nichols in the Teddy Charles quartet, were new members) and the programme, as well as a Mingus/John LaPorta duo, included Charles's *The Emperor*, Teo Macero's *Sounds of April*, and Mingus's *Minor Intrusion* and *Non-Sectarian*. Writer-photographer Burt Goldblatt shed a revealing light on this idealistic Newport venture when he quoted a member of the band complaining: 'We got paid five dollars for driving up from New York City and back. Unbelievable! And thirty-five dollars for the gig. We rehearsed quite a bit, three days rehearsing [unpaid], 6.30 till 11.'[39]

Teddy Charles, and for that matter Britt Woodman and Elvin Jones, were involved in Debut's first twelve-inch album (although the playing-time of twenty-six minutes suggests it was planned as a ten-inch but then cut 'making the grooves wider and deeper . . . giving more level and more bass than on the usual LP',[40] according to the sleeve). This is generally held to have been recorded on the Saturday before Newport weekend, although Bill Coss wrote of Miles Davis, the star of the sessions, that 'Just about one month before these tracks were cut, [he] had performed at the Newport Jazz Festival.'[41] It certainly would have made sense for Mingus to record Miles after what was a triumphant 'comeback', but perhaps there was more at stake than cashing in on the news value of this occasion, for Dannie Richmond (soon to become Mingus's friend and confidant) recalls that 'Miles was invited to join [Debut]. And he told Mingus he was crazy, it wouldn't work. He was bucking the establishment, and it was too big.' Of course, after Newport, Miles was being courted by Columbia Records, so it may be that the Debut session was done just as a favour to Mingus or, at least in Mingus's eyes, in return for his own appearance on the *Smooch* date. Musically, it is something of a damp squib for both of them, with all the arrangements except Mingus's on *Alone Together* being by Teddy Charles. *Nature Boy* is of interest as being another 'modal' popular-song (again in G minor) although Mingus's bass playing is much less forthright than on the Thad Jones session. This was not true, however, of Mingus as producer, to the extent that Elvin says 'If they had just printed the conversations that we had in that studio that time, that would have been a best-seller!'[42] Miles, in fact, later dismissed the album and also said of 'the things that Charlie Mingus and Teo Macero are writing for small groups, some of them are like tired modern paintings. Some of them are depressing.'[43] To which Mingus replied, in the first of his 'open letters' to *Down Beat*: 'I play or write *me*, the way I feel . . . If someone has been escaping reality, I don't expect him to dig my music . . . My music is alive and it's about the living and the dead, about good and evil. It's angry, yet it's real because it *knows* it's angry.'[44]

In the same month as the Debut session, July 1955, an incident that hit the headlines was the lynching of a fourteen-year-old (black) boy in Mississippi. It would be rash to surmise that this event in itself, just fourteen months after the Supreme Court decision which outlawed segregation, provided the necessary impetus for Mingus to amend his stance as a composer interested above all (or so it had seemed recently) in incorporating European classical techniques into jazz. However, one of the striking original pieces premiered when Mingus's own group made its initial appearances at the Café Bohemia for a week in late October 1955 also happened to carry his first-ever social-significance tune-title, *Work Song*. In the sleeve notes of the recording done two months later, Mal Waldron went so far as to paraphrase the lyrics of an actual folk work-song which had inspired Mingus: 'Fling that hammer over your shoulder, man grow bolder and bolder,' and commented that 'This is the only truly representative composition in the album.'[45] An especially revealing statement, since it is by far the simplest composition technically, and yet the rehearsals for Mingus's debut as a leader (in the meantime, he and Elvin Jones had worked with Bud Powell) had probably taken much longer than the Jazz Composers' Workshop's three days, for the crucial reason that Mingus was now returning to the roots of jazz in another way also.

Encouraged by the musicianship – and no doubt the opinions – of former JCW members Eddie Bert, George Barrow and Waldron, Mingus was beginning to feel that new material could be learned more thoroughly if the performers not only did not read any written music on stage, but memorized it from the start by ear alone. Not all of the many musicians who worked with Mingus in the next few years had the patience for this method, but few have disputed its efficacy in freeing (or forcing) them to interpret arranged passages in a more musical, and more personal way, rather than merely reproducing something fixed. Of course, Miles's new group (formed at the same time as Mingus's) appeared to operate in the same way, but his entire repertoire – like part of the current Jazz Messengers' repertoire – consisted of standards and well-known jazz classics, which did not need to be learned and could therefore be played without written arrangements. It was, on the other hand, axiomatic that anything with pretensions to melodic or harmonic complexity was the province of composers and therefore just had to be written; but rhythmic complexities, except of a very stilted kind, didn't lend themselves to being written, and so could safely be left to 'conventional' groups like Miles or the Messengers. Almost the only parallel to his new reliance on teaching arranged passages by ear was in Thelonious Monk's tunes where, as Sonny Rollins says, 'He had them written out, but I remember guys would look at his music and say "We can't play this." But by the end of the rehearsal everybody was playing it anyway.' But Mingus had become the first 'jazz composer' (as opposed to a tune-writer such as Monk) whose pieces were not written down, and the first since Ellington whose definitive works were to any extent 'co-composed' by his sidemen.

Mingus's new and initially tentative approach to group creation naturally was to recur in the work of other innovators such as Cecil Taylor and Ornette Coleman in the second half of the 1950s. But its beginnings were already established by the time that Nat Hentoff reviewed the quintet, now known officially as the Charlie Mingus Jazz Workshop, at the Bohemia in early December 1955. Hentoff noted that 'Mingus was breaking in a new drummer,' namely Willie Jones who had been recommended by Monk, and that Eddie Bert, who was much in demand for studio work, was not intending to become a regular member of the group, which, however, 'certainly should be recorded'.[46] By the time that the review appeared, Mingus had already taken this advice and the resultant album *Chazz!* – partly because it was taped live by a regular working band –

shows several dramatic improvements over Mingus's last sessions a year earlier, particularly that through his influence over the rhythm section Mingus is now capable of directing the ebb and flow of intensity throughout a performance. Nevertheless, the evolution of the repertoire used was still a gradual one, and of the numbers described by Hentoff and recorded for Debut two are similar in approach to the 1954 *Tea for Two* and *Body and Soul*; but, instead of harmonic resemblances, it is the melodic element which links the standards combined in *Septemberly* (namely, *Tenderly* and *September in the Rain*), while *All the Things You C Sharp* takes as its starting-point the three-note phrase used both in the Gillespie/Parker introduction to *All the Things You Are* and, with different timing, Rachmaninov's *Prelude in C Sharp Minor*. (The resemblances in question are mainly exploited in the ensemble choruses, but on *All the Things You Are*, whose basic chord-sequence changes key so often that it contains chord-roots on all twelve notes of the chromatic scale, Mal Waldron interjects the three-note phrase in different keys behind the solos of Bert and Barrow.) Of the other standards heard by Hentoff, *I'll Remember April* has its chord-sequence simplified and individual chords extended in duration, which also applies to *Love Chant* whose sequence is that of *Perdido* treated in a similar manner, while Dameron's *Lady Bird* theme is played with exaggerated contrasts between loud and soft, 'a study in dynamics for the average public'[47] according to Mingus.

Several of the above tracks show Mingus encouraging trombone and tenor to participate in each other's solo spots, even during rhythm-section breaks, so that the feel of collective improvisation permeates the front-line playing. To this end, Mingus's own numbers *Work Song* and *Haitian Fight Song* are presented not in unison but in canon (confusingly, *Work* is described by Hentoff as '*Fight Song*' but, although both these G minor pieces may conceivably have originated from the same idea, *Work* is an eight-bar format and *Haitian* a twelve-bar blues – the first that Mingus had recorded under his own name since *Lyon's Roar* almost seven years earlier). The tribute to Willie Jones's former employer, *Jump, Monk*, begins with the *Eulogy* turnaround in F minor and, like *Eulogy* and *Thrice upon a Theme*, has a B section in B flat minor, but its sixty-four bar A/A/B/A chorus is enlivened by a hard-bop melody which, played in unison and covering a range of two-and-a-half octaves, highlights the virtuoso playing required of Barrow and Bert. Setting the seal on an important and almost wholly successful recording session is the guest appearance of Max Roach, then enjoying a week off between engagements with his quintet featuring Clifford Brown and Sonny Rollins. Roach, incidentally, had asked Mingus to write for his group and, according to the composer, he submitted *What Love*, which 'the horn men looked at . . . for weeks, then said it couldn't be played'.[48] On the night in question, Roach replaced Willie Jones for two numbers, one of which was Mingus's *Drums* (which he described as 'Afro-Cuban and Afro-American rhythms combined with Caucasian and Afro-American harmonies'),[49] and created a duet with Mingus called *Percussion Discussion*. Their freely improvised interplay, a resounding demonstration that neither of them was any longer a mere supporter of soloists, also became the object of Mingus's first consciously creative use of overdubbing* when he added an extra part played on a three-quarter-size bass (similar to what Ron Carter calls a 'piccolo bass' but not necessarily tuned, like his, a 4th higher).

Mingus's successful second engagement at the Bohemia was extended until 4 January, and around this time he acquired a booking agency (Willard Alexander) and a personal manager, in the shape of Monte Kay, who fulfilled the same function for Chris Connor and for the Modern Jazz Quartet, both of whom made their first albums for the Atlantic label in January 1956. But, before Mingus too recorded for Atlantic, the problem of personnel continuity raised its head. Eddie Bert bowed out and was replaced by french-horn player David Amram (at least the requirement of memorizing the material saved someone from having to rewrite the parts for instruments of different pitch!) and shortly after, Barrow made way for altoist Jackie McLean, who had been recommended by Waldron. Then, towards the end of January, Amram was replaced by tenor-player J.R. Monterose, so that, when *Love Chant* was re-recorded on the *Pithecanthropus Erectus* album, not only was the front line quite new to Mingus's music but their interpretation was, tonally, very different from the Bohemia version. Indeed, although the change was again a gradual one, it is noticeable that from now on Mingus sought players whose personal tone-colour was extremely individual – in the case of McLean, one might say unique – and who were capable of varying it expressively in a way totally opposed to the more even, linear approach of John LaPorta and Teo Macero. McLean, in fact, inspired Mingus's third

---

* A single written chorus (the fourth) of *Trilogy Pogo* also uses this facility for artistic ends, as opposed to the technical reasons behind *Four Hands* or the Massey Hall bass work.

recorded 'portrait', *Profile of Jackie*, a continuously unfolding ballad which, after two minutes, alludes to *Chelsea Bridge* and *This Subdues My Passion*. *A Foggy Day*, subtitled *In London Town* by the Gershwin brothers, was now subtitled *In San Francisco*: although based on the arrangement already taped at the Bohemia (and originally 'whipped up in answer to a request' on the night of Nat Hentoff's review), this version overlaid (live) with sound-effects produced by, for instance, detached saxophone mouthpieces, was designed to conjure up images of the San Francisco waterfront. One of the first Mingus works to create controversy, it brought Mingus face to face with the tendency of critics and commentators to pigeonhole artists on the basis of isolated examples of their output. As he once said, 'That's what you do on one tune. There's the ocean and there's a million waves and each piece is like one of the waves and different as each wave.'[50]

The album was also revolutionary for the period in that nearly thirty-seven minutes of playing-time were devoted to a mere four pieces, of which only one was not based on totally original material. The title-track, *Pithecanthropus Erectus*, also included what were considered mere sound-effects by some, but were in fact high-register saxophone screams created for a more specific dramatic purpose. It takes its name from the earliest human-related fossil discovered at Olduvai Gorge in Kenya (since renamed *homo erectus*) and describes Mingus's 'conception of the modern counterpart of the first man . . . [in] four movements: (1) evolution, (2) superiority-complex, (3) decline, and (4) destruction'.[51] This four-part scenario is enacted in each chorus, with the high-register shouts and trills reserved respectively for the second and fourth sections of each chorus. The A/B/A/C structure has been erroneously termed an eighty-eight-bar chorus (which is true only of the opening ensemble), whereas this piece represents the first fully integrated example on record of Mingus's 'extended form'. The B and C sections, in fact, not only have no chord-sequence (replaced by modal improvisation on two alternating chords of I minor and IV7) but they are of indefinite length, variable according to both the inspiration of the soloist and the rhythm section's decision to cue the next section. This is quite different in character to the open-ended introductions and codas being featured by Max Roach's group, by virtue of being an essential part of each chorus and by having distinctive rhythmic patterns (heavy accents on the second beat of every other bar in the B section, and 6/4 figures in C). Furthermore, the cumulative intensity of the whole piece is predicted, and therefore augmented, by the dramatically motivated use of exaggerated dynamics in the A sections of the opening ensemble, while the cataclysmic finale of the closing ensemble is heightened by a collective *accelerando*. (The insistent bass-line of the A sections, far from negligible in the overall effect, begins with the *Eulogy* turnaround immediately followed by the first seven bars of *Extrasensory Perception*; see Appendix A.)

This startling and innovatory piece, with its pioneering incorporation of non-Afro-Cuban modal improvisation into the tradition of black jazz, seemed at the time to have sprung full-grown from the head of Mingus, despite previous tests of its various components. Being understandably excited when he had first achieved a successful club performance, Mingus had accepted the earliest opportunity to record it, causing J.R. Monterose to comment that 'It could have been much more soulful.'[52] And it was a musical disagreement which in March led to Mingus falling out with Jackie McLean. Years later, Mingus explained, 'When I hired him, he was a bebopper, but I didn't know they were so stuck with the stuff they couldn't play my music,'[53] and McLean has confirmed that he was 'fixed in my ideas and set in my ways . . . [Mingus] said, "I don't want Charlie Parker, man, I want Jackie." '[54]

Although emphasizing how much this eventually helped him find his own musical personality, McLean now recollects how, during a week in Cleveland, he became so 'disturbed because Charlie was always talking . . . behind solos and giving commands and reprimanding the rhythm section' that he handed in his notice. Mingus, unconsciously re-enacting phase 2 of the modern counterpart of the first man, tried to alter the profile of Jackie with a punch in the mouth, at which McLean retaliated with a knife:

Had the bartender not grabbed my arm at the particular time, I believe I would have wounded Charlie pretty bad, because the nick was right over his heart. Went about an eighth of an inch into his skin, and I came down with quite a bit of force because I was really angry. And, incidentally, I haven't carried a knife since that day.[55]

Although McLean's notice became effective immediately, it is perhaps surprising in retrospect that this was not quite the end of a beautiful musical partnership.

4

Fifty-First Street Blues

With the release of *Pithecanthropus Erectus* in September 1956, Mingus was at last seen to be getting into his stride musically and becoming not merely an interesting but an innovative composer. Particularly the title track, with what were previously thought of as freak tonal effects an integral part of the conception, had far-reaching implications for jazz itself; and, like Ellington's *Sophisticated Lady* (which he first recorded at exactly the same age, to within a few days), the 'jungle-style' primitivism of Mingus's piece seemed to indicate a radical change in his direction. The parallel with Duke is illuminating in another way: the critic Martin Williams has written: 'As [Ellington's] message of form began to take effect, revolutionary improvisers arrived. The maturing of Ellington's sense of form was followed by Parker's innovations, but Ellington had a lot to do with planting the seeds.'[1] At the time, however, this fact was hardly very widely recognized and, while Mingus is clearly the only pre-'free'-jazz composer of whom the equivalent may be said, even the musicians whose freedom he had licensed tended to ignore his role in stretching the conventions of the time. A notable exception was John Coltrane, who played opposite Mingus at the Bohemia as a member of Miles's increasingly popular quintet, and who told the french-horn player David Amram that 'he was quite an admirer of Mingus's music' and of his attempts to go beyond the thirty-two bar chorus.[2] By and large, however, both Mingus and Ellington were often thought of by their contemporaries as standing outside the mainstream of jazz development, and Duke, indeed, had to wait until he was in his sixties for

71

the historical significance of his work to be fully understood. In this respect, Mingus was more fortunate, by a decade or so, but without the kind of mass popularity that kept Ellington going he had some hard times ahead.

All too often, though, Mingus's response to hard times – or, at least, to hard times aggravated by sudden additional pressures – made matters worse, despite mingled regrets and excuses after the event. Doubtless this applied particularly to the self-styled 'Chazzanova's' escapades with other women, especially the rich ones he cast in the role of prospective patrons of his art such as 'Vassarlean', a slim college girl of wealthy background similar to the character 'Jane' in *Beneath the Underdog*. Guitarist-bandleader Alexis Korner, who heard a lot of Mingus's largely autobiographical conversation later in London, observed: 'He tries to carry his intolerance through to his personal relationships, and it didn't always work . . . And I think that must have been very, very difficult for him. Because, actually, he didn't really dislike these ladies whose penthouses he inhabited in New York City, but he had to give the impression of despising them.' Celia too must have borne the brunt of his intolerance from time to time, as well as alternately turning a blind eye and pouring oil on troubled waters. When Nat Hentoff, describing her 'forthrightness and courage equal to her husband's', also mentioned her 'reservoir of perceptive wit including the easy ability to laugh at herself',[3] it sounded as if she sometimes needed it.

If Mingus's personal life was somewhat unstable at this point, then so throughout 1956 was the personnel of the Jazz Workshop, and not solely through his own attempts to force his musicians' growth. Shortly after Jackie McLean abruptly left the band, J.R. Monterose was asked to join Kenny Dorham's new Jazz Prophets, the first of a series of Jazz Messengers breakaway groups. Coming in on tenor was Joe Alexander (a recent member of the Hampton band, and much later briefly with Woody Herman) while, for the first time since starting his New York group, Mingus found in Cleveland a trumpeter capable of playing his music, namely Bill Hardman; he indeed remained a whole six months although, after the next Café Bohemia residency ended on 27 April, there was very little work. (As an illustration of the fact that neat diagrams of stylistic development may not seem so clear-cut to the protagonists, and certainly do not fully coincide with activity in the marketplace, Mingus worked at least one weekend in a duo with Lennie Tristano before any further Jazz Workshop gigs came up.)

Simultaneously with starting his own group, Mingus had moved to an apartment on West 51st Street which provided a good base to rehearse new musicians, and for his next advertised appearance he announced personnel for a quintet including drummer Wilbert Hogan (shortly to join Hampton) and altoist Lou Donaldson, who was still trying to make a career as an out-and-out jazzman before realizing that his strength lay in the then embryonic soul-jazz field. In fact, though, when the gig took place on 5 July, Mingus actually fronted a sextet consisting of Ernie Henry (whose alto work, like Donaldson's and McLean's, was a somewhat strident simplification of Parker), Teo Macero, Hardman, Waldron and drummer Al Dreares. The set in question was at the rapidly expanding Newport Festival (the first one to be held during Independence Day weekend) where the fruits of Mingus's exploratory work at the Bohemia were aired before a crowd of 4,000, who not only sat entranced despite continuous heavy rain but, according to Mingus, gave him a standing ovation at the end. At the beginning of the set, he had stepped forward and commanded, 'First of all, I want it to stop raining right now.'[4] Although unsuccessful in this respect, he drew a tremendously exciting performance from the band, with Teo Macero, interestingly, adopting a more urgent, vocalized tone than hitherto on *Tonight at Noon*. This new composition, which like its longer companion piece on this occasion (*Tourist in Manhattan*) was to be recorded the following year, was again in F minor with extended passages on a single scale but this time at a hectic up-tempo, and was the first Mingus original to begin with a repeated bass-figure (see Appendix A). Immediately after this triumph at Newport, Mingus gave out the news that Willard Alexander, who he felt had not capitalized sufficiently on his growing New York reputation, would no longer be handling his bookings, and he switched his allegiance to the Moe Gale agency. This resulted in a week in Philadelphia in early August and the first week of September in Norfolk Virginia, and the further announcement that Mingus hoped to bring altoist Sonny Criss from the West Coast to join the Workshop. However, the sudden tie-up with Moe Gale obviously caused some quick thinking by Willard Alexander, and indeed by Celia, for the net result was that not only did Mingus rejoin Alexander but Celia went to work for the agency in their office. Her explanation is that 'Mingus was a tough character for anyone to handle. Because he would go into clubs and . . . make announcements about the men's room . . . and the acoustics, or they had no dressing-rooms. Mingus was not popular with clubowners by any means, and so it was hard to book him.'

Meanwhile, at the very end of August, Mingus was one of the guest speakers at the first Music Inn in Lenox, Massachusetts, a prestigious affair largely devoted to other forms of music but with the Modern Jazz Quartet as a resident group. He had previously made an unscheduled contribution to a panel discussion at Newport, saying of the festival 'that he thought four or five smaller concerts would be much more effective than the three larger ones', while George Wein had claimed 'I've been trying to get the Mingus group [to the Storyville] for three years,' but that such a group would lose him money by not attracting a large enough audience.[5] At Music Inn, in whose organization Wein had also had a hand, Mingus was an official guest along with such figures as Nat Hentoff, John Hammond, Bill Coss, Gunther Schuller, Lennie Tristano and Billy Taylor. Unfortunately perhaps, this required Mingus to attend an official reception and, unfortunately too, 'A Texas cop kind of cat – he had a hat on like a cop – made some racial remarks. Pettiford tried to pull me away and I did come away but he kept following me and I was afraid, so I popped him down . . . But I don't know if I hit hard or not. I think it's hypnotism.'[6]

Reactions such as this, however understandable in general terms, may also have been fuelled by Mingus's frustrations with the booking agency and with having a band personnel still in a state of flux. Ernie Henry, having been reintroduced to the jazz scene by Mingus, had by now left to work with Thelonious Monk so that, when in mid-August Mingus returned to the Bohemia, he reached a détente with Jackie McLean, who then promptly departed along with Bill Hardman as they both joined Art Blakey. As well as being documented in a broadcast which, interestingly enough, features a version of Parker's *Confirmation*, this Bohemia appearance was reviewed by Barry Ulanov who heard *Tourist in Manhattan, East Coasting*, a contrapuntal blues (possibly the number later recorded as *Conversation*), and a Mingus solo interpretation of *Memories of You* 'that had all the rugged individuality of a suite for unaccompanied cello by Bach and some of its contrapuntal style as well'.[7] It is not known whom Mingus took to Chicago for a fortnight in October but, back in New York at a new club called the Pad, it was George Barrow and Willie Jones once again alongside Waldron; and it was here at the Pad that an event of incalculable importance took place one night when Mingus, again trying to force the pace (this time literally), counted off a performance of *Cherokee* at a tempo which Jones found impossible to maintain. As the number disintegrated in midstream, Mingus proceeded to explain to the audience how he felt about Jones's efforts while Lou Donaldson, still part of the floating membership of the Jazz Workshop, went up to Mingus and introduced a drummer he was confident could play fast enough. This was the young Dannie Richmond who, still a couple of months shy of his twenty-first birthday, had only been seriously playing the drums for half a year. He recalls that he was overcome with nervousness and embarrassment (saying 'Oh, man, don't do that!'), but Donaldson prevailed: 'Man, go on! You don't have nothing to lose.'

The musical rapport between Mingus and Richmond was instantaneous. Announcing the intermission, 'He called me in the corner, and he said, "Where can I get in touch with you?" He wanted to explain that he had certain jobs coming up, and he could pay this certain amount, and it would be good for me to join him 'cause then people would know about me.' So not only did Dannie join Mingus but, as the relationship deepened over the months, which then turned into years, Dannie became Mingus's equivalent to Harry Carney in the Ellington band, an indispensable ingredient of 'the Mingus sound' and a close friend as well. Coincidentally, the gap of thirteen years in their ages was similar to that between Ellington and Carney, although Mingus and Richmond were both somewhat older when they first met. This aspect of their association began to develop almost immediately, as the promised tour got under way at the Sugar Hill in Newark, New Jersey; for this first fortnight of November the band actually included Lou Donaldson, who had got to know the New York-born Richmond when the drummer was visiting his mother in Greensboro, North Carolina.

Richmond had already been on the road as a tenor-saxophonist with Paul Williams (who had made the hit rhythm-and-blues record *The Hucklebuck*, based on the same traditional riff as Parker's *Now's the Time*) and had studied for a term at the Music Center in the Bronx. Willie Jones had been adept at interpreting Mingus's ideas, but this wider musical experience put Richmond potentially in the Max Roach class, and Mingus's ambition was that he should realize this potential. As Mingus put it, 'When I met Dannie several young drummers had just about burned me out time-wise, and they were sound deaf and tone deaf . . . [He] gave me his complete open mind . . . to work with as clay – I didn't play drums so I taught Dannie bass.'[8] And Dannie himself says:

Some people said that Charles actually taught me how to play, which in a sense is true . . . I, for example, did not know anything really about dynamics. My playing then was very flashy, and I wanted to be very fast. You know, a young boy showing off. It was only after Charles saw this that he was able to say, 'No, at this point you have to whisper, and there have to be other points where there's planned chaos!' There were many other lessons, of course, that I learned. Not only from the musical standpoint but about living, and doing certain things certain ways. And, of course, he would also make a point to drop some of his philosophical things on me.

The rest of the tour found altoist Bunky Green, also recommended by Donaldson, joining Willie Dennis and pianist Wynton Kelly (Mal Waldron having decided to stay in New York), for a week each in Washington D.C. and Los Angeles, followed by a December booking at the Black Hawk in San Francisco which lasted until the holiday period. When this engagement was completed and the band were at liberty for a few days before driving to Vancouver and then to New York for Mingus's first Birdland date under his own name, he decided to escape his former hunting-ground and, doubtless to celebrate Dannie's birthday a few days earlier, said, 'Come on, Dee, we're going to Tijuana.' That Richmond felt happy to join Mingus in such a trip confirms that he found the bassist very protective towards him:

> He had already proven that twice in that short space of time . . . Well, he liked to rumble. And, being that he was on a hair-trigger at that point – which he stayed on for years, it didn't take but a second and he was *ready* . . . OK, so I knew that we could go any place and not be bothered by anybody.

It was this trip to the somewhat tawdry tourist-trap at the Mexican border which formed the basis of Mingus's sexual fantasia in *Beneath the Underdog*, of which Dannie says:

> I was baffled. Because, you see, I had never been in the company of any prostitutes, and I found that Mingus really dug that. He wanted to be like a pimp, he wanted to be a gangster, he wanted to be a musician, he wanted to be a great lover. And, you know, he considered himself all of these people.

Mingus's first published description of this episode is also of interest: '[I was] trying to forget the blues that I had brought with me – and minus a wife. It actually ends in a contest between Dannie and myself to see who could outdo who in Tijuana's tequila-wine-women-song-and-dance. Dannie lost: he was very hungry; I was starved.'[9] The blues that Mingus had brought with him included the fact that Celia had recently suffered a miscarriage and, during the seven-week separation before the Birdland gig, 'He was very possessive, very jealous – and, by saying that, I'm not saying that it was all his fault . . . Yes, it *was* during that period that it started to get a bit rocky.'

On his return to New York, Mingus was due to record his second album for Atlantic, which producer Nesuhi Ertegun had originally planned to cut on the Coast during December. But, instead of taping the band during the gig at Birdland, Mingus decided to wait, possibly because Wynton Kelly was leaving to join Gillespie while Willie Dennis (anticipating, wrongly, that Mingus would now have a full touring schedule) had given his notice in order to be available for studio work. He had, however, recommended another trombonist to Mingus, who was to fulfil all the promise that Dennis had shown in the Mingus context and whose fluid legato style was to become an important part of Mingus's music over the next few years – namely Jimmy Knepper who, now twenty-nine, had just settled in New York. Continuing his search not just to populate the bandstand but, in Richmond's words, 'trying to find just the right ingredients musically', Mingus also hired a former Gillespie pianist Wade Legge and a new saxophonist with an impressive combination of bebop and blues phraseology, named Shafi Hadi. With this quintet Mingus set about preparing for his record date, and Jimmy Knepper rapidly learned about the leader's unconventional method of rehearsing new pieces: 'He sang them to us, or played them on the piano. And he'd teach us four bars at a time . . . It was a very time-consuming process to learn his tunes.' In another interview, Knepper has noted how Mingus's piano-playing was responsible for the delightfully rough sound of some of the band's ensemble passages: 'He would sometimes fake the fast runs and aim for the high notes, and you'd try to figure out what he was playing in between. He didn't want anybody to write out his parts. He wanted you to play like you just thought of it yourself, even if it wasn't exactly what he wrote.'[10] And Mingus's use of the piano was crucial in another way, as Dannie Richmond points out:

He definitely wanted a certain sound from the chords contained

77

in whatever piece he was writing. *And* he wanted the piano-player in his right hand to reinforce the melody line, *or* play a third part . . . Once he said, 'You can't bend the notes on the piano, so at this point the bending will be done by the horns while we'll play a contrapuntal melody to accompany the original line.'

According to a *Down Beat* report, the material Mingus had been planning to record included a new tribute, *Profile of Bud Powell*, along with *Tourist in Manhattan* and *Tonight at Noon*. The latter was in fact recorded at this stage although Knepper, unconsciously echoing J.R. Monterose's verdict on *Pithecanthropus*, says 'It was so ragged and so impossible and it sounded so bad at the time, I said "Oh God, I hope they don't release it." ' And indeed it was not issued until seven years later, as was the intriguing *Passions of a Woman Loved:* this has a theme in five sections but (unlike *Minor Intrusion* or *Pithecanthropus*) the passions depicted vary widely in mood, in key and in time-signature, and even incorporate *accelerandos* and *decelerandos*. Of the material which was issued immediately on the album *The Clown*, Mingus said, 'I selected these four [compositions] over two others that were more intricate because some of the guys had been saying that I didn't swing,' and the most striking refutation of this is the new version of *Haitian Fight Song*. Among many other things, it is notable for the use of just two four-bar riffs to fuel the entire twelve-minute performance; the wide range of pitch and texture obtained from all five instruments; and, more obviously than on any previous records, the variety of rhythmic feelings generated and their direct influence on the dynamics of the front-line instruments. Also heard for the first time on record is Mingus's vocal encouragement of the group, in the form of falsetto cries seemingly replacing another line in the ensemble passages (and closely approximating the sound of a plunger-muted trumpet); this and the leader's amazingly powerful introduction and subsequent bass solo heightens the contribution of everyone else. Bearing in mind that this piece (which, according to Mingus, 'could just as well be called *Afro-American Fight Song*')[11] was first recorded in the same month that Martin Luther King initiated the civil rights struggle in Alabama, it is as if the hope expressed in Parker's music has been bypassed and, in the abrupt change into tempo at the end of Mingus's two bass passages, he is enacting the transition from 'It's hopeless' to 'Everything *better* be alright – and soon!' (see Appendix A).

Once again, all four tracks of the album are worthy of comment, even if *Blue Cee* (a probable reference to Celia) is more gripping in theory than in practice: as well as establishing the mood of melancholy which pervades the remainder of the pieces, it is one of Mingus's earliest attempts at a twelve-bar blues deviating from the standard blues sequence, an idea which John Coltrane took up in his 1959–60 recordings. Despite Mingus's comment that in 1962 'Max Roach, Duke and I were recording and Max asked if I had ever heard a two-chord blues . . . It's based on different scales – C major to Bflat7, a bar apiece,'[12] this actually describes what he himself had attempted here. *Reincarnation of a Lovebird*, titled in wishful thinking of Parker and his belief in the possibility of reincarnation, is a long-lined ballad traversing more than two octaves in its opening phrases (like *Jump, Monk*), and its complex phrasing in a difficult key (F sharp minor) is played with apparently effortless delicacy by all concerned. The chorus is seventy bars long, and each A section begins with two *Eulogy* turnarounds; thematically, it uses much of Parker's vocabulary (bar A11 is a subliminal quotation from his famous *Just Friends* solo) and it is preceded by a dramatic thirty-five-second medley of fragments from tunes written by or associated with Parker. The dramatic element was considerably more to the fore in the title-track of the album, *The Clown*, Mingus's first attempt since *The Chill of Death* to blend words and music, and his first attempt to include improvisation in both elements. Depicted in a stiff waltz rhythm reminiscent of Kurt Weill, the character of the clown (as we have seen, a word with a special meaning for Mingus) is here a struggling artist who 'had all these greens and all these yellows and all these oranges bubbling around inside him and . . . all he wanted was to make people laugh'. One night in Dubuque, Iowa – a synonym for Hicksville – he discovers that people laugh most at the corniest gags ('Right about here, things began to change . . . A lot of grey in there now, a lot of blue'), until his greatest success: a fatal accident on stage. The track closes with a sardonic reference to the booking agency: 'William Morris sends regrets.'[13]

It is perhaps revealing that, in Mingus's original conclusion of the story, the event which the audience applauded, happily thinking it was all part of the act, was the clown shooting himself. But, for the recording, the narration was improvised (live in the studio alongside the band) by a hip radio commentator named Jean Shepherd, who was later paid the ultimate compliment of having one of his raps included in an anthology edited by Marshall McLuhan (*Explorations in Communications*, 1960). Thus the verbal content of this piece was a collaboration between author and improviser in exactly the same way that Mingus's music had become during the last couple of years. While Duke Ellington had started out approaching the problem of jazz 'composition' in somewhat the same fashion, before gradually assuming greater control and drawing on the soloists in order to flesh out his own conceptions, Mingus's development was largely in the other direction and thus the composer's control was often more dearly bought.

When the Jazz Workshop finally played the Storyville for a week in March (featuring, among other things, a solely instrumental version of *The Clown* in which Jimmy Knepper's trombone replaced the narrator), Boston-based Jaki Byard recalls that 'He used to stop the band and everything . . . I thought he was nuts, "What the hell is he doing?" . . . 'Cause you never did see that in a club, you know, where people are paying admission and paying for drinks, to see this guy stop the band in the middle of a number and say, "No, it don't go like that, blah, blah, blah." '[14] Knepper remembers that such occasions were often intended to prevent the players from becoming glib and facile, and simultaneously to improve the attention-span of the audience:

> One of his trademarks was to put the audience down, because of their drinking and clinking glasses. He'd say, 'Hey, you're supposed to be here to listen to my music.' And they weren't there to listen to his music at all, they were there because that's where the girl wanted to go and the guy wanted to get into the girl's drawers. One of the very first jobs we played, at Storyville in Boston, he went into a thing about the audience, and I told him, 'You know, there are some people here that came to hear you, and they're the poor people sitting in the back, nursing a Coke.' . . . It became kind of a requirement for him to act like that. It's always the way that somebody who's eyeworthy, who has stage presence, will go down better with the audience than someone who doesn't know how to sell themselves.

Another approach to encouraging audience participation was shown when in May Mingus played for a whole month at the Continental Lounge in Brooklyn, which had a dance floor, and, as composer-conductor Gunther Schuller has written, Mingus 'embarked on a crusade to revive jazz dancing' and used the multi-tempoed *Passions of a Woman Loved* 'to stump the fantastic dancers that competed in contests' there.[15]

Between these two engagements, Mingus had also appeared for

the first time at the Five Spot Café, a Greenwich Village coffee-house run by the Termini brothers which had only recently begun to use jazz groups, starting with the David Amram–George Barrow Quintet, then Randy Weston and then Cecil Taylor, and it seems unlikely that he would have been booked into such a minor-league venue by his agency, especially so soon after playing at Birdland. Similarly, the Continental Lounge (where Mingus had opened with altoist John Jenkins, Teddy Charles and Willie Jones, before rehiring Hadi, Legge and Richmond) sounds very much like one of those 'bars that has a piano in it', where Mingus himself had talked the owner into letting him play, especially as one of the attractions announced was the availability of free ice-cream for all comers! The agency would still be receiving its percentage, however, since Mingus was still under contract. It is also doubtless relevant that Celia and an agency colleague, Rudy Viola, had both left Willard Alexander the previous month to set up their own company, Superior Artists Corporation.

Unfortunately, around this same period, the ambitious recording policy of the Debut label came to a halt, the last issues in the spring of 1957 being an album by Alonzo Levister (one of whose items was re-recorded by John Coltrane), the twelve-inch compilation of the two Thad Jones albums, and the final selection from the 1953 four-trombone session. Further releases were planned, namely the second volume of the Café Bohemia date and sessions by singer Faron Taylor and by Jimmy Knepper (a seven-inch album actually appeared on Danish Debut), and Shafi Hadi has claimed that he recorded under his own name for Debut. But nothing more was issued in the US because, in Mingus's words, the A.F.M. 'stopped our licence . . . and . . . said we didn't pay our debts'.[16] It is not known who filed the complaint against Debut, whether fellow A.F.M. members or perhaps pressing plants or studios, but, either at this stage or earlier, there had been dissension between Mingus and Max Roach about the running of the company. As a result the name Jazz Workshop – which Mingus copyrighted to prevent its use by others – became not only the name of his group, but of his new publishing company and, briefly, of a new record-label. The only material issued on Jazz Workshop records, however, consisted not of original sessions but the two albums *Bird at St Nick's* and *Bird on 52nd Street*, live recordings collected by (and, in the first case, recorded by) Jimmy Knepper, one of whose other favours to Mingus was to build him a hi-fi set. When the Debut and Jazz Workshop catalogues subsequently reappeared on Fantasy, Mingus

81

noted that 'Jimmy Knepper had a whole suitcase full of Charlie Parker tapes; they only used one-tenth of them.'[17]

Despite the administrative problems which seem to have plagued Mingus's career, he had one stroke of luck in 1957 through the good offices of Gunther Schuller. Involved with John Lewis in the Jazz And Classical Music Society (an organization with similar aims to those of the Jazz Composers' Workshop), Schuller had also been responsible for having 'third-stream' works by such as Teo Macero, Teddy Charles and George Russell performed in the 'Music In The Making' concert series run by the noted classical conductor David Broekman (who, Mingus claimed in his autobiography, was aware of *The Chill of Death* although he is not known to have performed it). For the fourth Brandeis Festival, Gunther Schuller found himself in the fortunate position of being allowed to commission six new works all intended to reflect the influence of both jazz and European music, to be played by an ensemble including Macero, Charles, John LaPorta and other JCW sidemen plus Jimmy Knepper and the pianist Bill Evans, who had already worked with George Russell and Tony Scott. The six composers involved were Milton Babbitt, Harold Shapero (who taught at Brandeis), Schuller himself, Russell, Jimmy Giuffre and, of course, Mingus. But for the commission, Mingus might never have associated himself with such a project since, as Schuller describes him, he 'was a very fiery, often belligerent battler for a place in the sun, fiercely independent'. It is fortunate that he did, though, for critic Max Harrison has noted that:

Mingus takes greater risks than the other composers. The unity of his works depends not on their technical organization . . . but is largely of an emotional order . . . [*Revelations*] extends itself as a succession of moods, feelings, atmospheres, melting into and out of each other. This was something which had not then been widely attempted in jazz.[18]

It is, however, similar to Mingus's early, fully written works, namely *The Chill of Death* and *Half-Mast Inhibition*, with the exception that it incorporates a highly successful two-minute collective improvisation over alternating I minor and IV7 chords (as in *Pithecanthropus*). According to Schuller, 'Part of my recollection is his telling me that this was going to be the first movement of a multi-movement opus', but what there is of it stands as the most convincing attempt extant of Mingus's efforts to combine jazz and European music.

Around the same time, Mingus played under Schuller's baton on television's *Steve Allen Show* in a tribute to Duke Ellington, and recorded another piano trio album in which he featured Hampton Hawes and, among other standards, an arrangement of *Laura* (also heard on a Jazz Workshop broadcast from the Bohemia) in which *Tea for Two* is used as a countermelody. As well as a return visit to the Bohemia, the Workshop's other live performances had included a mid-June concert organized by promoter Art D'Lugoff at the Loew's Sheridan cinema in Greenwich Village, where, unlike headliners Billie Holiday and the MJQ, Mingus played wearing Bermuda shorts. Reviewer Jack Maher noted that 'in his gruff, exuberant way [he] also explored two additional forms of improvisation with the jazz form',[19] featuring Jean Shepherd on *The Clown* and, most remarkably, flamenco dancer Ysabel Morel in a piece called *Tijuana Table Dance*. There was also a week in Washington, D.C., and the first Great South Bay Festival held at Great River, Long Island, during the weekend of 19–21 July. By the time of these two engagements, the personnel of the Workshop had seen both a change of pianist (Bill Triglia) and the valuable addition of Detroit trumpeter Clarence (Gene) Shaw. Jimmy Knepper points out that Shaw 'came down on a job every now and then, and just sat in' but, during his brief stay, he provided Mingus with a very personal style and a gift for playing the unexpected, both rhythmically and tonally. The music in Mingus's two Great South Bay feature spots (he also played bass for Blossom Dearie with Roy Eldridge on drums!) included a solo performance of *Haitian Fight Song* of which *New Yorker* critic Whitney Balliett wrote, a trifle hyperbolically, that 'his instrument became a totally inadequate medium for all it was forced to do';[20] and two numbers from the album he had begun recording the Thursday before, namely *Dizzy Moods* and *Tijuana Table Dance*.

The album in question, *Tijuana Moods,* was actually done originally for Victor's jazz subsidiary Vik as part of a settlement of Mingus's suit against RCA-Victor for having used Thad Jones on two 1955 Al Cohn albums during the period of Jones's exclusive Debut contract, and was Mingus's first to be done in stereo and his first for a major label. It is important not only for the composer's ability to recollect musical impressions in tranquillity and bring them to the boil in the studio, but for further developments in his writing, and especially in combining earlier ideas into larger forms.

Tijuana Table Dance, later retitled *Ysabel's Table Dance* (but only for the record, not for live performances), is the emotional highspot in which repeated climaxes are created by the use of brief unisons disintegrating into collective improvisation, a technique which became widely influential during the 1960s. The overall structure is problematic since, like all the remaining tracks on the album as issued, it has been subjected to some sloppy editing. Whoever supervised the editing (the producer was probably Jack Lewis), it seems a fair bet that Mingus himself was not present; nor could George Avakian, who was responsible for getting the album released, have done it, since he had already proved himself capable of counting both beats and bar-lines. *Table Dance*'s main sections are based on the *paso-doble* rhythm heard in the Norvo trio's *Time and Tide* and on the alternation of E7 and Fmajor7 underpinning the archetypal 'Spanish' scale later used in part of Davis's *Flamenco Sketches* (1959), Coltrane's *Olé* (1961) and Chick Corea's *La Fiesta* (1972). These sections are balanced by out-of-tempo cadenzas and lighter, more boppish passages over alternating chords of C and Bflat7 (the principal chords of *Blue Cee*). Although the vocal encouragement and castanet-playing of Ysabel Morel do add to the impetus as well as the atmosphere, it was clearly a wise decision on Mingus's part to omit the narration originally intended, in the manner of *The Clown*, to complement a piece which turned out to be complete in itself (see Appendix A).

Dizzy Moods, apparently conceived while driving to Tijuana, was described by Mingus before it was ever recorded: 'Try a song like Dizzy's *Woody'n You*, for example, and make some changes; fit a church minor mode into the chord structure,'[21] and in fact a bluesy phrase in B flat minor is reiterated throughout the D flat circle of 4ths that constituted Gillespie's original A section (based on the sequence of Fats Waller's *Blue Turning Grey* and *I've Got a Feeling I'm Falling*). Mingus's B section, however, is in 6/4, but phrased in such a way that the 4/4 time-signature is still felt subliminally, and it may be that the idea of adapting this polyrhythmic approach (hinted at in the C sections of *Pithecanthropus*) surfaced after the trip to Tijuana, since it is a fact that Mexican popular music is typically in multiples of three syncopated by multiples of two. Of his rapport with Mingus in negotiating such novel terrain for jazz, Dannie has said:

I could see that he stayed completely on top of the beat, so much so that, in order for the tempos not to accelerate, . . . I had to lay back a bit. And, at the same time, let my stroke be on the same downbeat as his, but just a fraction behind it . . . So that, when I would play on the 2 and 4, and sometimes switch it around to 1 and 3, he liked these different kind of changes that were taking place just between the two of us. And I think it was when we first started to play something in 6 that we knew the magic was there, and that we could within a second be out of the 6 into a smashing 4/4 and not lose any of the dynamic level that had preceded it.[22]

One of the Tijuana-inspired pieces, *Los Mariachis*, has 'extended' sections in a slow 6/4 blues feel, forming part of another miniature suite, which also has brief out-of-tempo passages and other sections directly descriptive of the street-bands – indeed, the light-hearted Latin rhythm and calypso-type chord-sequence seem to be deliberately contrasted with the soulful laments of the North American blacks. The Latin rhythm is heard again in *Tijuana Gift Shop*, contrasted this time with a straight-ahead bebop theme whose harmonic complexity, changing key three times in the first eight bars, sets it apart from the rest of the original material; while the standard song *Flamingo*, imaginatively reharmonized in the key of E, allows all three front-line men to play an obviously fixed arrangement in a personal and seemingly unpremeditated way, something Mingus had been groping towards since the Trombone Workshop performance of *Chazzanova*.

It is worth noting that Knepper and Hadi had now been with Mingus for a whole six months, longer than any previous Workshop front line, and Richmond for nine months. Without exaggeration, it could safely be said that Richmond was the most important member of the Jazz Workshop for, although there were seldom any drum solos, his remarkable combination of fire and precision enabled him to play the frequently complex routines as if they were his own creation. Indeed, at about this stage, Mingus said to him:

You're doing well, but now suppose you had to play a composition alone. How would you play it on the drums? . . . OK, if you had a dot in the middle of your hand and you were going in a circle, it would have to expand and go round and round, and get larger and larger and larger. And at some point it would have to stop, and then this same circle would have to come back around, around, around to the little dot in the middle of your hand.

Dannie adds, 'That did more for me, in a compositional sense, than anything else he's laid on me.'

The musical solidarity of the group now not only accommodated the temporary addition of Shaw but survived an even more temporary pianist on a new album, recorded shortly after *Tijuana Moods*. Bill Evans, whom Mingus had remembered from the Brandeis concert, told me, 'I came in from my one-nighter some place around New York, and there was a wire waiting for me at four in the morning that said "Can you make a record date this morning at 10 a.m. with Charlie Mingus?" ' Not only was Evans quick to take up the suggestion but he was quick on the uptake musically: in fact, on *Celia*, Evans takes the option of extending the form (by repeating the last bar) more literally than the leader – just as he was to do on *Flamenco Sketches*. The first of Mingus's personal portraits to describe a non-musician, and a non-musician who was again carrying his child at the time, *Celia* is the first follow-up to *(God's) Portrait* in the D flat ballad series.

Given the excellence of *Tijuana Moods,* it is no criticism to say that the Bethlehem album *East Coasting* displays certain musical similarities to it. Despite the fact that they were already in the performing repertoire a year earlier, the title track has much in common structurally with *Tijuana Gift Shop*, while *Memories of You* (in A major) is another standard rendered in the same melancholy tone-colours as *Flamingo*. Indeed, while this seems a more conservative album, it is a tribute to Mingus's maturing methodology that ideas are shown to be capable of repetition and re-arrangement, and *West Coast Ghost* (whose alternation of two riffs is descended from *Work Song* and *Haitian Fight Song*) incorporates passages of G minor twelve-bar blues with an 'extended' two-bar turnaround only slightly different from the opening of *Eulogy* (Im/bVImaj7|bII7|V7 instead of Im|bVImaj7|IIm7b5|V7). Although the two remaining tracks also involve simple twelve-bar blues (*51st Street* having a non-standard sequence), the one entitled *Conversation* is remarkable for developing Parker's contribution to the 'language' of jazz both in its opening theme and its four-bar, then two-bar, one-bar and finally half-bar exchanges between Shaw, Knepper and Hadi.

In connection with Mingus's often lengthy gestation (and sometimes even cross-breeding) of his compositional materials, a perfect illustration came about in September 1957, possibly at the Bohemia, when Governor Orval E. Faubus was earning himself international news coverage – and, thanks to Mingus, immortality – by attempting to block the integration of the school system in Little

86

Rock, Arkansas. Mingus, who believed that the process of integration would be the way ahead for blacks, was hardly the only person incensed by the Governor, but he alone had a piece of music ready for the occasion. As Richmond explained: 'At the beginning, it didn't even have a title . . . We were playing it one night and the line, "Tell me someone who's ridiculous", just fell right in with the original line, and I happened to respond with "Governor Faubus!" At that time, Mingus and I had a thing where if something of musical importance happened on the bandstand, we'd leave it in.'[23] Ironically, this was also a trademark of Louis Armstrong, who must have earned at least some temporary admiration from Mingus by publicly condemning President Eisenhower's lack of action over the incident. Mingus's indignation about such matters, however, not only fuelled some fine compositions but spilled over into his stage patter, which at times developed into a sort of reverse Tomming. When Mingus again visited the West Coast in 1961 with Jimmy Knepper in the band, Patricia Willard recalls that:

He was going on and on to the audience about this white guy in the group, and about what a drag it was to tour down South with him. And they hadn't even been down South! A friend said to Mingus afterwards, 'Why are you saying all these terrible things about this nice guy, who really loves you?' And Mingus's reply was, 'Don't mess with my act!'

There was other music which, lying dormant in Mingus's mind, came together during this period, although not recorded until much later. Quite probably, this includes *Better Git It in Your Soul*, of which Mingus once observed: '[George Mraz] said it felt like it was written for the bass . . . We used to improvise with each other in the group. Jimmy Knepper and I would play it for a minute and play it in the next set. *Better Git It* was written on the bandstand. Not quickly, but over a period of time.'[24] Together with its contemporary *Wednesday Night Prayer Meeting* (first recorded, very briefly, in March 1958), *Better Git It* represents Mingus's first combination of the melodic idiom of gospel music with an entire performance in 6/4. Thus, apart from Bob Haggart's remarkable arrangement of *I'm Praying Humble* for the 1938 Bob Crosby band (based note for note on a record by Mitchell's Christian Singers) and despite the mid-1950s attempts of Horace Silver and the Adderley Brothers, Mingus did most to crystallize the influence of gospel on what became known as soul-jazz. It would be pleasing to find a link with vocal 'soul' as typified by Aretha Franklin or Stevie Wonder, but here the influence came much more directly through gospel-based singers Dinah Washington and Ray Charles.

Also dating from this time is the variously titled piece dedicated to Jelly Roll Morton, at least in its original form which, according to Knepper, was the saxophone line heard on the 1959 Atlantic recording but played by only two horns. Mingus wrote that he had 'bought a book of Jelly Roll Morton tunes that I planned to arrange',[25] but, although like the late *Eat That Chicken* this piece comes dangerously close to a parody of 1920s jazz, Knepper claims Mingus's basic idea was that each of the soloists 'had to play one old-style chorus, then a more modern-style one . . . It was meant to be sort of a novelty.' By this same period, Mingus also had begun featuring the occasional Ellington and Parker standards in his performing repertoire, as a change of pace and perhaps to emphasize his continuity with their tradition of jazz 'composition', although, *Flamingo* and *Memories of You* apart, only his own works found their way on to record at the time. Asked if any of the latter failed to get on record, Knepper chuckles: 'Oh, that's unlikely! Mingus used all the material he could get.'

One inevitable, and not totally welcome development was that, as he finally established himself as a leader, Mingus could no longer be considered a sideman except in an all-star context (one such recording, *A Sleepin' Bee*, features him in a duet with Herbie Mann 'alternating one bar ad libbed with one bar written',[26] according to Quincy Jones). Ironically, this also meant that he was no longer a 'star' on bass for, as he featured his instrumental prowess less and his compositions more, his image became blurred and his position in the popularity polls slipped accordingly. Possibly as a way of filling the extra time made available by his lack of employment on other people's gigs, Mingus's creative urge once again expressed itself verbally as he began to get seriously involved in the task of writing his autobiography, doubtless inspired by the appearance the previous year of Billie Holiday's *Lady Sings the Blues*. But, unlike the collaborative effort of Billie's story 'as told to William Dufty', Mingus 'would just write down whatever he was thinking about at the time, and then I would type it up – without editing, you know', says Celia. Two more record sessions in the autumn and winter of 1957–8 bore witness to Mingus's continued interest in the spoken as well as the written word. And concurrently, in early November, the Workshop (in which Horace Parlan, a recent arrival in New York, was the new regular pianist) began a new club residency by featuring Jean Shepherd in *The Clown* both on opening night and on several subsequent weekly appearances. The agreement with the Half Note Café on the lower West side, was actually somewhat more than a residency, since the owner Mike Canterino is said to have offered Mingus a lifetime contract to play there as often as he wished. The rather grandiose title of Mingus's second Bethlehem album produced by Lee Kraft, who had supervised the trio session on Jubilee and also recorded Jimmy Knepper under his own name (and possibly Shafi Hadi) for Bethlehem, was *A Modern Jazz Symposium of Music and Poetry with Charles Mingus*. In fact, the majority of the contents were non-verbal, with three of the tracks (*Nouroog, Duke's Choice* and *Slippers*) forming a suite which Mingus intended should be programmed together, and which was inspired by a lady-friend for whom 'Nouroog' was a sort of code-name.

The two longer compositions, *New York Sketchbook* and *Scenes in the City*, are both descriptive and episodic in the manner of *The Clown* and, although *New York Sketchbook* – the same piece played at Newport fifteen months earlier as *Tourist in Manhattan* – has no narration, it could easily have been conceived with one in mind. The brilliant self-assurance of the band's playing is shown in their handling of the frequent tempo-changes, especially in *Scenes in the City* which has a narration by actor Melvin Stewart, written with assistance from Langston Hughes by Lonnie Elder (who had originally performed on the *Tijuana Moods* session). The theme addressed by *Scenes in the City* is not the sensitive artist, as in *The Clown*, but black sensitivities in a hostile environment. This is also the subject-matter of Langston Hughes's own 1951 sequence of poems *Montage of a Dream Deferred*, containing the proverbial lines, 'What happens to a dream deferred? Does it dry up, like a raisin in the sun? Or does it fester like a sore, and then run?' When a selection of these Hughes poems were taped in March 1958, Mingus used one new piece, *Consider Me,* plus material from his existing repertoire such as *Wednesday Night Prayer Meeting, Double G Train* (both recorded separately the following year) and *Jump, Monk,* '[setting] changes of mood, tempo and theme, often quite spontaneously',[27] according to producer Leonard Feather. By the time of this latter session, however, not only was Dannie Richmond temporarily unavailable, but during the taping of the *Symposium*, trumpeter Clarence Shaw had parted company with Mingus:

There was this record date, and I had the flu. I tried to call his home to let him know that I couldn't make it, but I couldn't get through . . . So he called my house and – Where am I? What am I doing? Trying to ruin the record date? We went through those changes until he threatened – he didn't threaten, he told me – 'I'm going to have some cats kill you' . . . There were only two tunes left to play; he got Bill Hardman. Later on in the day, Celia Mingus, his wife, called up and then the story came out – Mingus had left the phone off the hook . . . 'Oh, Clarence,' he says, 'I love you. You know I didn't mean any of those things I said.' I say, 'Mingus, I have had it. I'm finished.'[28]

Langston Hughes, however, performed with the Jazz Workshop for a series of Sundays in March at the Village Vanguard, after initially appearing with just a duo of Mingus and pianist Phineas Newborn, whose backing was described by Daniel Filipacchi (co-editor of the French *Jazz Magazine*) as 'rather sad and ill-defined . . . would-be avant-garde music which had something over-decorative about it'.[29] And Melvin Stewart, an actor whose delivery resembled Hughes's quite closely, made guest appearances with the Jazz Workshop when Mingus returned to the Half Note Café for a six-week stay from the start of May. But what ought to have been Mingus's most enduring collaboration with actors also took place around this time, and indirectly thanks to Jean Shepherd's radio show. 'It was a Jean Shepherd idea to have his listeners send money and write in ideas for a movie. The listeners would pick the director, writer, etc. They chose me to do the music,'[30] said Mingus. *Shadows*, John Cassavetes's first film as a director, stands up extremely well today, with improvised dialogue and visuals which say much about living in New York and a plot which hinges on tensions between the races, especially as they affect those of mixed race. Shot on a tiny budget over a long period, it is not known whether the film had even been edited at the time Mingus recorded his background music. Unfortunately, not much of this survives in the finished movie, although among the fragments is the atmospheric *Nostalgia in Times Square*, an altered twelve-bar blues sequence in E flat. Mingus's comment about the lack of music on the soundtrack was that 'You can't write a score that quickly. It takes months,'[31] but according to Jimmy Knepper the problem was that, for this prestigious venture, Mingus had reverted to his attempts at 'writing it correctly' and, as a result, 'It came out very stiff 'cause it was written so precisely – it was all eighth-note triplets and sixteenth-note triplets – and they wanted to record all the music in one date. But we took so long over this one tune that it never did get finished.' Probably at Mingus's suggestion, Cassavetes solved this particular budget problem by inviting Shafi Hadi to improvise a solo tenor track for the remainder of the underscore.

At this point things began to change ('A lot of grey in there now, a lot of blue'). It was not only the relative failure with *Shadows* which increased the pressures on Mingus. For, on 30 December 1957, he had been presented with a son, who was named Dorian. And, while Celia may have been able to carry out the work of Superior Artists – and indeed to take orders for unsold stocks of Debut records – from their home, Mingus's own comparative lack of employment must have been a considerable worry. Despite the amazingly high level of artistic success on records cut between February 1957 and March 1958, only *The Clown* and *East Coasting* had so far been released, and in-person appearances during this same period had totalled no more than twelve weeks (mostly at the Half Note Café) and a few concerts. It may even have been in pursuit of a gig that at the end of February, after the Half Note engagement, Mingus visited the Bohemia and ended up in a brawl with Alonzo Levister which, in the chatty prose of Dorothy Kilgallen's nationally syndicated newspaper column, caused the arrival of 'the Bohemia's owner – in pyjamas – to appraise the damage, which included four broken chairs and an assortment of shattered glassware'.[32] Dan Morgenstern, who knew Levister well at the time, says:

> Mingus had been very kind to Lonnie . . . and they were quite close for a while. However, given their respective tempera- ments, it was bound to end like it did, and I wouldn't blame either one . . . In my experience, [Mingus's] violence was at least 75% verbal and those who wished to maintain some sort of regular relationship, professional or personal, with him would walk away from him when he got belligerent. Those who returned his compliments risked physical attack.

It may also have been at this period that Mingus had an argu- ment with Max Gordon, owner of the Village Vanguard, when not enough ready cash was available at the end of an evening. Accord- ing to Gordon, 'He smashed a couple of bottles on the floor, grabbed a kitchen knife, which he held threateningly in front of me, and, still unmollified, stood on a chair and punched his fist through a light fixture. He knocked the fixture askew but the bulb inside stayed lit . . . You can see it if you ask a waiter.'[33] Nor had life at the

Half Note been calculated to make Mingus any calmer; the Italian restaurant that his autobiography rechristened 'The Fast Buck' (owned by 'Mr Caligari') had a high level of background noise, and Jimmy Knepper tells the story of an evening when Mingus's protest took the form of operating a record-player on the stage while members of the band read a book or played cards – apparently, no one in the audience noticed the difference. Furthermore, the lifetime contract had come to a premature end because, as the Half Note was only just establishing itself as a jazz venue, it was receiving the attentions of the Police Department. In a reference to Mingus's habit of talking to white female admirers between sets, an officer was quoted by Nat Hentoff as suggesting pointedly that Mingus's residency be terminated, with the words 'That guy encourages miscegenation.'[34]

As a second-generation product of that most practical form of integration, Mingus might have been forgiven for preaching what he himself practised, but he can hardly have been surprised that the forces of reaction were so strong. In 1953 he had predicted that 'Those studio contractors won't hire Negroes,'[35] and, so far, it seemed that the only musical result of the moves towards integration was the breakthrough of rhythm-and-blues artists such as Fats Domino, Little Richard and Chuck Berry to the white teenage audience. In jazz, integration was mainly the other way round, and Mingus quoted Lester Young as saying of Stan Getz in 1958, 'There's a guy who's driving a Cadillac on money from the way *I* play.'[36] And, despite Mingus's own awareness and appreciation of R&B, he was deeply suspicious of the power and manipulation of the music 'industry':

I feel that society doesn't want the best – I mean, Madison Avenue, for instance, doesn't want the best to sell because they can't overcrowd the field. It would be a monopoly as to who made the money if the more trained musicians, or the more serious people, were pushed one-half as much, one-tenth as much . . . Plus they use other gimmicks: I was reading where people booed Little Richard. Well, see, I know there's a possibility that somebody could have hired twenty guys to say 'Boo', and people are like ants or birds – they follow the leader . . . I mean, Madison Avenue doesn't fool me. If they want to push – pardon me – horse manure; clean it, wash it, sprinkle it and spray it with perfume, and put it inside a cellophane package with a blue ribbon on it, and say 'This is a new powder, and the best made, and it also has vitamins in it for your skin,' they will sell it! So you can't tell me, if they wanted to sell somebody, if they knew his music was good and knew he'd convince twenty people, that they couldn't make him convince twenty *thousand* people! But they don't want to, because there's not that many Charlie Parkers . . . I think they're afraid, when you know you could turn around tomorrow, change your clothes, change your hair-do, start Uncle Tomming and singing, give up your career and your love of music, and become a clown of some sort. They know, if you're that strong a man to stick to your guns and believe in music the way you believe in it, they're *afraid* of you the same as they're afraid of Martin Luther King.

One of the points illustrated by this discourse is that, apart from the rash of small one-off concerts in the 1950s, jazz musicians were still stuck in the ghetto of night-club work, whereas the R&B performers were playing to huge audiences on nationwide package tours. Although he complained frequently that night-club clienteles and managements were inappropriate to the dignity of the music ('I'm not saying all night-club owners are pimps or gangsters but, you know, even the old movies used to tell you that, that they needed someplace, because they didn't do a legitimate job, so they needed a place to say, "Well, here's the money I made, Mr Uncle Sam!"'),[37] there was another side of him which so relished the atmosphere that he wanted to be a gangster. When he visited Europe in 1961, he told many of those he met, 'I am going to see Lucky Luciano in Italy . . . Lucky was framed a few years back as a gangster but there are no gangsters now – they're all legitimate businessmen.'[38] And Dannie Richmond recalls:

> He would say 'Dee, you know that broad so and so' or 'I want you to take a message to Somebody'; I know for a fact that many of his wives knew nothing about some of these things – I'm referring to contacts with some people about certain recording executives that Mingus wanted to have an accident happen to them – oh, yes! . . . That's why there are records that are on different labels, because he swears that not one record company did what they said they were going to do.

It is an irony which would have pleased Mingus, always assuming he knew, that one of his later affiliations was with a record company believed to have Mafia connections. But he also wanted to have it both ways, saying that he was in the habit of phoning J. Edgar Hoover 'to inform all the white folks that I'm trying to be a good boy'.[39]

Although Dannie confirms that the accidents under discussion never actually took place, something of the sort must have crossed Mingus's mind when in mid-1958 he learned that the *Tijuana Moods* album was unlikely to be issued, since not only was the Vik label to be scrapped but this was only one aspect of RCA-Victor's corporate disassociation from jazz, which was probably the result of adding up the total sales of their jazz LPs and comparing them with one Elvis Presley album. At the same time as this outcome of Mingus's involvement with a major record company, he discovered that the powers-that-be at Bethlehem felt that his first album was not going to earn back his relatively large advance as speedily as they had hoped ('My best recording contracts came from Lee Kraft,'[40] Mingus once said); therefore, they had decided not to take up their option on his services. Similarly, and almost simultaneously, he was informed that his agency contract was not going to be renewed and, while fifteen months earlier, he would have been delighted to break with the Willard Alexander office, the artistic successes of his current group must have made this seem a cruel blow. In consequence, Mingus spent much of July trying to interest other agencies, but from a position of considerable weakness, for the word was out that the agency were dropping him because he was 'difficult'. 'I found out recently,' Mingus said a couple of years later, 'that one agency wanted me but the cat in the office who was supposed to book me kept telling the head of the agency, "I don't like that guy, there's something about him" . . . He knew that if I ever made it, he was the kind of person I would help to get rid of.'[41]

Doubtless it was because of these extra-musical problems that Mingus's appearance in the second (and last) Great South Bay Festival at the start of August was not all that it promised to be. Advance publicity claimed that Mingus would perform with a seven-piece Jazz Workshop in the 'premiere' (presumably, therefore, the entire work) of *Revelations*. But the rest of the music was either not written or not rehearsed with a septet, for Mingus brought the quintet and, as well as a Melvin Stewart poetry-reading accompanied by Mingus on piano, featured 'three superior numbers, which included a blues ingeniously hooked up to an extremely attractive melody, several rhythms, breaks, and some first-rate solos . . . And then, the pot on the lip of boiling,' wrote Whitney Balliett, 'the group packed up and left.'[42] Inevitably too, without exactly packing up, the members of the quintet had begun drifting, for, though they had always been available when Mingus called, the amount of work he provided was insufficient to prevent them accepting other gigs. Jimmy Knepper, for instance, was now working regularly with Tony Scott's group, while Dannie Richmond had started an association which lasted a year on and off with Chet Baker. But this wavering of his men's loyalty, which is how Mingus saw it, was nothing compared to his sense of betrayal when Celia walked out on 2 April, their seventh wedding anniversary. Obviously, both she and Mingus had hoped that the birth of Dorian would bring them closer together again but, equally obviously, there was another mouth to feed and the pressure caused by Mingus's intermittent employment was redoubled. As Celia recollects:

> I also found it very difficult to function as his wife and his manager, which in effect I was. Because he didn't want his wife telling him what to do, and at the same time I couldn't be a manager and *not* tell him what to do, where working was concerned . . . The only way we could survive at that point, as I saw it, was if I completely sacrificed anything I wanted, and just spent my life doing what Mingus wanted me to do. And I couldn't do that.

Already during the previous year, Mingus had discovered psycho-analysis, and the analyst to whom he was recommended aggravated rather than eased the marital tensions: 'He talked to Mingus about other patients, which I thought was very unprofessional. And he indulged a lot of Mingus's whims, which created problems between Mingus and me.' But now Mingus lost his trust in the analyst as well, and this and the combined weight of all the pressures he was undergoing finally led him later in 1958 to refer himself to Bellevue Hospital. As Nat Hentoff has written, he 'naively thought that if he knocked at Bellevue's door, he might get some counsel. To those in charge, however, the act of asking admission was highly suspect and Mingus, instead of receiving advice, found himself confined. He was soon released when friends pointed out that there was nothing wrong with him except an excess of innocence.'[43] Hentoff omitted to point out that he was one of the friends in question, but an interesting sidelight on Mingus's situation at this point is offered by Sy Johnson's recent comment, clearly based on a statement by Mingus himself, that he 'pretended to be crazy and went to Bellevue in order to escape a personal management contract with [gangster] Joey Gallo'.[44] Whether this was a part of the truth, or merely wishful thinking at a later period when Mingus felt free to fantasize, the fact remains that he was admitted and, whatever indignities he suffered while in Bellevue, the brief contact with those actually certified insane left him better able to cope with his own problems.

5

All The Things You Could Be By Now

'From every experience such as . . . [being] an inmate of a Bellevue locked ward, Mr Mingus has learned something and has stated it will not happen again,'[1] wrote the analyst who treated him subsequently, Dr Edmund Pollock (the 'Dr Wallach' of the autobiography). One thing Mingus was determined should not happen again was to let circumstances get on top of him and reduce him to the state he was in before going to Bellevue. So, with a renewed vigour which must have surprised those who knew what had been going on, he set about reforming a band and obtaining engagements for it, beginning with a fortnight at the Half Note Café in November for which he rehired Dannie and Horace Parlan, and added tenor player Booker Ervin. Discovered on his arrival in New York six months earlier by Shafi Hadi and brought by Parlan to sit in during Mingus's previous Half Note gig, Ervin's scorching tone and polytonal improvisation added an intensity to Mingus's music hitherto only occasionally matched by Jackie McLean or Jimmy Knepper.

Finding such a soloist may have helped to convince Mingus that it was after all possible to express himself without resorting to violence and, as well as making himself this promise, he clearly decided also to speak what was on his mind as much and as often as necessary. Thus, when he called in at the Five Spot Café and heard saxophonist John Handy (another newcomer to New York) sit in briefly with the band, 'Charlie yelled from the floor, "Hey man, why don't you let this cat play?" It was kind of loud. I looked around and realized I was the cat he was talking about . . . But the guys on the stand were embarrassed. They said something like, well, he can play if he wants to. Mingus insisted that I play again.' He also insisted that Handy join his new band opening at the Five Spot the following week, opposite Sonny Rollins. 'It lasted four weeks,' said Handy. 'Sonny quit the gig after the first week because Mingus was so rude to him.'[2]

Mingus also lost no time in starting a relationship with another fair-haired lady ('He had a thing about blondes,' claims Jimmy Knepper) called Diane Dorr-Dorynek, who became his assistant, typing up further pages of autobiography, and his publicist. She it was who wrote – like other writers, unconsciously echoing the tone of Mingus himself – 'How is a musician to gain the financial security he must have to remain creative . . .? And who will listen to him? . . . On one of those hellish, noise-filled nights, [Mingus] almost gave up – and how many other musicians *have* given up trying to reach an audience at the level of honesty and love?'[3] And she it was who transcribed Mingus's address to the audience on that night at the Five Spot, the 'condensed' version of which runs over a thousand words:

I listen to your millions of conversations, sometimes pulling them all up and putting them together and writing a symphony. But you never hear that symphony . . . You haven't even heard the conversation across the table, and that's the loudest! Have you heard the announcement of a single song title during the night? Or a pause in between tunes, hoping you'd hear yourselves, then quiet down and listen? Joe [Termini] says he has two very loud bands and he's going for a walk. Maybe the other band has no dynamics, but if my band is loud in spots, ugly in spots, it's also beautiful in spots, soft in spots. There are even moments of silence. But the moments of beautiful silence are hidden by your clanking glasses and your too wonderful conversations. [*Shouts from the audience of 'Bravo!' 'Tell 'em, Charlie!'*] . . . You haven't been told before that you're phonies. You're here because jazz has publicity, jazz is popular, the word jazz, and you like to associate yourself with this sort of thing. But it doesn't make you a connoisseur of the art because you follow it around. You're dilettantes of style. A blind man can go to an exhibition of Picasso and Kline and not even see their works. And comment behind dark glasses, Wow! They're the swingingest painters ever, crazy! Well so can you. You've got your dark glasses and clogged-up ears. [*Someone has been needed to say that for years!'*] . . . And the pitiful thing is that there are a few that do want to listen. [*'Most of us want to listen!'*]

A better opportunity to hear the new quintet (with the last-minute substitution of pianist Richard Wyands for Parlan) was provided by their concert at the Nonagon Art Gallery on 2nd Avenue, one of a monthly series also featuring Tony Scott, Cecil Taylor, Jimmy Giuffre and George Russell. As well as Handy's feature on *I Can't Get Started*, based on the format of the Thad Jones recording, the concert included a sprightly and rhythmically varied *Nostalgia in Times Square* and a two-part ballad also originally intended for *Shadows*, called *Alice's Wonderland* whose meandering line also has an off-key countermelody. But most impressive is perhaps the sardonically titled *No Private Income Blues*, a themeless up-tempo twelve-bar blues whose heated exchanges and counterpoint between the saxes looks forward directly to the celebrated *Folk Forms*. The concert was also a formal recording session produced by Nat Hentoff for Jack Lewis (now at United Artists) and including, unlike the self-produced 'live' Debut albums, several brief retakes and rearrangements (Whitney Balliett quoted Mingus as telling Richmond, 'Don't get so fancy. This is *my* solo, man').[4] The resultant LP *Jazz Portraits*, is exciting enough to give cause for regret that the remainder of the material has disappeared without trace.

Interestingly, when the *Modern Jazz Symposium* album was prepared for issue in 1959, Mingus said: 'This is almost my time, maybe this year. I know one thing. I'm not going to let anybody change me any more . . . If Bird were to come back to life, I wouldn't do something just because he did it.'[5] And now, in his thirty-seventh year, at exactly the same stage of life as Ellington had produced his first compositions to feature a single musician (*Echoes of Harlem* and *Clarinet Lament* for Cootie Williams and Barney Bigard respectively), Mingus addressed himself to a new problem, namely how to capitalize on his advances of the last few years in an enlarged group, without sacrificing the amount of interpretative freedom and spontaneous interplay between leader and sidemen. This interplay was a touch-and-go thing even in the small group (Handy has corroborated the feelings of McLean and others that 'Mingus was in the way so much, you couldn't play for it. The man'd stop your solos – he was totally tyrannical'),[6] so that his three 1959 albums with larger forces represent not only a major breakthrough in Mingus's own development but a complete break from the currently accepted methods of handling a seven- to nine-piece group. As in his attempted compositions for *Shadows*, it was axiomatic that such a group was really a miniature big band, and therefore had to be carefully structured and shrewdly orchestrated, but Mingus's method was the now trusted one of dictating lines for each player, and leaving structure and orchestration to emerge spontaneously. Pepper Adams, who took part in the *Blues and Roots* session in February, says 'Certainly that was the way *that* date operated. If there was any music written down, I don't remember having seen any of it . . . I don't recall any rehearsal, there may have been *one*. But, with Charles, everything got changed up by the time you got to the record date, anyway. So having a rehearsal was really not of much benefit for the most part.'

It was therefore necessary that Mingus should surround himself with musicians familiar with this method, and so the regular quintet was augmented not only by Adams and two alumni from the early 1956 band, Jackie McLean and Mal Waldron, but both the great individualists of the trombone, Jimmy Knepper and Willie Dennis (any other band of comparable size would suffer from the absence of any trumpeters, but not this one!) The compositional materials were a turbulent and contrapuntal brew of blues and bop phraseology organized more on the lines of a gospel choir than a standard jazz big band. Mingus explained in the sleeve notes, 'Nesuhi Ertegun suggested that I record an entire blues album in the style of *Haitian Fight Song*, because some people, particularly critics, were saying I didn't swing enough. He wanted to give them a barrage of soul music: churchy, blues, swinging, earthy.'[7] In fact, only three of the six numbers are twelve-bar blues but the remainder display a compelling blend of Mingus's earlier bebop-derived sequences with countermelodies which add an altogether more vehement flavour. *Tensions*, based on the G minor turnaround from *West Coast Ghost*, has an involved ensemble in which four-bar phrases are regularly contradicted by the four-bars-plus-six-bars of the trombone and tenor figure, while *Moanin'* (unrelated to the tune of the same name by Art Blakey) is actually based on the *Jump, Monk* sequence. However, as in *Tensions*, thematic figures are introduced pyramid-fashion for six whole sixteen-bar sections before the sudden contrast of dynamics and texture in the first B section.

The driving up-tempo blues *E's Flat Ah's Flat Too* has a chord-sequence similar (except for bars 5–6) to *Nostalgia in Times Square* (that is, in E flat but landing on A flat in bar 11, the traditional resolution point of a blues chorus), which is outlined in an introductory Mingus chorus consisting entirely of octave leaps of varying pitch. *Cryin' Blues* could hardly be more different, a slow but exhilarating performance with Ervin improvising the opening chorus and McLean the last two, over the most straightforward chords possible apart from a change in bar 10 to the ♭ VI7, fore-shadowing its use in Miles's *All Blues* less than three months later. (Summoning up the final ensemble, Mingus repeatedly yells 'Going home', which, as well as recalling gospel lyrics, promptly became a fashionable phrase for signalling closing choruses, while before the final chord is ended he may be heard saying 'I want to run it through,' which may indicate a retake that could be responsible for the abrupt edit preceding the bass solo. *Tensions* and *My Jelly Roll Soul* appear to be the only unedited tracks on the album.)

However, the masterpiece of planned chaos here is *Wednesday Night Prayer Meeting*, not only for Mingus's hollering and its instrumental equivalents, and the equally gospel-inspired section of Booker Ervin's solo accompanied only by handclapping, but for the first successful jazz use of a fast 6/4 time-signature. Deriving from the polymetric ambiguity of *Dizzy Moods* rather than the relevant parts of *Los Mariachis* or *Pithecanthropus*, still less the 3/4 feel used in *The Clown* or *Passions of a Woman Loved*, this combines both the 6/8 feel (two beats to the bar) implied by the opening bass chorus, and the 6/4 feel of the later 'walking bass' line, with the conventional 4/4 of most jazz; as Ervin said later, 'A fast 6 is really strange, the first time you try . . . And then again, you can count in 4/4 against Mingus's 6.'[8] It is perhaps helpful to observe that four and six are based on a highest common factor of twelve, as heard in many slow blues and R&B items, and that in *Wednesday Night* (a) the repeated figure in the piano solo, (b) the riff added behind the piano solo, (c) the riff played first on piano and then by the horns behind Ervin, and (d) the figure used in Richmond's drum solo, all imply three simultaneous time-signatures (see Appendix A).

Shortly after completing this recording, Mingus was contacted by his former colleague Teo Macero who, after working a couple of years for Columbia Records, was now being allowed to produce albums such as Miles Davis's *Kind of Blue*, with the result that Mingus signed a one-year contract with Columbia. This liaison with a major label may have been the chief reason why Atlantic, then a relatively small company still a long way from becoming WEA International, held back the release of *Blues and Roots* (Atlantic 1305) until April 1960; Atlantic 1304 (by David Newman) was issued by the summer of 1959, whereas 1311 and 1317 (respectively

101

Coltrane's and Coleman's first albums for the company) had been released by the time that *Blues and Roots* was mastered on 29 January 1960. Characteristically, Mingus said, 'Do you know how long that was on the shelf? Two or three years,'[9] but the delay of fourteen months had served to obscure the fact that Davis's *All Blues*, a distinctly non-polymetric 6/4 blues, was predated by the definitive *Wednesday Night Prayer Meeting*.

The first album for Columbia, *Mingus Ah Um* (the jokey title needs no explanation to anyone who has had to study Latin adjectives) was perhaps the first deliberate attempt to show off Mingus's many and varied compositional approaches on one record, and *Better Git It in Your Soul* is closely related to *Wednesday Night*. The fact that it has a thirty-eight-bar chorus melody before getting down to the twelve-bar blues makes the whole somewhat more diffuse, as does the absence of editing on this track. Also, despite the recurrence of the *Wednesday Night* riff (see Appendix A, ex. 8b), the straight 6/4 feel tends to win out over polymetric ambiguity, an impression emphasized by the recording balance. Perhaps because of this, it became quite a hit and was later covered via the Bob Hammer arrangement for a Woody Herman band that included subsequent Mingus sideman Bobby Jones; and it would also have been covered by the Adderley Brothers, but for Mingus's reaction to their suggestion: 'I told them I had done it for Columbia and would they wait until it came out.'[10] Another track is a sibling of the Atlantic *My Jelly Roll Soul,* which had contained Mingus's original saxophone melody decorated with an arranged trombone countermelody. However, when Jimmy Knepper (then regularly employed by Stan Kenton) arrived at the Columbia session, Mingus 'changed the melody right there in the studio' – in other words, over the same fourteen-bar sequence and with an improvised trombone countermelody, the saxophone phrases are of the same length and rhythm, but melodically upside down!

The tribute to Parker, *Bird Calls*, ends with some high-register effects (saxophone squeaks and bass bowed below the bridge), which, unlike the violence of *Pithecanthropus*, are made to sound gently ethereal – a point not lost on the avant-garde of the 1960s. While there is no resemblance between his earlier *(God's) Portrait* and the ballad *Self-Portrait in Three Colors* (the title evokes the famous opening line of the autobiography, 'In other words, I am three'),[11] what looks like another portrait, *Open Letter to Duke,* turns out to be a six-minute compression of the entire *Nouroog* 'suite'. Beginning with Ervin improvising over a double-tempo

Nouroog chord-sequence, Handy's alto is featured on the slow *Duke's Choice* which leads directly into the *Nouroog* melody (both of these bolstered by new, often atonal-sounding countermelodies), and the closing B flat piece becomes instead of the up-tempo *Slippers* a brief Latin vamp providing the same change of mood. Naturally, Mingus's tributes no longer show any attempt to imitate their dedicatees but, whether or not *Open Letter* refers to Ellington, there is a distinct reminiscence in one of the other tracks which were not released until 1979. *Pedal Point Blues* begins with a two-minute shuffle-rhythm vamp, with repeated riffs and alto interjections all based on a single major scale, before becoming a twelve-bar blues in the same key; although the tempo is somewhat different, this would also describe the format of Duke's *Happy-Go-Lucky Local* of late 1946, the year in which Mingus first attempted a pedal-point figure on *Shuffle Bass Boogie*.

Returning to the originally issued tracks, *Boogie Stop Shuffle* (although announced at Newport two months later as *Shuffle Stop Boogie*!) has no connection with the above-mentioned 1946 piece, but is a fast B flat minor blues with a first ensemble chorus influenced by piano boogie patterns recurring at the start of each solo, while *Pussy Cat Dues* is a D major blues taken at a slow-medium bounce tempo. Not only is the second chord the characteristic ♭V17 (as in the *Eulogy* turnaround) but its reappearance in bar 10 (as in *Cryin' Blues*) is used to start a key-change to E flat while, with John Handy on clarinet, Knepper contributes another remarkable improvised counter-melody. The ♭V17 is also the second chord, and makes several further appearances, in the famous ultra-slow blues *Goodbye Pork Pie Hat* whose creation was set in motion on the bandstand at the Half Note Café, just after the quintet began a fortnight's stay in mid-March. Sy Johnson has repeated Handy's account that 'They were playing a very slow, minor blues and, in the middle of the tune, a man came in and whispered to Charles that Lester Young had died. And his response was, immediately, to start fashioning what became *Goodbye Pork Pie Hat*, and, by the time they were finished, the germ of it was there.'[12] As recorded by the quintet with both Handy and Ervin on tenor (Handy taking the solo, which includes some eerie flutter-tonguing in the second chorus), the simple, blues-ballad melody had been reworked with a heavily disguised but haunting twelve-bar chord-sequence. The first four and the last four chords, like the *West Coast Ghost* turnaround, represent a further variation on the *Eulogy* sequence:

I7/ ♭VI7| ♭IImaj7/ ♭V7|♭VII7/ ♭VI7| ♭VII7/I7|
IVm7/ ♭VI7|IIm7/V7|VI7/II7| ♭VI7/ ♭IImaj7|
♭V7/IV7|V7/ ♭VII7|I7/ ♭VI7| ♭IImaj7/♭V7||

Incidentally, the first cover version of *Goodbye Pork Pie Hat* appears to have been the 1966 recording by Bert Jansch and John Renbourn (guitarists with the folk/jazz/rock group, Pentangle), whose version largely ignores this chord sequence and may thus have inspired the harmonically correct, overdubbed two-guitar interpretation by John McLaughlin. A less successful but note-worthy overdubbed version was recorded (1977) by 'classical' bassist Bertram Turetsky.

Although now probably the best-known item of a highlight-filled album, this piece was slow to catch on as a standard but the album, the first to be released by a major label, earned excellent reviews and healthy sales, even if Mingus's estimate of the latter was not confirmed by Columbia: 'Well, let's say it sold well. But 90,000 [in nine months] is a bit, shall we say, exaggerated.'[13]

The tie-up with Columbia did, however, include at least two appearances with the associate company, CBS–TV. Apart from a couple of one-nighters at Birdland and a series of jazz-and-poetry gigs with Kenneth Patchen at the off-Broadway Living Theater (shortly to become the home of the jazz-play *The Connection*), in the spring of 1959 Mingus was also involved with a television play. Interestingly, his contribution to the series *Theater for a Story* was originally announced as part of a single half-hour programme to feature the groups of Miles Davis, Ben Webster, Billie Holiday and Mingus, all selected by music adviser Nat Hentoff, but while both Miles and Ben ended up in separate half-hour shows – Billie may have been unable to appear due to her failing health – Mingus's talent for combining with other media led producer Robert Herridge to use him in a trilogy of plays by S. Leo Pogostin. The first play, *A Song with Orange in It* starring Martin Balsam, was accord-ing to Mingus 'about a rich girl who supposedly fell in love with a piano player. She liked to bug him and so she bought an orange dress and told him to write a song dedicated to her dress, figuring that no one could find a word to rhyme with "orange".'[14] It was the author's intention that the actors, who would be videotaped and not filmed, would use his script as the basis for a certain amount of improvisation, and Mingus not only felt free but was presumably encouraged to contribute to this approach. Diane Dorr-Dorynek wrote that:

> During the week of rehearsal and the three dress rehearsals, musician and actors worked in close relation to one another. For the actual taping of the show, however, the music was cut down so low as to be inaudible to the actors, to avoid a feed-back into their mikes. Two of the actors said they missed it – the bass had seemed to be another actor and had become an integral part of the play.[15]

What Mingus said about the situation is not documented, but it caused his non-participation in the remaining parts of the trilogy. He did, however, record a band version of *Song with Orange* in November 1959, and later a piano version of the same tune retitled *Orange Was the Color of Her Dress, Then Silk Blues*; this would appear to indicate that *Orange Was the Color of Her Dress, Then Blue Silk* [*sic*], which is actually a different tune recorded several times during 1964, also stems from the television play. Mingus was also commissioned to write a band score for the CBS–TV ballet presentation based on *Frankie and Johnny* featuring dancer Melissa Hayden and singer Jimmy Rushing, among others, and likewise two pieces survive from this music, the opening number of the ballet *Put Me in That Dungeon* and the longer *Slop*, which accompanied a bar-room scene. Of the latter, Mingus commented, 'If you notice a similarity to a . . . composition on my last Columbia album, it is not coincidental. The choreographer had rehearsed his dancers to *Better Git It in Your Soul* and asked for something like it,'[16] and indeed not only is the piece in 6/4 but its eight-bar B section contains a quotation from the A theme of the earlier number. Strangely enough, the two cellos which have a couple of important figures in the LP version of *Put Me in That Dungeon* are virtually inaudible on *Slop*, despite Mingus's reference to them in his notes and, for that matter, in the studio conversation included in the 1979 reissue album.

Three more new compositions were premiered during the appearance at the 1959 Newport Festival. Perhaps because none of Mingus's splendid albums of the first part of that year had yet been issued, the festival programme devoted scant attention to him, and he himself was led to introduce his band as 'all new musicians', which was particularly true of trumpeter Richard 'Notes' Wiliams, pianist Roland Hanna and, deputizing for Handy, Leo Wright (whose father had played professionally in Texas alongside Booker Ervin's father). Mingus had in fact intended to present a seven-piece band but his former colleague, Teddy Charles, whose boating hobby is referred to in *Beneath the Underdog*, had chosen this mode of transport to Newport and had been becalmed at Guilford, Connecticut. Hence the announcement of the second number: 'Originally, George Wein booked this group for five pieces, and I kept adding men. So this next piece has been titled *Box Seats at Newport* – subtitled *Seven Pieces for the Same Bread*.' After this oddity, whose chord-sequence is reminiscent of Columbia stable-mate Dave Brubeck, played in a strangely uneasy 6/4, Mingus had been on stage less than twenty minutes when he was impelled to make further reference to Wein: 'We had a different programme scheduled, but he said "Last one", so I'll do [*pause*] half of two!', which is followed by eleven minutes of *Diane* (formerly *Alice's Wonderland*, now with a further atonal-sounding countermelody) and five minutes of the exciting 6/4 blues *Gunslinging Bird*.

Both Hanna and Williams, and come to that Teddy Charles, were included in the ten-piece band which recorded these three numbers in November, with Jerome Richardson taking Wright's flute part on *Diane* and that on *Farwell's, Mill Valley*, a piece dedicated to Farwell Taylor which combines an opening *Eulogy* turnaround with the 'Spanish tinge'. Mingus's notes to the album *Mingus Dynasty* (the word-play was a highly appropriate follow-up to *Ah Um*, given Mingus's Chinese ancestry) contain a 400-word analytical description of *Farwell's* showing it to be, unlike the rest of the material, composed and doubtless written out in a manner reminiscent of *Revelations* and some of the pieces for the Composers' Workshop big band. (It may not be too fanciful to suggest that *Diane* and *Farwells* could have been intended as the second and final movements of *Revelations*. Certainly, because of the similarities in orchestration and method, *Revelations (1st Movement)*, *Diane* and *Farwells* in that order would make a fine suite.) While Dannie Richmond claims, contrary to John Handy, that Mingus said his responsibility was to create the original melody while 'the musicians were responsible for the interpretation, and their solos', certainly in this instance Mingus was more demanding:

All solos in [section B] are ad libbed from a . . . tone row scale against a pedal point rhythmic pattern . . . When Roland Hanna takes the first solo . . . the written flute line takes up the melodic mood. When the flute line dissolves from written part to solo, the written alto part continues the melodic line . . . The soloist can't play a 'wrong' note, but he can make a bad choice of notes not related to the composer's melodic conception. . .

The solos in [section C] were written to be ad libbed from open 5ths. That means there is no major or minor 3rd or tone centre. All the chromatics are at the soloist's disposal which would allow a pivot point type of atonal solo. The solos by Handy on alto and Richard Williams on trumpet are fine solos, but they are executed in a diatonic Charlie Parker chordal manner that doesn't utilize the possibilities given by the open 5ths.[17]

The remaining recording by this line-up, along with the *Ah Um* version of *Self-Portrait in Three Colors* constitutes the final recording of material associated with *Shadows*. In this, *Nostalgia in Times Square* is preceded by a ballad melody not heard in the film, and the whole (now retitled *Strollin'*) has lyrics written by Nat Gordon and sung by Honey Gordon, seemingly inspired by the film's plot. From the same session, *New Now Know How* is a boppish unison line on the chord-sequence of the 1954 *Four Hands* (and thus related to *Extrasensory Perception*) with an A/A/B/A chorus in which the A sections can only be construed as being eight bars if bar 4 is in 6/4, while the B section consists of three plus four bars; it also has a fine solo by one of the few European musicians ever to record with Mingus, the Dutch pianist Nico Bunink. Finally, Mingus displayed on record for the first time his habit of using Ellington tunes, with apparently casual but energetic performances of *Mood Indigo* and *Things Ain't What They Used To Be*, the latter starting with a brilliant pastiche of the Ducal piano style by Roland Hanna. Reviewing a reissue of this material, Bruce King concluded that 'While these recordings are very good, I cannot help but feel that Mingus's continual recreations of Ellington and Parker . . . [and] his reliance upon European musical developments (especially 20th-century offshoots of late 19th-century impressionism) reflects an orchestral sense less original and brilliant than Ellington's or Morton's.'[18] What Mingus had achieved in his 1959 sessions, however, was to serve notice that he was now demanding consideration in the same league as Duke and Jelly Roll. Nevertheless, Mingus's and Columbia's disagreement over sales figures left them unable to renew their contract the following spring.

Before that, several events took place which were to have an important direct or indirect influence on Mingus's general well-being. Firstly he became, at least informally, a patient of psycho-somaticist Dr Luther Cloud, who had attended Lester Young during the last year of his life. He has commented that, at this period, Mingus 'drank a lot more than was good for him, particularly when he had an ulcer, and with his weight and hiatus hernia'.[19] Whether the treatments prescribed by other specialists at various periods were suitable is at least open to doubt; a year or so later, *Down Beat* made anonymous reference to the 'periodic explosions' of a certain bandleader who was 'under medication, and one of the side-effects of the drug causes extreme irritability'.[20] Dan Morgenstern recalls that 'For years . . . Charles would be alternately tranquillized or pepped up and fluctuate from grossly overweight to rather haggard.' Secondly, after an engagement in the autumn, probably at the Village Vanguard, and a booking for a month beginning on 28 November at the Half Note, Mingus moved directly to an indefinite stay at a new Village club on West 4th Street called the Showplace, where Lennie Tristano and Lee Konitz had been playing. This apparently inconsequential move in fact pro-vided the sort of working relationship Mingus had originally hoped for with the Half Note, for he stayed there (with one brief interlude, at his own request) for the next ten months. Not only was he able to bring in guest artists of his own choosing, rather as when he was recording other musicians for Debut, but the fact of working con-tinuously in the same club for so long had an enormously beneficial effect on his new group. What effect it might have had on the hitherto regular group, to which Jimmy Knepper had returned in the autumn to replace Ervin, while Paul Bley and Nico Bunink had alternated on piano, is not known; indeed the Showplace is, for Knepper, 'the place where we all got fired'. No doubt it was Diane who took up her typewriter to formalize the dismissal, for Knepper has recently stated, 'I've still got the letter at home, a typewritten thing which gives his reasons for firing all of us. It says John Handy is practising high notes on the job, Dannie's in another world, and I disagree with him on orchestration.'[21]

Dannie Richmond, who may have picked up some of the habits which ravaged Chet Baker's career among others', was as usual rehired. But the remainder of the group was created by phone-calls from Diane, hastily summoning to the club first Eric Dolphy and then a young trumpeter called Ted Curson (who had previously auditioned alongside Richard Williams, when the latter displeased Mingus by forgetting his wa-wa mute):

That first night was very interesting. No one knew what to do! I knew Dolphy a little through meeting him at a friend's place. We looked at each other kind of scared, saying like 'Go ahead, man, blow!' Suddenly I was out front on my own, with Mingus waving me to carry on. So I played like half-an-hour and then it was Dolphy's turn . . . Later he taught us the pieces on the stand. He knew how to make that go down well with the people.[22]

With due respect to Curson, however, it was the acquisition of Eric Dolphy which set the seal of quality and innovation on this new group. Having left Los Angeles at the comparatively late age of twenty-nine to fill what was originally Buddy Collette's chair with the Chico Hamilton Quintet, he had just taken up residence in New York during the autumn of 1959, and joining Mingus not only gave a considerable boost to his career but placed him in the most challenging environment he had yet encountered. As the first wholly convincing multi-instrumentalist in jazz, Dolphy had a distinctive and influential approach to both alto saxophone and bass-clarinet, and to a lesser extent the flute, and he was able to bring to Mingus's music a new and (in the eyes of the New York jazz public) untried voice, which blossomed markedly in the months to come. As Dolphy said later, 'You never know what [Mingus] is going to do because every night he comes on the stand with something different. He's so creative, and in that way it was so stimulating to work with him.'[23]

However, one further event, which partially obscured the significance of the Dolphy/Mingus collaboration, was the simultaneous arrival also from Los Angeles of Ornette Coleman. As well as generating an impressive amount of controversy with his first two West Coast-recorded albums, Coleman's debut engagement in New York had begun on 17 November at the Five Spot and, during the ensuing months, caused thousands of words to be poured out by everyone from Leonard Bernstein and Kenneth Tynan to Cannonball Adderley – not to mention the established jazz critics, who felt under some pressure to declare themselves *pro* or *contra*. Being an articulate, even opinionated, thinker about other people's music, Mingus contributed his three cents' worth and expressed genuinely mixed feelings:

Now aside from the fact that I doubt he can even play a C scale . . . in tune, the fact remains that his notes and lines are so fresh. So when [disc jockey] Symphony Sid played his record, it made everything else he was playing, even my own record that he played, sound terrible. I'm not saying everybody's going to have play like Coleman. But they're going to have to stop playing Bird.[24]

Ted Curson even reported that Mingus not only went down to the Five Spot to hear Coleman, as it seems did every other musician in New York, but sat in on piano; he also took Curson and Dolphy along in his car. 'After a while he said "Do you think you can play like that?" Of course, we could. I'd just got my pocket trumpet. Eric said OK. We rehearsed a bit, and soon we were playing that style, and just as good.'[25] Unfortunately the success, or even the seriousness, of this attempt can only be evaluated from records made many months later; but it is clear in retrospect that, while Coleman did not think in terms of tonality yet usually played in one identifiable key for at least several bars at a stretch, Dolphy on the other hand thought consciously of key and chord-sequence while frequently playing on the verge of atonality. He was, therefore, for all the unconventional phraseology and sometimes honking tone which linked him in many observers' minds with Ornette, much more suited to the Mingus approach.

However, even the few reviews accorded to the group during its residency at the Showplace give no indication of this, and merely confirm that there was considerable fluctuation of personnel, especially at the start. French jazz journalist Daniel Filipacchi, who paid another visit to New York in January 1960, described performances of *Jelly Roll* and *Fables of Faubus* but mentioned only Dannie Richmond of the frequently changing sidemen.[26] Whitney Balliett, who reviewed tap-dancer Baby Laurence guesting with the quintet, mentioned Richmond and the returning Roland Hanna and quoted Mingus as saying to Laurence: 'Baby, you want a job, I'll fire my piano player who's always late anyway and hire you.'[27] Ted Curson mentioned not long after that 'Leo Wright, Elvin Jones, Wilbur Ware, Jimmy Knepper were a few of the people who were in the group at one time or another while I was there,'[28] and Dannie Richmond reports that, as in 1957, the turnover of piano players was particularly high: 'Kenny Drew was there, Jaki Byard, Kenny Barron – there was a lot of different people in and out. [Mingus] said they were wearing him out!' (Byard has also mentioned attending a rehearsal at Mingus's apartment for the *Mingus Dynasty* recording in 1959, with his associates Don Ellis and vibist Al Francis.)[29] The fact that after a couple of months Mingus ended up with a group which, like Coleman's, had no piano at all, seems fairly coincidental, for *Down Beat* editor Gene Lees, covering a performance in late February or early March, gave the personnel 'on the night of review' as Curson, Booker Ervin (briefly substituting for Dolphy), Mingus, Richmond and Teddy Charles.[30] The last pianist to work at the Showplace, Sy Johnson, had sat in during the period when Baby Laurence was already on the payroll and been told by Mingus that 'Laurence was going to work for two more weeks, and that he'd like me to come in every night and play for nothing . . . "As soon as Baby Laurence leaves, the job is yours." ' After accepting this proposition, Johnson found that, as soon as the two weeks were over, Yusef Lateef was added to the band and, when Mingus finally acknowledged Johnson's presence, 'He made as though he was going to walk right by me, and then he said to me, "If it was up to you, and you had a choice between hiring Yusef Lateef and you, who would *you* hire?" And then he walked out, he figured there wasn't any answer for that. And he was quite right, as a matter of fact.'[31]

Lateef, who had just moved from Detroit to New York in January, played alongside Dolphy and Curson for nearly three months, and tells the following story of one of Mingus's more specialized approaches to communicating his ideas without written notes: 'For example, on one composition I had a solo and, as opposed to having chord symbols for me to improvise against, he had drawn a picture of a coffin. And that was the substance upon which I was to improvise.' Apparently this composition was unconnected with Lateef's feature, also in the repertoire at the Showplace, called *Prayer for Passive Resistance* (the start of 1960 had seen the first of the famous lunch-counter sit-ins, in Greensboro, North Carolina). The recorded version of this piece, in which Lateef plays a slow 4/4 blues over a 12/8 backing, was the only entirely new work in the album *Pre-Bird/Mingus Revisited*, most of whose items have been discussed in the chronological order of their composition. Apart from *Prayer*, the recordings of the nine-piece group are disappointing, viewed as the first documentation of an augmented Showplace group; but it is worth underlining the unusual nature of the album for, whereas Ellington had thirty years of hits behind him at the time of his *Historically Speaking*, here was Mingus at the age of thirty-eight doing a retrospective of his early career and including music which another more fashion-conscious, or less single-minded writer might have dismissed as his adolescent trivia. Ted Curson's account of how *Half-Mast Inhibition* even came to be recorded at all was that producer Leonard Feather:

> said he wanted to record the quartet. What Mingus did was say, 'OK, come tomorrow, but I got something for you to hear . . .' He had twenty-seven [*sic*] pieces there, which ended up getting Leonard Feather fired from his new position at Mercury Records . . . He said he had this music he did when he was seventeen and nobody would record it. He brought a box in and the music was yellow, crumbling in your hands. He had told Leonard Feather, I just want you to hear it, but he forced it on Leonard.[32]

The return of Booker Ervin in place of Lateef had taken place by at the latest mid-June, when the personnel was announced for Mingus's first visit to Europe, for the first of what turned out to be annual festivals at Antibes/Juan-Les-Pins on the Côte d'Azur. The fact that Mingus was invited at all to an event principally for European bands is a little surprising, but it may be not unconnected with the role of the French record company Barclay, who not only issued an album of some of the European participants such as Dusko Goykovic and Albert Mangelsdorff but, as the local licensee of Atlantic, recorded on their behalf both of the American bands involved, Wilbur DeParis's 'New' New Orleans Jazz and Mingus. (The DeParis album was, of course, issued at the time whereas Mingus's was apparently overlooked by Atlantic until after his death, but this may have been partly because of the delayed release of *Blues and Roots*, containing the studio version of *Wednesday Night Prayer Meeting*.) The European visit may, in fact, have been a little premature, as far as Mingus's reputation and musical accessibility were concerned. An unsigned photo caption in Filipacchi's *Jazz Magazine*, quoting a Mingus announcement 'I'm going to play something slow and quiet, quiet like an atom bomb,' summed up as follows: 'Admired unreservedly by a few, he remained a mystery for everyone else but was applauded nevertheless.'[33] Charles Delaunay, director of *Jazz Hot*, put it the other way round: 'Without the slightest concern for presentation, and without any concessions, the famous bassist presented an audience not really prepared for it with his latest musical research, which for most of the listeners must have felt like a cold shower, but intrigued and excited the majority of musicians present.'[34]

While *I'll Remember April* is chiefly remarkable for its blend of the group's heated style with that of guest Bud Powell, by then resident in France, it is particularly interesting to have versions of both *Better Git It in Your Soul* and *Wednesday Night Prayer Meeting*, from a single concert. *Wednesday Night* seems to have acquired additional backing riffs, possibly to distinguish it better from the former, but follows the same general outline of lengthy solos with a regular series of riffs interspersed with rhythm-section-only backings. (Both routines also include brief use of the piano, as Mingus leads the riffs behind the respective drum solos from the keyboard.) The third twelve-bar blues in F, this time basically in 4/4, apparently dates back to the early Jazz Workshop period of the mid-1950s. Called *Folk Forms,* it justifies its title by superimposing not the 6/4 of gospel (with the brief exception of the penultimate chorus) nor the 12/8 of slow blues, but the straight 8/8 common to ragtime and early country music, as well as Afro-Cuban music and subsequent fusions. The difference, outlined in Mingus's bass intro, is especially marked in the work of Dolphy, who along with deliberately simple folk-like phrases plays several bebop ideas borrowed from Charlie Parker but, instead of the dotted rhythms (eighth-note triplets) associated with Parker, uses even eighths throughout. Far from being put on especially for this piece, this was a general characteristic of Dolphy's playing, as it was of Coleman's, and can be heard particularly clearly in the unaccompanied choruses where each soloist is really out front on his own, without even the trampoline of handclapping which accompanied Ervin on *Better Git It.* Indeed, the polyrhythmic freedom is so total that the tempo is slightly unsteady, and disaster is sometimes only just avoided when bass and drums re-enter. But what is really extraordinary about this performance (like *No Private Income Blues*, entirely themeless) is the amount of collective improvisation for, although the shape of the whole is ultimately controlled by the changing contributions of Mingus and Richmond, the excitement generated by the continual fluctuation between accompanied solos, unaccompanied solos, improvised duets and improvised ensembles represents a new peak in Mingus's recorded achievements.

The other major item introduced on record here is *What Love*, which had been resurrected because 'Eric Dolphy found the manuscript and remarked on how much like Ornette Coleman's music it sounded.'[35] However, unlike most 'free' jazz before at least the mid-1960s, the piece spends most of its time going into and out of tempo. And it contains an example of the most unusual aspect of this group's work, the out-of-tempo 'conversation' between bass and bass-clarinet which, according to eyewitness Ted White, had begun one night at the Showplace as a result of 'Mingus making fun of Dolphy and Dolphy's spirited response'.[36] Intriguingly, Mingus's opinion of the genesis of his saxophonist's style changed, at least for interview purposes, saying in 1960: 'He played the style he does now in high school,'[37] and in 1971: 'I thought he was crazy, man, because he wasn't playing anything like I heard him play before.'[38] For my benefit the following year, he related Dolphy's speech-like lines directly to Charlie Parker: 'See, in bebop which I was raised with and so was Eric – he came a little later in it – but, aside from the chord changes and patterns and lines that there were, there was another expression on the bandstand that was called "conversation". That is the only thing that developed out with Eric *past* (not any *better than*) Bird.' While this too was characteristic of all Dolphy's work generally, what happens after his second middle-eight in *What Love* is an out-of-tempo interlude in which the only melodic or rhythmic content arises from Dolphy's and Mingus's imitation of speech patterns. 'We used to really talk and say words with our instruments . . . We had different "conversations", we'd discuss our fear, our life, our views of God – which is still the main subject today.'

This historic, if unexpected, trip to the South of France naturally required a leave of absence from the Showplace (where John Handy's group kept it in the family), as did the possibly even more significant event that had immediately preceded it. Mingus had spent the week before 4 July in Newport, Rhode Island, for 1960 was the year in which he launched the now commonly accepted idea of an 'anti-festival'. It was also the year in which, as if by an act of God, the official festival was cancelled in midstream because of rioting in the streets of Newport. In previous years, some commentators had begun to write off the musical content of the festival, and even a relatively sympathetic account of the 1960 debacle by *Down Beat* editor Gene Lees blamed George Wein's programming for attracting hordes of college students uninterested in jazz *per se*, noting that by Saturday afternoon 'A few of the boys were nude on the beach . . . [and] a young couple were engaged in the indoor sport outdoors in full daylight.'[39] (The only stimulant mentioned, nine years before the Woodstock era, was alcohol.)

The alternative festival, which took place at the nearby Cliff Walk Manor Hotel, had been put together during the preceding few weeks by Mingus and his old colleague Max Roach, their reconciliation dating from the previous autumn when Roach was briefly admitted to Bellevue Hospital (although, unlike Mingus, not of his own free will). Although their effort was conceived as a challenge to the jazz establishment in general, night-clubs and festivals alike, the Providence *Evening Bulletin* reported that Mingus's protest was fuelled two months before when he was advertised as being booked for the main festival: 'Festival officials say Mingus had agreed, over the telephone, to appear for $700, but later insisted on $5,000, mentioning the [Benny] Goodman fee. Wein says Goodman received $7,500 for an entire evening's programme and out of this paid his seventeen-man band.'[40] So, with only the moral support of Nat Hentoff and Elaine Lorillard (who had her own axe to grind as the recently divorced wife of the official festival's chairman), Mingus and Roach had done all the organization of the festival, including preparing the site and creating such publicity as there was. Burt Goldblatt described Mingus being driven through the centre of the town 'standing on the seat of a convertible, his bass in hand, appealing to one and all "Come to my festival!" ',[41] while Mingus himself recalled 'putting up tents . . . [and] walking around with a sledgehammer' while 'a well-known critic . . . was asking me questions and I was trying to answer him . . . "Don't you know I could break you, . . . destroy your whole professional life. You're supposed to give me respect." "Kiss my ass, m...r," I said' [dots in the text].[42]

Mingus seems to have been in a state of heightened emotion throughout the week, initially perhaps because a motel room he had reserved by phone turned out to be suddenly unavailable when this 'musical director' of the Cliff Walk Manor festival was found not to be white. There had also been an ugly scene on Wednesday 29 June, the day before the festival opened, when after the City Council had delayed in issuing a licence for Cliff Walk Mingus accused George Wein of trying to obstruct his efforts. Wein, on the contrary, claims his attitude was, 'By all means, if it's possible, let that "rebel" festival go – make sure it's not cancelled, 'cause they will accuse us of cancelling it.' In this confrontation, Wein told the Newport *Daily News* that Mingus had threatened to kill him 'in front of 10,000 people' and throw acid at Louis Lorillard.[43] Later, Gene Lees elicited from Mingus the information that what he had intended to use was black pepper and, when asked what that might achieve, he answered with a straight face, 'Make them cough and sneeze and things.'[44] (Having made a promise to himself not to be the initiator of physical violence, Mingus was now in the habit of

115

carrying a handful of pepper wrapped in Kleenex inside his back pocket. Nat Hentoff has described one of Mingus's attempts to use this pre-emptive self-defence in the presence of his then wife: 'When Mingus pulled out the Kleenex, the wind blew the pepper the wrong way – into her face. When she finally could see again, Charles and his antagonist were embracing.'[45] Mingus may possibly have picked up the idea from singer Babs Gonzales, whose autobiography *I, Paid My Dues . . . Good Times, No Bread* makes it clear, however, that he favoured red pepper.)

On Sunday, when the official festival's cancellation was announced, and even his colleagues at Cliff Walk Manor were dismayed at the implications, Mingus said, 'They deserve it because they confused rock 'n' roll with jazz'[46] and yet, on the Monday, he agreed to Jon Hendricks's suggestion of a reconciliation with George Wein. The most impressive aspect of the alternative festival was its musical quality and integrity. The full list of performers, who played in set groups and in unconventionally grouped jam-sessions, included Mingus's quintet with Booker Ervin; Max Roach with Booker Little, Walter Benton, Julian Priester, Ahmed Abdul-Malik and Roach's wife-to-be Abbey Lincoln; a Kenny Dorham group with Allen Eager, Kenny Drew, Wilbur Ware, Art Taylor and Teddy Charles; Cecil Payne, Duke Jordan, Nico Bunink, Baby Laurence, and vocalists Hendricks and Marilyn Moore; the representatives of the new free jazz, Ornette Coleman, Don Cherry, Charlie Haden and Ed Blackwell; and three elder statesmen, Jo Jones, Coleman Hawkins, and Roy Eldridge. Among many other notable moments recounted by Whitney Balliett, the Saturday evening indoor concert ($5 entrance fee, half-price for the press) included 'a nearly vicious rendition' of *Better Git It in Your Soul*, a twenty-minute duet between Mingus and Roach, and a free-form session (continued the following afternoon) by these two plus Kenny Dorham, Julian Priester and Ornette Coleman which 'provoked Mingus into one of the best solos he has ever played'.[47]

Sadly, and no doubt because of the hasty organization, none of this exciting and in some cases unrepeatable music seems to have been recorded, but there was a sequel four months later. For in the autumn of 1960 the Cadence record company announced the inauguration of its jazz label, Candid, directed by Bob Altshuler and with none other than Nat Hentoff as producer. The Jazz Artists Guild, a collective formed by Mingus, Max Roach and Jo Jones on the Monday after the Newport festivals (Independence Day, as it happens) was responsible for a Candid album under the title *Newport Rebels*; and, though the organization fell apart rather rapidly from internal dissension, its two sessions – one on which both Roach and Jones played, and one with Jones and Mingus – do give a taste of the music and the catholic line-ups featured at Cliff Walk Manor. In particular, the contrast between Roy Eldridge and Eric Dolphy and the powerful blues work of both Eldridge and Mingus on *Me and You*, justify the attempt to preserve the creative atmosphere of the festival. Roy must have especially delighted the bassist by what he said about his playing at the session: 'I wanted to find out what bag you're in. Now I know you're in the right bag. I'm not naming names, but a lot of them are so busy being busy on their horns that they forget the basics. They don't get all the way down into the music. You did, baby.'[48] Although doubtless unaware of his own contribution to Mingus's musical education way back in 1940, Eldridge had in fact put his finger on one of the main factors responsible for the bassist's growing maturity of the past five years.

Eric Dolphy too had recently paid tribute to his employer when, in August 1960 on his album *Out There*, he had become simultaneously the first person to record a Mingus tune without the man himself (namely *Eclipse*) and the first person to create a piece inspired by Mingus, aptly titled *The Baron*. And Mingus's example shows not only in the musical content, but in the fact that this and some other Dolphy numbers of the period were assigned to Jazz Workshop Inc., instead of being published by the record company. But perhaps Dolphy's most lasting tribute to Mingus at this time was his brilliant work on two other Candid albums, called simply *Mingus* and *Charles Mingus Presents Charles Mingus*. Three weeks before the session with Eldridge, on Thursday 20 October, he was in the studio with the nucleus of the original Showplace group: just Mingus, Dolphy, Ted Curson and Dannie Richmond. Starting at midday, the quartet had by late afternoon completed five long numbers – according to visiting French journalist François Postif, all of them first takes – before adding six more musicians for an enlarged group. Postif noted that Mingus had the studio lights switched out (an aid to relaxation first tried by Miles Davis) as he addressed an imaginary audience:

Good evening, ladies and gentlemen, we'd like to remind you that we don't applaud here at the Showplace, or *where* we're working. So restrain your applause and, if you must applaud, wait till the end of the set – and it won't even matter then. The

117

reason is that we are interrupted by your noise. In fact, don't even take any drinks, I want no cash register ringing. Et cetera! Like to open the set with a composition I wrote in 1941 that was a huge success at the time – Nat, you're going to make a lot of money! This piece is pretty far-out and it's called *What Love*. This is how it goes.[49]

All the first part of which is reproduced on the record, as a muted reminder of Mingus's famed night-club speeches, but there is an audible edit after the word 'composition' as the rest of the sentence (on disc) refers to an item recorded later in the afternoon.

What Love follows the same outline as the performance at the French festival, but, while the bass-clarinet solo is still two choruses of the chord-sequence with an out-of-tempo conversation between the second middle-eight and the last eight bars, at Antibes the conversation grew naturally out of Dolphy's solo and lasted about seventy-five seconds; here it lasts four minutes and forms an entirely separate episode, launching immediately into 'words' and the bass calling 'Dolphy!' and his wary reply 'Yeah?' on bass-clarinet. The conversation in fact becomes so animated that any audience hearing the record today is still likely to break up at the imitated swearing and screaming, and apparently at the playback (with the lights switched back on) Mingus and Dolphy were translating each other's 'remarks' for the onlookers. This was followed by a version of *All the Things You Could Be By Now If Sigmund Freud's Wife Was Your Mother*, the furiously up-tempo theme of which recalls the sound of Ornette Coleman and Don Cherry, although Mingus's autobiography claims that it was written in Bellevue. However, elements of this piece are also supposed to date back to the early 1940s, although this may well refer to the chromatic reharmonization which forms the start of each soloist's 'obstacle course', as Sy Johnson termed this arrangement.[50] In the out-of-tempo middle-eight which is the second 'obstacle', Dolphy, whose command of high harmonics sometimes seemed limited to a couple of favourite notes, creates a beautiful new melody rising to the high B (concert D) at the third bar capped by the altissimo C (concert E flat) at the seventh bar, before launching into up-tempo again.

This version of *Folk Forms*, the only one generally available until the rediscovery by Atlantic of the Antibes tapes, is a classic: with only two horns, the collective improvisations sound simpler if no less wild, while the slightly slower tempo and dry studio sound bring the contrapuntal brinkmanship of all four players into even clearer focus. Mingus's solo combines his virtuosity and his soulfulness in a single statement (see Appendix A), while the entire performance is spontaneously organized around a couple of simple rhythmic figures, one of which is much used by both Dolphy and Richmond and, first heard as a drum fill (bars 13–14 of the Antibes version, and bars 23–24 on Candid), is rhythmically identical to the 'Oh, play that thing!' of King Oliver's 1923 *Dippermouth Blues*. The remaining quartet titles are equally interesting, the poised yet powerful *Stormy Weather* presenting an interesting contrast to the tight-lipped 1954 version, while the final *Original Faubus Fables* is a bitter comedy compared to the gentle parody in the 1959 Columbia recording. Part of the reason lies in the lyrics, not recorded hitherto simply because Columbia was a major label with nationwide distribution (1960 was the year in which Dave Brubeck cancelled a concert and Norman Granz a national television spot, rather than bow to southern prejudices about presenting racially mixed groups).

(Intro) Oh Lord, don't let them shoot us
Oh Lord, don't let them stab us
Oh Lord, don't let them tar and feather us
Oh Lord, no more swastikas!

(A) Oh Lord, no more Ku Klux Klan!

(A¹) Name me someone ridiculous
[*Dannie:*] Governor Faubus
Why is he sick and ridiculous?
[*Dannie:*] He won't permit integrated schools
(Then he's a fool)

(B) Boo! Nazi Fascist supremists / Boo! Ku Klux Klan!

(A¹) Name me a handful that's ridiculous
[*Dannie:*] [Inaudible,] Faubus, [Inaudible,] Rocke-
feller, [Expletive,] Eisenhower
Why are they so sick and ridiculous?
[*Dannie:*] Two, four, six, eight [*All:*] They brainwash
and teach you hate[51]

Obviously, no one could find a word to rhyme with 'Faubus' but, nevertheless, this is a satisfyingly barbed culmination of Mingus's interest in combining words and music, and whether or not it played any part in the speedy discontinuation of the Candid label must be left to conjecture.

The remaining musicians added later the same day (and again on the day of the Eldridge session) were all Mingus alumni known from previous recordings except for the young Detroiters (recommended by Yusef Lateef) Charles McPherson and Lonnie Hillyer, and although they contrast well with Dolphy and Curson, being dedicated disciples of Parker and Gillespie, these eight- and ten-piece performances are, like those on *Pre-Bird*, somewhat disappointing in comparison to the 1959 sessions. *MDM* is a long, exciting but unexceptional blues with solos led off by Britt Woodman, who had just left Ellington, and with a theme-statement which combines Duke's *Mainstem* and Monk's *Straight, No Chaser* (despite the sleeve-notes, there is no audible reference to Mingus's own *51st St Blues*). *Lock 'Em Up* is another, more hectic blues with a double theme, Mingus's *Hellview of Bellevue* being counterpointed by Charlie Parker's *Passport*. One suspects the Parker tune should have been *Relaxin' at the Camarillo*, also titled in honour of a mental hospital, but the track does illustrate the session's loose organization as one of the rhythm-section breaks is filled with an insane yell, Mingus's way of cueing in Booker Ervin. When this second Candid album appeared, an otherwise favourable review by Dick Hadlock opened with the words, 'Mingus, a resolute independent of many faces, . . . has had a fling at every trend in jazz that has come along – cool jazz, hard bop, Third Stream, soul jazz, and more recently "all-out" jazz – yet has failed to make a lasting stylistic impression.'[52] Superficially, there is a lot to be said for this accusation, and for similar accusations levelled at Ellington, but Mingus's 1959–60 work had enabled him to discover that, for all he may have influenced the new avant-garde and enjoyed flirting with it, his allegiance to an overriding compositional form was far stronger.

However, a couple of straws in the wind signalled the end of this particular peak of activity. One day after the Candid quartet session, John Coltrane recorded for the first time with his famous quartet which, with the participation of Elvin Jones (and later a bassist who had studied with Mingus, Jimmy Garrison), adopted and simplified some of Mingus's modal devices while gaining the popularity which Mingus felt should have been his. And, secondly, by the time of the Candid dates, both Curson and Dolphy had officially left his group, and Hillyer and McPherson had taken over at the Showplace. Unfortunately, relations with the management there were no longer so stable either: Dannie recalls an occasion when he asked Mingus for an advance against his pay, 'And when the manager said that he couldn't do it, [Mingus] said "Now, wait a minute, hold it. I want this money for my drummer, it's not for me." And when the guy still said something about he didn't have it, that's when Mingus was getting ready to tear the place apart.' But that was nothing to what happened when Mingus showed up one night at the end of October to discover that his bass, which he habitually left on the stand, had been accidentally damaged. He would obviously have had an excellent case for suing the club, but this would have ended their working relationship in any case; so Mingus demanded immediate payment, and the manager refused. Instead of threatening to kill him in front of 10,000 people, the Bull vented his anger not on the owner but on the club piano, pulling out some of its upper strings, and then got on the phone to the Half Note.

6
Money Jungle

The year 1960 had also been notable for a new development on the personal front. Already by the start of the decade, the relationship with Diane was foundering. Mingus, of course, prided himself on going his own way but this time, despite collaborating with him on the notes for *Mingus Dynasty* and *Blues and Roots* (both prepared in early 1960), his partner also decided to do her own thing. 'She wanted to paint, take pictures – and write. She was a talented lady,' says Dannie Richmond, adding:

> The thing as far as the ladies – from what I could see – is that they didn't even *know* Charles. Just they heard his music and they heard, I think, the cry in it and the sorrow that was in some of it, and just took it upon themselves to make themselves known. And, as a result, you know, things started to happen. Even then, though, he was still talking about other women.

This temporary impasse inspired Mingus to invite Celia back to New York, where she lasted about two days. Dannie's recollection is that 'Celia was one of the female personalities in Mingus's life that was as heavy as he was – and he didn't like that,' while she describes her reunion with Mingus as 'A Mexican standoff – in other words, neither of us would give an inch.'

By the late spring of 1960, Mingus had arranged to sell his apartment and move to Suite 11P, 2186 5th Avenue in Harlem. Part of the reason was undoubtedly the blonde-haired Judy Starkey, whose lightning courtship provides a somewhat premature happy ending in the penultimate chapter of *Beneath the Underdog* and who, by the time of the move, was already pregnant; Carolyn, Mingus's only daughter, was born early in 1961. Mingus was now not only entering a period of at least some emotional stability, and musical satisfaction from his residency at the Showplace, but was beginning to feel a little more affluent. For, despite disagreements about album sales and therefore about artist royalties, his records past and present were certainly selling well enough to generate some visible publishers' royalties for the 200 compositions Mingus claimed were now handled by Jazz Workshop Inc. And, because of the interest created by his record sales, perhaps also because of the threat to the established order represented by the Newport anti-festival, booking agencies had begun to take an interest again. Thus, after a couple of years handling his own bookings, Mingus signed late in 1960 a one-year contract with Milt Shaw's Shaw Artists Corp. (who already had, among others, Miles Davis, Art Blakey, John Coltrane and Ornette Coleman on their books).

By the spring of 1961, apparently serious discussions were going on about an all-star group to consist of Mingus, Max Roach, Sonny Rollins (who was shortly to return from 'retirement') and possibly Thelonious Monk. This eventually came to nothing, but, earlier in the year, Mingus struck lucky with another compatible club residency for his own group. Unfortunately, as Dan Morgenstern pointed out, 'It would do great business in Manhattan, but not enough people feel like taking the half-hour drive out to Queens . . . The more's the pity, since this club is owned by a lady who loves jazz and is concerned for the welfare of musicians and audience.' The management of the club in question, Copa City, in fact allowed Mingus (at least on opening night) to use the entire group which recorded *Lock 'Em Up*, with the sole exception of Booker Ervin. As well as items by the nine-piece band such as *Original Faubus Fables* and *MDM* (now titled *Duke and Monk*), the music played on this occasion included a quintet performance of *Tijuana Table Dance* featuring Jimmy Knepper, who joined the Hillyer/McPherson front line for the several weeks of the engagement, and something called *Copa City Titty*. Mingus was quoted as saying 'It doesn't mean what you think. When I was working with Kid Ory, he used to call a gig that. "We're going to make that titty tonight," he would say.'[1] And there were multiple nods in the direction of the bop era, for example McPherson playing the Parker versions of *If I Should Lose You* and *I Didn't Know What Time It Was* and, with

123

guest Max Roach (who also did another duet with Mingus), ultra-fast small-group renditions of *Ko-Ko* and *Dizzy Atmosphere.*

The stay at Copa City not only gave the young Hillyer and McPherson a chance to settle in but, as Mingus recalled eleven years later, McPherson was also initiated into the art of 'conversation':

> There's a Dr Somebody, he came with his wife because he heard that we could talk and send messages. So he wrote a message down and – Eric had just left, McPherson was just learning the book. I forgot, so I told McPherson to go in the corner and I'd send him a message . . . [The Dr] told me and McPherson didn't see it, his wife went with McPherson. So I played the message, and Mac said 'I hear *something*'. A voice said in the corner 'Play it again!', it was my drummer Dannie Richmond. He says 'It's all mixed up . . . Why I couldn't hear it, and why McPherson didn't hear it, is he spoke backwards: "Mingus, I think, is a genius." But I knew he was saying "I think Mingus is a genius." ' That's what he wrote, and that's what I played to McPherson.

At least the anonymous doctor (Mingus actually said in introducing the anecdote: 'I'll tell you his name later 'cause I don't want to waste time thinking of his name') could identify genius when he saw it, but, at the press reception for his opening at Copa City, Mingus had declared his own genius by unveiling his concept of Rotary Perception.

It is interesting to speculate how far this theory was derived from his work with Richmond, and how far it may have been stimulated by the similar partnership, then a few months old, of John Coltrane and Elvin Jones. Expanding on the idea a little later in the year for an article he wrote in the *Jazz News* series entitled *What I Feel about Jazz* (ghosted from an interview by Kitty Grime during his visit to Britain), the subject only came up after slightly sour comments about Coltrane, Free Form and Third Stream:

> When I first introduced the name to the press, I admit it was only a gimmick like 'Third Stream'. I was tired of going hungry and I wanted to catch the public ear but, although the word was a gimmick, the music wasn't . . . Swing proceeds in one direction only – but this rotary movement is, of course, circular. Previously jazz has been held back by people who think that everything must be played in the 'heard' or obvious pulse . . . With Rotary Perception you may imagine a circle round the beat . . . The

notes can fall at any point within the circle so that the original feeling for the beat is not disturbed. If anyone in the group loses confidence, one of the quartet can hit the beat again.[2]

Seen as an explanation of rhythmic principles derived from the work of Lester Young and Parker, and specifically of most performances in which Mingus himself participated, this is quite revealing. Indeed, Mingus must have found the whole article/interview to be one of his more revealing moments, for it forms the basis of the two-page conversation with the unnamed 'English critic' which provides one of the few musical discussions in his autobiography. Despite the compression of the narrative causing it to take place in 'The Fast Buck' on the same night he got together with Judy Starkey, the author clearly had the printed article to hand when writing this passage. Not only is the progression from one topic to the next identical but, apart from the deletion of names such as Coltrane and Max Roach in the more critical remarks, Mingus's replies in *Beneath the Underdog* are almost word for word the same as in *What I Feel about Jazz*.

The fact that he was in Britain at all at the time of the interview seems so unlikely in retrospect that it deserves some clarification, especially since it was in connection with his sole appearance in a full-length movie. The idea for *All Night Long* (which must have looked a good one on paper, especially at the time of a considerable commercial boom in jazz) was to translate into contemporary terms the plot of *Othello*. Set in the jazz milieu, this meant that the Othello character became a black pianist-bandleader, among whose white sidemen Cass (Cassio) doubled as his road manager and Johnny Cousin (cousin Iago, no less) was planning to start his own band – with 'Othello''s wife Delia as his vocalist! According to Michael Relph, who produced and directed the film jointly with Basil Dearden for the Rank Organization, the script had come into their hands ready-made and presumably after failing to gain backing in the US. 'It was written originally as an American script, set in a loft in New York . . . I don't think our experiment in translating it to the London scene really carried credibility.' The writers concerned were Paul Jericho, who (under the pseudonym Peter Achilles) had worked in Europe in the post-McCarthy period, and a middle-aged New Yorker named Nel King. 'She was the one that was mainly the jazz authority . . . I think particularly Nel King took a very strong interest in the people who should be involved from the jazz point of view, and she particularly wanted Mingus. I think

Brubeck was [musical director] Phil Green's idea.'

Perhaps it should be emphasized that the two American guest stars did not take the leading dramatic roles but rather played themselves, as did the large number of British musicians who appeared on screen. Clearly the original idea was for the music to intertwine with the story-line and to comment on it, as in the recent off-Broadway success *The Connection* or indeed the television production of *A Song with Orange*. The possibilities are dimly realized in the use of the one original Mingus composition, and in the opening ninety-five seconds when the bulky figure of the bassist, projecting a huge shadow on the wall behind him, is seen playing vaguely menacing solo phrases and exchanging dialogue with actor Richard (now Sir Richard) Attenborough. But the gradual filling-up of the set with all manner of musicians (occasioning lines such as 'Hey, it's Johnny Dankworth!'), and the semi-Americanized accents of the other 'musicians' 'Iago' and 'Cassio', soon lead to the suspension of belief – even without the finale in which 'Othello' walks off into the night with his 'Desdemona' after merely *trying* to strangle her. Musically, as well as dramatically, the film falls some way short of John Cassavetes's achievement in *Shadows*.

But, for the seven weeks following his arrival on 16 June, and despite the fact that his playing was restricted to work on the film, Mingus loomed large over the London jazz scene. Everyone who met him seems to have been taken aback by the physical size of the man, not to mention his prickliness, and even those who got on well with him recall moments of embarrassment. When critic Charles Fox inadvertently brought up their joint forename by using the slang phrase 'a proper Charlie', Mingus glowered and said sternly 'Whadyamean, a proper Charlie?' Alexis Korner remembers taking him to a normally reliable Indian restaurant, where both the chef and the quality of service had taken a day off:

And then at the end of the evening he wanted this cup of coffee with cream, and the Indian waiter came up to him: 'I'm afraid we have no cream, sir.' And he said 'Whadyamean, you got no cream? Well, send someone out to go and fetch some.' 'At this time of night, sir, I'm afraid we can't get any cream.' 'You got *ice cream*?' [*pause*] 'Yes, we have ice cream.' 'Well, *melt* it!' And I actually said to him 'You're getting a bit heavy, aren't you?', and he said 'Who, me? Some of my best friends . . .', pointing at the waiter . . .

[He talked about] how he wanted to get himself a motor-car,

big sports wagon with white wall tyres, 'and then we could ride down South on white wall tyres'. All the time, on and on and on about that. He was perfectly amiable, but he went into his diatribes on racism, because that really was the main topic of conversation with him at the time. I mean, rotary perception and racism.

Michael Relph, while naturally aware of the racial theme of his film and having already made a similarly liberal message-movie on a similar subject called *Sapphire*, was somewhat shocked by Mingus's discussions with him:

Things that you take for granted are really subtle insults to black people, like the term 'black market' and 'black mass'. I thought 'Really, well, this is a little bit far-fetched,' but really if you take it back to its root I suppose that's what it is . . . But he was inclined to see slights where no slights were intended. If somebody else had a better car sent for them in the morning or something, he would interpret this as being an anti-black attitude.

Mingus got on surprisingly well with Brubeck when he arrived in the first week of July, and the result (only thirty-five seconds of which is used in the finished movie) was issued ten years later on a Brubeck album and called *Non-Sectarian Blues*, which although credited to Mingus seems to have no connection with his 1955 *Non-Sectarian*. But by this time he had already completed the shooting of the two numbers in which he is seen playing with Tubby Hayes (one of which, *Scott Free*, finds him miming to what is probably the work of white bassist Kenny Napper – an interesting reversal of the situation when he was prevented from appearing on American television with Red Norvo). He was also refusing to have anything more to do with any of the band seen on screen; his reported comment on the way his role seemed to be circumscribed was: 'Who invented jazz? Tubby Hayes and Kenny Napper?'[3] Instead of spending the long delays between shots sitting on the canvas chair marked 'Charles Mingus', he was rehearsing a band of his own backstage 'which was much better than the one they got on the set', as Alexis Korner recalls him emphasizing.

This consisted of Harry Beckett, Harold McNair and Scottish drummer Jackie Dougan, and, when asked about British musicians for *What I Feel about Jazz*, Mingus's first complimentary remarks were for Joe Harriott, McNair and Beckett, all three West Indian, followed by: 'Of the white boys, Ronnie Scott gets closer to the Negro blues feeling, the way Zoot Sims does.'[4] Beckett, then a complete unknown as a jazz player, was originally hired for the film as an extra (miming a two-trumpet feature with the veteran Dave Wilkins, who was on Fats Waller's 1938 London recordings) and was then heard by Mingus at his regular night-club gig on a Saturday evening. The following Monday on the set, he was commandeered by the bassist who, Beckett recalls, carried with him every day 'as if it was gold dust' a briefcase containing 'all his compositions on little bits of paper'. Countering Harry's initial hesitation with the words 'Well, do you want to do it or not?', he assured him that he, Mingus, would guarantee payment for his additional work. What has been overlooked, partly because there was to be no American recording available for comparison for a further three years, is that music cue no. 22 was a ninety-second extract from this group's version of what was to become a staple Mingus item, *Peggy's Blue Skylight* (which takes as its opening phrase bars 13–15 of *Reincarnation of a Lovebird*). The five-minute performance does not appear on the soundtrack album (as with *Non-Sectarian Blues,* Mingus was doubtless unwilling to surrender the publishing rights, unlike most of the British musicians who wrote originals for the film) and yet, with Mingus's heavy piano chording being mimed by an 'Othello' increasingly troubled by jealous forebodings, it is one of the few effective moments in the film. Although Mingus dubbed in his bass part subsequently, even the recording of this more personal work was not without incident, according to Harry Beckett:

> Mingus wanted to do a lot more takes, but the musical director said that this is the one he wanted, so they disagreed . . . The whole thing was, he said that he was brought over to supervise the film musically. He was saying the band should be people relaxing at a party and having a blow, not a band put on a stage and having music-stands . . . What he was trying to do was to make the music play a dominant part instead of the story playing the dominant part. So he tried to make that happen but, of course, the director didn't want to. 'You should do *this*, you should change *this*,' he was taking over the director's job.

Apparently Mingus's departure from London on 4 August followed only shortly after the recording of this number. At just about the same time, the BBC commissioned Alexis Korner to record a Mingus interview for transmission on 9 August, which in the event was replaced by a Korner script with records. 'I did an interview with him which the Beeb wouldn't use, because he said "fuck" every other word. And they wiped the tape.' But Alexis remembers distinctly another contributory factor in the termination of Mingus's stay, to be precise another blonde and, by all accounts, another Diane:

He had this torrid affair with this press lady, who was hired to look after him and keep him reasonably happy while he was here. But she was not prepared to go further than *reasonably* happy. In front of us, he was trying to get her to say yes to a weekend in Paris, you see, so she said yes to keep him quiet, and then she shot off so he couldn't find her. So he went and got a gun . . . He left suddenly, his work on the film was 'discontinued' after he'd broken down a hotel door and threatened her with a gun.

Among the more positive benefits of this London visit should be numbered the purchase, shortly after his arrival, of a fine German bass. One might also point to his one discernible contribution to British music via Alexis Korner himself, whose new band Blues Incorporated was formed out of his admiration for Muddy Waters and Mingus in equal proportions, recording some Mingus tunes and a 1963 original tribute *Blue Mink*. Not only this, but by dint of sparking off the whole 'British rhythm-and-blues' movement which begat the Rolling Stones, among others, the band had an incalculable indirect influence on American pop and rock music of the next two decades.

It is tempting to think also that the *Peggy's Blue Skylight* band may have been responsible for the fact that, immediately on his return, Mingus began rehearsing new material for a band which he would lead from the piano bench, something he had already threatened in 1957 before discovering Horace Parlan. This had a preliminary try-out as early as 15 August, when Oscar Peterson, also signed to Shaw Artists, was indisposed for what should have been an opening night at the Village Vanguard. Mingus replaced him for the evening, playing piano throughout his sets with two bassists, Nabil Totah and Wilbur Ware, plus Dannie Richmond, Charles McPherson and Jimmy Knepper. Knepper, who worked with Mingus again for the next few months, pointed out that 'When he had the band with Ted Curson and Eric Dolphy, he didn't use the piano. He needs a piano player of very high ability, but a piano

129

player of the calibre that Mingus needs would probably be working with his own group. So Mingus took it over himself.'[5]

The following month he was briefly back on bass, however, when his interest in the religious expression involved in musical improvisation (a subject dear to many other jazz players at this period, including Dolphy and Coltrane) led him to appear with Max Roach and Randy Weston on NBC-TV in a programme featuring the 'jazz pastor', Reverend John Gensel. In mid-October he performed versions of *Take the 'A' Train* and an original piece during a service at the Lutheran pastor's Advent Church in New York. (This service was then 're-enacted' early the following year on CBS-TV.) His group for the occasion, as during a preceding week at Pep's in Philadelphia, now had Yusef Lateef back in place of McPherson and Doug Watkins as the bass player, but when it opened at Birdland on 19 October it had become a sextet with the notable addition of multi-simul-instrumentalist Roland Kirk. The somewhat sensational-seeming Kirk had visited New York a couple of months earlier to make an album under his own name and had made a point of meeting Mingus, possibly at the Village Vanguard although he claimed it was the Five Spot. Anyway, Kirk sat in with Mingus who 'dug me right after the first number – he was hollering. After the gig, he rode me round in his car and asked me did I want to make a thing with him at Birdland that October.'[6] An inveterate listener to jazz, and by that very fact something of a historian of the music, Kirk was an obvious asset to Mingus during his short stay and was 'one of the few musical people . . . who came to New York knowing my music that he'd heard on records'.[7]

The first evidence of his contribution, on a broadcast from Birdland two days after the opening, includes a sprightly manzello solo plus chording to fill out the theme during *Ecclusiastics*. This (Gensel-inspired?) piece was not only re-recorded by Kirk (1963) and Knepper (1979) but mentioned in conversation by both Knepper and Lateef, speaking quite independently, because of its unique construction. In other words, while it is possible to think of this as another distorted twelve-bar blues, so much is packed into it that each chorus seems to consist of four separate sections, of four bars, two bars, four bars and two bars again. Apart from Mingus at the piano, Kirk is the only soloist, on tenor this time, in the (edited) studio recording done a couple of weeks later. While there had been talk in August of taping the piano-led group for Candid (where, although Mingus was still theoretically under contract, a halt had been called to all new recording) and towards the end of the year talk of Mingus signing with Frank Sinatra's new 'artist-owned' Reprise label, in his enthusiasm to put down some tracks featuring Kirk Mingus concluded a one-shot deal with Atlantic, which in fact yielded an album and a half.

Of the other tracks on the album *Oh Yeah*, there are many notable moments from Kirk including his stop-time chorus on *Wham Bam Thank You Ma'am* (an angular new theme based on *What Is This Thing Called Love*), his raucous tenor solo on *Hog Callin' Blues* (which is a major-key *Haitian Fight Song*), his counter-melodies during the ensembles of *Eat That Chicken* and *Oh Lord Don't Let Them Drop That Atomic Bomb on Me*, and snatches of flute on *Passions of a Man*. The last-named, a collage of musical and spoken mysteries, has the out-of-tempo and often distant-sounding group overdubbed with voices (all of them Mingus) speaking what sounds like a fake African language, apart from words such as 'America', 'Russia', and 'Mau Mau'. But Mingus's voice is most evident on the three tracks in which he actually sings with the band: the previously mentioned *Eat That Chicken* finds him attempting to reincarnate the personality of another paunchy pianist-vocalist-bandleader Fats Waller, while *Oh Lord* and *Devil Woman* are both slow blues in C, the former conventional and the latter constructed in phrases of three, four and a half, and eight bars (the last of which is strongly reminiscent of the last phrase of *Pussy Cat Dues*, although the autobiography claims Mingus was working on a version of *Devil Woman* in the mid-1940s).

While this first exposure on record of Mingus's current piano playing revealed a bluesy but unclichéd style overriding minor technical inadequacies, and the same might have been said of his singing, it was the singing that drew the most critical fire. A *Down Beat* review by Harvey Pekar, which dismissed this aspect of his work in less than thirty words, drew the following well-argued – and relatively brief – riposte from Mingus:

> My efforts at blues singing were not meant to challenge such diverse masters as Joe Turner, Ray Charles or Big Bill Broonzy, and I don't think their singing was meant as a challenge to each other or to me. Joe sang for Turner, Ray Charles for himself, just as did Big Bill. No one could sing my blues but me (if you must call it singing), just as no one could holler for you if I decide to punch you in your mouth. So don't come near me ever in this life.[8]

Earlier the same year (1962), when former colleague Howard McGhee expressed reservations about Mingus's music, the bassist had replied with these rather more personal comments inspired by the old photograph of McGhee printed alongside the interview: 'Howard McGhee said "I don't see any changes." Wrong. Most of the "jazz" musicians aren't gassing, processing, straightening their hair nowadays.'[9] And yet this insensitive blast must have provoked a reunion between the two for, in November 1962, McGhee was playing with Mingus's group at the Village Vanguard!

The three tracks left out of the *Oh Yeah* album and not issued until the summer of 1964 include, as previously noted, the D flat *Peggy's Blue Skylight* and the only ballad of the date, the B flat minor *Invisible Lady*. Adding to the listener's slight impression of *déjà vu* about the material from this session is the fact that *'Old' Blues for Walt's Torin*, like *Devil Woman*, borrows the last phrase of *Pussy Cat Dues*. And it may be that Mingus himself was somewhat dissatisfied with this date for, immediately afterwards, *Down Beat* reported him as complaining about 'the poor quality of most records, including his own'. Recalling that in those days jazz albums were made with absolutely minimum studio time, one can understand Mingus's plea 'to a major independent' that they sign him to 'a three-year contract during [which] the artist would be recorded, generally in jazz clubs. Then at the end of three years, the best of the recorded material would be . . . issued . . . with a guarantee that nothing else by this artist had been available for several years, and that these tracks were ones with which he himself was pleased.'[10] Unfortunately, this approach to documentation and promotion has never appealed to large corporations seeking a return on capital, and anything resembling the situation described by Mingus has only come about by default, which has necessitated more musician-owned labels.

Ironically, at this same period, Mingus was in fact receiving recognition for some of his earlier work with which he had pronounced himself pleased. For, on returning to San Francisco in 1958, Celia had been informed (by Bill Coss) of a record-company job as secretary to Fantasy Records' Saul Zaentz who, though nominally in charge of promotion and distribution, was one of the small company's few full-time employees aside from owners Max and Sol Weiss, and thus did a bit of everything. (One of his contributions to the sum of human happiness was, according to Ralph Gleason, the editing of all the early Lenny Bruce albums, while he was later responsible for producing films such as *One Flew Over the*

Cuckoo's Nest.) Celia explains that 'Even though I had Mingus sign a separation agreement, I never pursued it as far as child support or alimony was concerned . . . Mingus always had a good feeling about me. I guess time proved to him that I was never going to cheat him.' So, when Celia was about to marry Saul Zaentz, who thus became responsible for Dorian's upbringing, Mingus handed over all his Debut and Jazz Workshop tapes and gave his blessing to a reissue series on Fantasy, which began appearing in early 1962. Before the end of the previous year, he had also received the recognition of Joe Glaser's Associated Booking Corporation (then handling such modernists as Brubeck, Getz, Gillespie and Roach) and, thanks to his growing renown, RCA-Victor at last decided to issue in June 1962 the five-year-old *Tijuana Moods*, emblazoned with a quotation in bold type from the man himself calling it 'the best record I have ever made'.[11] One consequence of this belated issue was that, on a trip to Chicago, Mingus was reunited with Clarence Shaw, who, after being so upset by Mingus in 1957 that he had physically destroyed his trumpet, had been inspired to start playing again. At a party given by Shaw for Mingus, record-store owner Bill Chavers risked his luck by telling Mingus that he 'looked to me like Charles Laughton in *Mutiny on the Bounty* . . . He didn't say anything, and so then I told him that I expected to be hit in the mouth, because I heard about what a terrible temper he had. So he says, "Well, that was before I went to the hospital." '[12]

A week after the Atlantic session, the group had left for a trip to the West Coast, playing a fortnight at San Francisco's Jazz Workshop and a fortnight at the Renaissance in Hollywood, during which Jimmy Knepper recalls that he and Kirk constituted the whole front line. He also told trombonist-writer Mike Zwerin, 'When I got to [Mingus's] house to leave I found out that he and I were going alone in his Cadillac limousine. "You're driving," he told me. "But Mingus," I said, "I don't have a driver's licence." He didn't mind that at all. "That's cool. Nobody ever stops a Cadillac limousine." He was right.' But there were other more fundamental reasons why this trip marked a temporary end to Knepper's association with the group. 'Mingus just seemed to be unavoidable to me. I used to get very depressed. Good god, I'd say to myself, I'm stuck with this guy for the rest of my life. His music was so difficult, with all those time changes and different sequences . . . It seemed written to trip you up. I wanted to relax and play standards.'[13]

So for the first half of 1962, Mingus's group consisted of Richard Williams, Booker Ervin, and Charles McPherson (preceded briefly by John Handy and Charlie Mariano) on alto, with Doug Watkins replaced by Herman Wright on bass. According to Mariano:

> The poor bass player – God, [Mingus] would get up there, you know, and just literally take the bass away from him, like 'What, are you kidding? *This* is the way it's done,' you know . . .
>
> Anyhow, this radio interview. Charlie asked me to come along, so I did and, whenever he has the opportunity, he spouts about the racial situation and the police. So he was carrying on about, you know, the racial situation and Sid Mark happened to ask him . . . 'Well, how about Charlie Mariano?' . . . and he said 'Oh, well, Charlie Mariano's OK. He's not white, he's Italian!'[14]

However, as well as having trouble defining terms (prior to the popularization of the phrase 'White Anglo-Saxon Protestant'), Mingus was clearly worried about the bass situation. After frequently forsaking the piano bench to join in on bass, often bringing his own instrument to play a second part, he finally decided to take over again himself. For all that his communication with the equally sedentary Dannie Richmond had been unhindered, he must have found that the instantaneous command over the front line which he required was actually impaired by sitting at the piano. There is a tell-tale moment on the recording of *Hog Callin' Blues* when, three and a half minutes from the start of the track, Mingus stops playing briefly in order to shout out a new riff to Knepper.

Thus, early in 1962, Charlie Mariano's then wife Toshiko Akiyoshi replaced Mingus at the keyboard, and Knepper relates a story (probably from Pepper Adams) of how the diminutive pianist dealt with Mingus during one of those ritual trials of strength. This one culminated in a performance of *Fables of Faubus*, during which he instructed her that she too had to join in the vocal sections. 'So, when he got to "Name me someone who's ridiculous," she stood up at the piano and said "*You're* ridiculous, *I'm* ridiculous, we're *all* ridiculous." Then she sat down and carried on playing.' In fact a version of *Faubus*, with all but inaudible lyrics, is a feature of the series of broadcasts from two fortnights at Birdland, along with a hectic new piece called *Monk, Funk or Vice Versa* (melodically close to Monk's *Well You Needn't*) and a *Tijuana Table Dance* played (with two basses and no drummer) in order to tie in with the forthcoming record done 'seven years ago' [*sic*]. Despite seeming loose and disorganized, these heated performances are often extremely well ordered – even if on the spur of the moment – with the succession of soloists providing lots of contrast in terms of dynamics and textures, including of course those of the rhythm section. *Eat That Chicken*, used regularly as a closing signature-tune, also provided the finale of a 'three-part work . . . a curious mixture of humour, satire and respect',[15] which was described by Dan Morgenstern as alluding to the music of Ornette Coleman, Ellington and Waller, and which was played at the 1962 Newport Festival. (According to George Wein, now running the Newport Festival himself instead of being responsible to a board of directors, 'The first guy I hired was Mingus. You see, we made a big thing out of that, and we got a lot of publicity out of it, and worked very well together. Mingus was a calculating guy, as far as his career.') On this occasion at least, Mingus reverted to the piano for *Chicken* with Toshiko on bass!

Despite the fact that most things seemed to be going his way, Mingus was feeling dissatisfied with his lot. Not only was he beset by the problems of American society and his place in it, but the lemming-like qualities of those who influenced public taste disgusted him – and that was as true of those who hailed Coleman and/or John Coltrane as the new Messiahs, as of those who saw the Twist revitalizing their bank balances (and who, without realizing it, were softening themselves up for the Beatles' arrival during the following year). Thus it was that, at the first peak of his popularity, he proclaimed to the press that he was about to retire from active performing and to go and live on an island off the cost of Spain, variously reported as Majorca or Ibiza. Some indication of the interest in Mingus at this time may be gained from the reporting of his announcement in no less a journal than the *New York Times*.

The natural desire of a freelance artist to quit while he is ahead may have been fuelled by the occasion shortly before when the Rank Organization finally sent the right car for him. Just after his fortieth birthday, Mingus had been able to make a triumphal return to Toronto for a midnight concert featuring Canadian musicians in honour of the North American premiere of *All Night Long*, at which he arrived in a chauffeur-driven, air-conditioned limousine. However, a much more concrete inducement must have been the placing of what was already being termed his 'autobiographical novel' with a major publisher. As well as continuing to add to the manuscript and showing parts of it to his close associates, he had begun mentioning *Beneath the Underdog* to the press immediately after his return from filming in Britain. This fact, and the information that it was likely to run to 1,500 pages, finally brought him a

135

contract and what was described (in an early example of publisher's hype) as an 'unprecedented' advance of $15,000. McGraw-Hill announced that the book would be edited by author Louis Lomax for publication during 1963, and Mingus's retirement plan for at least two years ('maybe forever') included studying, composing and finishing his book.[16]

So, when Mingus opened at the Five Spot on Saturday 18 August, it was the end of an era – and in a number of different ways. As well as publicizing his imminent departure from the 'jungle with money', Mingus's was the last booking before the original Five Spot Café closed and the building was demolished. Also, on opening night, the band was missing both Toshiko and, potentially more damaging, Dannie Richmond, whose brief absence may well have been connected with his arrest earlier in the year in Philadelphia for possession of drugs. In their stead Wade Legge, who was to die a year later aged twenty-nine, and Omar Clay, now a member of Max Roach's percussion ensemble M'Boom, played with the quintet, as did a new discovery, former Berklee student, trumpeter Eddie Armour. Toshiko and Dannie were, however, present by the last night of the engagement on 27 August, which, like the opening at Copa City, gave Mingus the opportunity to field a bigger group. Working before a greatly enlarged audience with people queueing to get in until 3 a.m. (Dan Morgenstern commented 'How sad that it took a wake to bring all the people out'), he had an eleven-piece band including not only Armour and McPherson but Ted Curson, Eric Dolphy, Leo Wright, Pepper Adams, trombonist Julian Priester and tuba player Don Butterfield. Playing new music said to be destined for a record session the following Friday 31 August, they were apparently a replacement for Mingus's intended 'live' recording at the Five Spot with a twenty-seven piece ensemble since, according to Mingus, 'The engineers took one look and said the walls would collapse.'[17]

The engineers in question were undoubtedly those of United Artists, under whose auspices producer Alan Douglas had just launched a new jazz series with repackages of, among others, the 1959 *Jazz Portraits* album. In fact, by the end of the week, the recording plans had been postponed in favour of a public concert to be recorded at Town Hall on 15 November, which was supposed to be the start of a long-term contract bringing Mingus an advance of $10,000. This in turn brought about the postponement of his retirement, duly announced only two weeks after the retirement idea itself, since the music for the twenty-seven-piece ensemble had yet

136

to be written and as Mingus said later, he 'hadn't even tried to write [for a big band] since 1954'.[18] Remaining in New York had one other immediate consequence, which ought to have been wholly pleasurable but in the circumstances presented a distraction, because it was just at this time that Duke Ellington (very briefly in between two long-term contracts) recorded three sessions in less than six weeks, including one for United Artists with Mingus and Max Roach. Summarizing the situation in 1974, the bassist said 'I got a call from the record company, and then we went by to meet Duke at his office and discussed what he wanted to do . . . The A & R man, whatever his name is . . . begged me to do Duke's date; I told him I couldn't do it, I'd be behind in my music for my own date.'[19]

But Mingus did make the date on 17 September, which, as well as uniting Duke with two leading musicians of the next generation, both of whom idolized him, produced some splendidly forthright, if none too well recorded, playing by all three. The flying-by-the-seat-of-the-pants which characterizes the two twelve-bar blues, *Money Jungle* (Mingus's title?) and *Very Special*, was ample justification of the A & R producer's choice of personnel. Mingus's own playing, in fact, not only constituted an excellent summary of his mature style, thrown into relief by the context of his first trio recording since the 1957 Hampton Hawes session, but led Max Harrison to note that his 'astonishing bass work on the *Money Jungle* LP . . . provided an obvious precedent for a freer use of stringed instruments in jazz'.[20] Ellington himself recalled that *La Fleurette Africaine* had previously only been outlined at the piano during the meeting at his office, and yet it was completed in a single take with just a brief verbal description and a key-signature as instructions to his accompanists. 'Mingus, with his eyes closed, fell into each and every harmonic groove, adding countermelodies as though he had been playing the number all his life. It was one of those mystic moments when our three muses were one and the same.' But, whether because of working with Ellington again or because of his own worries, Mingus was extremely edgy during the date and, at one point, Ellington remembered, put the cover on his bass and was ready to leave the studio. ' "Man, I can't play with that drummer," he said. "Why, what's wrong?" I asked. "Duke, I have always loved you and what you're doing in music, but you'll have to get another bass player." '[21] Ellington's reminiscence concluded with him cajoling the bassist to remain by pointing out that United Artists had taken a full-page advertisement for Mingus in the forthcoming Christmas issue of *Billboard*. That Duke was perhaps more enthusiastic about Mingus's playing than his writing was shown a few years later when a question as to whether Mingus was one of 'the Ellington school' was answered: 'Well, that's what *he* says.'[22]

The foregoing may confirm that Mingus was worried about his Town Hall deadline but this was nothing compared to what he must have felt when, apparently after the Ellington session, the date of the concert was brought forward five weeks from 15 November to 12 October. It was at this point that he began attempting to draw a distinction between 'arranging' his large-scale works, which he still hoped to do himself, and the 'orchestration' which he decided to farm out. Bob Hammer, Melba Liston, Gene Roland and Pepper Adams were among those who assisted with the preparation of music for this concert, and Adams tells of visiting Mingus for this purpose at his Harlem apartment:

> It was one of these high-rise, modern, expensive apartment buildings where he had a nice big apartment – he was able to do well for himself then – with a doorman downstairs who would call and announce the visitor . . . He got the house phone and said 'Yes, send him up.' So I took the elevator up and, when I arrived, Charlie's door to the hallway was open. So I walked right in, and he's on the telephone. He's talking to somebody at Local 802, and he's cursing up a storm, 'You jive-ass white motherfuckers, if you don't quit fucking over me, I'm gonna bring my shotgun down there and blow your ass in –'. Then he puts his hand over the phone, points at me and says 'Cold beer in the refrigerator, Pepper.' Then he goes right back on the phone with this raving about 'you white motherfuckers at the Union'.

What caused the additional problems with the A.F.M. is not clear, unless it was the importation of Los Angeles member Buddy Collette to take part in a New York concert (Collette explained: 'A record company guy called me, in tears, saying they really didn't have the budget for it but needed me in New York because Mingus had said he wasn't going to do the concert unless I was there').[23] The mounting hassles eventually took their toll two days before the performance when Jimmy Knepper also visited Mingus's apartment:

> I was copying his arrangements, and the time got closer and closer. Mingus was writing very slowly, and he kept adding horns

to the band . . . Mingus called me up to go to his apartment, and he says 'I want you to write some backgrounds for solos.' And I said, 'Mingus, this is your music, you should write everything for it' and – I guess he was under a strain – he blew up and swung at me, and broke a tooth off. So we severed our relationship.

Already before he retired with a broken tooth, Knepper had found that the amount of music to be copied was growing at such a rate that he had to use the services of a copying agency, and thus it was that the total of thirty-five musicians, arrangers and copyists involved included two of the latter who sat working at a table at the front of the stage during the concert itself.

This occasion, far from being the highlight of Mingus's career which it should have been, was a fiasco. Initially there was tension because what had been agreed by all parties was to be a recording session done before an audience (as opposed to a live performance recorded just as it happens) had been promoted for the purpose of ticket sales as a concert pure and simple. Joe Glaser, hearing Mingus for the first time since he acquired an interest in him, and referred to in Bill Coss's review as 'prospective booker of Mingus'[24] (doubtless because of his option to renew their contract or not), had to resort to the lobby to placate disappointed customers, nearly a hundred of whom got their money back. But what fatally sabotaged the evening was that, although there had been at least two band rehearsals beforehand, there had been no liaison with the recording engineers. Mingus said afterwards, in a letter to *Down Beat,* naturally: 'United Artists' word was that they would tape our final rehearsal so the musicians could hear what I was trying to do. This was stopped when their engineer said he couldn't get into the hall and didn't have speakers but would have them there for the concert.'[25] However, there were no loudspeakers for playbacks to the musicians at the concert either, which surely argues a certain naivety on the part of Alan Douglas, whose job at United Artists terminated almost immediately. So indeed does the choice of a concert hall where the engineers could not see the musicians (reviewer Ted White noted that, as well as interruptions for musical reasons, 'Some of them [came] from engineers who would open the stage door to the right wing, peer out at us, whistle and wave their arms, and then shout, "From the top again, Charlie," or "You weren't on-mike, Charlie; do it again." ')[26] And, even if it was Mingus's idea originally, no doubt it was naive to agree to a 'guest appearance' by his uncle, clarinettist Fess Williams, who though no longer active as a performer was (surprise!) an official at Local 802. 'A record session for an LP usually takes nine hours. We're supposed to do a record session in two and a half hours with an intermission, plus bring on my uncle who is a genius.'[27]

Even though the concert was not abandoned until nearly midnight, Mingus was obviously exaggerating somewhat when he claimed in his subsequent letter to have produced 'two and a half hours of good taped music' and that he would 'pay my entire salary to United Artists for those tapes'.[28] (In fact, although Bill Coss claimed that United Artists had spent nearly $23,000 on the venture, Mingus was still waiting for payment over six months later and sued the company for $18,000 plus.) But Ted White, who reviewed the eventual album as well as the concert itself, was perhaps nearer the mark: 'Whether or not Mingus had adequately prepared for the concert/recording session . . . I would surmise that at least an hour of Mingus's music came off *well* – excluding the false starts, etc.'[29] If so, it seems a shame so little is on the finished album, edited after Alan Douglas's departure by George Wein (who was not credited because 'I don't want Mingus ever to know'), but it appears likely the recording quality is even more execrable on the portions that were not issued. These included, according to Bill Coss, a *Peggy's Blue Skylight* with Jerome Richardson on baritone; a *Portrait* featuring Charles McPherson; and Jaki Byard and Zoot Sims solos in *Please Don't Come Back from the Moon* (which is quite distinct from the incomplete track labelled *Don't Come Back*, in reality a version of *Duke's Choice* played on alto by Buddy Collette). It speaks volumes about the general lack of organization that the only well-recorded section of the album is Mingus's recitation of his *Suite Freedom* poem, while the only real musical excitements come in the rather chaotic *Epitaph* (which opens with a few bars of *Pithecanthropus Erectus* and incorporates brief references to Ellington's *Black, Brown and Beige* and *Just Squeeze Me*) and the jam-session on *In a Mellotone* played by some members of the band while the stage-hands were already attempting to clear the stage.

What with the concert reviews and then the album reviews, the accusations of United Artists and the counter-accusations, and the lawsuit over payments, it was an event that just would not lie down. But even more unfortunate were the consequences of the regrettable incident with Jimmy Knepper. His embouchure ruined, Knepper had lost not only a tooth but about an octave of his hitherto enviable range and, though fundamentally mild-mannered, was not content to let the matter rest:

Different people advised me 'Kill him,' and another fellow said 'No, don't kill him, you hire somebody to do it.' And other people said 'Sue him,' so we got a lawyer and he said 'First thing you do is bring a criminal action against him.' So we did, and Mingus convicted himself. And that was the end of that, the civil suit never did come up.

After preliminary hearings, Mingus was in fact committed for trial and appeared in the New York City Criminal Court on 6 February 1963, charged with third-degree assault. Knepper stated in evidence that, as well as knocking him to the floor, Mingus had brandished a chair until restrained by his wife Judy and that, after the incident, Mingus had made threatening phone calls including a threat to kill him. Mingus for his part claimed provocation, denied the subsequent threats, and maintained that 'other things attributed to him might legitimately be parts of his "act" '.[30] Despite the evidence of Judy and of three character witnesses (Britt Woodman, Buddy Collette and Reverend Gensel), his 'act' succeeded in obtaining a unanimous verdict of the three judges that he was guilty.

At the sentencing on 15 March, Mingus caused a slight stir by objecting to being described as a jazz musician by his attorney of long standing, State Senator Manfred Ohrenstein of Ohrenstein & Karpatkin. 'Don't call me a jazz musician,' he said. 'To me the word "jazz" means nigger, discrimination, second-class citizenship, the whole back-of-the-bus bit.'[31] He was given a short suspended sentence.

141

7

Black Saint

All in all, the Town Hall concert was to cause more fallout than the almost simultaneous Cuban Missile Crisis, which prompted Mingus's forecast of 'the day we should be blown up to preserve [our leaders'] idea of how life should be'.[1] Life did go on, however, despite the initial disappointment and frustration of the Town Hall venture, and the Thursday following the concert (18 October) Mingus began another two-week stand at Birdland with an augmented small group in which the front line of Armour and McPherson was joined by Don Butterfield and Pepper Adams. Adams, who earlier in the year had been added for a week in Philadelphia during Toshiko's tenure, notes that:

> When I would become available, and if he would have something he could fit me into, he would do so. So I wound up in some very different kinds of playing situations. Being added to what has already been an existing band for several months – they have at least learned their parts – that first night is quite an experience . . . Which is very nice for friendship, but it's not a very good way to do business. At least at first, it certainly doesn't help the band if he has something already organized and suddenly another piece is there.

On the other hand, personnel could change even during the course of an evening and suddenly the band would be one piece short, as a member was fired or quit in mid-set. 'I've seen both things happen,' says Adams, which, coming from a relatively infrequent Mingus sideman, is quite revealing.

But the most important acquisition was the widely experienced and vastly talented pianist Jaki Byard who, being a mere three weeks younger than Mingus himself, was the most mature musician to have joined the Jazz Workshop thus far. Equally proficient on several other instruments, and as a composer and arranger, Byard was particularly fascinated by the Dynamic Duo of Mingus and Dannie Richmond which, as he has modestly pointed out, now became the Almighty Three. 'Every time we played one of those tunes, you had to be alert and ready for constantly varying situations. Patterns would change from time to time, and if perchance any of us were caught off guard – watch out!!'[2] An example of Byard being almost caught off guard occurs during the B sections of his solo on *Monk, Funk or Vice Versa* during the second broadcast from this engagement, which also introduces the similarly boppish *O.P.O.P.* This has an A/A/B/A/C chorus, the C section being based on the interlude of *Night in Tunisia* despite the apparent dedication to Oscar Pettiford, who had died in 1960 aged only thirty-seven. As well as performances of *The Search*, a new line derived from *I Can't Get Started* and also heard on the Town Hall album, the broadcasts preserve a version of *Please Don't Come Back from the Moon*, an A/B/C chorus in which C is a modal section of indefinite length.

Mingus's next appearance four weeks later, as well as showing him already on the rebound, was the prelude to something far greater, and the ten-piece line-up featured at the Village Vanguard from 27 November to 19 December 1962 was (although used briefly at Town Hall) the descendant of the group heard at the closing of the Five Spot. Apart from the rhythm trio and Don Butterfield, the new personnel consisted of veteran trombonist Quentin Jackson (who, like Byard, had first worked for Mingus at Town Hall), saxophonists Jerome Richardson, Charlie Mariano and Dick Hafer, and two trumpeters – initially Howard McGhee and Snooky Young, subsequently Rolf Ericson and Idrees Sulieman. Ironically, the club was only paying him for a sextet and it was his own decision to provide 'ten pieces for the same bread'. Part of the reason may have been his desire to show how 'near-in' some of his music was, for visiting critic André Hodeir's reaction was that 'It's not the exuberant Mingus we know from the records, but a neo-classic Mingus, playing old Ellington hits (*Mood Indigo, Take the 'A' Train*) with plunger effects and piano choruses *à la* Fats!'[3] Certainly he managed to express his feeling that the jazz avant-garde, at least in the form that was showing signs of becoming increasingly fashionable, could be a haven for incompetents. It was during a Sunday matinée at the Vanguard that he pulled his trick of having the band pretend to play, while behind the screen three young children (one the son of drummer Charles Moffett) 'improvised' on instruments they had not yet learned. 'And it *did* sound avant-garde,' recalls Jaki Byard. Mingus later castigated the white imitators of Coleman and Coltrane who reproduced the externals of a style without its underlying emotion:

> They remember the keys they push, and they move them out the same way, but I'm sure they couldn't translate it as B-sharp-and-a-half or 1/132nd of a tone. They're bending, and making harmonics *true*. And it's not unmusical, it's just that – life has many changes. Tomorrow it may rain, and it's supposed to be sunshine 'cause it's summertime, but God's got a funny soul – he plays like Charlie Parker – he may run some thunder on you, he may take the sun and put it up at nighttime, the way it looks to *me*. You know, I mean, when people live so that they're only playing one mood, one emotion, there's something dangerously wrong there because it's like insanity in a way . . . You can play 'sad' with variations of sadness, you can play 'love' with variations of love. But, when I hear the same *tunes* wherever I go, man, it's almost impossible to follow it . . . Because some of that music came from some of the things I did with Eric Dolphy and Booker Evin, and things when I was playing introductions and endings that Barry Ulanov used to call 'avant-garde' years ago.

At the Vanguard, however, the band was also playing excerpts from a new piece with a written piano solo intended to simulate the sound of a Spanish guitar and 'to mirror the period of the Spanish Inquisition and El Greco's mood of oppressive poverty and death',[4] according to Mingus. Perhaps this is why the group was now billed as the 'Charles Mingus New Folk Band' and why the recording of *The Black Saint and the Sinner Lady* (the piece in question) – instead of carrying the usual legend 'The new wave of jazz is on Impulse!' – announced that 'The new wave of folk is on Impulse! Ethnic Folk-Dance Music'. Mingus had not only taken the initiative in contacting Bob Thiele, the producer of Coltrane's albums, but had suggested the terms of a possible contract; when this, however, was rejected by Thiele's bosses at ABC-Paramount, Mingus had signed a more standard one-year agreement allowing an artist royalty of five per cent, an advance against this of probably $10,000, and an option for a second year with the advance rising to $15,000. Releasing these details later, Thiele recalled that 'Just before signing the contract, Mingus wanted to know the schedule of *my* salary payments. I told him that I received my salary every two weeks. He said, "I want to be like an executive – like a white man – I want to be paid every two weeks." ' In the end, the 'advance' was paid in weekly instalments.

Thiele also mentioned 'much confusion with arrangers and copyists prior to and during the actual recording',[5] which sounds strangely similar to the Town Hall story, but the resultant albums are like chalk and cheese. As well as the *Black Saint,* the material from this excellent session also included two remakes of earlier compositions, *Celia* and *I X Love*, both of them elevated by the splendid solo work of Charlie Mariano (the latter being the same Bob Hammer arrangement of *Duke's Choice* issued in truncated form on the Town Hall album as *Don't Come Back*). At the same age, give or take a couple of weeks, Ellington had re-recorded three of his greatest hits and then created a series of masterpieces such as *Jack the Bear, Ko-Ko* and *Concerto for Cootie,* all before his forty-first birthday. *The Black Saint and the Sinner Lady* is not only the most monumental of Mingus's works but the one which most nearly combines his various compositional approaches in a convincing whole. It is also at the same time his most Ellingtonian piece and his least Ellingtonian. Certainly the Ellington references abound, in for instance Byard's introduction to the second movement, in Mariano's various melody statements recalling Johnny Hodges, and in the 'jungle-style' plunger work of Jackson whose eleven years with Duke himself had coincided not only with Britt Woodman's ten years in the band but also, of course, with Mingus's ten days. And Mingus in his notes pointed towards another reference: 'The three reeds . . . were placed in what I called a V balance with the tenor sax at the V's bottom and the baritone and alto closer to the mike . . . so as to give the sound of more than two obvious saxes playing but with the possibility of being perhaps four or five,'[6] without going so far as to underline the resultant similarity to the sound of Ellington's sax section and its domination by Carney and Hodges. But the basic simplicity of the materials and their poly-rhythmic development, the structural use of passages with acceler-ating tempo or with no tempo, the fact that *all* the improvised solos are modal (many of them based on the favourite 'Spanish scale') –

these show how far the work is a product of Mingus's own experience and experimentation.

Don Locke went further in his perceptive article published not long after the record's appearance:

> The scale of *The Black Saint* also invites comparison with Ellington, but here I think Mingus has achieved, at what appears to be first attempt, something which Ellington has scarcely even tried: a coherent and unified work of full LP length. Ellington's usual procedure has been to bind together a series of short pieces into a lengthy suite . . . The compositions which have been unified and organized into a whole, e.g. [the original] *Diminuendo and Crescendo in Blue* or *Creole Rhapsody*, have been much shorter; the longest, *Reminiscing in Tempo* and *Tone Parallel to Harlem* . . ., run to about twelve minutes.[7]

The complete version of Ellington's *Black, Brown and Beige*, unheard by Locke (or by Mingus) at this date, consists of a continuous 'organized' section of about twenty minutes followed by a suite, which is then followed by a last movement that falls uneasily between the two approaches. Mingus himself confirmed that *Black Saint* 'was conceived first of all as a continuous piece, but I was urged to make it into several pieces for marketing reasons',[8] and Locke highlighted the way in which the whole work hangs together:

> Now if the composition consisted solely of a series of episodes repeated and contrasted in various ways then, no matter how compelling the rhythm, it would tend to fall apart into disconnected fragments, perhaps interesting in themselves despite their brevity, but failing to build up into any complete whole. Mingus manages to avoid this trap – the main difficulty he has to face – by the skilful way in which the parts are dove-tailed together.[9]

What was not known at the time was that this had been largely achieved by a combination of overdubbing (which, as we have seen, had interested Mingus in the past) and editing. While the latter technique had been used on Mingus albums to shorten improvised performances and, doubtless, where these were not single takes, sometimes to combine different versions of the same piece, the idea of editing in order to create previously nonexistent repetitions was practically unknown at the time (except for certain pop records such as Little Richard's *Keep A-Knockin'*). Not only was this how the shape of the composition was ultimately created, but the superimposition of Charlie Mariano in certain passages provided a new dimension: 'He said "OK, when I point to you, start playing and, when I wave at you, stop. And, when I point, start again."And that's how the whole last thing was made. Because there wasn't any alto jazz written in that thing at all, it was all dubbed in a week later.'[10]

While not purporting to be a complete breakdown of the various takes used, and certainly stopping far short of a detailed analysis of the various melodic, rhythmic and key relationships, the table on page 245 does help to elucidate the structure of the piece. And it will be noted that, whereas Mariano appeared to refer to merely the last part of the last movement, there is overdubbing in other sections where he can be heard playing with the ensemble as well as soloing over the top. Mingus was later to claim that this post-recording work was only necessary because Bob Thiele and/or the engineer mislaid the best takes of the last movement ('They could take that track and put it out as a whole new tune'),[11] but the copious editing on the first side also seems to imply that he had this in mind all along. According to Thiele, 'There were literally fifty splices to be made after the date – all in Charlie's head.'[12] Certainly, although hardly equalling the 550 hours' studio time spent on the Beatles' *Sergeant Pepper*, a lot more effort was devoted to this album than to the average jazz record of those days. And, while Bill Evans was working concurrently on his first multi-track album, *The Black Saint* marks the first occasion in any field where the combination of overdubbing with creative editing actually determined the nature of the product. Mingus himself was extremely happy with the result, explaining:

> The difference between now and twenty years ago is that I went back to what I originally was. I took out the space. When I met Bird, there was the confusion of adding another self to me . . .As a perfectionist I say I have only two records on the market, on Fantasy* and Impulse . . . And I was satisfied with one of the Candid albums, the one with [*What Love*].[13]

How interesting that the first Candid album gives the illusion of spontaneity despite the constraints of the studio, while the Impulse

---

*Which of the Debut repackages is meant was unfortunatley not clarified.

simulates compositional form through a certain amount of juggling after the fact. Interesting, too, that Mingus was only able to complete the latter by courtesy of his probation officer, for, as soon as the pre-trial hearings had established that there was a case to answer, his movements were restricted. Not so his contacts with the underworld, perhaps, for Jimmy Knepper has alleged that one morning he received an envelope containing heroin, closely followed by two Treasury Department officials. ('We got an anonymous phone call.' 'Well, this guy I'm filing a suit against is trying to set me up.')[14] In any event, after the verdict, Mingus was subject to the New York State law providing that, no matter what the sentence might be, anyone convicted of a crime was not allowed to work more than one day a week in premises catering to the public. Obviously, the weekly salary from Impulse came just in the nick of time, because apart from a Carnegie Hall benefit concert for the Student Nonviolent Coordinating Committee in February, Mingus made almost no playing appearances until August. For the concert, the full *Black Saint* personnel performed, with the exception that Jerome Richardson was replaced by Marvin Halliday and that Dannie Richmond unexpectedly failed to appear (as compared to his expected non-appearance six months earlier at the Five Spot). Mingus had often said, 'I'd rather not use a drummer if [Dannie] weren't available,'[15] and, as during the Birdland broadcast the previous May, he now had the chance to prove it.

Mingus naturally used this interlude of public inactivity to bring his autobiography up to date, and indeed this was virtually the first opportunity since signing the publisher's contract to devote any time to it. Not only was he planning to include his court case, but it was doubtless at this period that he wrote the party sequence (Chapter 31) with its barbed references to Gene Lees, Leonard Feather and others. He also had time to play host to his eldest son Charles III who, having now finished high school, was shortly to settle in New York; this visit was the occasion of Mingus's comment on the latest twist in the racial situation:

My son was telling me about walking by a Muslim temple in Harlem and looking in the window at the books. A guy . . . introduces himself with a Muslim name and a southern accent. 'We don't mind you coming in the temple, the weak off-spring of the white man's sin' . . . When these fellows start talking about their 'black brothers and the weaker tribes', I think it's a lot of

Mingus as a member of The Strings And Keys; 1944

Red Callender's Pastel Sextet: Jimmy Bunn, Callender, Mingus, Kenny Bright, Bill Douglass, Teddy Edwards; 1948

The Lionel Hampton Band: (front row) Mingus, Charlie Harris, Hampton, Leo Shepherd, Harpo Wormack, Al Hayse, Andrew Penn, Sonny Graven; (middle) Milt Buckner, Billy Mackel, Johnny Sparrow, Morris Lane, Charlie Fowlkes, Bobby Plater, Ben Kynard; (rear) Earl Walker, Duke Garrette, Teddy Buckner, Walter Williams, Wendell Culley; late 1947

Guido Caccienti, Tal Farlow and Red Norvo celebrate the marriage of Mingus and Celia; San Francisco, 2 April 1951

Mingus at twenty-eight, ready to storm New York; Black Hawk, San Francisco, March-April 1951

Leonard Feather, George Wein, John Hammond and Nat Hentoff admiring the music of Lee Konitz and Lennie Tristano with Max Roach (hidden) and Mingus; Brandeis University, 13 June 1952

The 'Quintet of the Year' with Mingus, Max Roach and Dizzy Gillespie — (Charlie Parker and Bud Powell not shown); Massey Hall, 15 May 1953

'This is almost my time, maybe this year.' Mingus in 1959

Jimmy Knepper, John Handy, Shafi Hadi and Booker Ervin recording the **Mingus Ah Um** album;
5 May 1959

Suitably attired for a reception, Mingus meets up with Britt Woodman; opening night at the
Jazz Gallery, December 1959

Newport 'rebels' Mingus and Roach with Kenny Dorham and Ornette Coleman; Cliff Walk Manor Hotel, 3 July 1960

Mingus leads both Charles McPherson and Eric Dolphy; closing night at the old Five Spot,
27 August 1962

The Almighty Three: Jaki Byard, Mingus and Dannie Richmond play while McPherson and Lonnie Hillyer listen

Mingus with the new releases on his own record-label

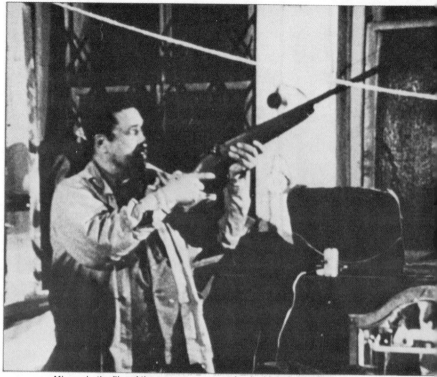

Mingus in the film of the same name, preparing for his eviction; 21 November 1966

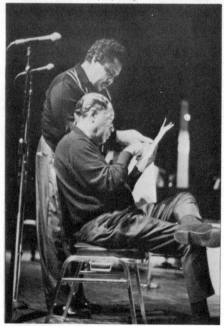

Rehearsing with Duke Ellington; University of California at Berkeley, 29 September 1969

CHARLES MINGUS

Mingus on the cover of the **Changes** album; Newport Jazz Festival, 3 July 1971

Recording **Let My Children Hear Music**; September 1971

Roy Brooks, Mingus, Jon Faddis, McPherson and Bobby Jones with microphones; Munich Jazz Festival, 17 August 1972

Mingus with his and Judy's children, Carolyn and Eric; c.1973

George Adams, Mingus and Dannie visit Jasper Hampton; Chicago, October 1974

The spirit is willing…Mingus at Châteauvallon; 17 August 1976

President Carter and Sue comfort Mingus; The White House, 18 June 1978

The shadow of death...Mingus in Mexico; November 1978

Sue prepares to scatter Mingus's ashes in the River Ganges; January 1979

crap, especially when Muhammad X is lighter than Max Roach and as light as I am.[16]

Mingus's own religious leanings led him to take part in the spring of 1963 in a series of Sunday night workshops at the Church Of The Master organized by Reverend Eugene Callender (a very distant cousin of Red Callender). And in the summer, possibly coinciding with the receipt of a lump-sum payment from United Artists, he took a ten-year lease on one floor of 386 3rd Avenue for the new headquarters of Jazz Workshop Inc. and for a proposed School Of Arts, Music And Gymnastics. Willie Jones (who was involved in the Church Of The Master workshops), Max Roach, Buddy Collette and dancer Katherine Dunham(!) were to be among the tutors, and financial assistance was anticipated from Harlem Youth Opportunities Unlimited (HAR-YOU) whose board of directors included Reverend Callender. Certainly Mingus was still taking selected private pupils at this period and, having moved with Judy and two-year-old Carolyn to a new apartment at 1160 5th Avenue, needed somewhere to teach undisturbed; but, within a few months, he had moved his 'studio' to a much smaller building on 26th Street, east of 2nd Avenue. 'The real one was on 3rd. I got beat out of it . . . I was going to have to pay the police and the Fire Department and I got tired of all that crap, so I gave away some of my equipment and moved the rest of it here,'[17] he commented. Meanwhile, he was practising seriously again himself: 'I just played bass with the bow for about the first time since 1945 [*sic*]. I explained to my old lady how most bassists who use the bow sound as though they were sawing wood – bzzzz, bzzz, bzzzz.'[18] The desire not to be tarred with the same brush bore fruit in the opening theme of *Meditations*, widely performed during the following year, but in the summer of 1963 Mingus's popularity had for the first time pushed Ray Brown into second place in the *Down Beat* Critics' Poll. The irony of this announcement during his months of virtual invisibility would not have been lost on Mingus, but he was in any case pretty sceptical about the value of such recognition. Jaki Byard has noted his reaction: 'Why the hell didn't they give me that award when I was in my youth? I'm getting old now, but I was hell on wheels then, ask any of the cats.'[19]

His interest in the piano too was considerably increased by his enforced leisure, to such an extent that he approached Bob Thiele with the idea of a solo album to be titled *Mingus Plays Piano*. Although his own reaction to his playing is preserved on the disc ('I don't think I should improvise, man. It's not like sitting at home, I can tell you that'),[20] there are many insights into the improviser-composer-arranger who worked out his material at the keyboard first. The out-of-tempo *She's Just Miss Popular Hybrid*, for instance, opens with a typical Mingus phrase which can be related to the 1970 *Man Who Never Sleeps* and, more distantly, to one of the lines of *Don't Be Afraid, the Clown's Afraid Too* (also, indeed, to *(God's) Portrait*, here performed as *Old Portrait*), while the phrase in bars 9–12 recurs in *Once There Was a Holding Corporation Called Old America* and in an untitled piano piece in the film *Mingus*. There are also slightly Tatumesque, and slightly Monkish, versions of *I Can't Get Started* and *Memories of You* using the altered chord-sequences already heard on group recordings. *Roland Kirk's Message,* the only down-home number of the set, turns out to be a version of *'Old' Blues for Walt's Torin,* while *Meditations for Moses* incorporates a quotation from *Invisible Lady*. The chord first heard in the second bar of the latter, and the piece's B flat minor orientation (as in *Black Saint*), recur during the longer and more episodic *Compositional Theme Story: Medleys, Anthems and Folklore* (with its references to, among others, *When Johnny Comes Marching Home, I Dream of Jeannie with the Light Brown Hair* and *God Bless America*) and during *Myself When I Am Real*. This last, placed first on the album, is the piece of which Mingus was most proud 'because', as he said years later, 'to me it has the expression of what I feel, and it shows changes in tempo and changes in mode, yet the variations on the theme still fit into one composition . . . I would say the composition is on the whole as structured as a written piece of music.'[21] It also combines Mingus's idiosyncratic chording, as heard in the third movement of *Black Saint*, with a waltz theme which anticipates the 1964 *Meditations* (see Appendix A).

As well as being perhaps a suitable title for a successful improvisation, the phrase *Myself When I Am Real* is reminiscent of a remark made by Mingus to his psychiatrist, as recorded in the autobiography: 'Doctor, you're everything I could be myself if I could just find my hang-out, my notch on the stick, my crowd of people'[22] (which in turn recalls the tune title *All the Things You Could Be By Now If Sigmund Freud's Wife Was Your Mother*). Mingus's search for self-fulfilment was indeed the theme when Edmund Pollock, Ph.D. contributed a thousand-word sleeve-note about his patient to the *Black Saint* album – another first. Although it was treated by many as a gimmick when the album appeared in the summer of 1963, Mingus felt that his analyst's comments would be

150

appropriate to accompany such profoundly emotional, cathartic and indeed orgasmic music. (Don Locke's comment on the sections S1, S2 and S1(0) –'Presumably the idea was that three accelerandi one after another would produce the climax to end all climaxes . . . but . . . perhaps . . . the musicians no longer felt up to it'[23] – offers a veiled explanation for the languorous urgency of the third and final effort.) To Mingus's surprise, the initial sales were acknowledged when, in addition to his weekly salary, he received ABC-Paramount's first half-yearly payment of publisher's royalties. According to Thiele this was in August, when these royalties would have been fairly negligible; nevertheless 'He phoned immediately to thank me . . . and stated emphatically "I'm sure with the right company – boy, any company that pays publisher's royalties on time is a legitimate company." '[24]

At this point Mingus went back to work at the Village Gate, for the last two weekends in August and then a full week, and the Gate's owner Art D'Lugoff recalls, 'He sent me a telegram saying he's coming in with ten people instead of five . . . I think there was some arrangement that Mingus was paying them.' As well as dropping the guitar from the *Black Saint* line-up, Mingus had brought in new sidemen Eddie Preston, Garnett Brown and Joe Albany for Ericson, Jackson and Byard, while the three reeds were old hands Eric Dolphy, Booker Ervin and Pepper Adams. (During this stint, Detroit native Adams was contracted by the Motown record company for their short-lived Workshop Jazz series – no connection with Jazz Workshop! – to do the first non-Mingus album of Mingus compositions, with Teddy Charles as producer. Mingus not only wrote a new tune especially for the session called *Carolyn* but, according to Zoot Sims he 'was running around, whispering things to do . . . He'd come over to the saxes, you know, and he'd hum real quiet: "Now here, play this behind the trombone." ') And shortly afterwards Mingus did another session for Impulse with similar personnel, this time consisting entirely of remakes. *(Suite) Freedom* now has its central section, the Town Hall version of which was issued as *Clark in the Dark*, taken by Ervin, who also enlivens *Better Get Hit in Yo' Soul* (the minuscule change of title being perhaps explained by the take-off of two-beat Dixieland rhythms in the coda). But *Mood Indigo*, despite a fine bass solo, sounds rather limp because arranger Bob Hammer attempted to reproduce the original Ellington voicings, which sound far less personal than Mingus's 1959 scoring. In connection with this same session, Joachim Berendt compared Ellington's and Mingus's 'inner compulsion to work over and modify the music which they had previously played with success . . . They forget that the creative process which took place during the original recording cannot be replaced by any amount of technical perfection.'[25]

By the time of this recording, however, Mingus had undertaken a few days at the new Five Spot (deputizing for Monk) with just Dolphy, Ervin and Richard Williams in the front line, and Roland Hanna joining drummer Walter Perkins in the rhythm section; and, although Dannie Richmond was due to make the album date and only missed it through a mix-up, the fact remains that for the first time in over five years Mingus recorded without Dannie's assistance. As the year neared its close, in fact, Mingus took a few more blows, and it is difficult to say which hurt the most. First of all, McGraw-Hill decided not to publish *Beneath the Underdog* because, as Mingus revealed some months later, 'They say it's dirty in parts . . . I'm gonna publish it myself and sell it door-to-door.'[26] It is possible also that the publishers were afraid of libel actions, for Mingus subsequently complained that this 'book about my childhood [*sic*] which was never intended for release *until* properly edited, with the names of persons I wrote about changed for the protection of individuals . . . was taken and unlawfully distributed to various persons in its unedited form which brought great mental anguish and undeserved condemnation to its author'.[27] And it is at least possible that this is a description (slightly exaggerated) of the publisher circulating those named in the manuscript to obtain their reactions to the eventual publication.

However, the end of the year also saw ABC-Paramount deciding that Mingus's sales, while encouraging them to take up their option, did not merit increasing his royalty advance to $15,000. Given that only the first album had been issued and this for a short while, this was probably an over-reaction, as was Mingus's incredulity 'that a company like Impulse could not manage to sell just as many records as my own company, Debut, did nine years ago'. He claimed that RCA-Victor, who had paid royalties since issuing *Tijuana Moods* eighteen months ago, had 'sold almost ten times more than my recent recordings for Impulse and Columbia'.[28] Bob Thiele, feeling that everyone would see increasing sales if only the contract was renewed, recommended a compromise whereby the current arrangement would continue for the second year. ABC-Paramount and apparently Mingus agreed to this initially, but, 'About two weeks later Charlie called me – "Forget it; they're just trying to take advantage of me." ' Thiele later stated that, according to the grapevine, 'Mingus thought I would call him again and urge him to accept the new "deal" . . . A perfect example of his approach to life and business.'[29]

At the same time, only a couple of months after the violence surrounding Governor Wallace of Alabama's attempts to do a Faubus, the country was now reeling from the impact of President Kennedy's assassination and its apparent implications for any racial liberalization. Mingus himself, with the prospect of no further weekly payments, had just learned that Judy was pregnant again, which, along with his recently restricted activity keeping him around the apartment much more, may have brought to the surface some of the underlying tensions between Mingus and his much younger wife. Certainly, his attendance at a New Year's tap-dance party showed the tensions at full strength, for his complaints about the quality of the dancers were sufficiently vociferous to break up the party in disarray. During 1964, journalist Bill Whitworth reported that Mingus 'often stays at the Earle [Hotel] or the Gotham because he and his wife are separated, more or less'.[30]

A promised return engagement at the Five Spot, which was now planning to rotate Rollins, Monk and Mingus on a more or less permanent basis, had been postponed by the extension of what proved to be a record-breaking nine months' residency by Monk. This only came to an end in late January when Monk stood down in anticipation of a long European tour, and again Mingus was allowed to appear on opening night with a ten-piece band similar in personnel to the last Impulse session (but with Ken McIntyre in place of Dolphy, Tommy Turrentine and once again Snooky Young on trumpets, and Dannie Richmond back in the drum chair). But now unable or unwilling to finance this group out of his pocket, Mingus reverted for the remainder of his two-month stay to a quintet, with Turrentine and then Johnny Coles on trumpet, and Booker Ervin followed by Dolphy on saxophone. But Mingus also used some very special and very mainstream guest stars, such as Illinois Jacquet who briefly preceded Ervin. Between Ervin and Dolphy, he filled in with Coleman Hawkins for one night, followed by Rollins also for one night, and then, when Dolphy contracted a mouth infection, Ben Webster joined the group for an evening. Unfortunately, Ben became somewhat drunk and challenged Mingus to fisticuffs. The 'temperamental' bassist, preferring discretion in the face of one of his Ellingtonian idols, retreated from the club in a cab with the portly saxophonist chasing him.

Strange though it may seem to mention the above names in the same breath, Mingus did just that in a 1971 interview:

> One thing about Charlie Parker, Eric Dolphy, Ben Webster, Coleman Hawkins – well, Ben's still with us – those were the days when guys used to play in dance-halls. They didn't have these things, microphones . . . Bird didn't need no mike, Hawk didn't need no mike . . . To get the balance of my band in Europe, I put Eric Dolphy back by the curtains, because my tenor sax and the trumpet were so soft.[31]

In fact, the choice of guest stars at the Five Spot seems to have been part of Mingus's growing anti-avant-garde stance (from which Dolphy was always specifically excluded): 'When I was a kid and Coleman Hawkins played a solo or Illinois Jacquet created *Flying Home*, they (and all the musicians) memorized their solos and played them back for the audience, because the audience had heard them on the records. Today I question whether most musicians can even repeat their solos after they've played them once on record.'[32]

Having incorporated into his performing repertoire not only bebop standards but Ellington hits, Mingus undoubtedly would have adapted his programme further to include *Flying Home* for Jacquet, *Cottontail* for Webster, etc., taking delight in meeting the masters on their home ground and proving that the rest of his group was aware of the classics too. He was writing nothing new for any larger line-up at the moment, although a Canadian television special was being discussed by the start of the year (also two soundtracks for the Canadian National Film Board, which seem to have come to nothing) and there was talk of a commission for the following September's Monterey Jazz Festival. What did emerge, and was rehearsed Ellington-fashion, fragment by fragment, at the Five Spot, was a new small-band composition known under a variety of titles starting with the word *Meditations*, and also as *Praying with Eric*. The reason for the titling is given in Mingus's spoken introduction to the piece's official premiere at Town Hall during a 4 April benefit concert for the National Association for the Advancement of Colored People (NAACP):

> Eric Dolphy explained to me that there was something similar to the concentration camps once in Germany now down South . . . and the only difference between the barbed wire is that they don't have gas chambers and hot stoves to cook us in yet. So I

wrote a piece called *Meditations*, as to how to get some wire cutters – before someone else gets some guns to us.[33]

As well as indicating Mingus's desire to avoid the polarization caused by violence, the announcement confirms that, unlike some of his other evocative titles, this one refers to a deliberately descriptive composition. According to Jaki Byard, 'That really depicted his feelings for the '60s, what was happening then and what happened previously . . . He used to talk about slave ships, . . . and you had to play something to depict the relationship between the struggle and the slaves.'[34]

Although the overall structure is much simpler, *Meditations* does share the same mournful-sounding B flat minor key-centre as *The Black Saint* and *Myself When I Am Real* but, unlike that passionate music, the opening theme played in octave unison by Dolphy's flute and the leader's bowed bass (with the tenor playing rhythm!) establishes a mood of profound sadness at the folly of mankind. Doubtless in part because of this instrumentation, and also thanks to his hard-earned evolution towards maturity, the composition represents the final fruition of Mingus's leanings to European classical music, and at the same time the summation within a single piece of all his musical experience to date.

The group which finally came together to play at this Town Hall concert was a sextet. For, while Dolphy appears to have been still absent (as was Dannie) for the last night at the Five Spot in late March, his regular replacement Clifford Jordan – who had just returned from a European tour with Max Roach – stayed on when Dolphy rejoined. This was the band which the following week set out on Mingus's own tour of Europe, organized by George Wein who had also been responsible for touring Monk and Roach in the preceding weeks. The proliferation of recordings – some for national radio and television stations, others unofficial – from this European tour suddenly gives an in-depth coverage of Mingus's live performances hitherto unmatched in his discography. Thus, at the time of writing, no less than four versions of *Meditations* from the same month (including the Town Hall concert) have been issued on record, none lasting less than twenty-five minutes. Other numbers are played over comparable distances, with the Wuppertal *Fables of Faubus* running thirty-seven minutes and the Stuttgart version three-quarters of an hour. *Faubus* had by now, in fact, developed into quite an extravaganza with out-of-tempo sections for each soloist heralded by a chord-change to E7, which allows quotations from *Tijuana Table Dance*; while Byard's solo contains all manner of allusions to Garner, to Ellington, to the 'hip' soul-jazz of the Adderley Brothers etc.

> I played the Negro national anthem [*Lift Every Voice and Sing*] in Sweden, and he didn't like it. He thought I was putting that whole situation down, you know . . . And somebody in the audience said 'Yeah, brother!', it must have been one of the only black cats in the audience. And I said 'See? Everything's cool'. . . He didn't like it then, but then we kept it in and he used to play it on the bass.[35]

Many of the concerts included a polytonal Charlie Parker medley which was like a greatly elongated version of the introduction to *Reincarnation of a Love-Bird*, while the opening number of each concert was usually Byard's brilliant pastiche of Art Tatum and Fats Waller called, *AT, FW, YOU, USA*.

The most impressive aspect is not merely the all-embracing nature of these references to other music but that each of the longer pieces, as in earlier but less extended broadcast performances, has a distinctive architecture dictated by the order of the soloists and the way in which the accompanying textures are varied during their lengthy solos. Byard has written of Mingus's 'ability to relieve some of the obligations to the soloist that can otherwise turn accompaniment into an endurance test',[36] and there is a dramatic example during Jordan's solo on the Stuttgart *Peggy's Blue Skylight* when, at the most unexpected place eight bars before the end of a chorus, Mingus brings the rhythm section to a ragged but total stop. Less dramatically but very effectively, the use of different rhythmic approaches for textural reasons is particularly evident on a blues which, by the middle of the month at least, was known as *Farewell Eric Dolphy* or *So Long Eric*, because the saxophonist had once again announced his intention of leaving the group and spending several months in Europe after the tour. By way of contrast, this feature is absent from another new composition, the slow *Orange Was the Color of Her Dress Then Blue Silk* (not to be confused with the piece originally titled *Song with Orange*). This has an A/A/B chorus, the A section having a blues-derived sequence similar to *Nostalgia in Times Square* (which is in the same key) and an opening phrase related to that of *What's Your Story Morning Glory, Black Coffee, Heartbreak Hotel* and several other popular songs. The first six bars have a three-part harmonization which, interestingly, is in the patented semi-atonal style which was by now beginning to disappear from Mingus's vocabulary.

The trip to Europe as a whole was full of incident in a number of ways. It was during a performance of *Orange Was the Color* on Friday evening, 17 April, just one week into the tour, that Johnny Coles collapsed on stage suffering from a stomach rupture which was the after-effect of a recent operation. Thus, for the concert at midnight the following night, the top line of the *Orange* harmonization was played on piano and Coles's trumpet stood on an empty chair, while Coles himself spent the next couple of weeks in the American Hospital at Neuilly, where he had been operated on overnight. The following morning, the band and their instruments were supposed to travel by train to Liège, arriving around 11 a.m.; instead, they arrived by coach at seven in the evening and still managed to complete a filmed studio session for RTB. Unfortunately, this later caused some dissension, because: 'It was in the contract as part of the deal but Jaki wanted extra money. He was on salary and I had to tell him that the TV money just paid our trip over.'[37] Nevertheless this programme, produced by Belgian bassist Benoit Quersin just six months before the one for CBC, probably represents the first television special devoted exclusively to Mingus. But the tour schedule was clearly a demanding one, with the band travelling all the way to Marseilles for a concert the following evening, before heading the next day (Mingus's birthday) towards Switzerland and Germany. While delayed starts to concerts were almost expected in French-speaking areas, they were openly resented by the German-speaking public, and especially the promoters; the Hamburg and Zurich concerts started an hour late and those in Wuppertal and Frankfurt forty-five minutes late, while in Biel, Switzerland, the audience were already in their seats when the musicians left to partake of a pre-concert meal.

Mingus's reaction is interesting for, just as stories of his own prickly personality had preceded him to Europe, he was not unaware of the Germans' reputation for foolproof organization combined with social conformism, and may therefore have taken a perverse delight in confounding them. However, what Mingus saw also – perhaps what he expected to see – were signs of racism: 'We couldn't eat or drink or nothing. In the hotels our rooms weren't cleaned. George Wein, who was booking us there, was Jewish; he spoke the language . . . When he got downstairs, everybody stood to attention, the elevator operator, the desk clerk! . . . After that, as soon as it happened, they put swastikas on Eric's door.'[38] But

157

Mingus was perhaps most irked by what happened at the actual concerts, saying in Stuttgart at the end of the tour:

> They give us instructions how to set up, how to sit or stand, what direction to play in. Then there's a forest of mikes, nobody knows what for, and some other people come on and move the mikes about, nearer to us or further away. *We're* not allowed to touch them, we're expected to pick our way through the mike-stands and cables, like a ski-run . . . And people turn up with movie-cameras and tape-recorders, and we know nothing about film and recording rights.[39]

Thus, in Biel, Mingus had the film confiscated from a fan's camera and aimed a well-judged kick at a portable tape-deck, while in Hamburg he took out his feelings on mikes and telephones and broke down doors in both the concert-hall and the hotel, before being restrained by the police while brandishing a knife. All of this was widely reported in the European press, including daily papers such as *Die Welt,* while the jazz periodicals, though bending over backwards to be fair, were hardly overjoyed. For his pains, the editor of *Jazz Podium* received a stream of handwritten letters from Mingus, some only published after his death (including the comment, 'I was practically a saint until I ran into your Germany Nazi treatment')[40] and of course he wrote to *Down Beat* with his version of the Biel incident. But, as well as finding it unfair that his actions were more newsworthy than what led up to them, Mingus must also have regretted that the end of the tour marked the departure of Dolphy. Perhaps because of the impending separation, the relationship seems to have been rather fraught, but years later Mingus recalled that in Europe Dolphy 'talked about God – that seemed to be his only subject . . . He and John Coltrane were eating honey, I think it was a vegetarian diet, and trying to find the Lord.'[41]

With Dolphy and, of course, Johnny Coles remaining behind, the band effectively broke up on its return to New York, where Jaki Byard too found other work for a while. Dannie and Clifford Jordan, however, accompanied Mingus to San Francisco in late May for a fortnight at the Jazz Workshop, where John Handy was now available, and the group was completed by pianist Jane Getz. The last two nights were recorded for a new album on Fantasy, which consisted of further long versions of *Meditations* and *Fables of Faubus*, and which may have been intended to compensate

Mingus for the greatly increased sales of the Debut material since its reappearance on Fantasy. (Max Roach had also been accorded a live date at the Jazz Workshop, on his first visit to San Francisco since the issue of the repackages.) But more important in the long run was the fact that renewed contact with Celia and Saul Zaentz led Mingus to suggest that sales of the new album, and especially of his back-catalogue, might be sufficient to warrant regular 'salary' payments such as those he had received from Impulse during the previous year; whether such a deal was concluded immediately or only a couple of years later is unclear.

Returning from the Coast with Jordan, Richmond and pianist Getz, Mingus once again went into the Five Spot and, adding Lonnie Hillyer and Charles McPherson to make the group a sextet once more, he remained in residence with only brief interruptions until well into the autumn. Once again, the ability to play most of the year in the same club (despite problems with audience noise) led to both increased musical stability and increased experimentation. Some of it was rather theatrical, as in the Parker medley when, according to Rafi Zabor, 'Mingus would have the reedmen hide in the cloakroom so the ghost of Charlie Parker could come in like Eliahu and play fragments of old bop anthems.'[42] Jane Getz soon gave way to Byard again, while Jordan was followed by Calvin Newborn (the first guitarist to work with the regular group), who was followed by Booker Ervin, replaced at Monterey by John Handy and then by Joe Farrell.

The news of Eric Dolphy's death, on 29 June, was a terrible shock to Mingus. That his friend and colleague – after Dannie Richmond, his second musical 'son' – should die in mysterious circumstances, and in Berlin, seems to have burst the dam of Mingus's emotions. Dannie Richmond (prefacing his remarks with the statement, 'It was for me very, very special to have been on the stage with two geniuses at one time – and I would say three when it was Jaki Byard also in the band') confirmed that 'At Eric's death, I know that it affected Charles very, very deeply; I have a feeling that there was something left unsaid between the two of them.'[43] Which is echoed in a passage from the *Jazz Podium* letters:

> I just kinda feel like if I just believed a little more inside my self, and not the outside, I'd see Eric Dolphy somewhere way back in my mind's eye of conversation unfinished . . . [dots in the text] This time I'd just end my thoughts out there with him, and everyone I know in jazz circles would be much happier without

us both . . . Some would say I died of some foolish thing like a heart attack.

Here Mingus referred to the heart attack which was the supposed cause of Dolphy's death. In another passage he discounts the apparent diagnosis of previously unsuspected diabetes: 'I believe Eric was murdered. So does his N.Y. doctor Dr Finkelstein, who checked Eric just before we left for Europe. He was operated on for a tumour on the forehead. This would not have been done if Eric had been diabetic.'[44]

Mingus attended the funeral in Los Angeles on 9 July, despite what is known of his reaction to the last rites of Charlie Parker. And he christened his new son Eric Dolphy Mingus. But his emotional state showed when, on 2 September at the Five Spot, he paused in the middle of trying to play *Meditations* and kicked over one of the front tables, announcing to the audience that a woman seated at the table had been rejected by Sonny Rollins and was now chatting up Mingus every night during his performance. The woman in question responded, inaudible to most people, and, when a heckler at the bar joined in the conversation, Mingus picked up his bass and left the stand. According to eyewitness Jerry De Muth: 'As he walked past the tables to the rear of the Five Spot the two voices still criticized and ridiculed him. He reached the door to the kitchen, paused, and then suddenly dropped his bass to the floor. As it cracked and broke Mingus stormed through the doors.'[45] Later, as the instrument Mingus had bought in Milan (valued at $2,200) lay in pieces, he offered the remains to Charles Mingus III, now a budding artist: 'If you can't paint on that, you can't paint on nothin'.' And, suitably contrite about the hasty departure of the Five Spot's embarrassed clientele, he said to Iggy Termini: 'I'm sorry, Iggy, I owe you an apology. Maybe it's time to end the job. I'm so sick I want people to listen.'[46]

Before this famous incident the club had become a mecca for foreign journalists, just as the Showplace had been four years earlier. Benoit Quersin taped a two-hour radio interview with his idol and the bassist also talked to Ray Coleman of *Melody Maker*. Sporting his English suit, bowler hat and rolled umbrella for the occasion, he issued a challenge to the Beatles to play opposite him: 'Let the kids . . . find out that there's more to life than rock and roll and fringes.'[47] The fact that this ploy might have had some success, if the music business had been able to see the wood for the trees, was demonstrated during the next decade, but, back in 1964, it seemed like two different worlds when another visiting writer Victor Schonfield described a typical Five Spot set, including re-creations of Parker (by McPherson), Gillespie (by Hillyer) and now Jaki Byard's facsimile of Erroll Garner. Revealingly, in the light of this part of the programme, the reviewer observed that:

> Unlike most jazzmen, Mingus does not repeat what you know already, in either his person or his playing. Rather he conveys a liberating sense of openness and exploration, of being truly and happily aware of the actual place and time and their potential . . . There is no attempt to dovetail the ingredients, and it sounds like more of a jam-session and blues orgy than you would have thought possible.

Schonfield also included several personal vignettes, including a sartorial note:

> [The band members] look like modernists anywhere, more or less respectable and a bit anxious. A man in shorts and sandals emerges from the kitchen. He is wearing a floppy sweater with a V-neck which shows he has nothing on underneath, . . . and stuffing crumbs into his mouth. He moves through the well-dressed, multiracial audience, . . . systematically dealing with a shower of genial greetings or brief enquiries, . . . while conducting a shouted exchange about cheese with the barman at the other side of the room.[48]

The man whom Jaki Byard describes as a 'foodaholic' ('He found out that chit'lins was a delicacy in France, so he always used to order chit'lins – you know how fattening chit'lins are')[49] was obviously trying to deal with his weight problem at this period. For he told Ray Coleman, while ordering his second steak of the interview, 'You know, I lost ninety pounds in weight through exercise and less eating. [To be precise, he had reduced from 287 pounds to 190, according to Bill Whitworth's 1964 article.] Sonny Rollins is in this game. He put me on to it.'[50] On the other hand, Byard remembers that 'He started to lose weight when he started taking those pills, grey, red and white pills.'[51]

Indirectly, this may relate to another theme of Mingus's conversation at this time, as shown by another part of Victor Schonfield's acount:

I introduced myself, and in no time he was including me in a discussion about the need for rich women, and the precise definition of 'a billion'. . . When I ventured that I could not rely enough on my prowess with women whose bodies attracted me to divert it to women whose money attracted me, Mingus briefly and clearly said that this was how it was with him, too.

This may sound surprising in view of Mingus's self-confessed prowess, though less so considering his sense of morality (all the same, when Schonfield next attempted to speak to him, he 'turned away to usher some rich women into a taxi').[52] However, another passing phrase from an interview done by Nat Hentoff for the BBC during this period strikes a similar chord: 'The Negro has become the phallic symbol to America's sexual scene but the musician, I've found now, is the *first*! It's embarrassing, they think that musicians are some kind of strange, great, beautiful lover, and I'm probably the world's worst lover there is.'[53] The false modesty may have been acceptable to make a point about media manipulation (if hardly as publicity for the unpublished autobiography) but, given that a few years later he was talking cheerfully about Max Roach having undergone his 'whadyacallit, male climactic period – going through his changes',[54] it may be that Mingus had received his first intimations of the same phenomenon.

Or it may just be that Mingus was feeling somewhat careless of life itself. Just before the bass-throwing incident, Mingus had, in the words of journalist Bill Whitworth:

[written a letter to] a famous booking agent who is powerful enough to harm Mingus's career. It accused the booking agent of stealing Mingus's jobs, of associating with gangsters and killers, and of various crimes against the Negro race. It informed him that Mingus had worked out a plan under which the murder of Mingus would be answered with scores of retaliation killings, before sundown of the following day. A note at the bottom of the last page said that copies had been sent to President Johnson, the US Labor Department, the FBI, the Black Muslims, Malcolm X, and Charles de Gaulle . . . 'He came to a jazz concert once in Paris,' Mingus explained.[55]

Perhaps this is why, during his Ellington medley at the Monterey Festival that month, 'I had a pain in my chest and the fear of the possibility of my death surged through me . . . I had been so tired and overworked and I had a funny feeling as I looked up to the sky.'[56] Maybe Mingus's dieting was also partly responsible, but the audience of 7,000 must have been blissfully unaware as the small group continued with a new unison-front-line arrangement of *Orange was the Color* (this being the version which inspired Gil Evans to do his 1978 recording with Mingus's then alumnus George Adams). But the piece which drew a standing ovation from the audience, and rave reviews not only in the jazz press and the San Francisco papers but also in *Time* and *Newsweek*, was the big-band performance of *Meditations*. Six Los Angeles session musicians chosen by Buddy Collette (and unusually for those days all of them were black except for the baritone player) had gone up to Monterey two days earlier for a series of rehearsals which, according to Jaki Byard who had orchestrated the written sections, only came together when he was allowed to conduct, whereas initial attempts had failed 'largely because of C.M.'s lectures to the musicians'.[57] (Mingus's 'instinctive' approach to directing larger groups for a live performance, although anathema to the consciously 'professional' musicians involved, may be likened to that of the conductor Sir Thomas Beecham. Speaking of his live recordings, clarinettist Jack Brymer said 'There is an immediacy of impact which makes the work sound as if the orchestra were just discovering it for themselves . . . So often we ended a rehearsal knowing very little of what Beecham intended us to do at the concert; he mostly simply joked his way along, so that there were inevitably great areas of doubt in even well-known works.')[58] Following the arranged passages, in which Red Callender plays what had been the tenor part on his tuba, the excitement of the audience is carried to another plane altogether in the out-of-tempo second part, which begins with a brief piano duet by Mingus and Byard before an ethereal improvisation by Mingus on bass and Collette on flute gradually introduces the other instruments one by one, and all apparently improvising. But, as Mingus wrote, 'They're playing a written part. Then comes the ad lib section, then the written section and then ad lib again. Ad lib, in this case, is not *what* to play but in what range to play. One guy is playing a written section while another is ad libbing. It's chaos but it's organized chaos.'[59] In other words, it's a further use of the system employed in *Farwell's, Mill Valley* and a further definition, established just a few days before the 'October Revolution in Jazz' concerts in New York, of Mingus's preference for incorporating avant-garde sounds within a controlled form.

Given that this triumph took place on the West Coast, and given the programmatic subject-matter of *Meditations*, one might draw a further chronological parallel with Duke Ellington who spent the first half of *his* forty-third year also on the Coast, working on his race-relations musical *Jump for Joy*. And, having been at the centre of one of those performances in which musicians and audience feed off each other to create a memorable event, Mingus lost no time in taking the tapes to Bob Simpson (who had engineered *Tijuana Moods* and the Impulse sessions) to be edited and mastered for an album release. He had already been contemplating starting his own label again ever since the end of the Impulse contract, and since a rumoured recording with Dizzy Gillespie for Philips had fallen through. Given his previous partially unsatisfactory dealings with the major companies, and the distribution problems of smaller operations such as Atlantic (not to mention Debut), he decided that this time his records would only be available by mail-order. Though extremely unusual then, this has since become standard procedure for small musician-owned companies, even involving establishment figures like Stan Kenton (one of the first to follow Mingus's precedent was pianist Don Pullen, who was to play with Mingus in the next decade). Thus the rhetoric of his advertisement for the two discs, sold separately in plain covers, was not entirely unjustified: 'Among the causes of deprivation in which most musicians live are the avarice and corruption existing in the big business of record companies and their cohorts . . . [*heavy type*] I am doing something more to help free the next, younger generation of jazz music.' As well as the invitation to order direct from the New York postbox number of Jazz Workshop Inc., the ad concluded with: 'LEGAL NOTICE: $500.00 REWARD for evidence which secures conviction of any person for selling these records . . . in tape or any other form not bearing our code number sequence.'[60]

It is perhaps revealing that no interest was shown in mounting a big-band performance of *Meditations* in New York but, apart from the visits to the West Coast and to Canada for the television special, Mingus's stay at the Five Spot was only interrupted late in the year for a fortnight at Birdland which, during September and October, had hosted the homecoming of Bud Powell. Powell, absent in Europe for five years, had been lionized by everyone from Max Roach to Ornette Coleman and indeed had made a point of sitting in with Mingus at the Five Spot, but Mingus's own foray from Greenwich Village to the more conservative midtown club was less satisfactory for all concerned.

The fact that earlier in 1964 Birdland, with its reputation as the figurehead of a whole generation of jazz night-clubs, had temporarily abandoned a jazz policy altogether in favour of pop groups was one of the early warning signals of a difficult period for the musicians involved. Not only had the rise of the avant-garde, and the identification of some of its performers with black militancy, scared off a part of the mainstream jazz audience, but the bandleaders who still wooed this audience were leaning more and more towards formulas which oversimplified the once-fresh hard-bop and soul-jazz of the late 1950s. And, when the music industry realized that even the most successful of these bandleaders sold peanuts compared to the mushrooming market for Top Forty records, the jazz albums and most of the jazz radio shows which had promoted them suddenly began to dry up.

Mingus would seem to have been well placed to withstand this impending drought, having already sidestepped the established record companies and having at his disposal a faithful audience and a stable group. From mid-1964 to mid-1965 he had retained the services of Hillyer, McPherson, Byard and Richmond, and they joined him for a couple of months at the Village Vanguard (terminating in an abrupt departure on 13 April).

But, apart from a few one-night stands such as the Minneapolis concert which took place after the Vanguard stint, there were now gaps between engagements and it is doubtful whether Mingus was writing any new music for this particular line-up. Byard recalled him telling McPherson:

'Too bad you don't play flute and bass-clarinet and alto, like Eric did, so I could turn you on like I used to turn him on' . . . I remember he used to do this to Eric Dolphy. He'd pick a certain tune and Eric would take out his flute and get his flute ready to perform, then he [Mingus]'d change his mind, go to another one, this meant he had to do a tune with his sax. And so on and so forth, till Eric went around his three or four instruments about three or four times! But he said 'I wish I had never done that,' I'll never forget that.

Interestingly, this story is told in relation to the *Cocktails for Two* routine which, unlike the merely inappropriate treatment of standards such as *A Foggy Day* or *Flamingo*, was the first – at least on record – to be openly satirical of an earlier and cornier style of playing and which, according to Byard, he initiated 'to sort of relieve the tension that we had with the band'.[61] Byard eventually decided that enough was enough and, shortly after ending his association with Mingus, went on record as saying 'I can do without the dictator approach in music . . . I like to play a certain thing, but sometimes I don't have that feeling, and when it's forced on me, it becomes another thing entirely.'[62] As with the restrictions experienced by both McLean and Handy, this merely indicates something of the perennial problems of improvisers working with composers, and vice versa.

Mingus was, however, writing at this period, and his recorded introduction to *Once There Was a Holding Corporation Called Old America* describes it as part of a ballet score (as indeed was *The Black Saint and the Sinner Lady*, it seems). But his vehicle for writing was not the regular working band, now reduced to a quartet with Mingus occasionally doubling on piano, but an eight-piece group similar in instrumentation to the Miles Davis *Birth of the Cool* band. With a view to playing entirely new material at a second Monterey Festival appearance in September 1965, he had added trumpeters Jimmy Owens and Eddie Preston (later Hobart Dotson), the brilliant french-horn player Julius Watkins and Howard Johnson on tuba and, having introduced this line-up during several weeks at the Village Gate spread between June and September, was reasonably well rehearsed by the time of the West Coast trip. Nevertheless, the album taped at UCLA one week after Monterey preserves the first recorded example of Mingus's intolerance towards his musicians, when the somewhat Kurt Weillesque opening of the aforementioned *Once There Was* begins with half the band missing the downbeat for the first note. Mingus's comments simultaneously addressed to audience and performers (one of whom appears to be saying 'Blah, blah, blah') include the phrase, 'If we can't play together, let's go play with *us*,'[63] doubtless accompanied by masturbatory gestures, judging by the mirthful reaction. A new start, lasting about twenty seconds before the tension induces a cracked note, leads Mingus to give a piano demonstration which doesn't actually help in any discernible way, followed by a third attempt that barely reaches the second bar. After five seconds of glowering silence, Mingus exclaims 'For God's sake' and proceeds to dismiss the additional brass, while continuing with the quartet alone in yet another bebop potpourri called *Ode to Bird and Dizzy*.

The music composed for the octet, however, is consistently impressive if also somewhat oppressive, probably as a result of Mingus once again doing his own orchestration. The performance

166

at Monterey, where he had this time to follow on stage the hugely successful appearance of John Handy, was less than totally relaxed and ended prematurely with Mingus leading his men offstage while playing *When the Saints Go Marching in.* Jimmy Lyons, now the producer of the Monterey Festivals, has said that the reason for Mingus's disgruntlement was the non-arrival of a batch of his records of the previous year's concert, which he had planned to sell, and, somehow blaming the non-arrival on Lyons, had threatened not to play at all: 'Okay, you get down on your knees and beg me.'[64] However, the UCLA concert not only demonstrates the growing maturity of McPherson and Hillyer, but *The Arts of Tatum* provides the only lengthy documentation of Mingus's contemporary, Hobart Dotson. Having left Los Angeles with Billy Eckstine in 1946 and moved to Chicago and then New York (taking part in the *Pre-Bird* album), it is perhaps appropriate that his feature, a contrapuntally disguised *Body and Soul*, goes back in spirit to Mingus's writing of the mid-1940s. Dotson also plays all the lead trumpet work, includ-ing the off-key fanfare which introduces *Don't Be Afraid, the Clown's Afraid Too*, whose fifteen-bar A-section has several contrapuntal themes (partly contributed by McPherson and Jimmy Owens, according to Sy Johnson) while the satirical B-section is in 3/4, reminiscent of the 1957 *Clown. Meditation on Inner Peace* has ostensibly no connection with the previous year's *Meditations*, unless it was derived from extending the bowed-bass intro added for the 1964 Monterey version. But that the search for inner peace was inseparable from wider concerns was shown by Mingus's latest piece of words-and-music, *Don't Let It Happen Here*. Charles Fox has pointed out that this is in fact a free adaptation of a poem by the German anti-fascist Pastor Niemöller, but Mingus's motivation was surely not unconnected with the fact that, in a year of continuing racial violence in pursuit of civil rights, the worst confrontation had come just one month earlier in his own home town of Watts.

One day they came and they took the Communists,
And I said nothing because I was not a Communist.
Then one day they came and they took the people of the Jewish
   faith,
And I said nothing because I had no faith left.
One day they came and they took the unionists,
And I said nothing because I was not a unionist.
One day they burned the Catholic churches,
And I said nothing because I was born a Protestant.

Then one day they came and they took me,
And I could say nothing because I was as guilty as they were,
For not speaking out and saying that all men have a right to
    freedom.[65]

The freedom of an eight-piece group to find regular employment, however, seems to have been severely restricted for, apart from a fortnight in San Francisco immediately following the UCLA concert, Mingus did not resume public performances until 21 December when he began a six-week booking at the Five Spot, which was eventually extended to twice that length. But, during that period, the band was reduced first to a septet (trombonist Tom McIntosh replacing the two added trumpeters) and then to a sextet, and, despite attendance at a February benefit concert for the striking faculty members of St John's University, there seemed to be little interest in booking the group for further appearances. Meanwhile Mingus was replaced at the Five Spot by a Charles McPherson-Lonnie Hillyer quintet.

In some ways he may not have been too distressed by this turn of events. For, in the spring of 1966, he was soliciting advance orders for a further batch of records to be issued in June on the Charles Mingus Enterprises Inc. label and, at least according to Nat Hentoff, his initial release of the Monterey concert had 'awakened more response than even he anticipated'.[66] The records in question were the NAACP benefit – 'Eric [Dolphy]'s last appearance in USA' – which Mingus, perhaps attempting to cash in on the notoriety of the United Artists episode, billed with the same title as the 1962 album *Town Hall Concert*; the Minneapolis recording by *My Favourite Quintet*; and *Special Music Written for (and Not Heard at) Monterey*, in other words the UCLA tapes. The largest type in the advertisement, however, was reserved not for the musical details but for the heading '$1,000 IS YOURS! . . . if you can provide information leading to the arrest and conviction of any person or persons etc.'[67]

This concern with counterfeiting records (as compared to taping live performances without permission) is partially explained in the sleeve-notes to the *Town Hall Concert* album for, as well as photos of the composer taken by Charles Mingus III, the covers of these latest issues were adorned with what were described as 'Notes from Charles Mingus's book *Beneath the Underdog*'. The author refers to one 'John Hamhead', a 'main investor for one of these major record-labels' and 'liberal tongued beast of high finance', who explained away the low official sales figures of a particular album by alleging that the record stores 'are probably black-marketing your music, Mingus Ah-Um'. By contrast:

> After [Mingus Enterprises] pay[s] the musicians, the band, as a cooperative group, will receive a minimum of 7–10% . . . This will be the first American company to make a step to give justice to all employed. When we succeed, we will also practise fair employment – and not just blacks . . . compared to the mathematician's statistics of integrated peoples in the N.Y.C. area, or any other city we expand to.[68]

These dreams were not in fact to be realized, and meanwhile there were problems which were more pressing, especially in their effect on Mingus's inner peace. Although the gymnastic equipment for the proposed School of Arts, Music And Gymnastics had gone the previous year, the idea of a music school was still in Mingus's mind; but, in the spring of 1966, he had moved his instruments and other effects from East 26th Street and taken a loft apartment at 5 Great Jones Street. He had not been living with Judy for some while now and, though not short of lady friends, he was not staying regularly with anyone else either. Instead, he was using the loft as his home.

The feeling that the various supports he had been leaning on were being gradually withdrawn must have been accentuated by the case of Dannie Richmond, whose earlier occasional unreliability had been solved, but only by leaving New York. Dannie says:

> I was having problems myself, you know. The gigs were really hard, and I was hanging out with the wrong people . . . I had gone back to Greensboro, and was doing local things at the time. Even to the point where he would maybe have a weekend, he'd send for me; I'd meet him in New York, finish the gig and go back to Greensboro.

One such gig, Mingus's first in nearly six months, was a fortnight in September opposite Herbie Mann at the Village Gate, where the motley personnel (including Dannie, Britt Woodman and pianist Walter Bishop) shows that he was no longer even trying to maintain a regular group. And his behaviour was again on a knife-edge, as Dr Cloud recalls:

> Herbie was trying to play African music. And [Mingus] said

'What does a Jew like you know about African music?' and threw a drum at him. And then busted up a microphone, and these things cost $1,000 – Art D'Lugoff wasn't too happy about that . . . And then he [Mingus] had a little pistol around his neck as a charm, but it happened to be a Derringer with two bullets in it! And John [Reverend Gensel] and I took him out, and we took Charlie home.[69]

Meanwhile he completed a commission to write the music for a National Educational Television documentary called *Blues for the Jungle*, and was booked to appear on a George Wein tour of Europe with the long-awaited Rollins-Mingus-Roach trio. But at the last moment he backed out in order to take part in a documentary film by Tom Reichman, at whose son's funeral he had played in the summer of 1964.

Being himself the subject of the documentary, he was filmed in November at Lennie's-on-the-Turnpike with a group including Dannie, Bishop, Hillyer, McPherson and saxophonist John Gilmore playing standards such as *Take the 'A' Train* and *All the Things You Are* and quartet performances of *Peggy's Blue Skylight* and *Portrait*. But, as well as incorporating a bit of 16mm footage of the 1962 Town Hall concert, the unique value of this documentary is that it faithfully captures his persona just as he approached one of the lowest points of his life so far. For on 22 November 1966 he was evicted by city marshals from 5 Great Jones Street for alleged non-payment of six months' rent, and Reichman filmed a long soliloquy as Mingus packed his belongings in readiness the previous evening. Not only does he briefly vent his anger by firing his shotgun at the ceiling of the apartment, but earlier he sits at the piano playing for a young lady who had been allowed to visit him:

At one very touching moment, Mingus's extraordinarily articulate five-year-old daughter reminds her father of the days she misses – the days when the family was living in luxury on Sutton Place. The once prosperous Mingus simply embraces her, lovingly and painfully . . . The climax is a newsreel sequence showing television reporters and press photographers plying their trade before the harassed musician on the morning of the eviction. As he is escorted by police to the paddy wagon, Mingus comments to the reporters, first seriously, then sarcastically, finally on the verge of tears.[70]

Since Michael Cuscuna's review above only deals with the film, it necessarily omits the punch-line of *Down Beat*'s news item on the event itself. For Mingus's visit to the police station was in order to produce a permit for his gun and a doctor's prescription for vitamin B injections, after which he was permitted to leave, with the words: 'It isn't every day that you see a Negro walk out of a police station with a box of hypodermic needles and a shotgun.'[71]

8
Put Me In That Dungeon

One of the only hopeful signs for the future was that Mingus was accompanied on eviction day by his most frequent female companion, Susan Graham Ungaro. The fact that this led to her appearance in the film *Mingus*, walking beside him in an anti-war march and sharing the calamity of the actual eviction, may have caused a certain confusion because of the other sequences with Carolyn. Dannie Richmond articulates the understandable error of many who have seen the film; 'One would get the impression that it was Susan's daughter.' But Sue had in fact known Mingus off and on for only two years before this event. Having first come into contact with jazz through playing the lead in a 1963 Robert Frank short *OK, End Here*, for which Ornette Coleman was commissioned to write the music, she had become aware of Mingus the following year at the Five Spot. 'What was absolutely striking and marvellous was the way he was eating a turkey bone at the time, completely involved and concentrated, sitting all by himself at a table . . . He was on a diet at the time, and food was doubly important as a result.'[1]

But this relationship, though obviously supportive, was less than totally involving for Mingus at the time, and partly for reasons also outlined by Dannie: 'Susan was still married, and raising a boy and girl of her own. And it was only at certain times that she was able to go . . . and see Charles.' Had Sue been immediately available and on a permanent basis, it is possible that the next couple of years in Mingus's life might have been different, but, on the other hand, perhaps no one could have been enough of a saviour to help Mingus at this stage. Certainly the progression from the Harlem apartment to a loft where, despite the assistance of NAACP and CORE (Congress Of Racial Equality) lawyers at the hearing beforehand, his right of abode was not recognized, seemed symbolic. Surveying his possessions in the film, Mingus is heard to say, 'It looks like junk that's thrown away – naturally, 'cause it's not unpacked – but everything, my whole life since I was a baby is in these boxes, my music and everything I got.'[2]

Clearly the public humiliation of the eviction was the last straw that broke the Bull's back. Dannie Richmond again: 'Later on, he really went "out" because he did a Charlie Parker. I mean, no clothes on in Central Park, cursing the police, going to jail . . . There was definitely something wrong.' So that, when Mingus wrote a year or so later of 'the destruction of my record firm and music school . . . and the wilful burning of my piano, bass, musical scores and other personal belongings by the City of New York – the city I live in',[3] he was reliving the anguish which caused him to be referred, this time for real, to Bellevue Hospital. On the other hand, he may have also been exaggerating, for the damage to his property, as opposed to his self-esteem, may have been less wanton. Certainly much of Mingus's written music, going back at least as far as the Hampton scores of 1947–8, was irretrievably lost (Susan Graham's voice is heard off-camera in the film, complaining 'There are sheets of music all over the floor, that people are stepping on')[4] but, even after a lengthy period of living down and out when his possessions were minimal, Mingus claimed that: 'All that's left are a Steinway and my basses.'[5] Therefore it would seem that, if nothing else, his basses were reclaimed within the required thirty days by someone with Mingus's interests at heart. He himself, according to a *Down Beat* news item, had been 'spending some time with friends in Mill Valley',[6] and it seems extremely unlikely that he was in any shape to have made his scheduled appearance at the Village Gate for the last two weekends of January.

Apparently it was this particular trip to San Francisco which suggested the idea that recuperation could shade off into a graceful retirement, and by 1970 he had rationalized his actions as being just that: 'I quit after Monterey . . . everybody should retire sometime.'[7] And, as previously indicated, it was Celia and Saul Zaentz who had come to the rescue. 'I do know,' says Dannie Richmond, 'that he was able to go into this semi-retirement only because of the tapes that existed from Debut . . . The agreement was like for so much money, and then they would pay him so much per month for so long a period. Pay his rent, get him a piano, you know. And that's when he kinda decided to just cool it.' So, when Mingus arrived back in New York after a couple of months in California, he found a relatively cheap apartment on the lower East Side at the corner of East 5th Street and Avenue A, and at least contemplated the notion of just cooling it.

In practice, it was not so easy. For a start, the money from Fantasy would hardly provide more than the bare necessities of life and, in any case, Mingus must have had very mixed feelings about deliberately cutting himself off from live audiences, however tiresome they sometimes were. Besides, having benefited from his layoff in California, he felt ready to get back on the treadmill. Yet, even here, his mixed feelings were in evidence for, after asking for work at the Half Note where he had agreed to play four weeks up to 14 May, he suddenly appeared in the third week of April at a new establishment just across the street from the Half Note called Pookie's Pub. It may be that he was attracted by the idea of working at Pookie's because it had only recently been opened by young people and originally with the intention of catering to the Village youth crowd – although, by the time of Mingus's appearance, it was charging the same prices as the Half Note. Nevertheless the quartet (with Hillyer, McPherson and Richmond) was a success, a brief review by French writer Jean-Marie Hess mentioning in particular an 'excellente et ultra-swingante parodie des époques Dixie et Chicagoan'[8] on the lines of the UCLA *Twelfth Street Rag*.

Sadly, this comeback was decidedly premature. For, when the residency at Pookie's (begun on the eve of Mingus's forty-fifth birthday) terminated in late June, it turned out to be his last documented public performance for over a year. There was, of course, a combination of reasons for this. Firstly, everyone involved in jazz in night-clubs was definitely crying the blues about bad business, and a further indication of this was the end in August of the jazz policy at the Five Spot. Joe Termini was quoted as saying 'Jazz just isn't profitable any more . . . For college kids, the place to go used to be a jazz club. Now they have other interests.'[9] Mingus was always hopeful of the profit-motive being removed from the area of jazz promotion, no doubt influenced by writers such as Nat Hentoff, and in their 1964 BBC interview had said: 'This is my dream too, I look forward to that. Or even roping off an area and having a block party . . . It's a funny society that's raised mainly on hearing records, they very seldom get the chance to know what the difference is, hearing live music.'[10] And, for all the hopes and indeed European examples of subsidizing jazz in order to take it to the people, the only tentative steps in this direction in America were being taken by private pressure groups such as Jazz Interactions, not by official agencies.

In this connection Dannie Richmond mentions other factors which affected Mingus's situation:

> He was just sick of the 'system', the way he told *me*. But at the same time, there was the black revolution going on in the States . . . And then, with a lot of the white musicians coming on the scene and getting credit for certain things, I do know for a fact – from many of the long talks that we had – that he was bitter about that . . . Along with the fact that, you know, black people themselves were not helping the issue, see? And, in fact, I can't really put my finger on any one real thing with black musicians during that period, but I do know that some of them were saying that what Mingus was doing was not 'what was happening'. That he was crazy.

And, as if this were not enough, financial worries were obviously a not insignificant part of Mingus's problem at this time:

> Well, he was about to get into a lot of trouble about that mail-order thing, because there were people that sent cheques for records, that were never fulfilled. So there was about to be some static about that. Well, I mean, it caused the thing to fold. I can't remember just what followed what, but we were doing our income tax and I never did get a statement. So I said 'Mingus, you know, the date is getting near and I don't have any statement.' He said, 'Well, I didn't pay you none.' 'So, er, what am I supposed to do now?' He said 'Well, you just tell them that I spent the fucking money, and they can come see *me* if they want to!'

It had been one of Mingus's constant themes that such difficulties were part of the normal lot of jazz performers, for example citing in his record-label advertisement 'Fats Waller, King Oliver, Art Tatum, Bird, Lester Young . . . How many people realize that many of the jazz greats have lived lives of utter poverty?'[11] Certainly Mingus considered his talent worthy to be mentioned alongside such names as these, the only difference being that he was still alive.

Just in the last few years, Eric Dolphy had died suddenly and tragically, having survived a whole year and a half longer than Bird. Then Bud Powell, who had returned to America a hero in August 1964, had died a virtual derelict less than two years later at the age of forty-one. And now John Coltrane, whose compositional style he actually disliked but whose popularity among musicians and listeners alike he recognized, had died in July 1967 without even reaching his forty-first birthday. In his darkest hours – and there were some very dark hours indeed during this period – Mingus must have called out to God and demanded to know why he was still here. In later years, he spoke openly and even a little melodramatically about having had one foot in the grave, and he told Nat Hentoff: 'For about three years I thought I was finished. Sometimes I couldn't even get out of bed. I wasn't asleep; I just lay there.'[12]

What kept him going at all was the discovery that, after music, there is yet life:

> In that neighbourhood, they didn't know me from the man in the moon, but they took an interest in me. I'd go into a bar, sit by myself, and I'd hear someone say 'There's something wrong with this guy. He doesn't come out of his house for four or five days at a time.' And they'd invite me to join them. I got to know what friends are. Ukrainians, blacks, Puerto Ricans – a house painter, a tailor, a woman who owns a bar, her bartender, a maintenance man who says, 'I'll walk you home tonight if you get drunk. And if I get drunk, you walk me home.' . . . There was a time when I had no money left at all, but the tailor on the block made sure I had enough to eat.[13]

And intermittently even his interest in music was revived. Just over a year after his eviction, Mingus was reported to be writing a new ballet, part of it entitled *My Arrest*, and at the same time to be dabbling with the increasingly popular electric bass. This may simply have been a ploy to obtain a new instrument from Framus, to whose advertisements he had lent his name while a pollwinner, and who had pioneered the solid-body upright electric bass (as distinct from bass-guitar). Certainly he later pronounced anathema on all electronics, especially as applied to basses.

But sheer survival was the foremost problem, and the Charles Mingus Enterprises record-label had become another millstone. A reply to a British record retailer from their (unnamed) American agent advances the theory 'that the receivers simply grab every

dollar that reaches the address', while a later communication contradicts this by saying 'I have just had my letter to that P.O. Box
address returned, marked "No longer box holder." '[14] Once again
Saul Zaentz, who in the autumn of 1967 had taken over effective
control of Fantasy from the Weiss brothers, had made arrangements to handle the records concerned and, in mid-1968, the
Monterey album reappeared with the original pressing of the discs
enclosed in a new Fantasy sleeve bearing the legend 'A product of
Debut in California'. But, although Debut apparently still existed
on paper, and whatever contribution it may have made to the profits
of Fantasy, it seems to have made no additional contribution to the
well-being of Charles Mingus. For the repackage of the Monterey
set also enclosed a sheet headed 'A Living Benefit for Mingus' and
containing the words 'Saul Zaentz, who is an honest person and who
is now distributing my records for the first time in public stores, has
consented to include this letter in my album. Anyone who cares to
alter my deplorable financial condition which has resulted from the
misfortunes I have suffered, may send a contribution to–', followed
by the same box number which, by the time of the re-release, had
been discontinued.[15]

At exactly the same period, Mingus made an almost subliminal
reappearance by playing bass with poet Sayed Hussein for four
Thursdays in July 1968 at a pub called Joey Archer's, and that
summer he also appeared on film as Tom Reichman's documentary
had its first showings in the art houses. But his interest in music at
this time might almost be said to have been equalled by his interest
in photography, as, for a short while, he not only explored the
medium but managed to get hired by a theatrical group to take their
publicity shots. And yet, all the while, he was still poised pre-
cariously on the knife-edge and, rather than courting disaster as he
used to do, was waiting passively and almost fatalistically to slide off
into the abyss. Susan Graham speaks of not one but a couple of
nervous breakdowns, one of which kept Mingus in hospital for three
months. 'It was one of the pretty down periods of his life, and I
would say he was not happy principally because he *wasn't* involved
in music. His life was all for music, and I think it was extremely
difficult for him to have put it aside for that long a period.'

The very gradual rehabilitation which followed was partly an
inner one, and partly induced by medication. As Susan points out,
'You know, when you have breakdowns in this country, very often
drugs are dispensed with great irresponsibility, to make people
simply easier to handle. And he was given quantities of thorazin,

which can be extremely debilitating.' But, however distressing some of the side-effects of this prolonged treatment, it seems to have allowed Mingus the space in which to breathe once more. Given this, music could now become, if not yet the all-consuming interest it once had been, then at least a form of therapy. So it was not surprising to find him in January 1969 sitting in a couple of times with his former sideman, Nico Bunink, at a small piano-bar in the Village called Casey's. And, earlier the same month on 8 January, he made his first appearance in over eighteen months with a band during a benefit concert at Fillmore East for the *New York Free Press* (an 'underground' weekly co-published by Susan Graham). Also on the spectacularly heterogeneous bill were Peter Yarrow of Peter, Paul and Mary, Norman Mailer, and the Fugs. Dannie Richmond, who travelled from Greensboro to play the single thirty-minute set, recalls that 'He said he could get him a bunch of girls and do better than that,' though whether 'that' refers to the Fugs or to Mingus's own personal and financial situation is an open question. Susan Graham says of this concert, 'It was the first time he ever used a bass amplifier, as I remember, and he was very upset by it.'

Although not exactly heralded in the press, this brief gig did mark the start of Mingus's slow re-emergence on the jazz scene. It was to be a few months before he put together anything resembling a regular band, but he was gradually resuming his contacts and eventually agreed to try a two-week stand at the Village Vanguard in June. The month before this, he even attended one of those celebrity-packed New York funeral services, conducted by Pastor Gensel, in order to pay his respects to the late Coleman Hawkins. The renewed interest in Mingus, and perhaps relief at the relative success of the Vanguard appearance, led to a booking at the Village Gate in August also for two weeks, with his 'new' quintet featuring Dannie Richmond, Bill Hardman, Charles McPherson and the only new element (recently arrived in New York from Fort Worth), tenor player Billy Robinson. At the start of July, this band had also taken part along with the quintet of Lee Morgan (who the following year was active in forming another pressure group, the Jazz And People's Movement) in a second anti-George Wein protest, playing once again at Cliff Walk Manor on the Friday and Saturday of the main Newport Festival. Mingus 'seemed relaxed and happy to be back in action, but' according to Dan Morgenstern, 'took no solos and left the announcing to Richmond'.[16]

Nat Hentoff too has written of this period, 'Mingus rarely appeared in public, and when he did his music was almost dispassionately retrospective. In the daytime I'd see him occasionally wandering around the lower East Side, uncommonly subdued, abstracted.'[17] But the one event which, while not producing any new music from Mingus, began to restore his faith in himself was actually one of the relatively few celebrations of Duke Ellington in this year of his seventieth birthday. For on 28 and 29 September the University of California at Berkeley presented a two-day 'extension course' consisting of lectures and tributes to Ellington by such as John Handy, Stanley Dance, Gunther Schuller and John Lewis and a concert by the Ellington band. Mingus had been invited to take part in two separate capacities, and his 'tribute' comprised the quintet playing some of its normal repertoire plus a Ducal medley similar to that done at Monterey five years earlier. But, during the concert which formed the last evening session of the event, Dick Hadlock noted that 'Ellington attempted something quite extraordinary, even for him. He presented Charles Mingus's extended piece, *The Clown*. Mingus was slated to direct the orchestra while Ellington narrated but the composer failed to appear and Duke did it all.'[18] Sue Graham recalls the last-minute change of plan:

> Duke said 'I don't know if I can play this. You know, Charles Mingus is a difficult composer.' And, of course, a number of the musicians were outraged and didn't want to play at all, because it was hard music. And Charles did not want to get involved himself on stage, with all those musicians who were furious to begin with. Duke was calling 'Is Charlie Mingus in the house?' in this packed auditorium, and Mingus was hiding way up at the top of the balcony.

This unique big-band version, orchestrated from the record and featuring Paul Gonsalves, must have been a fine vehicle for Duke's speaking voice, although *The Clown* was hardly the piece to show Mingus's link with Ellington, who promptly christened him 'The Two-Beat Waltz King'.[19] Perhaps it was after this performance that Mingus suggested to Ellington that they make 'a real avant-garde record' together, and Duke replied 'Charles, let's not go back *that* far.'[20]

This initiative of the organizer of the Berkeley event, Marvin Chachere, which had turned it into an Ellington tribute to Mingus as well as vice versa, did not have any immediate effect in terms of inspiring new compositional activity. But, as Sue notes, 'I started actually booking him following this tribute to Duke. It was obvious that he needed and wanted to play music again, and I started asking other musicians and clubowners how to go about it.' So that, as well as the fortnight at Chicago's Plugged Nickel and a similar period in San Francisco at the Both/And, which were part of the same cross-country trip which included Berkeley, the quintet appeared in December at Slug's, a bar in Mingus's own neighbourhood of the lower East Side which had been featuring jazz for the past couple of years. Mingus the bass soloist took part in a February concert at Town Hall opposite Kenny Dorham's band, and the group made a return visit to Berkeley in April (by which time Jimmy Vass had replaced Billy Robinson) for the first of innumerable festival appearances Mingus was to undertake during the 1970s.

An increase of activity of a different kind that took place in 1970 was brought about partly because Sue Graham was now publishing another 'alternative' periodical called *Changes*. The fact that Vol. 1, No. 3 of *Changes* contained an extract from Mingus's by now somewhat legendary autobiography was instrumental in arousing the interest of publisher Regina Ryan of Knopf, who not only sought out the author with a view to bringing out the book at last but also agreed with Mingus that the best person to edit the manuscript would be Nel King, of the *All Night Long* screenplay. While acknowledging that the *Changes* extract was responsible for the appearance of the much longer extract (365 pages out of the original 1,000 plus) which we know as *Beneath the Underdog*, Sue feels that:

> What was most responsible was a negative factor: that, as a result of this nervous breakdown, Mingus was under a lot of medication and was operating on two cylinders, and very agreeable to many things he would not have been, had he been his normal self . . . He got along much more easily with the editors that he met. He left a lot of decisions to Nel King that, I think, under other circumstances, he never would have. Then again, it was a good thing in many ways, the book had become a huge nightmare for him . . . because it had circulated for so long, he had used real names of people in the book and he was very paranoid about that. He'd used names of gangsters and society women and clubowners and so forth, and he often felt that things happened as a result of people trying to get back at him because he had maligned them in his book. Or, in maligning them, had told the truth about many dangerous subjects.

As we have seen, many of the names of the dramatis personae were changed, the major exceptions being close musical associates such as Buddy Collette, Britt Woodman, Teddy Charles and Nat Hentoff. Furthermore, despite Mingus's earlier references to 'Musicians . . . virtually enslaved by union and big business over-seers, by callous and cynical business practices . . . payola, bootleg records, under-the-table kickbacks, phony contracts . . . All this and more I expose in my forthcoming book, *Beneath the Underdog*,'[21] there is hardly a trace of such matters in the published version. Nor is there any evidence of his seven years with Celia. And, despite the confirmation of the original's great length by the many people to whom it was shown by its author (including, for instance, Red Callender, Jimmy Knepper and Pepper Adams, who had in fact said to Mingus, 'Are you going to write the longest autobiography since Gibbon, who wrote eight volumes?') the sub-stance of the deleted passages must forever remain a mystery. Although in the autumn of 1974 Mingus said 'The rest of it's lost, so I'm dictating it again,'[22] it would doubtless differ in outline at least as much as the re-recordings of his compositions.

A correspondence initiated by the British collector Roger Rowland about one of the business practices complained of, an apparently unauthorized reissue of the first Candid album, affords some insight into Mingus's comparatively docile attitude at this time. His first reply written in July 1970 (although, perhaps reveal-ingly, he dated it '1967') expresses gratitude for the information, while the second letter comments, 'I don't know what can be done since the world is still pretty big, even though people can fly over it in what seems minutes, also the laws don't work from one country to the other.' A third letter was written on *Changes* notepaper from Sue Graham's new address since her separation from her husband (to be precise, an apartment on East 10th Street formerly owned by photographer Diane Arbus), although Mingus was still based at East 5th; it contains the phrase 'My manager "Sue" will do all she can to try and trace who Candid sold to,'[23] which sounds worlds away from the indiscriminate threats Mingus would have issued in earlier days. This approach was also rewarded by the appearance the following spring of a legitimate reissue on the Barnaby label.

During the summer of 1970, however, Mingus had completed further stints at Slug's, the Vanguard and the Gate, while Sue had been to Europe in order to set up a long tour which was to begin in early October and end with three weeks in November at London's Ronnie Scott Club. By the time of the Gate residency, the touring band was taking shape, with Eddie Preston and Carlos Garnett replacing Hardman and Vass, while Jaki Byard made his peace and sat in on occasion. But, during this period, another change took place in typically Mingusian fashion. Bobby Jones, a then-obscure white reedman formerly with Woody Herman and Jack Teagarden, had first sat in during the first week at the Gate and then, probably on Tuesday 11 August, he arrived before the band's first set; when Carlos Garnett also arrived, Mingus invited Jones to the stand and Garnett left the club, never to return. However, at the end of the night, Mingus told Jones to come back tomorrow, as he did each night until, at the end of the week, 'He laid some money on me. The same thing happened next week, and the week after, each time more money. So I finally discovered that I was a member of the group.'[24] Almost simultaneously Mingus lost one of his most individual ex-sidemen, who had often been willing to rejoin the group for a couple of weeks, when Booker Ervin died on 31 August; and he discovered a new potential audience when on 9 September the Jazzmobile (a truck providing free concerts in the streets of Harlem sponsored by Jazz Interactions) featured his sextet. Although one of the band advised against playing their usual repertoire, Mingus said 'I did more. I took the music as far out as I could, and they still liked it. All those kids following the truck, wanting more . . . It's *their* music, man. It's their lives.'[25]

It was the European tour which gave rise to Mingus's first new albums in five years, indicating that record companies in Europe were more interested in Mingus (and indeed in jazz) than their US counterparts. While taping the band officially for their 'America' label, Musidisc not only made amends for their *sub rosa* Candid reissue but negotiated the first public issue of the 1964 concerts. The 1970 recordings do include the D flat *The Man Who Never Sleeps*, actually a ballad-tempo reworking of the piano sketch *She's Just Miss Popular Hybrid*; but it must be said that the studio session, and to a lesser extent the Rotterdam and Berlin concerts, still suggest the 'dispassionately retrospective' and comparisons with the originals of *Pithecanthropus* or even *Reincarnation* make these performances seem almost polite, despite flashes of brilliance from Preston and the occasionally striking similarity to Clifford Jordan in the work of Jones. One new piece described by Jones, however, apparently started life during a sound-check in Berlin. 'He sat down and played a little of it, and one by one we picked out our parts. Then Jaki Byard decided to write another section – actually two sections – and after only a day and a half, we had come up with what Mingus called a history of jazz . . . Some parts were very difficult, but we debuted it in Berlin after practically no rehearsals.'[26]

One of the more remarkable surprises awaiting those seeing Mingus's band for the first time, in fact, was that the front-line players were actually reading the various ensemble sections from written parts placed before them on music-stands. Jaki Byard explains:

I used to write all my parts out so I'd remember them, and . . . specifically so I could say 'Well, you told us to do *this*,' till finally later on he accepted that fact. I explained 'This is out of respect for your music, that's why *I'm* doing it.' I remember after I did it, then Bobby Jones used to write everything out, until finally we took to writing everything out so that the book was always there and he didn't have to go through that ritual of rehearsing it the way he usually rehearsed.[27]

But more distressing perhaps for people brought up on the fables of Mingus was that, not only did he make no announcements (nor did Dannie Richmond), he took no bass solos and displayed an adequate but hardly very dynamic approach to keeping time in the rhythm section. Certainly, signs of the famed empathy between Mingus and Richmond were few and far between and, although the musical concept was still Mingus's, the driving force behind the band was Richmond. Questioned in London about the reasons for Mingus's return to playing, Dannie said 'Maybe it's the new young lady he's met, Miss Sue Graham. Personal relationships mean a lot to him,' adding that 'I'm still worried about him. He's putting on a lot of weight.'[28] Mingus's own explanation in one of the only interviews he gave on this tour was that he was 'just tired . . .But I don't have enough to live on – otherwise I wouldn't still be playing. I had to come back just to make a living.'[29]

In the comments quoted above, Dannie had also said 'Although I don't seem to get as close to him as before, he never considered coming to Europe without Jaki Byard and me,'[30] a reference to the fact that, at the Gate three months earlier, drummer Al Hicks (who had been with Kenny Dorham at Town Hall, as had a subsequent Mingus sideman Danny Mixon) substituted for Richmond while he worked with singer Johnny Taylor. Ironically, during the stay at Ronnie Scott's, first Byard left after a week because of teaching commitments back in the US and then Dannie started sitting in with the support group the Mark-Almond Band, whose joint leaders had played with John Mayall at the same 1969 Newport Festival against which Mingus had demonstrated at Cliff Walk Manor. In fact, Richmond's extra-curricular activities at Ronnie's led directly to a lucrative offer to join Mark-Almond in touring the States, and the fact that their own pianist Tommy Eyre also sat in with Mingus in London hardly compensated him for the double defection of Byard and Richmond.

Thus the Japanese tour, which followed December engagements at the Club Baron and Slug's, was undertaken with a quartet consisting of Eddie Preston, Bobby Jones and Al Hicks, and this was the basic format of the recording session augmented by Toshiyuki Miyama's New Herd. Despite the simple but effective arrangements commissioned from Byard prior to the tour, and despite the comparative lack of soloists forcing Mingus to feature himself on bass once again, *Charles Mingus with Orchestra* is one of his more forgettable albums. A moment to treasure, though, must have been Mingus's brief appearance later the same month on the *Ed Sullivan Show*. As a result of the demands of the Jazz And People's Movement for more media exposure, the 24 January edition of this American institution included a few minutes devoted to the group of Roland Kirk (now Rahsaan Roland Kirk) augmented by Archie Shepp, Roy Haynes and Mingus. Doubtless in deference to Mingus's status as senior protestor, the music performed was a version of *Haitian Fight Song*.

Two months later, the Jazz And People's Movement were active again without Mingus's participation, protesting against the 'racist policies' of the John Simon Guggenheim Memorial Foundation. Whether or not this demonstration influenced their decision-making, the Foundation's awards, announced a fortnight later, included a fellowship for composition to Charles Mingus and, although not the first jazz artist to be so honoured, it must be said that most of his few predecessors had been white. By this time Mingus had completed return visits to Slug's and the Vanguard with a revised sextet in which Lonnie Hillyer and newcomer John Foster had replaced Preston and Byard, while Virgil Day had taken over from Al Hicks. Interestingly, Mingus himself had missed the first couple of nights at Slug's and been replaced by Wilbur Ware, after which Sue Graham 'got him to a pill authority in New York . . . who went through an enormous encyclopaedia and showed us what Charles had been ingesting, and how lucky he was to be alive . . . In fact Charles got rid of all the side-effects of this enormously strong medication he'd been taking, and got his personality back and his feelings.' It was to be some while yet, however, before Sue could make the comment reported by Sy Johnson: 'He's his old self. He just yelled at the band.'[31]

What sparked renewed interest in Mingus much more than the Guggenheim award was, of course, the publication in May of the long-awaited 'autobiography', and the very mixed critical reaction which greeted it served if anything to increase interest still further. The same phenomenon had already been observed fifteen years earlier on the appearance of Billie Holiday's book, as it was nearly a decade later with the revelations of Art Pepper, when general readers dimly aware of their music, but not of their scandalous in-group reputations, suddenly caught up with the disarming spectacle of a jazz musician 'telling it like it is' in print. Certainly George Wein lost no time in contacting Mingus again, and this time the price must have been right, for the sextet enlivened the 1971 Newport Festival (the last to take place in the town of Newport itself) with performances of *Pithecanthropus Erectus, Cocktails for Two* and *Oscar Pettiford Junior* (formerly *O.P.O.P.*).

Another celebration of Mingus which came to fruition in the autumn of 1971 had also been initiated the previous year, when the black choreographer Alvin Ailey contacted him about doing a ballet based on his music. Either Ailey could not commission Mingus to do any new writing, or he had already derived such specific inspiration from existing Mingus music that he wished to restrict himself to it, for the outcome of their discussions was that trombonist-arranger Alan Raph prepared full orchestral versions of nine previously recorded pieces, the most recent of which, the piano solo *Myself When I Am Real* was actually orchestrated by Jaki Byard. Performed by the City Center Joffrey Ballet and conducted by Walter Hagen, *The Mingus Dances* consisted of five 'dances' interleaved with four 'vaudevilles', all described rather pompously by their tempo markings: *Andante Con Moto* (danced to *Pithecanthropus Erectus*), *Prestissimo* (*O.P.*), *Adagio Ma Non Troppo* (*Myself When I Am Real*), *Pesante* (*Freedom*), *Lento Assai* (*Half-Mast Inhibition*), *Vivace* (*Dizzy's Moods*), *Andantino* (*Diane*), *Scherzo* (*Ysabel's Table Dance*) and *Allegro Marcato* (*Haitian Fight Song*). While the choreography was dismissed by *New York Times* critic Clive Barnes at the premiere ('Good, bad and indifferent, . . . it was also incomprehensible'), he described the music as 'cool, with a sinuous energy. It is at times Oriental in its melodic curves, and always gently beating, unassertively powerful, music with satin muscles rippling unobtrusively, music perfectly pulsed for dance.'[32]

Due acknowledgement of the reality of Mingus's comeback came in December 1971 with his election in the *Down Beat* Readers' Poll to their Hall of Fame, and with a marathon tribute on WKCR-FM which included a two-and-a-half hour live interview, parts of which have already been quoted. During the inevitable section on critics, as well as a sideswipe at ballet writers – 'particularly the guy on the *Times*', he protested that 'I haven't even read a *Down Beat* magazine in ten years, or none of those things, but I picked up one or somebody told me that there was one where I'd won some kind – whatdyacallit? – Hall of Fame.'[33] It must have been at this same time that Mingus did another interview/monologue which formed the notes of a forthcoming album recorded in the autumn, and which included the comment: 'There has never been a contest to decide who is the King of the Trumpet in the Symphony. Or who is the Best Violin Soloist – Jascha Heifitz, Yehudi Menuhin, Isaac Stern, Salvatore Accardo? Or which is the Best String Quartet of the Year – Budapest or Juilliard?'[34] The Columbia album which set the creative seal on Mingus's resurgence was *Let My Children Hear Music,* produced once again by Teo Macero and in many ways a direct follow-up to *Pre-Bird*. Mingus told me that this came about because 'I wanted to do *Chill of Death* only, but [Columbia] said "Why bring musicians in for that one tune? Just do a whole big-band date." And I'd been writing some things for a Guggenheim, you know, that I got. So I decided to do some of those.'

Apart from *The Chill of Death* and two new pieces, Mingus also revisited three items from the 1960s. The track called *Adagio Ma Non Troppo* is, of course, the Jaki Byard orchestration of the originally improvised piano piece *Myself When I Am Real*, played straight with hardly any improvisation and with Mingus's piano (from the original record?) used briefly as one of the orchestral textures, as well as a bowed cello solo by Charles McCracken. This particular session also provided a reunion – of sorts – since Alan Raph, who also conducted, had booked one of his favourite fellow instrumentalists, Jimmy Knepper, to play in the section. As Knepper recalls, 'Mingus didn't say a word, he just sat over in the corner.' But the sight of his former sideman doing a reading gig reminded Mingus that the ballet score had included a transcribed Knepper solo which, according to the classical trombonist who read it, 'was one of the most technical exercises he had ever attempted to play. And he was just playing the notes – not the embellishments or the sound that Jimmy was getting.'[35] Also in connection with these sessions, however, Mingus said of Dannie Richmond: 'I sent for him recently for my record date, and he'd forgotten everything we learned together, so I don't send for him any more.'[36]

The other revivals, *Don't Be Afraid, the Clown's Afraid Too* and *The Shoes of the Fisherman's Wife Are Some Jive Ass Slippers*, the latter a simple(!) retitling of *Once There Was a Holding Corporation*, are expanded orchestrations of the numbers heard on the UCLA album, the only one of the Mingus Enterprises records not already reissued by Fantasy. A chance meeting in copyist Emile Charlap's office resulted in this task being entrusted to Sy Johnson, who had to start by transcribing from the record since no written versions had survived. 'I would go over with questions about something, and he would say "I don't remember," you know. Or he'd sit down at the piano, and take a left-hand turn and wind up with the tune some place other than the way he had written it to start with! So that it was a lot of work to make that music come alive.'[37] But come alive it did, partly due to faster tempos than those of the original performances and partly due to the general excellence of the all-star big band. A lot of work went also into the use (for the first time since *Scenes in the City*) of sound-effects, such as the animal and crowd noises which are so effective on this version of *Don't Be Afraid*. As Mingus explained to me, 'Teo helped me . . . We used the arena sound with the chariot races to get that effect, rather than the circus crowd. 'Cause the circus crowds sounded too shallow, there wasn't any depth to it.'

Of the new pieces written for the Guggenheim fellowship, *Hobo Ho* is 'composed, orchestrated and arranged' by Mingus and merely 'scored' (presumably from Mingus's verbal instructions) by Bobby Jones. Featuring an extended tenor solo (extended in part by repetition at the editing stage) from James Moody, it has an insistent rhythmic figure based on the 'even 8ths' heard on *Folk Forms*, over which Moody frequently uses a half-tempo feeling. It comes closest to capturing the sound of Mingus's medium-sized ensembles, even down to what seems like a quotation from *The Black Saint* in the coda. On the other hand *The I of Hurricane Sue* (not only a typical word-play, but a reference to the childhood nickname 'Hurricane' bestowed on Sue Graham by her brothers) is a more conventional big-band item. But it is distinguished by Sy Johnson's warmly Dameronesque voicings, the sprightly french-horn work of Julius Watkins and by the overdubbed wind effects created by Mingus and Bobby Jones. Johnson recalled that Mingus:

was very supportive and quiet, even through the recording

sessions for the most part. But, once that was over, he turned into a tiger. The first argument we had was to do with arranging credits, and he suddenly turned to me and started yelling at me in the middle of a mixing session up at Columbia, about 'how dare I assume that I was going to get arranging credit for doing these things' . . . We went and got a dictionary to find out what the dictionary definition of 'orchestration' was, as opposed to 'arranging', and we went through this whole ridiculous scene, all so that he could cloud the credits on the album . . . It was very calculated, he knew that he was doing it. As soon as he got approximately what he wanted, he turned into a pussycat again.[38]

Unfortunately, after devoting so much attention to this aspect of the finished album, neither Mingus nor Teo Macero remembered to ensure that the full line-up of participating musicians was listed. Apparently the assistant responsible for this omission 'was moved to a different division of Columbia, because he goofed', Mingus told me matter-of-factly. 'He has a different job now.'

But both Mingus and Macero were sufficiently enthused about the big-band music, as well as the sextet appearances (including an end-of-year stint at the Vanguard during which Julius Watkins's french horn replaced Lonnie Hillyer), that they began planning a big-band concert at Philharmonic Hall on 4 February as a foretaste of the record. Appropriately the actual promoters called themselves New Audiences, for not only was the concert a sell-out but, as Mingus pointed out, 'The ticketron broke and they oversold 300 seats at least, so in a way it gave confidence to promoters to start booking jazz again.' For the most part, this was another retrospective of Mingus's music from *Eclipse* onwards, with an even more 'all-star' line-up including Lee Konitz, Gerry Mulligan and Gene Ammons (plus walk-on parts for James Moody, Randy Weston and a vocal by Dizzy Gillespie!). However, apart from the totally improvised and very effective *Mingus Blues* featuring Ammons, the only new music was a simple sixteen-bar tune at medium tempo called *Us Is Two* and the more ambitious *Little Royal Suite*. Both (like *The I of Hurricane Sue*) are 'back home' in the key of D flat, and, if the latter with its further references to *The Black Saint* seems a trifle bitty, it would have been extremely interesting to hear it played as first conceived – which was as a tribute to and feature for Roy Eldridge. In the event Eldridge went down with laryngitis, and the star role was given to eighteen-year-old newcomer Jon Faddis, 'a newcomer to improvisation actually', according to Mingus. 'At least he said he was before he came in – he sounds like he's been doing it before,' and, as the concert recording shows, the youngster originally hired just to play in the section came through with flying colours. The record also demonstrates that new drummer Joe Chambers, previously known for his sensitive small-group work, was an excellent choice and that the whole concert, though overbalanced by too much amorphous blowing, was undoubtedly an 'event'.

As a result, when the Thad Jones-Mel Lewis band went on a lengthy European tour, Mingus took over their Monday night residency at the Vanguard for seven successive appearances beginning 20 March, followed by the week of 9–14 May, all with slightly differing versions of the big-band line-up heard at Philharmonic Hall. This ensemble also played the last week of June and the first of July at the Mercer Arts Center in New York and, during this period, did two concerts in one night for the Newport Jazz Festival, which had now been transported to the metropolis. (In addition, Mingus's solo involvement in one of the Newport midnight jam-sessions allowed him to repeat the success of *Mingus Blues* with a *Lo-Slo-Bluze* which was capped by the high-note work of retired Ellingtonian Cat Anderson.) At the time that this short-lived big band was getting off the ground, Mingus received one of his only commissions to write something 'classical', or at least not specifically 'jazz', when the Whitney Musuem's concert series called Composers' Showcase concluded on 23 April with a programme of new music inspired by the poetry of the recently deceased Frank O'Hara. The composers involved, who each contributed one short piece, included Aaron Copland, Virgil Thomson and Lukas Foss as well as Jimmy Giuffre and Mingus. His setting of an O'Hara poem for voice and string quartet doubtless replaced the standard two-violins-viola-cello with his preferred instrumentation of two violins and two cellos, and Mingus commented that 'The guys read it at sight. I rehearsed for months with the big band and the music hasn't been played yet. And the string quartet was 9,000 times more difficult.'[39]

His own lengthy European tour, arranged to take in such festivals as Loosdrecht, Châteauvallon and that organized for the Munich Olympics, was of course undertaken with the sextet. And, although during separate weeks at Slug's in March and a club called Fiddlestix in May, the trumpeter had been Charles Sullivan, it was Jon Faddis whom Mingus invited to Europe while the drummer, as at the Newport concert, was now former Horace Silver sideman Roy Brooks. This second European tour of the 1970s, if not quite as action-packed as the 1964 tour, certainly showed Mingus back on form, both musically and personally. Harry Beckett mentions, for instance, that two years earlier in London he had tried to renew acquaintances but Mingus had apparently not recognized him, whereas this time Mingus greeted him with an expansive '*Sure* I remember you!' Ronnie Scott, at whose club the group played another two weeks and two days, recalls that one day Mingus received an income tax demand arising out of his previous visit: 'We said "Well, don't worry about it, it'll all be taken care of," but he was really quite concerned about receiving this very official letter. And he went on the bandstand . . . and went up to the microphone – everybody went quiet – and Mingus said "I've just had a letter from your Queen!" '

One of the many interviews he gave this time round, in fact for BBC-TV, betrays a temporary estrangement from Sue Graham (who confirms 'That was a particularly tempestuous period' and chuckles in recollection of their up-and-down relationship). But Mingus sounded quite forlorn when mentioning 'my woman' and then in the same breath correcting this to 'my manager – my *ex*-manager'.[40] However, as usual when American bands tour Europe or Japan where they are inevitably more in demand than at home, it was not only the leader who was giving interviews and, as a result of statements to the press by Bobby Jones, friction between the musicians was on the increase. Indeed, in the same BBC-TV interview, Mingus brought up the problem of 'my saxophone player':

> This happened over and over again, he would insult me and say – to an audience – 'You beat me out of some money.' What he means is I didn't pay him in the time he thought he should get paid, 'cause he's not counting the days the way I have to count them . . . Plus he'll say 'Nigger', you know, and the whole band – the drummer wants to fight him right now . . . I don't know if Bobby knows how serious it's gotten, because it's not only me that feels this way, some other guys in the band feel it, that he's not one of us. I mean, we're not trying to be one of him, we're trying to just play music together as we're hired to do. And it's too bad there's still a racial thing going on. Because he does interpret the music, and sometimes more than the other guys, 'least what I write.[41]

However, at the Bilzen Jazz Festival the following week, writer Bert Vuijsje observed the end of this problem with the 'wilfully recalcitrant' Jones, when 'Mingus pelted his sideman with several handfuls of onions, a cucumber and a plastic bag full of food. "I'll break your back" were his last words.'[42] Probably as a direct result of this incident, Jon Faddis too departed before the tour was over and, by the time of the Châteauvallon Festival, McPherson was the only front-line player, with Mingus's son Eugene, originally taken along as road manager, making up the numbers on conga. For the final dates in Aarhus and at the Montmarte, it was Copenhagen resident Dexter Gordon who sat in alongside McPherson, playing the trumpet parts on tenor! Then, the tour over, McPherson also left the band, and for the last time.

All of which should not obscure the fact that immediately prior to this, and perhaps even aided by the growing tension, the band was playing magnificently (which makes one long for the rediscovery of the live tapes said to have been done by British CBS at the Scott Club on 14 and 15 August). The material ranged from favourites such as *Faubus* to a long, exciting, multi-section piece called *Mind Readers' Convention in Milano* to a slow blues featuring John Foster on vocals(!) and drummer Roy Brooks on musical saw(!!), the first two of which formed the highspots of an even-better-than-usual first set on the night of 12 August. To my great good fortune, this put Mingus in excellent spirits for my own extended dressing-room interview between sets, snippets of which have been quoted throughout this book, although this has naturally involved wrenching them from their originally freely associative context. The manner in which the interview was conducted – by Mingus of course, not by me – is instructive in itself; for a start, he had told Charles McPherson to stay behind and participate (during a brief preliminary discussion of my intention to broadcast the interview along with appropriate records, he said 'Are you going to play one of McPherson's too?') and, after answering mainly factual questions about his recent activities, he not only steered us into the realms of opinion but often allowed McPherson to 'solo' at some length first, before engaging him in a dialogue and finally using this momentum to launch into his own solo statement.

It was when the subject of God came up in answer to my question about Eric Dolphy that Mingus really got into his stride:

There must be something right about Jesus, or they still wouldn't be talking about him. He must have said something good . . . I heard two doctors on television here, talking about people are ashamed to say 'God' . . . and they're afraid to mention Jesus or Buddha or Allah, they're afraid to say they believe in God. You look funny or corny, but I'm not afraid no more, man. Yeah, I believe in God, I just jumped some bars. And that's what my music is about, man. When we did that arena in Italy, I said 'That's where we belong, right in there where they killed the Christians – for kicks.' I was saying, if I was here now under the conditions those people were in, would I say I didn't believe in God? I hate to tell you, man, I *think* I'd just go down and have to fight the lions. And *might* win – might win.I got a feeling that the lion might say by now, man, 'These cats really believe, man, we better be careful.' [*Laughter*] Not that those were particularly black Christians in those days they were destroying, were they? [*To McPherson*] What's your views on that, man? . . . I think, what I've been through now, especially being fifty, and having believed it and all, they'd have to call [?] one of the guys and send the lions out. 'Cause the way I've lived, I haven't done anything to take revenge on those people who don't believe so, if they're going to destroy me for how I believe, then they've got it! Even though I use a couple of dirty words, I still believe in God, you know . . . And I think now it's time that young kids started realizing there's something else to life too besides baring their breasts – for instance, I notice something in your town that's very sad. The girls wear dresses that they don't *believe* in. See, if they believed in that, they would *be* like that. I notice that some of the women that wear longer dresses, and cover their bodies a little more carefully, are a lot more free and open about sex than the ones who show more. I notice if you look at them – you know, I may be looking at a *flower* in her hair, they be ducking and trying to cover their legs up. So something's wrong, when they walk around like they – they dress a lot more revealing than a prostitute does, 'cause she has to be careful that she don't get busted. So they look worse than prostitutes, I'm not saying it's *sinful*, I mean, but it gets to a point where it's not even beautiful any more, man. It just don't move me no more, man, I don't even look at them no more. I'm trying to do something to make them look at me. Run me a zip up on my shoulder, or something. Put an arrow on my tie, pointing down towards my shoe. You know, what is that? What are they saying? 'Look at my breasts, I don't wear brassieres no more.' So what? I know a woman who said she's very sorry – in Chicago, remember? – she said 'I'm very sorry that I ever took off my brassiere, 'cause now they're down to my navel.' You know, and this is ridiculous 'cause they may not have to be as strong and pull a woman up as they were, but I was told it's healthier if they carry themselves like that, the same as when a man plays football he wears a support for his testicles. Right? If he's going to play any athletic sports, they have this jockstrap they wear so they won't get a rupture. Well, you know, maybe you can get ruptured breasts. I'm not saying I dig that they have no right to do things, they can do anything they want to do. I got a feeling that Women's Lib in America can go as far as they want to go. I think nuns can become popes if they want to, maybe God's a *she*. You know, if they want to run it like that, they can even let the women who wrestle don't wrestle women [but] wrestle men, and they'll find out where they really stand. There *is* a Women's Lib, but they may train a woman with karate or something to beat an ordinary wrestler, but there'll be another karate guy, a man that can still beat her. I'm not saying men are better, it's just that they were born from our rib, weren't they? One rib! They're not as *strong* as we are.

Amid the self-mocking guffaws with which Mingus capped this final twist of his improvisation, the audience of two (plus Charles McPherson) felt the same sense of release as after a particularly audacious bass solo. One final question and answer obviously reminded him of the factual intro to our conversation for, following my gaze as I watched the tape nearing its end, he briefly reprised the main theme which he had outlined much earlier:

Thanks for the interview, I'm glad you – 'cause I got something I want to say that might help somebody to free their kids enough to let them have equal education, instead of just limiting them to the black scene as is, from the past. I say that we're completely right to do anything, we have a right to do it. Give us a chance to be a doctor or lawyer or something else we want to be. Or king or queen or president, you know. '*Least* give them the education for it. Don't limit him to make him think he has to stay the way that [it] looks like he can make a living being a rock singer only, or just a jazz musician. Give him the whole field, he may be another Jascha Heifitz, you know, or Isaac Stern or somebody – I said that already, goodbye!

Conscious of form as ever, Mingus managed to fit his five-word coda on to the last one and a half seconds of my tape.

193

9

Myself When I Am Real

As in 1964 and 1970, although each time for different reasons, Mingus returned from Europe in the summer of 1972 with only half a band. This time he not only bounced back quickly with a new front line but, thanks to George Wein, he very rapidly found himself back in Europe. And, despite the fact that the European tour that autumn turned out to be, shamefully, the last tour on which he was to appear in England, interest in his music on the Continent was such that in the mid-1970s he seemed to spend almost as much time in Europe as at home. Before that, however, he went through a further period of regular personnel turnover which lasted over a year, in order to get a band with the right ingredients once more.

The new line-up which Mingus introduced for the last week of September at the Vanguard retained John Foster and Roy Brooks, while adding a young trumpet discovery, Joe Gardner, and Hamiet Bluiett, the virtuoso baritonist who had arrived in New York from St Louis some three years earlier. Unlike even the younger musicians whom Mingus had used up to this point, Bluiett's allegiance and (such as it was thus far) reputation lay definitely within the field of avant-garde jazz, yet it was clear that Mingus's ear for talent-spotting had not deserted him. Therefore, whereas the sextet which had reached its peak a couple of months earlier had sounded rather traditional (especially compared with the high-speed-electric bands and fellow Columbia artists, Weather Report and John McLaughlin's Mahavishnu Orchestra, both simultaneously making their first European tours), Mingus's new group seemed at least superficially, and particularly in the context of a George Wein package, more far-out than any he had led since the death of Eric Dolphy.

And yet because of his respect for the traditional – no doubt also because the contract called for a six-piece group – Mingus decided to add a guest star for the trip to Europe, in the shape of Cat Anderson. Appearing again in London on 21 October and bringing on his guest after a couple of quintet numbers, Mingus introduced him as 'a musician I've always wanted to play with, the man with the strongest chops in the world'. This personnel enabled him to combine in one slow blues Brooks's musical saw speciality and Anderson's sustained high-note work as heard at the Newport jam-session; the number now closed with a Dixieland-style finale with Bluiett on clarinet and Anderson paying tribute to Louis Armstrong. But Mingus also resurrected *Perdido* in order to give Anderson a plunger-mute workout which was much lengthier and more coherent than any of his feature numbers when with the Ellington band. Just before going on stage to play this number in Berlin (the version now preserved on record), Anderson told me how he welcomed Mingus's invitation to show his versatility and creativity, but that 'Whether I work with him again depends on whether I can get time off' (in other words, from his busy schedule of studio work). Perhaps too, being on the road with George Wein was too much like being on the road with Ellington, for, in the intervening two weeks, he had been from one end of Europe to the other, from Spain to Norway to Yugoslavia to Poland. Whatever the reason, this interesting combination was never repeated.

Another tangential contact with the Ellington orbit had taken place before the European tour on 6 October, during a special ceremony at Yale University. Although Mingus had accepted the patronage of the Guggenheim Foundation, he had not so far received the formal invitations into the groves of academe which (after Black Studies had been given the green light by the actions of the Johnson administration) had seen even Max Roach gain a professorship the previous year. But, on this occasion, Mingus was one of nearly forty major figures invested as Duke Ellington Fellows at the instigation of former professional bassist and french-hornist Professor Willie Ruff. The celebration called for participation in a mammoth jam-session on *How High the Moon* with five other bassists (George Duvivier, Milt Hinton, Joe Benjamin, Slam Stewart and Ray Brown) and four trumpeters including Jon Faddis and Dizzy Gillespie.

It may have been this musically rather chaotic situation which inspired Mingus to renew his playing relationship with Gillespie, by choosing him as the sole guest with the quintet for a second New Audiences concert, this time at Carnegie Hall. But shortly before this event on 19 January two personnel changes had taken place within the quintet. The first, on Roy Brooks's recommendation, was the hiring of Don Pullen, whose critical reputation as an avant-garde player in the mid-1960s had been supplemented by commercial gigs on both piano and organ (including records on the latter instrument with one Charles Williams), and who for the next three years was to help revitalize Mingus's music. Meanwhile writer Gary Giddins, attending a press-conference-cum-public-rehearsal for Carnegie Hall, reported that 'When Charles has a problem . . . he likes to hit you over the head with it. The group's saxophonist, it seems, isn't making the music. Emergency action is called for and Howard Johnson . . . is inducted as a replacement.'[1] The concert itself, once again a sell-out, was not only enlivened by Johnson (who played baritone with even more facility than his better-known tuba work) but highlighted by Gillespie's contribution to a new Mingus 'tribute', *Profile of Dizzy*. And, as well as Dizzy-associated bebop repertoire such as *Wee* and *Woody'n You*, Mingus chose to revive both *Pithecanthropus Erectus* and *Fables of Faubus*, now retitled *Fables of Nixon* to mark the start of the President's second term.

Since Howard Johnson was only available for the concert and its rehearsals, there was now a vacancy in the saxophone department which led to brief tryouts for players such as John Stubblefield (a former Chicagoan colleague of Pullen) and, possibly also at this period, Sam Rivers. In two interviews the following year, Mingus spoke of enjoying both Rivers's work with him and that of trumpeter Marcus Belgrave, who had been in his big band but was unable to accept gigs on a regular basis for the money that Mingus could have offered him. However, by the time the quintet did two weekends in March at the Village Gate, it had acquired the redoubtable George Adams who (like Sam Rivers) had played in everything from contemporary jazz groups to primitive blues bands. Reviewing this quintet the following month at Howard University, Don Locke said of Adams that:

These apparently disparate elements were welded together into a unified style, and used with complete control, so that his solos would move from relaxed moments of an almost mainstream quality to passages of frenzied avant-garde wailing and bleating, and back again, with no sense of discontinuity . . . There is more variety in Adams's playing, more control, more movement from idiom to idiom even with a single phrase, so that it is no longer appropriate to think of them as separate idioms.[2]

This approach was not only clearly in line with Mingus's own thinking but did much to prove, to sceptical audiences and writers and indeed to Mingus himself, the continuing validity of his music in the 1970s. A factor which immediately emphasized Adams's role was that there was now some instability in the trumpet chair, for Joe Gardner had left and been replaced by Charles McGhee and then by Lonnie Hillyer, who by the middle of 1973 had in turn been replaced by Ronald Hampton. At this period also, the group briefly expanded to a sextet with the addition of altoist Bob Mover, but sometimes it was just a quartet; as Adams has said, 'I can remember being out on the road and the cats would get bad with Mingus and the next thing I know I would come to the gig and there wouldn't be nobody there but me . . . and the rhythm section.'[3]

Shortly after Adams had joined the band, two other things happened which were both in different ways extremely encouraging signs. The Five Spot Café, now rechristened the Two Saints (not after the Termini brothers but after the address, 2 St Mark's Place), had re-opened its doors to jazz and in April gave the new group a chance to settle in with an extended engagement, for which Mingus cancelled a previous booking at the Vanguard. And during the same month he signed a new exclusive recording contract with the company which had first boosted his career when he was playing at the original Five Spot, namely Atlantic. The fact that the first album to be released under this contract was a reissue, *The Art of Charles Mingus – The Atlantic Years*, is significant for two reasons. For a start, with the exception of the unique circumstances governing Mingus's relationship with Fantasy, it was still most unusual for a reissue of any kind to alter the financial terms under which the material was first recorded. The reappearance of a selection of Mingus classics concurrent with the signing of a new contract acknowledged that he deserved to earn more from them than he had originally commanded anything up to seventeen years earlier. And, of course, it shows that Mingus was not bursting to record a new band and a bunch of new compositions as he had been, for instance, at his last Atlantic session in November 1961.

Details of his live appearances around this period show little evidence of new quintet or sextet material, with the exception of the unrecorded *Portrait of Dizzy*, and the reason may be a change in his compositional interests, which could have been reinforced by his work on the big-band recordings of the early 1970s. Certainly, as he entered the sixth decade of his life, his preferred listening had become concentrated on the peaks of musical experience, such as Ellington and Beethoven ('I like Beethoven string quartets, I like No. 9 [Op.59 No.3] and 12 [Op. 127]'),[4] and he often cited his earlier loves Ravel and Debussy, sometimes adding his more recently acquired taste for Indian music. His joint interview with Charles McPherson included the following passage:

> Bach is still the most difficult of any music played, man. It may not be atonal or dissonant, but you don't find guys playing it. And I ain't heard no jazz cats do it yet – not even on piano . . . I know, what's that piano player who played on my date?* – Hank [Roland] Hanna – I asked him to *improvise* some Bach I heard him play at home. He had to bring the *book*! Yet he's a great piano player and a great composer, he hasn't done it yet! . . . So that must be the baddest cat going. 'Cause a lot of guys come close to Stravinsky and Schoenberg and Bartok, a lot of *critics* say they do. But I ain't heard nobody say 'That cat has cut Bach' yet.

And certainly, in principle, Mingus felt ready to rise to the implicit challenge. At the time of receiving the Guggenheim Fellowship, he had begun work on an 'operatic ballet' which would incorporate 'jazz' and 'classical music'. Showing the other side of the coin to the comments above, he had said:

> Of course, there always has to be improvisation in it. A really creative improvisatory solo can be as priceless as Bach or Beethoven. And obviously, if you leave space for improvisers in a symphony, it's going to be different every time it's performed. But to have *that* kind of symphony played as it ought to be requires more so-called jazz players who actually compose as they improvise . . . So I've been working on developing new kinds of lines – foundations for improvising inside a composition – that will make it impossible for a musician to slip back into playing something he's used to in order to fill the time . . . But I want to get to the point where everyone playing something of

*Probably a reference to recording *The Shoes of the Fisherman's Wife* mine will be able to think in terms of creating a *whole*, will be able to improvise compositionally so that it will be hard to tell where the writing ends and the improvisation begins . . . When I get enough players who can do that, I'll be able to write that two-hour symphony that's been in my head – all the parts of my life, like a book.[5]

And, in pursuit of this elusive goal, Mingus explained to the listeners of WKCR-FM:

Thank God that, in jazz, they've improved the virtuosity of the instruments, mainly the trumpet. I say 'mainly the trumpet' because that's the most obvious. Everybody white knows that the trumpet is not gonna go over B flat, and yet Louis Armstrong busted Gs and As back in the 1800s, you know . . . For instance, I'm saying that like hiring Dizzy Gillespie with the Boston Symphony isn't enough. They should have hired Dizzy to orchestrate for them and everything – [let] the whole thing be Dizzy – not just stand out in front and play a solo. When that day comes, . . . you gonna have to change your trumpet men 'cause you gotta get a first man like Snooky Young . . . He *is* the greatest, man. Well, there's a slight touch between he and Ernie Royal, but I'm thinking about a guy who doesn't just solo, does everything the white man wants to do and does it better.[6]

Obviously the combination of virtuosity and accuracy, of interpretive and improvisatory ability possessed by such a top studio musician prompted Mingus's 1970 nomination of his front line for an 'ideal band' as 'Ernie Royal, Jerome Richardson, Jaki Byard and it would have to be Dannie Richmond. Elvin and Max couldn't – or wouldn't – play my music.'[7]

How much of Mingus's more ambitious music of the 1970s was performed (like the Composers' Showcase arrangement for the Whitney Museum string quartet, repeated at the 1972 Newport Festival) but not recorded, or rehearsed but not performed (apparently the case with some new material intended for Philharmonic Hall in 1972) – let alone how much was conceived in the mind but not successfully organized on paper– is difficult to assess. In 1964, he said 'I've written a symphony for a 120-piece orchestra, and the music is lying around the house in piles. But I can't see any opportunity to present it.'[8] This comment was made, however, in the same interview during which he claimed his brother had been lynched, so this may be the same symphony which in late 1971 was 'in his head'. In any case, if the music had been lying around the house in 1964, it would doubtless have been destroyed in the course of his eviction. What is certain is that the talents of the 'ideal band' were somewhat different from the very real qualities of the current working group, who had initially found themselves playing Mingus standards and whom he gradually felt the need to challenge with some new pieces. Both Adams and Pullen began to write for the band too, as throughout 1973 they kept busy with a full programme of college concerts, club dates as far away as Houston, and festival appearances including 'Newports' in New York, Los Angeles and Boston; the Pittsburgh Jazz Festival; and Ann Arbor in September, by which time the Mingus blues speciality which had been changing shape for eighteen months included a vocal by George Adams. Significantly, one more personnel change was to occur before Mingus felt ready to record once more. 'I hadn't seen the paper but Tommy Eyre, the pianist, had, and he told us that Mingus was playing at the Vanguard. We decided to go by there when we had finished. When we walked in the Vanguard, I turned around to go in the back and met Mingus in the kitchen doorway. He said, "I had a dream last night that my drummer was coming back and here he is!" '[9] Dannie Richmond had returned, and as he remembers he joined his mentor almost immediately, replacing Doug Hammond, who had taken over from Roy Brooks. He also mentions that, according to Don Pullen, Mingus had periodically said to the band during the preceding months, 'Man, everything would be alright if Dannie would just come back.'

Although Pullen was very soon to discover exactly what Mingus had meant, the album *Mingus Moves* hardly represents what this band could do. Elsewhere Dannie has stated that recording began within two days of his visit to the Vanguard, and that 'I had no time to learn the arrangements. If the album has faults, it's because of me.'[10] But it has to be said that Mingus's own playing is not all that lively, or even accurate, in places. In addition the material, at least as performed here, is strangely backward-looking, with a vocal by Honey Gordon and an *Opus 3* which adds a boppish new line over the *Pithecanthropus Erectus* format but misses the atmosphere of the original. *Opus 4* is in the same tempo and key as *Opus 3* and begins with the same four-bar turnaround, but the opening track *Canon* is even more of a disappointment: a throwback to some of the more sterile contrapuntal exercises of the mid-1950s, its choice of key and tone-colours make it sound like a pastiche of Coltrane's

Alabama. While the above three pieces by Mingus himself would make a respectable if restrained half-album, the impact seems more diffused by the inclusion of material by other composers such as Pullen's *Newcomer*, written to celebrate the birth of a daughter. This would have been even truer of his Bo Diddley-inspired *Big Alice and John Henry*, later known as *Sophisticated Alice*, which remained unreleased although part of the band's working repertoire.

Before this album was released in April 1974, Mingus had been recorded again at the third of his annual New York concerts, this one featuring a number of fairly famous alumni. The regular small group, which played the first half, was marked by the return in January of Hamiet Bluiett in place of the trumpeter, although Jon Faddis made up the numbers to a sextet for one night only. And then Charles McPherson, John Handy (who had sat in with Mingus at the Two Saints eight months earlier) and Rahsaan Roland Kirk joined the band for lengthy jamming on *Perdido, C Jam Blues* and a 'free' encore which went on for several minutes and which, like the first half of the concert, has not been issued on record. What was issued is fun, but once again hardly indicative of the qualities of the regular quintet, especially now that Bluiett was working alongside the man who had indirectly replaced him, George Adams. A review by Bill Smith of a Toronto performance on the night of Mingus's fifty-second birthday listed *Fables of Nixon, Goodbye Pork Pie Hat, Oui Oui Mademoiselle, Celia, Peggy's Blue Skylight,* an Adams vocal blues and *Big Alice* among the tunes played, and exclaimed:

> And that FRONT LINE . . . created such a stir with their passion cry that the whole week turned into some kind of black sanctified ceremony. It seems weird now in retrospect that the man who had done so much to create bebop music was here again, this time helping to untie the threads and let it be free. Even when the set ended with one of bop's national anthems, *Cherokee*, it was a wild humorous version quite unlike what we had always presumed it to be.[11]

Although Smith's presumptions were in some respects twenty years out of date or just plain wrong, his comments are instructive in that they typify the positive reactions of many people who only came to grips with Mingus in the 1970s, sometimes at rock venues like Max's Kansas City, which he played in 1973. This certainly in no way detracted from Mingus's growing reputation as a father figure, capable of spanning the history of the music and several generations of its listeners.

But the creative tension within a group of musicians who span the generations can easily spill over into personal tension, especially perhaps with all the seniority concentrated in the reunited bass-and-drums team and all the principal soloists being younger and more free-thinking. One tiny musical detail of the kind that can split an improvising band down the middle emerges in Mingus's answer to writer John Litweiler, who asked whether a soloist in *Pithecanthropus Erectus/Opus 3* can end the extended modal sections when he chooses: 'He has a musical cue, like a conductor does it. The drummer does it.' (The fact that 'On the record, piano does it'[12] merely shows that the audibility of the acoustic piano in a studio is not usually equalled in a live performance, hence the 'conducting' role of the drums.) Probably for reasons such as this rather than purely personal matters Don Pullen, who in fact remained with the group until the autumn of 1975, said after his departure: 'I had enough after the first month! . . . There was a lot of strength in that band, coming mainly from the horns. Bluiett, George Adams, both extraordinary musicians. I hope they'll soon be able to do their own thing the way they want to.'[13] Bluiett, for his part, has said 'I dug [Mingus] and he dug me, but I had some serious emotional problems at that time . . . I would play something that I thought was out of sight, and people would be looking at me like they wanted to kill me. I was twisted, and turned, and tormented, and I didn't show up for some of Mingus's gigs because I was afraid to play for people because of the way they reacted.'[14] When Bluiett left for the last time during an engagement in Chicago in October 1974, Mingus betrayed somewhat mixed feelings about his current soloists in an interview the following day: 'It's not gonna hurt me how they play a solo, if they're avant-garde, or weird, or whatever. What I'm saying is I don't have to like them as soloists. They just have to be able to play my music as it's written . . . Baritone player walked off the job, quit last night, on the third set. Said he didn't like playing that long. I didn't like him, to tell the truth.'[15]

Mingus's choice of a replacement on his return to New York was surprising, as usual. Recommended by Paul Jeffrey (the saxophonist and arranger who had collaborated with Monk in the early 1970s), trumpeter Jack Walrath was the product of a new generation of white musicians in that, after graduating from Berklee, he had elected on the one hand to play avant-garde jazz and on the other to work with black soul acts such as the Motown Revue and the Ray Charles Band. His forthright open tone and frequently bop-based lines, as well as the cardinal requirement for this group of being willing to take risks, seem to have stimulated George Adams to be even more of an all-rounder, and, without diminishing the tenorist's role as the superior soloist, to have effected an immediate shift in the stylistic balance of power between soloists and rhythm section. Certainly Dannie Richmond, who in interviews has described the band with Dolphy, Johnny Coles, Clifford Jordan and Jaki Byard as the First Band In Jazz, now says 'When there was finally Don, George, Jack, Mingus and myself, that in my opinion was something like the Second Band.' Reviewing the new line-up the following month in Montreal, Ron Sweetman noted that 'Mingus is composing again,'[16] and, as well as showing that the only items used from the *Mingus Moves* album were those by other writers, logged performances of Walrath's *Autumn on Neptune, Peggy's Blue Skylight, Just for Laughs Saps, Sue's Changes, Duke Ellington's Sound of Love,* and Sy Johnson's *For Harry Carney*. And the last four formed the main highlights of the *Changes* set recorded at the end of 1974, the year in which first Duke and then Harry Carney had died.

Mingus's last recorded tribute to his idol, already in the repertoire before Bluiett left, was cut in two different versions, the shorter featuring vocalist Jackie Paris dubbed over an arrangement by Sy Johnson. The lyric was clearly composed after the melody, and works better (with the exception of the last two lines) as a lyric than as a poem, unlike the equivalent eulogy of Parker quoted earlier, but it is interesting for its autobiographical flavour:

> I was young and carefree, / Not a song had found my soul,
> Lost in blues, jazz and ragtime, / No sound had got to my mood,
> I was searching for my melody, / Love blues that gets me wooed.
> All alone, sad clown with his circus closed down,
> Lost on my merry-go-round,
> Came a melody in my heart so yearning, / Taught me to hear
>   music out of love
> From the soul, for this life / We all live infinite,
> With a lover and beloved / As one Ellington sound of love.[17]

To complete the reverential tone, the last word is changed on the closing chorus to 'God' and the languorous, long-lined melody (see Appendix B) actually sounds as if it could have been written by Ellington – or at least by Billy Strayhorn. In fact, most unusually for

Mingus, there is a deliberate quotation in bar 3 of B which, although intended to be Ellingtonian, is from Strayhorn's *Lush Life*. The melody of 'Taught me to hear music out of love' (bar C9) comes from the *Blues* in *Black, Brown and Beige*, whereas the notes 'infinite' (bars C13–14) allude to that other famous Strayhorn item, *Take the 'A' Train*. The slower instrumental version of this important addition to the D flat series, although apparently shorn of a trumpet solo (the splice betrays a slight drop in tempo), does include a George Adams tribute to the school of ballad playing founded by Ben Webster (who himself had died a little over a year earlier) and extended by Paul Gonsalves; and there is a passionately elegiac bass solo from the composer.

While Mingus like many writers frequently quoted himself in his music, he did not often do so in the same utterance, so to speak. But, for some reason, bars C9–14 of *Duke Ellington's Sound of Love* are echoed by bars 5–16 of the fast-medium tempo tune originally called *Just for Laughs Saps* and now retitled *Remember Rockefeller at Attica*, whose fifty-one-bar chorus consists of forty-two bars' continuous melodic invention plus a repeat of the first nine bars; Mingus's only comment in the publicity interview concerning this album was 'I like this feeling of the quarter[-note] triplet, like a waltz against 4/4,'[18] which he illustrated by singing the opening phrase as if it was in 6/4. Unusually too, the companion piece (labelled *Free Cell Block F, 'Tis Nazi USA*, which looks like a challenge to anagram-lovers) contains six isolated bars of 5/4, possibly the only instance of this time-signature in Mingus's writing. If the evidence of Mingus's 1975 concert announcements is taken as the criterion, then the titles assigned to these two pieces were accidentally reversed on the record as issued, but speaking later about such titles, Mingus said: 'I just write tunes, and put political titles on them. *Fables of Faubus* was different, though – I wrote that because I wanted to. And Dannie made the words up and started calling it *Fables of Nixon*.'[19] What a shame that the President, who still had several months to go before resigning, probably never heard this tribute – unless he had a private tape – for the new lyrics concocted since Dannie's return went unrecorded. But the blues vocal featured on and off for the past couple of years, firstly with John Foster, was captured in George Adams's rendition of *Devil Blues* with its lyrics by Gatemouth Brown (whose own recording was entitled *The Drifter*); this performance, drawing on the rhythm-and-blues experience of the players without patronizing Mingus's widening audience, can be seen as the belated fulfilment of his early commercial efforts such as *Ain't Jivin' Blues*.

If the three new Mingus compositions mentioned above, with the long titles and even longer phrases, show an almost unstoppable flow of melody, then the *pièce de résistance* of this period is *Sue's Changes*, the second portrait of Ms Graham (or possibly the third, for she points out the word-play of the 1965 title *They Trespass the Land of the Sacred Sioux*). Originally called *Sue's Moods*, it is basically in D flat and it is worth noting that, among others, *The I of Hurricane Sue, Celia* and *(God's) Portrait* all share the same key-centre, while *Diane* was in C. Its mammoth chorus-structure (see Appendix B) is even longer than the fictitious 'eighty-eight-bar chorus', and melodically it is remarkable for a number of subliminal quotations. The tightly-voiced, high-pitched A theme is (coincidentally?) quite similar to *Portrait*, and the B and D strains respectively seem to borrow their initial ideas from the old pop tunes *With a Smile and a Song* and *No Two People*, while Sy Johnson has intimated that Mingus's original version of B was unintentionally closer to *The Things We Did Last Summer*![20] Nevertheless, what is really impressive is the linking of these melodies through the carefully orchestrated changes of texture and sometimes of tempo, and the fact that, as in *Pithecanthropus* or the unrecorded *Mind Readers' Convention in Milano*, each soloist has to negotiate the entire progression of moods from A through to the mandatory freak-out on E^1, often incorporating lengthy out-of-tempo spots in live performance. Jack Walrath, who does not solo on the record but can be heard doing so on concert versions, has said 'Your solo would last fifteen, twenty minutes and he'd always expect you to be all-out the whole time. And I found that's where the challenge was – just to keep the chops happening, you know.'[21]

Early in the new year, the quintet played a further Carnegie Hall concert with Milt Jackson, newly released from the bondage of the Modern Jazz Quartet, as guest, and then made a hit in Europe. Before this there had been one short trip to Italy in July 1974 including an appearance at the Umbria Jazz Festival, following which Mingus had undertaken a rigorous weight-reducing course at a health farm. Nevertheless John Litweiler, whose interview was done on the autumn tour which took the band to Chicago, reports that Mingus was still overweight and that even talking seemed difficult for him; despite attempting to keep to a meat-free diet, he ended a huge Chinese meal still feeling hungry and going in search of a Mexican restaurant. During the interview Mingus pointed out that he felt obliged to do a lot of touring 'because Dannie Richmond wants to make money'; however, 'I can't get enough money to have a valet to help carry the musicians' instruments around. Me and Dannie do all that work . . . I fly everywhere I go: it cost me a thousand dollars to come out here, over a thousand dollars' worth of tickets.'[22] Practical considerations such as these must have made Mingus aware that, if for nothing but financial reasons, his reunion with Richmond would not last forever. And Richmond recalls that, since rejoining Mingus, 'More and more he'd say "Dannie, what about the tickets?" or "Dannie, does the man know where we're going?" And one day he said "Do you know why I'm asking you to do all of these things for me? . . . Well, I've always had you under my wing, what I'm doing is grooming you to have your own band. These are the things that you're gonna have to do." '

These duties were obviously more onerous on the foreign tours such as the return visit to Italy in March 1975, including two nights at the Bergamo Festival, and the summer tour of Europe lasting all of five weeks from 26 June to early August which, as well as festivals such as those at Montreux and Antibes, took in several more dates in Italy. Whether Mingus enquired into the reasons or not, he must have been pleased to discover a whole new audience in Italy which had been created largely because, in the regions governed by the Italian Communist Party, considerable subsidies were now available for promoting the 'music of the people'. But his reputation in the marketplace was also at its highest yet and, back in the land of free enterprise, he stayed for a further five weeks in August and September at the Village Gate. And even George Wein, despite Mingus's lengthy presence in Europe during the summer, signed him up for his own series of European concerts in the autumn. Philippe Carles of *Jazz Magazine* noted that the concerts in Paris, and doubtless on the rest of the tour, were 'with the exception of *Fables of Faubus/Nixon* . . . a live version of the new double album *Changes*',[23] while agreeing with reviewers in other cities that Mingus's were the outstanding sets of the respective festivals. In Berlin, reviewer Herbert Lindenberger observed that Mingus was on form in another sense, for 'Backstage he picked a row about the television recording, comparing it with the gassing of the Jews by the Nazis and the exploitation of the Negroes by the Jews.'[24]

On the other hand this sort of behaviour must by now have been less typical. Sue Graham recalls that, after fully recovering from the efforts of the medical profession, 'As he got older, I think he got a longer view of some things. He spoke a great deal less than he had. You know, like Charlie Parker, "If you have to ask, you don't know." He got to the point, I think, of just being somewhat disinterested in what many people had to say and, if it didn't interest him, he sat like a Buddha and didn't say anything.' In addition, he had given up any pretence of leading a separate existence from Sue, and was settled in happy domesticity with her and her two children, Roberto and Susanna. And whether it was a conscious result of growing older or merely a natural acquiescence in his own ability to exploit others, he allowed himself to relax and place his reliance on Sue while at home, just as he was doing with Dannie when on the road. Dannie says, 'He just stopped as far as having things to say to other women, and was now totally dependent on Susan Graham . . . It got to the point where it was "Oh, *Sue!*" for everything.' Although it was the logical outcome for Mingus, now more genuinely stable than at perhaps any other time in his life, he showed that he was still capable of apparent spontaneity when, suddenly in 1975, he decided to get married again. As Sue told Mike Zwerin, 'We were married by Allen Ginsberg. One day Charles just said: "Hey, man, marry us." So Allen chanted for about an hour.'[25]

Mingus clearly felt that the best way to celebrate his new marital status was to continue working as much as possible. One of the fruits of this policy was a four-day stint in December 1975 at another rock-biz showcase, the Bottom Line, but at the same time the 'Second Band', after a year of steady working (which was more quantitatively than any previous Mingus group), was beginning to break up. Already before the George Wein tour, Don Pullen had left and been replaced briefly by former Yusef Lateef pianist Hugh Lawson, but he rapidly gave way to Danny Mixon, whose first gig with the band was a trip to San Francisco. He was with Mingus when in March 1976 he undertook yet another tour of Italy, one purpose of which was to record the soundtrack music of a film directed by Elio Petri called *Todo Modo*. As well as a mournful link theme, the music written for a ten-piece group (and written without seeing either the finished film or the script) includes a jaunty medium-tempo blues and a very slightly disguised *Peggy's Blue Skylight* which contains a higher-pitched and more loquacious bass solo than usual for this period. It also included a couple of solo spots for George Adams, one planned and one unplanned. Explaining that the story of the film concerned a series of political murders, without elaborating on his statement that this was somehow connected with Mingus's music not being used on the final soundtrack, Adams says:

I had a tenor solo during the part where a murder was being

207

committed, and I remember them telling me how to play. 'Play real forceful, and play like you're a matador hoping to kill the bull,' you dig . . . And after that particular thing we had the organ and the funeral and all that, you know . . . After we had recorded the music, then they had some more time and they . . . had Mingus and I play a bass/flute duet.

Although Adams was shortly to leave the quintet in order to join Gil Evans, when he next saw the by-then fatally ill Mingus more than two years later the bassist had been listening frequently to this improvised duet. Mingus greeted him with the words: 'George Adams, you played your ass off on that last date!'

Back in the States Mingus had several prestigious festival gigs lined up including the New Orleans Festival in mid-April, preceded by three days at Keystone Korner in San Francisco, and at the end of the month he made one of his last solo appearances on the anniversary of Duke Ellington's birthday at the New York Cathedral Church St John The Divine. Among those taking part were the former Ellington band now directed by Mercer Ellington, whose twenty-two-year-old saxophonist Ricky Ford (an alumnus of New England Conservatory, where he had made his recording debut under the baton of Gunther Schuller and gigged with one of his tutors, Jaki Byard) immediately became a new member of Mingus's band. His replacement of Adams, who was only four years younger than Dannie Richmond, emphasized even more Richmond's comparative seniority and his loyalty, since most band-leaders of Mingus's generation (such as Art Blakey or Miles Davis) were surrounded entirely by sidemen less than half their age. Now turned forty, Richmond's role even extended to taking an avuncular interest in the welfare of the rest of the group and, according to Danny Mixon, he got on particularly well with the next oldest member, thirty-year-old Jack Walrath. 'With Jack he's always putting on this act of an old black hipster telling a young greenhorn how it is – all for his own good. Jack is knocked out by this and makes like he's going along with it all until, very politely, very gently, he gives Dannie the bum's rush!'[26]

This new line-up played the latest Berkeley Festival in May and, with some important additions, the Newport Festival at the end of June. The Mingus concert at Carnegie Hall consisted of three sets; the first, by his small group, included *Sue's Changes, Goodbye Pork Pie Hat, Remember Rockefeller* and *Fables of Nixon* (who was certainly well remembered in this election year) and was followed by the flamenco dancing of the Azucena Y Edo group, whose singer Manolo Correa and two guitarists Guillermo Rios and Roberto Reyes then joined the Mingus sextet for a combined performance of *Tijuana Table Dance*. The composer's group was a sextet for the occasion because, doubtless recalling his important contribution to the original record, Mingus had called up Jimmy Knepper quite out of the blue and asked if he could make the date. Another link with the recorded version was that it was Ysabel Morel, for whom the piece had been retitled, who although not taking part herself had put Mingus in touch with the flamenco dance group when he was assembling the Carnegie cast. Apparently the inspiration for this presentation had come from a stopover in Barcelona on the tour the previous autumn, where Mingus had been very impressed by the dancing. According to Burt Goldblatt the first two sets were sufficienty exciting that the finale was a case of 'spontaneous combustion. The rhythms even propelled the giant proportions of Mingus to contribute a few choice movements at the close of the programme.'[27] Rewarded with a huge standing ovation, Mingus must have felt gratified that the highlight of the Bicentennial Year festival was a fusion of black and Mexican music organized by a 'yellow' outcast who claimed to be descended from President Lincoln.

But his spontaneous terpsichore at Carnegie Hall was to be one of the last signs of physical abandonment on Mingus's part. Another six-week European tour in August and September left him feeling quite exhausted, and indeed a photograph taken at the Châteauvallon, very near the start of the tour, shows a weariness and even anguish in Mingus's face much greater than that associated with merely wheeling a bass offstage. And it must have been for physical reasons that he had now begun using a pick-up on the bridge of his instrument, for he still had very ambivalent feelings about the desirability of such a move. A couple of months later, he answered a question from Arnold Jay Smith: 'You can't bow electric bass. The acoustic kind with a pickup is another story, but you can't bend it because once you put in that amplifier you can't bend your notes . . . Once a microphone touches that wood, the wood is no longer wood. It's something beyond human control.'[28] Hearing the somewhat ugly sound of his bass on Mingus's 1977 recordings, one can only agree and assume that he no longer felt able to cut through his acoustic group with his own acoustic tone. David Wild's review of an Ann Arbor concert (broadcast by National Public Radio) from February 1977, by which date Mixon had been replaced by pianist Bob Neloms, reported that 'the improvisatory fire comes more from the sidemen than from the bassist himself'. He also described how, in order to reach the stage, 'Mingus, his way lit by student-volunteers with flashlights, led his sidemen down the aisles like an aging disillusioned evangelist with three blank-faced acolytes. His remarks were delivered in the familiar fast, slurred style, but the voice has grown breathy and hoarse, like a shadowy echo of the more vibrant past.'[29] The fact that there were only three acolytes on this occasion is explained by the absence of Dannie Richmond – unlike his absences in the early 1960s, this one was caused by the death of both his parents.

Strangely enough, just as in 1966, Mingus had recently passed up an opportunity to play in a pianoless trio with Max Roach, although this time for markedly different reasons. Towards the end of the European tour Mingus's band had played on 11 September at an open-air gala organized by the French Communist Party alongside the groups of Roach and Archie Shepp (the latter including Mal Waldron, now resident in Europe). Max has recounted that 'After the tour was over, the Young Italian Communist Party asked us if we could do something. While we were negotiating that, Mao died. Mingus backed out because he had just signed a heavy contract with Atlantic, so he said he couldn't do it,'[30] with the result that Shepp and Roach performed and subsequently recorded as a duo. In speaking of Mingus's relationships with record companies, Richmond points out that: 'It was only in the end when he got back with Atlantic that everything was like they said. In fact, they did more than what they said they were going to do.' And, with this renewal of his contract, Mingus seems to have gained more in the way of studio budgets and promotional budgets, while at the same time coming under some pressure to play something which would reach a wider audience. This is clearly the rationale behind the inclusion in the early 1977 sessions of *Nobody Knows* (based on the spiritual *Nobody Knows the Trouble I've Seen*) and the versions of Mingus's 'greatest hits' *Goodbye Pork Pie Hat* and *Better Git It in Your Soul*, the latter with choral effects led by the composer himself. Doubtless it also explains some of the additions to the regular quintet, namely jazz-rock guitarists (and Atlantic artists) Larry Coryell and Philip Catherine.

According to Gary Giddins, 'When Mingus first heard the tapes, he was contemptuous and sent a scathing telegram to his producer, accusing the label of making him look ridiculous. When the record [*Three or Four Shades of Blues*] outsold all his others [50,000 units in a couple of months], he changed his mind.'[31] The long title track, the only arrangement not farmed out to Paul Jeffrey, is interesting for its attempt to link various kinds of twelve-bar sequences, including that of the opening theme which is hardly a blues at all. The so-called 'Ellingtonian' two-chord blues, which is heard three times, relates to Mingus's own *Blue Cee*, while the element of deliberate pastiche only really comes off in the Kansas City section and the 'superbebop' sequence. This, moving around the key-cycle in order to arrive at $B\flat 7$ in the fifth bar, begins a blues in F with an opening chord of $F\sharp m\flat 5$, which is also the opening chord of Mendelssohn's *Wedding March* (included by Mingus as an example of 'Caucasian white folks' blues'). Although Mingus had so often in the past shown himself capable of taking the influence of Ellington and bebop as the inspiration for something more 'Mingusian' than it was derivative of anything else, the incorporation of pastiche and even parody into this work seems rather ill-digested. And though some passages are an excellent illustration of his statement 'I used to play avant-garde bass when nobody else did; now I play 4/4 because none of the other bass players do,'[32] the piece does not flow as well as his other episodic compositions, including the contemporaneous *Cumbia and Jazz Fusion*.

Issued after *Three or Four Shades of Blues* and thus benefiting commercially from the success of the latter, *Cumbia* is a superior achievement, fit to be placed alongside *Tijuana Table Dance*. Although inspired not by personal experience but by another Italian film script, it takes the equally Spanish-influenced music of Colombia as a starting-point and builds it into a twenty-eight-minute composition that – unlike *Music for Todo Modo* or most other film scores, which seem to be written as a series of separate events – is continuously compelling. Beginning with the sounds of birdsong and ethnic percussion, it introduces a couple of particularly folky themes on the oboes, the second of which is underpinned by the first of a series of modal bass-figures. The first one is based on the alternation of $Bm7(\flat 5)$ and E7, which lasts for six minutes and contradicts the happy major-key feel of the folk theme with the Spanish scale heard in *Tijuana Table Dance,* probably as a deliberate metaphor for the natives' subjugation by the Conquistadores. A similar sort of culture-shock is experienced when the D flat bass-figure originally heard some thirteen minutes in as the foundation for some effective plunger-mute playing by Walrath and Jimmy Knepper, becomes, after nineteen and a half minutes, the excuse for some satirical vocalizing by Mingus and Dannie (shades of *Faubus/*

211

Nixon) based on the pseudo-black-folksong *Mama's Li'l Baby Likes Shortnin' Bread*.

The only slight drawback of the whole work lies in the scoring, and one might add the recording, of the ten-piece line-up (augmented by a percussion section) which veers from the nondescript to the slightly bizarre. Speaking of Mingus's writing for larger groups, Jimmy Knepper says: 'I don't want to malign the guy, but I never felt he was as great an orchestrator as some people made out. For instance, in *Cumbia* he would use the trombone with the bassoon and the bass-clarinet. If you put them all together, it just sounds like mud!' It is a fact that Mingus often seemed more interested in the lines he wrote than in the instrumentation which carried them, and yet with the restrictions imposed by a quintet or sextet he achieved some very precise and very varied orchestration, as in some of the 1957 classics with Knepper or indeed in the ensembles of *Sue's Changes*. Nevertheless, the power of the content plus the frequent originality of the structure is what often triumphs in his large-band writing. When *Cumbia and Jazz Fusion* closes with the long-drawn-out board-fade – a rare occurrence in Mingus recordings – during the repeated four-bar turnaround (on the first four chords of *Goodbye Pork Pie Hat*) which made its only previous appearance five minutes from the start, it becomes clear that this extraordinarily fulfilling piece could not have been created by anyone else.

But the creator himself was now having to seek medical advice about the recurrent discomfort he was experiencing in the entire lower half of his body. Dannie Richmond recalls: 'They thought it was his legs at first, that his legs were going as a result of carrying round all that weight.' There was also a rumour that he had suffered a slipped disc, a rumour which spread because Mingus could now only walk with the aid of a cane. This was certainly the case when the quintet played the Village Vanguard in May where, according to eyewitness Bruce Talbot, Mingus's once formidable authority on the bandstand seemed minimal; on the night in question, only Jack Walrath showed any apparent interest in producing a creditable group performance, and Mingus didn't help by choosing an identical programme on successive sets. During a Bob Neloms-accompanied solo bass set at the Newport Festival which included *I Can't Get Started*, Chuck Berg noted the 'rather thin arco sound and a passel of pitch problems'[33] which showed Mingus on less than top form. Still, despite his weakened condition, and doubtless believing more than one doctor who was not quite sure what caused it but was convinced it would go away, Mingus undertook his most extensive touring yet, covering not only European festivals such as Nice and Montreux and a few days in North Africa but subsequently dates in South America as well.

Performing quintet versions of both *Cumbia* and *Three or Four Shades of Blues*, sometimes in the same concert, in addition to older material such as a *So Long, Eric* which was preceded by a long free-form introduction, the work of the group was certainly more together than at the Vanguard in May. Dannie has pointed out that 'Charles placed a great importance on being your very best on all of the European tours, musically, and he wanted everything to be correct.'[34] Sadly though, the evidence of radio and television broadcasts and of the limited-edition album called *European Tour 1977* is that, as his physical condition deteriorated, so naturally enough did Mingus's bass playing, and, in place of his once forceful and even imperious sense of time, one hears (especially at up-tempo) the struggle to master his instrument which Mingus had first overcome nearly forty years ago. George Adams, who has doubtless had the opportunity to discuss the matter since with Dannie Richmond, notes that 'When I left the band, he still had his health, in the way where he was effective playing, you know. So I wasn't around when . . . the time element had really begun to take a retrograde motion.' While in other circumstances this could have created real friction in the band, their concern for the leader's condition caused them as far as possible to ignore the rhythmic problems, and even to carry the load in other ways. As Dannie has said, 'Towards the end of Mingus's career, Mingus was ill and nobody knew it. His contracts called for two sets, but he was really ill. So instead of going out for an encore he would say, "Here's my drummer." '[35] And sometimes Dannie would sing a short ballad or, as on the *European Tour 1977* album, he would milk the audience with a corny drum solo of the kind he had learned to play at rock concerts.

However, as Mingus's playing ability became unmistakably affected by his health – and he would of course have been the first to be aware of this and unbearably frustrated by it – he found an outlet in composition. The renewed burst of activity during much of 1978 had already been foreshadowed by a piece performed, along with *Cumbia*, at the Newport Festival by a group augmented with trombone, woodwinds and percussion. Jack Walrath has said, 'He'd have the trumpet and oboe playing together, the bassoon and trombone; whatever came to his mind seemed to work. There was no pattern where woodwinds *had* to play certain things. It was polyphonic, like everybody had his own melody to play. He fit it together, like Bach, almost. One of the high points was that it sounded improvisational.'[36] This apparent culmination of Mingus's concern with lines rather than instrumentation seems fairly untypical of his late works generally, and two other new pieces that surfaced during 1977 are simple, heartfelt, A/A/B/A ballads. The thirty-two-bar *Carolyn 'Keiki' Mingus* (in C) is the last in the series of portraits of ladies related to the composer, in this case his co-star in the film *Mingus* who was now a lady of seventeen summers, while the D flat *Farwell Farewell* (which has a nine-bar B section) was given this title after the death of Mingus's lifelong friend and mentor from Mill Valley, Farwell Taylor. These were the two most successful tracks on an all-star album put together as part of a series led by Lionel Hampton, who plays his short feature spots with great sympathy for Mingus's music, as does Gerry Mulligan. Mingus's bass playing (though suffering from the same problems as on the European tour) is at least more relaxed as a result of being able to play more quietly in the studio. But by and large the nine-piece line-up, plus occasional vibes from Hampton, is ill-served by the ponderous and rather too literal arrangements of Mingus's music by Paul Jeffrey.

Ironically, this session, done thirty years almost to the day after Mingus's first big-time recording, which was also with Lionel Hampton, was to be the last occasion on which he played bass in the studio. There had been another project in the autumn that never got beyond the discussion stage, which had paired Mingus with fellow Atlantic artist, and Mingus admirer, electric bassist Stanley Clarke. A couple of months later Mingus was saying: 'I know a guy who is a superstar bass player. "I don't need to play *'A' Train*. I don't need to know *'A' Train*," he said. He is so dumb he doesn't know *'A' Train* is *Exactly Like You*, he's not a musician. In the key of C he couldn't play *'A' Train*. And he's a superstar. I don't need that shit, man.'[37]

Whether or not the reaction of the other bassist was a response to some one-upmanship from a Mingus no longer confident of his ability on the instrument – and all too conscious of the apparently limitless technique of younger players who had drawn some of their inspiration from him – at the time it seemed to be Mingus who was in the wrong. For by the late 1970s there was a generation of players (and listeners) for whom the word 'jazz' signified the work of jazz-influenced electric groups. (Nevertheless, in the last few years, these players have followed the lead of Anthony Braxton, the Art

214

Ensemble of Chicago and, of course, Mingus himself in strongly reaffirming their knowledge of the jazz tradition. Even Stanley Clarke has recently recorded *'A' Train* with Freddie Hubbard and Chick Corea.)

Covering one of Mingus's last playing appearances at the Blue Note in Boulder, Colorado, in October 1977, Rafi Zabor wrote:

> At the end of the last night, when the audience raised up its insensitive cries of 'More!' like a house to what god, he made his way across to the piano, which was a good one, to play something for the people . . . Mingus leaned his cane against the instrument and sat down . . . but as he began to play, the man in the sound booth had already put on a Weather Report tape, and though Neloms and I waved him to turn the thing off Mingus had to stop and come offstage.[38]

Worse still, the European tour set up by Atlantic to feature Mingus's group plus Larry Coryell and Philip Catherine, in other words to promote the *Three or Four Shades of Blues* album and to prove that Mingus was still relevant to the young generation, had to be cancelled. Two weeks of concerts had been announced at places such as Dortmund (17 November), Paris (21 November) and London (30 November), but on 23 November, the day before Thanksgiving, he had a booking at the Neurological Institute of Columbia Presbyterian Hospital. And here at last came the verdict, not on Mingus's bass playing or on the relevance of his compositions, but on his physical condition: Amyotrophic Lateral Sclerosis.

10
Epitaph

He had had trouble with his leg for many, many months. When he toured Japan [in 1976] I remember he was using marbles to exercise the bottoms of his feet . . . so it's possible that it had started. You know, it's a disease that can strike you and take a while to develop. By the time it was diagnosed, the doctors said that he had three to six months to live. That's how fast it was, but of course nobody knows just how long he might have had it. They know virtually nothing about the disease, they don't know what causes it or what cures it. They think it may be a virus, that's one of the theories. Another theory is that it's a breakdown in the immunization system in the body.

The words of Susan Graham Mingus, now something of an unwilling authority on Amyotrophic Lateral Sclerosis or Lou Gehrig's Disease, so called after the star of the New York Yankees who died from it in 1941 at the age of thirty-nine. 'A terminal disease, for which the established medical profession offers no hope whatsoever. They tell you to make the best of it, and go home and wait. But, you know, Mingus was a fighter on every level, and he simply didn't accept the diagnosis.' In another interview, Sue illustrated his attitude by mentioning that in July 1978, in other words after his 'three to six months' had expired, 'A friend of ours called up in a state of depression, saying she was going to jump out of her third-floor loft, and he said immediately "Tell her to come over here, we're forty floors higher up!" It was his typical response to things, he had no pity for complainers and no self-pity for anything that he went through.'[1]

To protect himself as far as possible from the pity of others, Mingus and Sue made the immediate decision to try and keep secret the precise details of his illness, or at least to restrict the knowledge to the smallest possible circle of family and close associates. The fact that, since earlier in 1977, the Minguses had been living forty floors up in the federal-government-subsidized Manhattan Plaza on West 43rd Street, meant that he was surrounded by a community of 3,500 performing artists including 300 musicians, among them Ricky Ford, Jackie McLean's son René and the homecoming hero Dexter Gordon, and telling the neighbours would have been tantamount to telling the jazz press. Even Dannie Richmond learned the truth at third hand: 'Ricky Ford told me "Did you know, man, that Mingus is going to *die*?" Actually Mingus's son it was, told Ricky that he had this incurable disease. 'Cause they were trying to keep it very quiet, you know.' What was supremely important to Mingus was to maintain his immersion in music, despite the imminent prospect of exchanging his cane for a wheelchair as paralysis gradually made movement more and more difficult. Even though he didn't accept the diagnosis, he knew that at present he had no strength for playing the bass, but he could take the longer view that at least some of his bass work had been preserved on records. Any compositional ideas, on the other hand, which were 'in his head' would sooner or later die with him unless they could be got down on paper. The posthumous fame of Charlie Parker had made Mingus aware of posterity's mellowing attitude to artists who are no longer around (back in 1974 he had said sardonically, 'When I'm dead they'll probably do my string quartets. Like they're discovering Joplin, whatever his name is').[2] No matter that Mingus at fifty-five was more revered and renowned than Parker had ever been in his lifetime, there was still work to be done.

Of course Mingus, losing the use of his hands, was at a disadvantage compared to a Beethoven, who with his hearing impaired, could still write out the notes as he conceived them. A double disadvantage in fact because, unlike even a Frederick Delius who could dictate from his wheelchair to an amanuensis, the nature of the music Mingus was most involved in (and his incorporation of spontaneous composition into the act of performance) made it resistant to the process of composition at second-hand. Even the January 1978 recording sessions, at which Mingus was actually present, are not encouraging in this respect. There are acceptable remakes of

Devil Woman and *Wednesday Night Prayer Meeting* (the latter with vocal chorus, for the album *Me, Myself an Eye*, was, commercially speaking, a direct follow-up to *Three or Four Shades of Blues*), and Jack Walrath's arrangement of *Carolyn* is preferable on the whole to that of Paul Jeffrey, whose role this time was restricted to conducting the ensemble. But the longer works, *Three Worlds of Drums* and *Something Like a Bird,* suffer by comparison with comparable items in Mingus's output, and each in a different way.

Walrath's comments on *Three Worlds of Drums* make it clear that Mingus's role in its creation was perilously close to that of a Dmitri Tiomkin instructing one of his ghost-writers:

> Charles gave me a tape of himself noodling on a Moorish-sounding scale and said to me, 'Pick out some of my notes, organize a melody and write an arrangement on it' . . . The shout chorus was a melody which Mingus wrote and to which I kept adding counter lines . . . The trumpet-soprano melody near the end was organized the same as the initial melody, . . . the funereal ending I transcribed from a piano tape . . . All in all Mingus supplied me with one lead line, loose sketches for two more, a six bar ending and a basic chord consisting of two perfect 5ths a half-step apart sounded simultaneously.

It is perhaps the more surprising that Walrath 'told Mingus that all I wanted was credit for arranging and orchestration',[3] but for all the effort that went into this piece it comes across (no doubt partly because of the recording mix) as strangely static. And this is thrown into relief by the one small touch which is reminiscent of Mingus's organization of a long performance, namely having the most exciting soloist (in this case Larry Coryell) create a climax immediately before the drum solos. The boppish *Something Like a Bird*, a direct descendant of *Extrasensory Perception*, suffers even more from the absence of those peaks and troughs it would have had with Mingus fully in charge, for it is a jam-session on a repeated thirty-two bar chorus but segmented so that players of the same instrument do battle with each other. Jimmy Knepper says Mingus's intention was that 'The tenor player with the band, seeing another tenor player, will say "Oh, I'm about to lose my job, maybe I'd better play better." And they're supposed to spur each other on, but that really doesn't happen.' Dannie Richmond, while impressed with the willingness of Atlantic to pay for the number of musicians Mingus wanted, is even less complimentary about the results: 'You take a bag of diamonds, and drop them in a hole. With all those personalities, the top musicians in their field, putting all of them together to *read* music!'

Shortly after this Mingus was able to show his recognition of Richmond's constant support over the years, and briefly to escape the New York winter, by taking a holiday with Sue and Dannie and Dannie's wife on St Martin, some 200 miles east of the Virgin Islands. And then it was back to New York to concentrate on other urgent projects, one of which had been commissioned towards the end of 1977 for the next Ann Arbor Festival to be performed by the Mercer Ellington band. But the musical origin of the piece went back to 1972 when, according to Jon Faddis:

> One day I went to see him and he told me he wanted to write this piece for the trumpet that went from the very bottom – and I mean bottom – to the very top. He wanted to know if it was possible to play what he had in mind. I said sure it's *possible*. Then he asked if I could do it, and I said nope. But he wrote it out anyway.[4]

The same gag was tried out on a few other brilliant trumpeters and then 'It sort of got tabled for a while.' So says Sy Johnson, who saved it from oblivion by suggesting a big-band adaptation for the Ann Arbor commission, at which point Mingus 'sang some things into a tape-recorder and it became a piece for a three-horn front line, trumpet and alto and tenor, with the band in a very challenging role of both being a supporting agency and also sharing the melody . . . He disregarded what was possible and impossible, and so what he gave me was pure melody, and the most soaring kind of melody.'[5] At first called *Number 29*, when it was premiered by Mercer Ellington at Ann Arbor in September 1978 Mingus had given it the more positive title *Alive and Well in Dukeland*.

From now on, singing into a tape-recorder was to be Mingus's only means of composing new music, since he could no longer control his fingers enough even to play the piano. In this way, he created seven or eight pieces including *Pilobolus* for a New York dance group of that name, and was working on a commission arising from the South American tour for a jazz sextet plus symphony orchestra in Buenos Aires. Also (unless this was a version of the same project) he was contemplating:

> a piece of music based on T.S. Eliot's *Quartets* and he wanted to

do it with – and this is how he described it – a full orchestra playing one kind of music, and overlaid on that would be bass and guitar playing another kind of music; over that there was to be a reader reading excerpts from *Quartets* in a very formal literary voice; and interspersed with that he wanted me to distil T.S. Eliot down into street language, and sing it mixed in with the reader.[6]

The singer-songwriter quoted here is Joni Mitchell, Mingus's last and most unlikely collaborator, to whose work he had been introduced by the Italian film producer Daniele Senatore. Although the collaboration sounds like another record-company inspired idea (Mitchell's label being part of the WEA group), it was Mingus who not only first contacted her but, when she demurred on the Eliot idea, asked her to write lyrics for six of the new tunes he had written.

It was in April that she visited Mingus at the Manhattan Plaza tower-block to discuss the material, from which meeting came the title *A Chair in the Sky* ('He was a very commanding figure, because he just swallowed the chair up; it was like he was enthroned, very regal').[7] Of the three new songs which later found their way on to Mitchell's *Mingus* album and on to the first Mingus Dynasty album, the ballad *A Chair in the Sky* is the most affecting, particularly in Sy Johnson's arrangement for the Dynasty, while *Sweet Sucker Dance* is an expansion of the opening phrase of *Sue's Changes*. But although the Joni Mitchell recordings can hardly be considered part of the Mingus canon, it is worth noting that her lyrics for *Goodbye Pork Pie Hat* are far superior to those recorded by Rahsaan Roland Kirk, and that her singing is almost good enough to make one think of Sheila Jordan or Annie Ross. And the restrained but distinctly space-age bass playing of Jaco Pastorius which, fittingly, dominates the album, could never have existed but for the influence of Mingus on those who have influenced Pastorius.

It was in April too that Atlantic arranged a fifty-sixth birthday party for Mingus, to tie in with a performance of *Revelations* by the New York Philharmonic under Gunther Schuller on 29 April. 'It was supposed to swing more,'[8] he told Schuller afterwards. This rare public appearance meant admitting to the press that he was at least temporarily paralysed, but now, five months after the diagnosis of his disease, he was sometimes seriously troubled by the persistence and possible fatality of the paralysis which gripped both arms and legs. 'He would get terrified by a housefly,' Sue has said, adding that: 'There are terminal circuits for many diseases and we kept running after hope.'[9] The next attempt in this direction was a trip to Switzerland, which brought relaxation but no relief. Whether or not he believed it, Mingus publicly blamed his present condition on his attempts at dieting, just as a couple of years earlier he had attributed the death of John Foster to the same cause, telling Danny Mixon: 'Hey, you remind me of John Foster! What did he think he was doing trying to lose weight, the jerk? He lost his hide.'[10]

Mingus was back in New York by June in order to have further discussion with Joni Mitchell and attend her preliminary studio tryouts of the joint numbers (the issued recordings, of course, were not done until the following year). Dannie Richmond, not included in these sessions although he worked with Mitchell on the project later in the year, also visited Mingus regularly at this period and was distressed by his worsening condition:

Have you ever looked into his eyes? I used to look into his eyes, and he used to turn away and not speak. And I didn't know what to say either, I felt like crying. Those were just brief, like five-minute visits. I guess he didn't want me to see him like that. He'd just say, 'Well, I got to take my medicine now,' and then I would leave.

But Mingus was also available to give moral support to Paul Jeffrey for his forthcoming Newport Festival appearance at Saratoga Springs, where he was to conduct a twenty-four piece ensemble in the public premieres of *Three Worlds of Drums* and *Something Like a Bird*. And it was in this connection that Mingus received a surprise invitation to Washington, as a result of George Wein's suggestion that the twenty-fifth Newport (the twenty-fourth to be organized by Wein) should be the occasion for some Presidential recognition of the importance of jazz.

Thus it was that on the afternoon of 18 June 1978 Mingus and Sue were guests of honour at an unprecedented all-star concert on the south lawn of the White House, listening to performers such as Dexter Gordon, Roy Eldridge, Illinois Jacquet, Dizzy Gillespie, Lionel Hampton, Max Roach, Billy Taylor, Stan Getz and Ornette Coleman. But the most unforgettable moment of the whole event came when producer/compere George Wein called for applause in honour of the figure in the wheelchair. The assembled musicians and guests gave Mingus a standing ovation, President Carter went over to Mingus and embraced him, and Mingus himself broke down and wept. Ignoring the uncharitable thought that he was weeping because Wein had once again called him 'Charlie', it is easy to understand Mingus's frustration at being unable to express all the mixed feelings that would have flooded forth, had he been handed a microphone. Unmistakably, too, this represented the moment when the pity of others finally got through to Mingus, and his proud resistance snapped under the strain.

If this had been all, in fact, this moment of acclamation might well have actually hastened Mingus's end, but it also brought with it another ray of hope, in the shape of Gerry Mulligan. As Sue recalls, 'Gerry had just come back from Mexico and he had, I think, witnessed an operation of this legendary healer there by the name of Pachita, who was in her seventies and was reputed to have cured cancer and all kinds of terminal diseases.' And so, within a matter of days, Sue and his son flew with Mingus on the last trip to his beloved Mexico. Staying in Cuernavaca, about fifty miles south of Mexico City, and reputed to have one of the healthiest climates in the world, Mingus adopted a regime that involved herbs, herbal teas, mudbaths, biofeedback and hypnosis, and he once went so far as to drink some iguana blood. As musical concerns began to take more of a back seat to the serious business of trying to achieve a cure, the last week of July saw the Village Vanguard in New York featuring the Dannie Richmond Quintet, with the personnel of Mingus's 1977 group plus Eddie Gomez on bass, playing a largely Mingus repertoire including *Cumbia and Jazz Fusion*. (Of the bassist, Dannie says: 'In fact, he was named by Charles personally: if there was one bass player that could do it, Eddie Gomez was the one.') Not only was Dannie an obvious candidate as keeper of the flame, but he felt that he had received the blessing of Mingus himself before he left for Mexico. 'It's a drag in a way, how it came about . . . Charles told me, "You know the music. Just go 'head on." '[11]

In New York and elsewhere this development, following on the widespread coverage of his White House appearance, alerted Mingus's fans to the fact that his illness was indeed serious, despite the press maintaining their silence, in their published material at least, about its reputation for being terminal. One of the writers whose Mingus interviews have been quoted earlier visited London in August and said bluntly, as one journalist to another, 'Obituaries should be written now.' Also at this period Roger Rowland, writing to express concern about the health of his former correspondent, not only had his letter forwarded to Cuernavaca but actually received a reply from Sue:

Oct. 15, 1978
Dear Roger Rowland,
It is 7 a.m., I have been up all night with Charles and a substitute Mexican nurse who does not speak English, trying to ease the inferno of these nights and also trying to catch up on a bunch of mail which was sent to me down here . . . I have not written any personal letters since we came down here over three months ago, and at this hour I hardly expected to be writing anyone . . .

Whether or not there is any real hope of changing the course of the disease, the suffering Charles is going through is at least bearable in the sense that he does have hope that he may one day get back the use of his hands, that he may walk again, that he may live, whole. Sometimes I believe it and sometimes I lose hope entirely. But we are trying as hard as we can, and all things considered, I suppose we are better off here than anywhere else. We have a beautiful place with a garden and a car the wheelchair fits into, and we go off to the market during the day and often to restaurants at night. We have had visitors who are dear to Charles and we have full-time nurses to help as much as is possible. He has special massages and exercises through the day and night, many teas, and he has had two operations. He is beautifully tanned, looks wonderful, and is suffering a great deal. He has been heroic through all this, bearing up in a way which only someone with his great spiritual resources and energy and strength could have managed . . . His voice is very thin and not easy to understand, but the huge energy and will is as much there as ever, and he still has more vitality and humour and courage than anyone I know.
With love from both us,
Susan Graham Mingus[12]

This letter was posted by Celia ('Mingus made us both co-executors of his will,' says Sue, 'somehow knowing, I'm sure, that we would become fast friends'). One of Mingus's other visitors was Joni Mitchell, who noted that 'Every night he would say to me, "I want to talk to you about the music," and every day it would be too difficult.'

One final musical project which inspired Mingus, however, was the suggestion by New Audiences of a series of concerts, the proceeds of which would establish a Charles Mingus Fund for Musicians And Composers to combat record pirating and to aid new talent. As Sue has commented, 'It was of the few things that came along then that he showed any interest in . . . One of his suggestions was a concert with the Juilliard String Quartet, Sonny Rollins, a bowing bass player (he didn't identify anybody – he just said a bowing bass player), Sarah Vaughan and Joni Mitchell. It would have cost a fortune.'[13]

By this stage Mingus must have realized that he was losing the battle and that, as the grip of the paralysis became ever greater, he was using up more and more of his strength just in staying alive. And yet, no doubt because he was inspired by Sue's continuing display of optimism, he continued to do the same and to play the part of being Charles Mingus to the last. In another interview Sue said that the house in Cuernavaca had a staff of around eight, but 'There was no doubt who ran that place, even though Charles was in a wheelchair and came to have so hard a time talking. He orches-trated everybody.'[14] One of Mingus's last visitors was his old friend, Buddy Collette, who also came down from California and who, when the final hour came on 5 January 1979, had the task of informing the press of the heart attack which had terminated Mingus's illness. Sue had other duties, for Mingus's will made provisions for the disposal of his body which he had decided on some years before, and indeed can be heard discussing (while listening to the then-unreleased tapes of *Sue's Changes*) during the home-recording incorporated in Joni Mitchell's album. So Mingus was cremated and, within a few days, Sue had flown to an ashram in India, where Mingus had hoped to go from Mexico, and cast his ashes into the sacred waters of the Ganges at sunrise.

At the time of his death Mingus had survived fifty-six years and eight months (only eleven months longer than Jelly Roll Morton) and, on the same day that he died, it is recorded that fifty-six whales beached themselves on a Mexican coast, where the locals disposed of them by burning them. It may be that the Whale is a more apt metaphor for Mingus than the Bull, since those who try to bend the improvised folk-music of jazz to the designs of a compositional approach are now more than ever an endangered species. But, at least in death, Mingus reaped one of the benefits of being a writer rather than a mere instrumentalist, in the fulsome tributes of the international press. *Time, Newsweek, Der Spiegel* and others not only gave considerable space to his achievements, but all placed him first in their obituary columns ahead of, for instance, the architect Pier Luigi Nervi. The extent of the coverage in fact was such that some purist jazz fans, unaware of the growth of Mingus's fame as the 1970s progressed, were taken aback at his posthumous glory.

As at the passing of Charlie Parker – and seldom since – a flock of poems about the dead man were published, and there was even the true story of a poet phoning a jazz critic to discover the name of Mingus's final illness (it is not known whether he ever found a word to rhyme with Amyotrophic Lateral Sclerosis). And, after a while, pieces of music inspired by Mingus began appearing, in almost as great a profusion as at the death of Duke Ellington. Those by former sidemen included George Adams's *Metamorphosis for Mingus* (recorded on Timeless), *Farewell to Mingus* by Toshiko Akiyoshi (RCA), *I Heard Mingus* by Ted Curson (Interplay), John LaPorta's *Remember Mingus* for Herb Pomeroy (Shiah), *Ode to Mingus* by Dannie Richmond (Soul Note), *Mingus Lives* by Mal Waldron (ENJA), and (on Gatemouth) Jack Walrath's *King Duke* (the title, according to Walrath, describes a heavenly game of five-card stud in which 'Mingus turns over the last card and triumphantly reports, "It's a King, Duke!" ').[15] Among those by musicians merely influenced in different ways by Mingus, it is worth singling out *Charlie M* by the Art Ensemble of Chicago (ECM), *Blues for Mingus* by Stanley Clarke (Nemperor/CBS) and – if only for the title – Gunter Hampel and Jeanne Lee's *All the Things You Could Be If Charlie Mingus Was Your Daddy* (Birth). Of the many tribute concerts, sometimes by musicians who had no connection with Mingus but felt bereaved by his death, special mention should perhaps be made of an informal event organized by Eugene Mingus in Los Angeles, featuring Charles McPherson and Buddy Collette, who also played in a flute and bass duet at the Los Angeles memorial service. In addition, there was the debut of the group that soon became known as the Mingus Dynasty at the Walnut Street Theater in Philadelphia on 28 April, followed by two Carnegie Hall concerts on 1 and 2 June.

In some ways, the task of perpetuating Mingus's music is made easier for this group than is, for instance, the stated aim of the Mercer Ellington Orchestra, in that, rather than a musician with ideas of his own, the effective organizer of the Mingus Dynasty is Susan Graham Mingus. And it is, of course, true that Mingus's compositions allowed a much larger place for extended improvisation than many of Ellington's could comfortably accommodate, and thus more readily absorbed the efforts of changing personnel, as Mingus's own groups over the years amply demonstrated. With the on-stage leadership of Dannie Richmond and arrangements/transcriptions by Sy Johnson and Jimmy Knepper, the 1979–80 edition of the Dynasty featuring Charlie Haden on bass produced

the fine *Chair in the Sky* album and many vital concert performances, including a tour of Europe and also one for the State
Department. Appearances by the group have continued at a similar
pace since the departure of Dannie Richmond, who, in order to
counteract the problems of fluctuating personnel, has again revived
Mingus's 1977 band, in the flesh and on disc, with Cameron Brown
as bassist. Of course, Jimmy Knepper's verdict on the Dynasty,
which he has since left and rejoined – 'We're playing his tunes;
without Mingus there, you're not playing Mingus music' – is necessarily a verdict on all such groups. Nevertheless, in another sense,
any attempt to play Mingus perpetuates his influence and his presence in the music. George Adams recalls that, at the 1979 Berlin
Festival performance of the 'Original Charles Mingus Workshop
Ensemble' led by Dannie Richmond with Eddie Gomez on bass,
'Before we played and after we played, we were in the dressing-
room . . . and all of a sudden somebody said "You know, I feel
Charles in this room." And Gomez said "Yeah" and, you know,
everybody felt it at the same time.'

During the last weeks of his life, Sue 'asked him one day what he
was going to come back as. He said seriously: "I'm not going to
leave." '[16] While this is surely true of his musical contributions, one
wonders if even now he is planning his reincarnation. Certainly he
must be fretting in the double-bass section of that great orchestra in
the sky, directed by Duke Ellington, and is probably running a small
band of his own backstage starring Eric Dolphy, Booker Ervin and
Roland Kirk, doubtless augmented by Clarence Shaw, Hobart
Dotson and Willie Dennis, and with John Foster and Wade Legge
obliged to challenge each other for the piano chair. Perhaps he is
criticizing their interpretation of his latest tunes, and complaining to
anyone who will listen, 'Man, everything would be alright if Dannie
would just come here.'

Appendix A
Musical Examples

Example 1
Bass part from Illinois Jacquet version of *Ghost of a Chance* (Crosby, Washington, Young)

Example 2
Bass part from Lionel Hampton version of *Mingus Fingers*

Example 3
Bass part from Thad Jones version of *Get out of Town* (Porter)

Note especially (a) the use of *Perdido* as a countermelody and (b) the double-stops with successive open strings to form a cadence. Direct imitation of the trumpet solo is heard at (c), (d) and (f), while (e) is an imitation of the drum part.

231

Example 4
Quintet orchestration of *Pithecanthropus Erectus* (1956 version)

234

Example 5
Bass introduction to *Tonight at Noon* (1957 version)

Example 6
Bass solo from *Haitian Fight Song* (1957 Version)

The two quotations, (a) from the pseudo-spiritual *Shadrack* and (b) from *God Bless America*, not only symbolize the racial conflict implied by Mingus's title, but typify the polarization between the blues scale and the European diatonic scales which permeates the entire solo.

236

Example 7
Bass introduction to *Tijuana Table Dance* (*Ysabel's Table Dance*) (1957 version)

Example 8
Polyrhythmic figures from *Wednesday Night Prayer Meeting* (1959 version)

Example 9
Bass solo from *Folk Forms* (October 1960 version)

Mingus's vocal interjection at bars 64–65 illustrates the rhythmic figure which recurs in the work of all four performers throughout this piece.

Example 10
Piano improvisation *Myself When I Am Real* (*Adagio Ma Non Troppo*)

242

Appendix B
Non-Standard Chorus Structures in Mingus Compositions

This list is not exhaustive, but contains the main examples mentioned in the text.

This Subdues My Passion (rec. 1946)
  Intro (6 bars)/A(8 bars)/B(8 bars)/C(8 bars)/D(8 bars)/E(8 bars)/A(8 bars)
Chazzanova (1953) Intro (4 bars)/A(8 bars)/B(8 bars)/C(8 bars)/A(8 bars)
Purple Heart (1954)   A(12 bars)/A^1(12 bars)/B(24 bars)/A(12 bars)
Eulogy for Rudy Williams (1954)   A(8 bars)/A(8 bars)/B(8 bars)/C(8 bars)
Thrice upon a Theme (1954)
                A(12 bars)/A^1(14 bars)/B(12 bars)/C(14 bars)/A^2(12 bars)
Minor Intrusion (1954)
  Intro (12 bars, only 4 when repeated)/A(8 bars)/A^1(8 bars)/A^2(12 bars)/
  A^3(16 bars)/B(17 bars, omitted on repeat)/C(16 bars)/D(16 bars)/E(44
                                                                        bars)
Pithecanthropus Erectus (1956)
                    A(16 bars)/B(indefinite)/A(16 bars)/C(indefinite)
Profile of Jackie (1956)
                A(14 bars)/B(indefinite)/C(13 bars)/D(8 bars)/E(indefinite)
Tonight at Noon (1956)
            Intro (indefinite)/A(10 bars)/A(10 bars)/B(8 bars/A^1(14 bars)
Reincarnation of a Lovebird (1957)
                A^1(16 bars)/A^2(16 bars)/B(16 bars)/A^{1+2}(22 bars)
Fables of Faubus (1959)   A(19 bars)/A^1(18 bars)/B(16 bars)/A^1(18 bars)
Better Git It in Your Soul (1959)
                        A(10 bars)/A(10 bars)/B(8 bars)/A(10 bars)
Self-Portrait in Three Colors (1959)   A(5½ bars)/B(9 bars)

243

New Now Know How (1959)

A(8½ bars)/A¹(8½ bars)/B(7 bars)/A(8½ bars)

Peggy's Blue Skylight (1961)

A(8 bars)/B(8 bars)/A(8 bars)/B(8 bars)/C(8 bars)/B(8 bars)

Devil Woman (1961)   A(3 bars)/A¹(4½ bars)/B(8 bars)

Please Don't Come Back from the Moon (1962)

A(10 bars)/B(5 bars)/C(indefinite)

O.P.O.P. (1962) A(14 bars)/A(14 bars)/C(15 bars)/A(14 bars)/C(16 bars)

Orange Was the Color of Her Dress (1964)

A(11 bars)/A(11 bars)/B(10 bars)

The I of Hurricane Sue (1971)

A(8 bars)/A(8 bars)/B(9 bars)/C(7 bars)/A(8 bars)/D(4 bars)

Duke Ellington's Sound of Love (1974)

A(8 bars)/B(4 bars)/C(14 bars)/B¹(5 bars)

Free Cell Block F, 'Tis Nazi U.S.A. (1974)

A(7 bars)/B(9 bars)/A¹(5 bars)/B¹(12 bars)/A²(5 bars)/C(5 bars)

Sue's Changes (1974)

A(11 bars)/B(6 bars)/C(12 bars)/C¹(12 bars)/D(8 bars)/D¹(8 bars)/
E(12 bars)/E¹(indefinite)

Chair in the Sky (1978)   A(7 bars)/A¹(7½ bars)/B(16½ bars)/A²(12 bars)

Appendix C
Analysis of
The Black Saint and the Sinner Lady

Letter	Approx. timing	Description	Key
1st Movement (Track A)			
A	0.00–0.10	Polyrhythmic drum intro	B♭m
B1	0.10–0.50	Ensemble figure 1 with alto lead	B♭m
B2	0.50–2.30	Ensemble figure 2 with baritone lead	B♭m
C	2.30–3.10	Ballad (alto lead)	B♭m
B3	3.10–4.05	Ensemble figure 1 with alto + trumpet + new material	B♭m
D	4.05–6.20	Soprano solo with rhythm (later ensemble), out-of-tempo end	B♭m
2nd Movement (Track B)			
E	0.00–1.10	Piano intro with ensemble backing	D♭
F	1.10–2.00	New ballad (alto lead)	D♭
G1	2.00–3.05	Ensemble figure 3 with muted tpt + tbn (*accelerando*)	B♭m
G2	3.05–4.35	Longer take ending with tbn + drums out-of-tempo	B♭m
B4	4.35–5.35	Ensemble figure 1 with tbn muted (then open, cf. alto at B1)	B♭m
C	5.35–5.45	Excerpt from C	B♭m
B3	5.45–5.55	Excerpt from B3	B♭m
F	5.55–6.25	Second half of F	D♭
3rd Movement (Track C)			
H1	0.00–0.35	Piano out-of-tempo – Mingus	B♭m
J	0.35–0.50	Piano with ensemble chords	B♭m

H2	0.50–1.30	Piano out-of-tempo – Mingus	B♭m
K	1.30–1.50	Flute theme	B♭m
H3	1.50–2.30	Piano out-of-tempo	B♭m
K	2.30–2.45	Flute theme	B♭m
L1(0)	2.45–4.20	Intro + guitar (later collective improv.) with alto overdubbed	F7
M(0)	4.20–6.45	Ensemble figures (with *accelerando*) with alto overdubbed	B♭m
(0)	6.45–7.00	Out-of-tempo end of alto overdub	F7♭5

4th Movement (Mode D/Mode E/Mode F)

J	0.00–0.15	Piano with ensemble chords	B♭m
N	0.15–0.25	Bass intro	B♭m
P	0.25–1.35	Third ballad section (tbn lead then tpt)	B♭m/D
L2	1.35–2.50	Guitar, this time unaccompanied	F7
Q	2.50–4.20	Ensemble entry, then improv. by 2 tpts	A♭7
J	4.20–4.30	Piano with ensemble chords	B♭m
H4	4.30–4.45	Piano out-of-tempo	B♭m
K	4.45–5.00	Flute theme	B♭m
H5	5.00–5.35	Piano out-of-tempo	B♭m
K	5.35–5.45	Flute theme	B♭m
H6	5.45–6.10	Piano out-of-tempo	B♭m
R	6.10–6.40	Fourth ballad section (alto lead)	B♭m
P(0)	6.40–7.50	Third ballad section (with alto overdubbed)	B♭m
L2(0)	7.50–9.05	Guitar (with alto overdubbed + marimba – Mingus???)	F7
(0)	9.05–9.25	Continuation of alto overdub	A♭7
Q(0)	9.25–10.55	Ensemble and improv. (with alto + marimba overdubbed)	A♭7
R	10.55–11.20	Fourth ballad section	B♭m
S1	11.20–12.50	Ensemble figure with muted tbn (*accelerando*)	E♭
S2	12.50–14.35	Longer take (*accelerando*, ending out-of-tempo)	E♭
S1(0)	14.35–16.30	S1 also longer, ending out-of-tempo (with alto overdubbed)	E♭
B1(0)	16.30–17.35	Ensemble figure 1 (with alto overdubbed)	B♭m
(0)	17.35–17.52	Out-of-tempo end of alto overdub	F7♭5

Appendix D
Discography

The following summarized discography of Charles Mingus lists all known material, whether issued or not, up to 1962. From then on, because of the volume of private recordings, only those issued or available for issue by established record companies have been included. As in the appendix to *Miles Davis: A Critical Biography* by Ian Carr, one original catalogue number has been shown for each title, except in the case of simultaneous mono and stereo releases or nearly simultaneous releases at 78, 45 and 33 rpm. These entries are cross-referenced to an index of catalogue numbers for currently available issues, where applicable.

A single asterisk after the catalogue number shows that a particular issue includes less than the complete performance, whereas the designation 'theme' denotes a deliberately short version to open or close a broadcast. The double asterisk is reserved for known examples of deliberate editing of a performance, or composites of different takes. Overdubbing, which interested Mingus earlier than most other jazz musicians, has been mentioned in the footnotes to the relevant sessions.

Where the same tune has been given more than one title by Mingus, the newly issued title is shown first, with an explanatory 'i.e.' afterwards. However, where the original title was still used by Mingus but the piece was retitled by a record company (e.g. *Tijuana Table Dance*) or by a radio announcer (the 1956 airshot of *Confirmation*), the correct title has been listed first followed by the incorrect title in parentheses. The following abbreviations have also been used:

acc	accordion
AFRS	Armed Forces Radio Service
arr	arranger
as	alto saxophone

b	bass
bars	baritone saxophone
bcl	bass clarinet
btb	bass trombone
btp	bass trumpet
cga	conga
cl	clarinet
cond	conductor
D	Danish
d	drums
dir	director
Du	Dutch
E	English
el-p	electric piano
eng-h	english horn
F	French
fl	flute
fr-h	french horn
G	German
g	guitar
I	Italian
J	Japanese
mat no	matrix number
mc	master of ceremonies
narr	narrator
org	organ
p	piano
perc	percussion
picc	piccolo
ss	soprano saxophone
tamb	tambourine
tb	trombone
tp	trumpet
ts	tenor saxophone
tu	tuba
tymp	tympani
vcl	vocal
vib	vibraphone
VOA	Voice of America
vtb	valve-trombone

1943:

c. early 1943 LOUIS ARMSTRONG AND HIS ORCHESTRA
Los Angeles Prob. Louis Armstrong (tp, vcl); Shelton Hemphill, Frank
Galbreath, Bernard Flood (tp); Henderson Chambers, George
Washington, James Whitney (tb); Rupert Cole (as, cl); Carl
Frye (as); Prince Robinson, Joe Garland (ts); Luis Russell (p);
Lawrence Lucie (g); Charles Mingus (b); Chick Morrison (d)
Dear old Southland AFRS Jubilee 21 (or 22)
Ol' man Mose –
Note: If Mingus took part in this session, as stated in Hans
Westerberg's Armstrong discography, there are several other
AFRS transcriptions from this period on which he may be
present

1945:

c. early 1945 *Los Angeles*	RUSSELL JACQUET AND HIS ALL STARS Russell Jacquet (tp, vcl-1); Calvin Boaz (tp); Teddy Edwards (as); Maurice Simon (ts); Arthur Dennis (bars); Bill Davis (p); Charles Mingus (b); Chico Hamilton (d)

APP6A	**Penny's worth of boogie**	Globe 105
APP6B	**Look what you've done to me** -1	–

c. early 1945 *Los Angeles*	CHARLES MINGUS Britt Woodman (tb); Buddy Collette (as); Spaulding Givens (p); Charles Mingus (b); Roy Porter (d) **unknown titles** unknown label (unissued)

c. May *Los Angeles*	HOWARD McGHEE AND HIS COMBO Howard McGhee (tp); Teddy Edwards (ts); Vernon Biddle (p); Stanley Morgan (g); Charles Mingus (b); Monk McFay (d)

JM2	**Deep meditation**	Modern Music 111

c. June *Los Angeles*	CHARLES MINGUS SEXTET N. R. Bates (tp); Maxwell Davis, William Woodman Jr. (ts); Robert Mosley (p); Charles Mingus (b); Roy Porter (d); Oradell Mitchell-1, Everett Pettis-2 (vcl)

CM132	**The Texas hop**-1	(1) Excelsior CM132
CM133	**Baby takes a chance with me**-2	(1) Excelsior CM133
CM134	**Lonesome woman blues**-1	(1) Excelsior CM134
CM135	**Swinging an echo**	(1) Excelsior CM135

Note: Although previously listed as 'late 1945', these sides were issued at the latest by September 1945. CM132/CM133 are coupled as one single, likewise CM134/CM135

August 2 *Los Angeles*	ILLINOIS JACQUET AND HIS ORCHESTRA/WYNONIE HARRIS Russell Jacquet (tp, vcl-1); Illinois Jacquet (ts); Arthur Dennis (bars); Bill Doggett (p); Charles Mingus (b); Al Wichard (d); Wynonie Harris (vcl-2)

S1100-1A-2	**Jacquet mood**	Apollo 769
S1101	**Wondering and thinking of you**-1	(2) Apollo 758
S1102(?)	**Jacquet mood (Merle's mood)**	(2) Jazz Selection 518
S1103	**Memories of you**	(2) Apollo 760
S1104	**Wynonie's blues**-2	(3) Apollo 362
S1105	**Here comes the blues**-2	(3) Apollo 363

August
Los Angeles

John Brown (as); Ulysees Livingstone (g) added; Harris out

S1113	**Bottoms up**	(2) Apollo 756
S1114	**Merle's mood**	Apollo 760
S1115	**What's this**	Apollo 758
S1116	**(I don't stand a) Ghost of a chance**	(2) Apollo 756

Note: S1104 and S1105 issued as by WYNONIE HARRIS: remainder as by ILLINOIS JACQUET AND HIS ORCHESTRA. **S1102(?)** is reissued on Vogue LD087/LDE026 (and Apollo LP104??) as **Jacquet mood** and on Vogue CLDAP858 as **Merle's mood**, and is the item referred to in Chapter Two as **Jacquet mood; the Merle's mood** referred to in Chapter Two is **S1114**

249

October 4	ERNIE ANDREWS AND THE BARANCO TRIO
Los Angeles	Wilbert Baranco (p); Buddy Harper (g); Charles Mingus (b);
	Ernie Andrews (vcl)
GEM20A	**You go to my head**	G & G 1020
GEM20B	**Don't let the sun catch you crying**	–
GEM21A	**Paradise lost**	G & G 1021
GEM21B	**(I don't stand a) Ghost of a chance**	–

c. November	BOB MOSLEY AND HIS ALL STARS
Los Angeles	Karl George (tp); Marshall Royal (as, cl); Lucky Thompson
	(ts); Bob Mosley (p); Gene Phillips (g); Charles Mingus (b);
	Lee Young (d); Marion Abernathy (vcl-1)
BTJ34-3	**Voot rhythm**	Beltone J751
BTJ35-1	**Stormy mood**-1	Beltone J752
BTJ36-2/3	**Beggin' the boogie**-1	Beltone J751
BTJ37-5	**Bee boogie boo**	Beltone J752

Note: **Bee boogie boo** has **BTJ37-5** in the wax but **BTJ37-2** on the label

December 10, 12	DINAH WASHINGTON WITH LUCKY THOMPSON
Los Angeles	AND HIS ALL STARS
	Karl George (tp); Jewel Grant (as); Lucky Thompson (ts);
	Gene Porter (bars,cl); Milt Jackson (vib); Wilbert Baranco (p);
	Charles Mingus (b); Lee Young (d); Dinah Washington (vcl)
S1170-3	**Wise woman blues**	Apollo 368
S1171-2	**Walking blues**	Apollo 374
S1172-2	**No voot – no boot**	Apollo 368
S1173	**Chewin' woman blues (Chewin' mama blues)**	Apollo 396
S1174-2	**My lovin' papa**	Apollo 371
S1175-1	**Rich man's blues**	Apollo 374
S1176	**Beggin' woman blues (Beggin' mama blues)**	Parrot 20-001
S1177	**All or nothing**-1	–
S1178-3	**Mellow mama blues**	Apollo 371
S1179-2	**My voot is really vout**	Apollo 388
S1180-1	**Blues for a day**	–
S1181	**Pacific coast blues**	Apollo 396
	1-Jackson out

1946:

January	CHARLES MINGUS SEXTETTE (*sic*)
Los Angeles	Karl George, John Plonsky (tp); Henry Coker (tb); Jewel
	Grant, Willie Smith (as); Lucky Thompson (ts); Gene Porter
	(bars,cl); Wilbert Baranco (p); Buddy Harper (g); Charles
	Mingus (b); Lee Young (d); Claude Trenier (vcl-1)
OR162A	**Ain't jivin' blues**-1	(1) Excelsior 162
OR162B	**Baby take a chance with me**-1	(1)	–
OR163A	**Shuffle bass boogie**	(1) Excelsior 163
OR163B	**Weird nightmare**-1	(1)	–

January	WILBERT BARANCO AND HIS RHYTHM
Los Angeles	BOMBARDIERS
	Karl George, Snooky Young, Howard McGhee, 'John Burk'
	(Dizzy Gillespie) (tp); Ralph Bledsoe, Henry Coker, Vic
	Dickenson, George Washington (tb); Willie Smith, Marvin

250

	Johnson (as); Lucky Thompson, Fred Simon (ts); Gene Porter (bars); Wilbert Baranco (p,vcl-1); Buddy Harper (g); Charles Mingus (b); Earl Watkins (d)	
183-2	**Night and day**	(4) Black & White 41
184-2	**Weepin' Willie**	(4) –
185-2	**Every time I think of you**-1	(4) Black & White 42
BW 186-2	**Baranco boogie**	(4) –

Same period
Broadcast,
Los Angeles

poss. Hobart Dotson, unknown (tp); Britt Woodman, Melba Liston (tb), Buddy Collette, Jackie Kelso (as) replace McGhee, Gillespie, Bledsoe (or Coker), Dickenson, Smith and Johnson; Ernie Bubbles Whitman (mc)

One o'clock jump (theme)		AFRS Jubilee 175
Bugle call rag	(5)	–
Night and day	(5)	–
Every time I think of you-1		–
Where you at		–
Baranco boogie	(5)	–
One o'clock jump (theme)		–

January
Los Angeles

IVIE ANDERSON AND HER ALL STARS
Karl George (tp); Willie Smith (as); Gene Porter (ts); Buddy Collette (bars); Wilbert Baranco (p); Buddy Harper (g); Charles Mingus (b); Booker Hart (d)

BW203	**I got it bad and that ain't good**	Black & White 771
BW204	**On the sunny side of the street**	(1) –
BW205-1	**I thought you ought to know**	Black & White 772
BW206-3	**The voot is here to stay**	–

Spring
Los Angeles

THE STARS OF SWING
John Anderson (tp); Britt Woodman (tb); Buddy Collette (as); Lucky Thompson (ts); Spaulding Givens (p); Charles Mingus (b); Oscar Bradley (d)

unknown titles	unknown label (unissued)

April 26(?)
Los Angeles

BARON MINGUS AND HIS OCTET
unknown tp, tb; prob. Buddy Collette (as); unknown ts, bars; Lady Will Carr (p); unknown g; Charles Mingus (b); unknown d, vcl-1

	Ashby de la zouch	(1) 4 Star 1105
	Love on a greyhound bus	(1) –
388AS-2	**After hours**-2	(1) 4 Star 1106

May 6
Los Angeles

393AS	**Make believe**	(1) 4 Star 1107
394AS-1	**Honey take a chance with me**-1	(1) 4 Star 1108
395AS	**Bedspread**	(1) 4 Star 1107
396AS-2	**This subdues my passion**	(1) 4 Star 1108
397AS-2	**Pipe Dream** (i.e. **Weird nightmare**)	(1) 4 Star 1106

2-p, b, g only; issued as by LADY WILL CARR AND HER TRIO

Note: **397AS-2** issued as by LADY WILL CARR WITH BARON MINGUS AND HIS OCTET

251

Same period	HOWARD McGHEE AND HIS ORCHESTRA	
Los Angeles	Howard McGhee (tp); Teddy Edwards (ts); James King (ts, vcl-1); Jimmy Bunn (p); Charles Mingus (b); Roy Porter (d)	
KFI-23333	**Sweet potato**	Melodisc M1001
KFI-23337	**Hoggin'**	Melodisc M1002
KFI-23345	**Blues a la King**-1	–
KFI-22610	**Night mist**	Melodisc M1001

Same period	DARBY HICKS QUARTET	
Los Angeles	Buddy Collette (reeds); Darby Hicks (p); Buddy Harper (g); Charles Mingus (b); Norman Alexander-1, Carolyn Richards-2 (vcl)	
101A	**Lazy baby**-1	Indigo 101
101B	**Just count the days I'm gone**-2	–

Same period	GENE MORRIS QUINTET	
Los Angeles	Walter Morris (tp); Gene Morris (ts); George Williams (p); Charles Mingus (b); Lee Young (d); Lee Williams (vcl-1)	
KI-501A	**Riff G.M.**	Cleartone 501
KI-501B	**Is it a sin?**-1	–
FOTO-502A	**G-ing with Gene**	Cleartone 502
FOTO-502B	**Laughing at life**-1	–

1947:

c. February	CHARLES MINGUS	
Los Angeles	unknown large orchestra incl. Buddy Collette, Ted Nash (reeds); Red Callender, Billy Hadnott, Artie Bernstein, Art Shapiro (b); unknown cond; Charles Mingus (narr)	
	The chill of death	Columbia (?) unissued
c. Spring		
Los Angeles	unknown big band incl. Jimmy Knepper (tb); Charles Mingus (b)	
	unknown titles	unknown label (unissued?)

Note: This *may* be the Rex Hollywood session dated as c. Spring 1949

October	GERRY WIGGINS	
Los Angeles	Gerry Wiggins(p); Charles Mingus (b)	
	Cherokee	(1) Private recording
	These foolish things	(1) –

November 3	LIONEL HAMPTON AND HIS ORCHESTRA	
Los Angeles	Leo Sheppard, Duke Garrette, Snooky Young, Wendell Culley, Teddy Buckner (tp); Andrew Penn, James Robinson, Britt Woodman, James Wormick (tb); Bobby Plater, Ben Kynard (as); Jack Kelso (cl,as); Morris Lane, John Sparrow (ts); Charlie Fowlkes (bars); Lionel Hampton (vib); Milt Buckner (p); Billy Mackel (g); Joe Comfort, Charles Mingus (b); Earl Walker (d)	
W4528-3	**Goldwyn stomp**	(6) Decca 24505
WL4529-7	**Red top**	(6) Decca 24281
WL4530-2	**Giddy up**	(6) –

November 10		
Los Angeles	Walter Williams (tp) replaces Young	
W4543-5	**Hawk's nest**	(6) Decca 24505

WL4544-6	**Mingus fingers**	(1,6) Decca 24428
WL4545-5	**Muchacho azul**	(6) –
WL4546-12	**Midnight sun**	(6) Decca 24429

November 14
Los Angeles
LIONEL HAMPTON AND HIS SEXTET
Benny Bailey (tp); Morris Lane (ts); Lionel Hampton (vib, p-1, vcl-2); Dodo Marmarosa-3, Milt Buckner-4 (p); Billy Mackel (g); Charles Mingus (b); Earl Walker, Curley Hamner (d)

WL4560-10	**Cherokee**-3	(6) Decca 24430
WL4561-8	**No. 2 rebop and bebop**-3	(6) –
WL4562-7	**Zoo-baba-da-oo-ee**-1,2,3	(6) Decca 24431
WL4563-10	**Rebop's turning blue**-4,5	(6) –

5-Bailey and Walker out
Note: Unknown fl heard on **WL4544-6**

December 31
Chicago
EARL HINES AND HIS ORCHESTRA/CURLEY HAMNER AND HIS ORCHESTRA
Duke Garrette (tp); Bobby Plater (as); Morris Lane (ts); Charlie Fowlkes (bars); Bill Dougherty (vln); Earl Hines (p); Billy Mackel (g); Charles Mingus (b); Curley Hamner (d); Wini Brown (vcl)

SU2126	**The sheik of Araby**	Sunrise 525
	No good woman blues	Pickwick PR127, Bravo K134
	Bow legged woman	– –
	My name is on the doorbell	– –
SR2128	**Bama lama lam**	Sunrise 2115
SR2129	**Spooky boogie**	

Note: **SR2128** and **SR2129** issued as by CURLEY HAMNER AND HIS ORCHESTRA; remainder as by EARL HINES AND HIS ORCHESTRA

1948:

May 1
Broadcast,
Howard Theatre
Washington, D.C.
LIONEL HAMPTON AND HIS ORCHESTRA
As for November 10, 1947 except Fats Navarro (tp); Sonny Craven (tb); Billy Williams (ts); Charlie Harris (b) replace W. Williams, Robinson, Lane and Comfort; Woodman and Kelso out

	Hot house	(7) JDS JDS12-1*
	Wizzin' the wizz	Airshot*

July 1
Broadcast,
Geneva, N.Y.
Jimmy Nottingham (tp); Lester Bass (tb,btp); Wes Montgomery (g) replace Navarro, Penn and Mackel

July 7
Broadcast,
Geneva, N.Y.
Billie Holiday-1, Wynonie Harris-2 (vcl); Bobby Tucker (p-1) added

	Adam blew his hat	(7) JDS JDS12-1
	I cover the waterfront-1	JDS JDS12-1
	Good rockin' tonight-2	(7) –

July 21
Broadcast,
Geneva, N.Y.
Johnny Board (as) added; Holiday, W. Harris and Tucker out

	Brant Inn boogie	(7) JDS JDS12-1

August 4
Broadcast,
Peoria, Ill.
Roy Johnson (bs) replaces C. Harris

	Body and soul	(7) –

August 11
Broadcast,
Denver

	Satchmo's blues	(7) –

Note: According to contemporary reports, Hampton's appearance at the Howard Theatre, Washington, D.C. was for one week beginning April 23, the following week (incl. May 1) being an engagement at the Royal Theatre, Baltimore.

1949:

c. January　　CHARLES 'BARON' MINGUS PRESENTS HIS
San Francisco　SYMPHONIC AIRS
　　　　　　　　Vern Carlson, 4 unknowns (tp); Henry Coker, 3 unknowns (tb); 5 unknown reeds; Dante Profumato (fl); Richard Wyands (p); unknown g, b; Charles Mingus (b, cello); unknown d, tamb; Herb Gayle (vcl-1)

0-189	**He's gone**-1	(1) Fentone 2002
0-190	**Story of love**	(1)　　–
	God's portrait-1(?)	Fentone 2001 (unissued?)
	unknown title	–

c. January　　BARON MINGUS AND HIS RHYTHM
San Francisco　Herb Caro (bars); Buzz Wheeler (p); Charles Mingus (b); Warren Thompson (d); Herb Gayle (vcl-1)

Pennies from heaven-1	(1) Fentone 2003
Lyon's roar	(1)　　–

c. Spring　　Buddy Collette (cl. as); unknown p; Charles Mingus (b);
Los Angeles　unknown d

Mingus fingers	(1) Dolphins of Hollywood 200
These foolish things	(1)　　–

Same period　unknown tp, tb; poss. Buddy Collette (ts); unknown p; Charles
Los Angeles　Mingus (b); unknown d; Helen Carr-1, unknown-2 (vcl)

DH-300-A	**Say it isn't so**-1	(1) Dolphins of Hollywood 300
DH-300-B	**Boppin n' Boston**-2	(1)　　–

Same period　unknown big band incl. Charles Mingus (b)
Los Angeles

Story of love	(1) Rex Hollywood 28002
Inspiration Pts. 1 and 2	(1) Rex Hollywood 28014

1950:

May 3　　　RED NORVO TRIO
Los Angeles　Red Norvo (vib); Tal Farlow (g); Charles Mingus (b)

D305-1	**Swedish pastry**	(8) Savoy SJL2212
D305-?	**Swedish pastry**	(8) Discovery 135
D306	**Cheek to cheek**	(8) Discovery 134
D307-?	**Night and day**	(8) Discovery 135
D307-?	**Night and day**	Discovery DL3018
D308	**Time and tide**	(8) Discovery 134

October 31
Chicago

D375	**September song**	(8) Discovery 147
D376	**Move**	(8) Discovery 145
D377	**I've got you under my skin**	(8) Discovery 144
D378	**I'll remember April**	(8) Discovery 146
D379	**I get a kick out of you**	(8)　　–
D380	**I can't believe that you're in love with me**	(8) Discovery 144
D381-?	**Little white lies**	(8) Discovery 145
D381-?	**Little white lies**	Discovery DL3012
D382	**Have you met Miss Jones?**	(8) Discovery DL3014
D383	**Zing! went the strings of my heart**	(8) Discovery 147

Same period	**Tea for two**		Standard Q-261
Chicago	**I only have eyes for you**	(9)	–
	Budo	(9)	–
	Sweet Georgia Brown	(9)	–
	Night and day		–
	This can't be love	(9)	–
	These foolish things	(9)	–
	Good bait	(9)	–
	September song	(9)	–
	September in the rain	(9)	–
	I get a kick out of you		Standard Q-262
	Swedish pastry		–
	Blue room	(9)	–
	Move		–
	If I had you		–
	C jam blues	(9)	–
	Time and tide		–
	Godchild	(9)	–
	Crazy rhythm	(9)	–
	Rose room	(9)	–
	Where or when	(9)	Standard Q-266
	East of the sun	(9)	–
	Begin the beguine	(9)	–
	Honeysuckle rose	(9)	–
	Exactly like you	(9)	–
	Zing! went the strings of my heart		–
	My blue heaven		–
	I'm yours		–
	Sunday		–
	Cheek to cheek		–

1951:

c. early 1951	MEL TORME WITH THE RED NORVO TRIO	
Los Angeles	Red Norvo (vib); Tal Farlow (g); Charles Mingus (b); Mel Torme (vcl)	
	unknown titles	Capitol unissued

Same period	ANN MILLER WITH THE RED NORVO TRIO	
Los Angeles	Ann Miller (vcl) replaces Torme	
	Dynamite	Soundtrack

Same period	RED NORVO TRIO	
Los Angeles	Miller out	
	Time and tide	Soundtrack

April 13		
Los Angeles		
D480-?	**If I had you**	Discovery 166
D480-?	**If I had you**	(8) Discovery DL3018
D481-1	**This can't be love**	(8) Savoy SJL2212
D481-2	**This can't be love**	(8) Savoy SJL2212
D481-3	**This can't be love**	(8) Discovery 167
D482-1	**Godchild**	(8) Savoy SJL2212
D482-2	**Godchild**	(8) Savoy SJL2212
D482-?	**Godchild**	(8) Discovery 167
D483-?	**I'm yours**	(8) Discovery DL3018

255

D483-3	I'm yours	Discovery 166
Prob. same	**Mood Indigo**	(8) Savoy SJL2212
session	**Prelude to a kiss**	(8) –
	Deed I do	(8) –

April
Los Angeles
STRINGS AND KEYS
Spaulding Givens (p); Charles Mingus (b)

What is this thing called love	Debut DLP1
Darn that dream	–
Yesterdays	–
Body and soul	–
Blue moon	–
Blue tide	–
unknown titles	Discovery unissued

c. Summer
Christy's,
Framingham,
Mass.
CHARLIE PARKER JAM SESSION
unknown tp; Charlie Parker (as); unknown ts; Dick Twardzik (p); Charles Mingus (b); unknown d

I'll remember April	(10) Charlie Parker PLP404

September 29
Broadcast,
Birdland,
New York City
MILES DAVIS ALL STARS
Miles Davis (tp); Lockjaw Davis, Big Nick Nicholas (ts); Billy Taylor (p); Charles Mingus (b); Art Blakey (d); Symphony Sid (mc)

Move (Mod)	(11) Ozone 7
The squirrel	(11) –
Lady bird	(11) –*

prob. November 6
Broadcast,
Storyville,
Boston
BILLY TAYLOR TRIO
Billy Taylor (p); Charles Mingus (b); Marquis Foster (d)

What is this thing called love	(12) Roost RLP406
I'm beginning to see the light	(10,12) –
All the things you are	(10) –
Laura	–
Lady bird	(10) –

December 18
New York City
MELVIN MOORE
unknown fl, oboe, strings; Terry Gibbs (vib); Billy Taylor (p); Mundell Lowe (g); Charles Mingus (b); Charlie Smith (d); Melvin Moore (vcl)

K8150	**While I'm gone**	King 4519
K8151	**Possessed**	King 4539
K8152	**Hold me, kiss me, squeeze me**	–
K8153	**I'll be there**	King 4519

1952:
February 21
Broadcast,
WNYC Studio,
New York City
JAZZ '52
Lee Konitz (as); George Wallington (p); Chuck Wayne (g); Charles Mingus (b); Max Roach (d)

Yesterdays	Airshot

Note: All except Roach play final chord only of **Drum conversation** from this session

c. Spring
Broadcast,
Birdland,
DIZZY GILLESPIE/CHARLIE PARKER
Dizzy Gillespie (tp); Charlie Parker (as); Billy Taylor (p); Charles Mingus (b); prob. Max Roach (d)

256

New York City	**How high the moon**	VOA JC26
	Hot house	–
	Embraceable you	–

April 12
New York City

CHARLES MINGUS QUINTET
Lee Konitz (as); Phyllis Pinkerton (p); George Koutzen (cello); Charles Mingus (b); Al Levitt (d); Jackie Paris-1, Bob Benton-2 (vcl)

RKV5241	**Precognition**	Debut M101
RKV5242	**Portrait** (i.e. **God's portrait**)-1	–
E2CB6497-2	**Montage**-2	Debut M103
E2KB6500-1	**Extrasensory perception**	–

April 15
Broadcast,
Birdland,
New York City

STAN GETZ QUINTET
Stan Getz (ts); Horace Silver (p); Jimmy Raney (g); Charles Mingus (b); Connie Kay (d); Symphony Sid (mc)

	Potter's luck	Alto AL704
	I can't get started	–
	Parker 51 (Cherokee)	–

May 31
Broadcast,
Birdland,
New York City

Duke Jordan (p); Phil Brown (d) replace Silver and Kay; Mingus (definite on above session) may be replaced by Nelson Boyd or Gene Ramey (b) on the following

	Just you, just me	Alto AL704
	Yesterdays	–
	Long Island sound	–
	Round midnight	–

August 9
Broadcast,
Birdland,
New York City

	Woody'n you (Wouldn't you)	Session Disc 108*
	Yesterdays	–
	The song is you	–
	I only have eyes for you	–
	Move (Moo)	–

August 16
Broadcast,
Birdland,
New York City

	My old flame	Alto AL704
	Move (Moo)	–
	I'll remember April	Session Disc 108*

September 4
New York City

GEORGE WALLINGTON TRIO
George Wallington (p); Chuck Wayne (mandola-1); Charles Mingus (b); Max Roach (d)

351	**Love beat**-1	(13) Prestige 788, PRLP136
352	**Summer rain**	(13) Prestige 803, –
353	**Escalating**	(13) –
354	**Laura**	(13) –

Note: Mingus replaced by Oscar Pettiford (b) on other titles from this session

September 16
New York City

CHARLES MINGUS QUINTET
Paige Brook (fl,as); John Mehegan (p); Jackson Wiley (cello); Charles Mingus (b); Max Roach (d); Jackie Paris (vcl)

E2CB6494-2	**Paris in blue**	Debut M102
E2CB6495-2	**Make believe**	–

September 20
Broadcast,
Birdland,

CHARLIE PARKER
Charlie Parker (as); Duke Jordan (p); Charles Mingus (b); Phil Brown (d); Bob Garrity (mc)

| *New York City* | **Ornithology** | Mark MG101 |
| | **52nd street theme** | – |

October 16	OSCAR PETTIFORD QUARTET	
New York City	Billy Taylor (p); Oscar Pettiford (cello); Charles Mingus (b); Charlie Smith (d)	
R1102	**Cello again**	Roost 546
R1103	**Ah dee dong blues (Oriental cello blues)**	Roost 561
R1104	**Sonny boy**	Roost 546
R1105	**I'm beginning to see the light**	Roost 561

c. 1952	JOHN MEHEGAN	
New York City	John Mehegan (p); Charles Mingus (b)	
	King Porter stomp	Perspective PR1
	Maple leaf rag	–
	Pinetop's boogie woogie	–
	Rosetta	–
	Ain't misbehavin'	–
	Tea for two	–
	Don't blame me	–
	Sweet Lorraine	–
	This can't be love	–
	Untitled original	–
	Untitled blues	–*

Note: Incomplete takes of last title are used with Mehegan (narr) overdubbed

1953:

January 30	DUKE ELLINGTON AND HIS ORCHESTRA	
Broadcast,	Cat Anderson, Clark Terry, Willie Cook (tp); Ray Nance (tp,	
WMGM Studio,	vln,vcl-1); Britt Woodman, Quentin Jackson (tb); Juan Tizol	
New York City	(vtb); Hilton Jefferson (as); Russell Procope (as,cl); Paul	
	Gonsalves (ts); Jimmy Hamilton (ts,cl); Harry Carney (bars,	
	bcl); Duke Ellington (p); Charles Mingus (b); Louis Bellson	
	(d); Jimmy Grissom-2, Betty Roche-3 (vcl)	
	Take the 'A' train (theme)	Airshot
	Summertime	–
	Come on home-2	–
	The hawk talks	–
	Bakiff	–
	Take the 'A' train-3	–
	Monologue-4	–
	Rockin' in rhythm	–
	Smada	–
	Take the 'A' train	–*
February 2	**Take the 'A' train** (theme)	Airshot
Broadcast,	**Caravan**	–
WMGM Studio,	**Smada**	–
New York City	**Do nothin' till you hear from me**-2	–
	The mooche	–
	How high the moon	–
	Take the 'A' train (theme)	–
	Caravan	–
	Love you madly-3	–

VIP's boogie	–	
Jam with Sam	–	
St. Louis blues-1	–	
Things ain't what they used to be	–	

4-Procope, Hamilton (cl); Carney (bcl); Ellington (narr) only

March 21	BUD POWELL TRIO	
Broadcast,	Bud Powell (p); Charles Mingus (b); Roy Haynes (d)	
Birdland,	**I want to be happy**	Session Disc 109
New York City	**I've got you under my skin**	–
	Embraceable you	–
	Woody'n you (Wouldn't you)	–
	Salt peanuts	–
April 5	**I want to be happy**	(14) Elektra E1-60030
Club Kavakos,	**Somebody loves me**	(14) –
Washington, D.C.	**Nice work if you can get it**	(14) –
	Salt peanuts	(14) –
	Conception	(14) –
	Lullaby of Birdland	(14) –
	Little Willie leaps	(14) –
	Hallelujah	(14) –
	Lullaby of Birdland	(14) –
	Sure thing	(14) –
	Woody'n you	(14) –

April 29	THE GORDONS	
New York City	Hank Jones (p); Charles Mingus (b); Max Roach (d); Honey Gordon-1, George Gordon-2, George Gordon Jr.-2, Richard Gordon-2 (vcl)	
RM508	**Can you blame me?**-1	Debut M110
RM509	**You and me**-1,2	Debut M111
RM510	**Bebopper**-1,2	Debut M110
RM511	**Cupid**-1	Debut M111
	You go to my head	Debut DEB198

Note: Last title issued as by HANK JONES TRIO

May 15	QUINTET OF THE YEAR	
Massey Hall,	Dizzy Gillespie (tp,vcl-1); Charlie Parker (as); Bud Powell (p);	
Toronto	Charles Mingus (b); Max Roach (d)	
	Wee	(15) Debut DLP4
	Hot house	(15) –
	Night in Tunisia	(15) –
	Perdido	(15) Debut DLP2
	Salt peanuts-1	(15) –
	All the things you are/52nd street theme	(15) –

Note: Mingus overdubbed on all (except part of **Hot House**) of DLP4, and on reissues of DLP2

Same concert	BUD POWELL TRIO	
	As above minus Gillespie and Parker	
	Lullaby of Birdland	(15) Debut DLP3
	Cherokee	(15) –
	Embraceable you	(15) –
	Jubilee	(15) –
	Sure thing	(15) –

259

	I've got you under my skin	(15) Debut DEB198
	Bass-ically speaking	unissued
	Note: Mingus and Powell out on **Drum conversation** from this concert	
Same period	Billy Taylor (p) replaces Powell	
New York City	**Bass-ically speaking**	Debut DLP3

May 19	MILES DAVIS	
New York City	Miles Davis (tp); Charles Mingus (p); Percy Heath (b); Max Roach (d)	
482	**Smooch** (i.e. **Weird nightmare**)	(16) Prestige 884

May 22	CHARLIE PARKER	
New York City	Junior Collins (fr-h); Al Block (fl); Hal McKusick (cl); Tommy Mace (oboe); Manny Thaler (bassoon); Charlie Parker (as); Tony Aless (p); Charles Minguş (b); Max Roach (d); Dave Lambert Singers (vcl); Gil Evans (arr,cond)	
C 1238-7	**In the still of the night**	(17) Clef 11100
C 1239-9	**Old folks**	(17) –
C 1240-9	**If I love again**	(17) Verve MGV8009

May 30	BUD POWELL TRIO WITH DIZZY GILLESPIE AND
Broadcast,	CHARLIE PARKER
Birdland	Dizzy Gillespie (tp-1); Charlie Parker (as-2); Bud Powell (p);
New York City	Charles Mingus (b); Art Taylor (d); Candido Camero (cga-3)
	Autumn in New York	(18) Session Disc 109
	I want to be happy	(18) –
	I've got you under my skin	(18) ESP (J) SXF10028
	Moose the mooche-2,3	(18) Queen-Disc Q-002
	Cheryl-2,3	(18) –
	Lullaby of Birdland (theme)-2,3	Airshot
Same period	Max Roach (d) replaces Taylor	
Broadcast	**Budo** (i.e. **Hallucinations**)	Airshot
	Salt peanuts-1	–
	Algo bueno (i.e. **Woody'n you**)-1	–
	Dance of the infidels-2	Parktec 46271
Same period	**My devotion**	(15) Fantasy 6006, 86006
Broadcast	**Polka dots and moonbeams**	(15) – –
	My heart stood still	(15) – –
	I want to be happy	(15) – –

c. May	SONNY STITT	
New York City	Don Elliott (tp, mellophone); Kai Winding (tb); Sonny Stitt (as,ts); Sid Cooper (ts,fl,picc); George Berg (bars); Horace Silver (p); Charles Mingus (b); Don Lamond (d); Johnny Richards (arr, cond)	
R 1156	**Sancho Panza**	(19) Roost 571
R 1157	**Sweet and lovely**	(10) Roost 576
R 1158	**If I could be with you**	(10) Roost 571
R 1159	**Hooke's tours**	(19) Roost 576
c. July	Gerry Sanfino (fl); Al Williams (p); Jo Jones (d,bgo); Santo	
New York City	Mirando (cga) replace Cooper, Silver and Lamond	
R 1180	**Shine on, harvest moon**	(10) Roost 588
R 1181	**Opus 202**	(19) –
	Loose walk	(19) Roost RLP415
	Pink satin	(19) –

September 18	JAZZ WORKSHOP	
Putnam Central	J.J. Johnson, Kai Winding, Bennie Green, Willie Dennis (tb);	
Club, Brooklyn,	John Lewis (p); Charles Mingus (b); Art Taylor (d)	
New York City	**Move**	(20) Debut DLP5
	Stardust-1	(20) –
	Yesterdays	–
	I'll remember April	(20) Debut DLP14
	Blues for some bones	(20) –
	Ow!	(20) Debut DLP126**
	Trombosphere	(20) –
	Now's the time	(20) – **
	Chazzanova	(20) – **
	Kai's day	Debut DLP198
	Conversation-2	Roost OJ1

1-Green and rhythm only; 2-Johnson, Winding and rhythm only

October 27	CHARLES MINGUS OCTET	
New York City	Ernie Royal (tp); Willie Dennis (tb); Eddie Caine (as,fl); Teo Macero (ts); Danny Bank (bars); John Lewis (p); Jackson Wiley (cello); Charles Mingus (b); Kenny Clarke (d); Spaulding Givens (arr); Janet Thurlow (vcl-1)	
	Eclipse-1	Debut EP450
	Blue tide-1	–
	Pink topsy	–
	Miss bliss	–

November 30	PAUL BLEY TRIO	
New York City	Paul Bley (p); Charles Mingus (b); Art Blakey (d)	
	Opus one	Debut DLP7
	Teapot	–
	Like someone in love	–
	Split kick	–
	I can't get started	–
	Spontaneous combustion	–
	Santa Claus is coming to town	Debut DLP198
	Drum one	unissued
	Autumn breeze	–

December 5	TEO MACERO QUINTET	
New York City	Teo Macero (ts,as); Lanny Dijay (acc); Charles Mingus, Lou LaBella (b); Ed Shaughnessy (d)	
	Teo	(21) Debut DLP6
	Mitzi	(21) –
	I'll remember April	(21) –
	How low the earth	(21) –
	Yesterdays	–
	Explorations-1	(21) –

1-Macero only, overdubbed

December 29	OSCAR PETTIFORD SEXTET	
New York City	Julius Watkins (fr-h); Phil Urso (ts); Walter Bishop (p); Oscar Pettiford (cello); Charles Mingus (b); Percy Brice (d); Quincy Jones (arr)	
	Jack the fieldstalker	Debut DLP8
	Stockholm sweetnin'	–

261

Low and behold   –
The pendulum at Falcon's Lair   –
Note: Mingus out on **Tamalpais** from this session

1954:

August 11
New York City

THAD JONES
Thad Jones (tp); Frank Wess (ts-1,fl-2); Hank Jones (p);
Charles Mingus (b); Kenny Clarke (d)

Bitty ditty-1	(22) Debut DLP12	
Chazzanova-1	–	
I'll remember April		
(Chazzanova)-1	(22)	–
Illusive (Elusive)-1	(22)	–
You don't know what love is	(22)	–
Sombre intrusion-2	(22)	–

August 24
Hackensack, N.J.

J.J. JOHNSON AND KAI WINDING
J.J. Johnson, Kai Winding (tb); Billy Bauer (g); Charles
Mingus (b); Kenny Clarke (d)

Blues for trombones	(23) Savoy 4506, XP8140, MG15038
Lament	(23) Savoy XP8142, MG15038
The major	(23) Savoy XP8141, MG15048
What is this thing called love	(23) Savoy XP8140, MG15048

August 26
Hackensack, N.J.

Wally Cirillo (p) replaces Bauer

Bernie's tune	(23) Savoy 4506, XP8141, MG15038
Co-op	(23) Savoy XP8140, MG15038
Reflections	(23) Savoy XP8141, MG15038
Blues in twos	(23) Savoy XP8142, MG15038

September 17
New York City

THAD JONES/DON SENAY
Thad Jones-1, Louis Mucci (tp); unknown fr-h; John LaPorta,
Julius Baker (reeds, woodwinds); Billy Taylor (p); Jackson
Wiley (cello); Milt Hinton, Fred Zimmermann (b); Joe
Morello (d); unknown harp, strings; Charles Mingus, Alonzo
Levister (arr); Don Senay (vcl-2)

Edge of love-1	Debut 112
Fantasy-2	–
Making whoopee-2	Debut DEB198
Portrait-1	–

Note: Solos by Jones and Senay overdubbed

September 24
Hackensack, N.J.

J.J. JOHNSON
J.J. Johnson (tb); Wynton Kelly (p); Charles Mingus (b);
Kenny Clarke (d); Sabu Martinez (cga-1)

Jay-1	(24) Blue Note 45-1651, BLP5057

	Old devil moon-1	(24) Blue Note 45-1651, BLP5057
	Too marvellous for words-1	(24) Blue Note BLP5057
	Coffee pot	(24) –
	It's you or no one	(24) –
	Time after time	(25) –

October 31
Hackensack, N.J.   CHARLES MINGUS SEXTET
John LaPorta (cl-1,as-2); Teo Macero (ts-3,bars-4); George Barrow (bars-5,ts-6); Mal Waldron (p); Charles Mingus (b); Rudy Nichols (d)

SCM6914	Purple heart-1,4,6,7	(26) Savoy MG15050
SCM6915	Gregarian chant-1,3,5	(26) –
SCM6916	Eulogy for Rudy Williams-2,3,5	(26) –
SCM6917	Tea for two-1,3,5	(26) –
SCM6918	Getting together-1,3,5	(26) –
SCM6919	Body and soul-2,3,5	–
	7-Waldron out	

November 9
New York City   VIN STRONG
Vin Strong (org); Wally Richardson (g); Charles Mingus (b); James Smith (d)

SVS7900	Lovingly	Regent MG6044
SVS7901	Heart strings	Savoy 1145, –
SVS7902	Swinging the mambo	–
SVS7903	New Orleans mambo	unissued

c. December
New York City   CHARLES MINGUS JAZZ WORKSHOP
'Oliver King' (Thad Jones) (tp); John LaPorta (cl-1,as-2); Teo Macero (ts-3,bars-4); Jackson Wiley (cello); Charles Mingus (b-5,p-6); Clem DeRosa (d,tamb)

	Trilogy pogo (What is this thing	
	called love)-1,2,3,5,6	(27) Period SLP1107
	Minor intrusion-2,3,5,6	(27) –
	Abstractions-2,3,5	(28) –
	Stormy weather-2,3,5	(28) –
	Spur of the moment-2,3,5,7	(27) Period SL P 1111
	Thrice upon a theme-1,4,5,6,7,8	(27) –
	Four hands-2,3,5,6,7,8	(27) –
	7-Wiley out; 8-Jones out	

Note: On **Four hands** Mingus plays b and p simultaneously by overdubbing; on other tracks both instruments are used alternately

1955:
January 6
Hackensack, N.J.   TEDDY CHARLES NEW DIRECTIONS QUARTET
J.R. Monterose (ts); Teddy Charles (vib); Charles Mingus (b); Jerry Segal (d)

680	Violetta	New Jazz NJLP1106
681	Relaxo-abstracto	–
682	Speak low	–
683	Jay walking	–
684	The night we called it a day	–
685	I can't get started	–

January 21
Hackensack, N.J.   HAZEL SCOTT
Hazel Scott (p); Charles Mingus (b); Max Roach (d)

263

The jeep is jumpin'	Debut DLP16	
Git up from there	–	
A foggy day	–	
Like someone in love	–	
Peace of mind	–	
Lament	–	

January 30
Hackensack, N.J.   JOHN MEHEGAN TRIO
John Mehegan (p); Charles Mingus (b); Kenny Clarke (d)

SJM4650	**Blues too much**	Savoy XP8130,MG15054
SJM4651	**Thou swell**	– –
SJM4652	**The boy next door**	– –
SJM4653	**Cherokee**	– –

Same session   WALLY CIRILLO QUARTET
Teo Macero (ts); Wally Cirillo (p) replace Mehegan

SWC4654	**Transeason (Transocean)**	(26) Savoy MG15055
SWC4655	**Rose geranium**	(26) –
SWC4656	**Level seven**	(26) –
SWC4657	**Smog L.A.**	(26) –

Note: All reissues as by CHARLES MINGUS

February 5
New York City   LITTLE JIMMY SCOTT
Budd Johnson (ts); Howard Biggs (p,arr); Mundell Lowe (g);
Charles Mingus (b); Rudy Nichols (d); Little Jimmy Scott (vcl)

WJS4662	**When did you leave heaven**	Savoy 1154
WJS4663	**Guilty**	Savoy 1199
WJS4664	**Everybody needs somebody**	Savoy 1154
WJS4665	**Why don't you open up your heart**	Savoy 1174

March 10
Hackensack, N.J.   THAD JONES/JOHN DENNIS
Thad Jones (tp-1); John Dennis (p); Charles Mingus (b); Max
Roach (d)

	One more-1	(22) Debut DLP17
	I can't get started-1	(22) –
	More of the same-1	(22) –
	Get out of town-1	(22) –
	Ensenada	Debut DEB121
	Machajo	–
	Cherokee	–
	Seven moods	–

Note: DLP17 issued as by THAD JONES, DEB121 by JOHN
DENNIS

May 27
New York City   RALPH SHARON ALL STAR SEXTET
J.R. Moterose (as,ts); Teddy Charles (vib); Ralph Sharon (p);
Joe Puma (g); Charles Mingus (b); Kenny Clarke (d)

	Manhattan	London LL1488
	Two sleepy people	–
	Have you met Miss Jones?	–
	Man on the couch	–
	Just because we're kids	–
	Darn that dream	–
	Mood for Mitch	–
	There's a small hotel	–
	Love walked in	–

264

Can't get out of this mood	–	
Plutocrat at the automat	–	
Slightly Oliver	–	

July 9
Hackensack, N.J.

MILES DAVIS
Miles Davis (tp); Britt Woodman (tb); Teddy Charles (vib); Charles Mingus (b); Elvin Jones (d)

Nature boy	(29) Debut DEB120	
Alone together	(29)	–
There's no you	(29)	–
Easy living	(29)	–

July 17
Newport, R.I.

CHARLES MINGUS
Art Farmer (tp); Britt Woodman, Eddie Bert (tb); John LaPorta (as,cl); Teo Macero (ts); Teddy Charles (vib); Mal Waldron (p); Charles Mingus (b); Elvin Jones (d)

The emperor	VOA
Sounds of April	–
Minor intrusion	–
Non-sectarian	–

December 23
Cafe Bohemia,
New York City

CHARLES MINGUS JAZZ WORKSHOP
Eddie Bert (tb); George Barrow (ts); Mal Waldron (p); Charles Mingus (b); Willie Jones-1, Max Roach-2 (d)

Jump, Monk-1	(30) Debut DEB123		
Septemberly (September in the rain)-1	(30)	–	
Percussion discussion-2,3	(30)	–	
Work song-1	(30)	–	
Serenade in blue-1	(30)	–	
All the things you C sharp (All the things you are)-1	(30)	–**	
A foggy day-1	(30) Fantasy 6009,86009		
Drums-2	(30)	–	–
Haitian fight song-1	(30)	–	–
Lady bird-1	(30)	–	–
I'll remember April-2	(30)	–	–
Love chant-1	(30)	–	–

3-Bert, Barrow and Waldron omitted; additional bass part overdubbed

1956:

January 30
New York City

Jackie McLean (as); J.R. Monterose (ts) replace Bert and Barrow

1865	**Pithecanthropus erectus**-1	(31,31a) Atlantic 1237
1866	**A foggy day**-1	(31) –
1867	**What is this thing called love**-1	unissued
1868	**Love chant**-1	(31) Atlantic 1237
1869	**Profile of Jackie**-1	(31,31a) –

June 18
New York City

METRONOME ALL STARS
Thad Jones (tp); Eddie Bert (tb); Tony Scott (cl); Lee Konitz (as); Zoot Sims, Al Cohn (ts); Serge Chaloff (bars); Teddy Charles (vib); Billy Taylor (p); Tal Farlow (g); Charles Mingus (b); Art Blakey (d)

11740-3	**Billie's bounce**	(32) Clef MGC743

265

July 5	CHARLES MINGUS JAZZ WORKSHOP	
Freebody Park,	Bill Hardman (tp); Ernie Henry (as); Teo Macero (ts); Mal	
Newport, R.I.	Waldron (p); Charles Mingus (b); Al Dreares (d)	
	Tonight at noon	VOA
	Tourist in Manhattan	–

August 18		
Broadcast,	Jackie McLean (as) replaces Henry and Macero	
Cafe Bohemia,	**Confirmation (Purple heart)**	Airshot
New York City	**Bohemia**	–
c. Autumn		
Broadcast,	poss. Tommy Turrentine (tp); Willie Dennis (tb); George	
Cafe Bohemia,	Barrow (or Shafi Hadi?) (ts) replace Hardman and McLean	
New York City	**Laura**	Airshot
	Jump, Monk	–

September 14	QUINCY JONES	
New York City	Art Farmer (tp); Jimmy Cleveland (tb); Herbie Mann (fl,ts);	
	Gene Quill (as); Lucky Thompson-1, Zoot Sims-2 (ts); Jack	
	Nimitz (bars); 'Brother Soul' (Milt Jackson) (vib); Hank Jones	
	(p); Charles Mingus (b); Charlie Persip (d); Father John	
	Crowley (handclapping-3); Quincy Jones (arr,cond)	
	Sermonette-1,3	ABC-Paramount ABC149
	Evening in Paris-2	–
September 16	Phil Woods (as); Billy Taylor (p) replace Quill and Jones; Sims,	
New York City	Jackson and Crowley omitted	
	A sleepin' bee-1	ABC-Paramount ABC149
	Boo's bloos-1	–

November 12	TEDDY CHARLES QUARTET	
New York City	Teddy Charles (vib); Hall Overton (p); Charles Mingus (b); Ed	
	Shaughnessy (d)	
2188	**Laura**	Atlantic 1274
2189	**untitled original**	unissued
2201	**When your lover has gone**	Atlantic 1274
2202	**Just one of those things**	– **
2203	**Blue greens**	–

1957:

February 13	CHARLES MINGUS JAZZ WORKSHOP	
New York City	Jimmy Knepper (tb); Shafi Hadi (as-1,ts-2); Wade Legge (p);	
	Charles Mingus (b); Dannie Richmond (d,tamb); Jean	
	Shepherd (narr-3)	
2452	**The clown**-2,3	(33) Atlantic 1260
2453	**Love bird**-1(?)	unissued
March 12		
New York City		
2454	**Passions of a woman loved**-1	(31a) Atlantic 1416, SD1416
2455	**Blue Cee**-1	(33) Atlantic 1260
2456	**Tonight at noon**-1	(31a) Atlantic 1416, SD1416
2457	**Reincarnation of a lovebird**-1	(31a,33) Atlantic 1260
2458	**Haitian fight song**-1	(31a,33) –

266

June 18	BRANDEIS JAZZ FESTIVAL ENSEMBLE		
New York City	Louis Mucci, Art Farmer (tp); Jimmy Knepper (tb); Jim Buffington (fr-h); John LaPorta (cl,as); Hal McKusick (as,ts); Teo Macero (bars); Bob DiDomenica (fl); Manny Zegler (bassoon); Teddy Charles (vib); Bill Evans (p); Barry Galbraith (g); Fred Zimmermann (b); Teddy Sommer (d); Margaret Ross (harp); Gunther Schuller (cond); Charles Mingus (vcl)		
CO58202	**Revelation (1st movement)**	(33a) Columbia WL 127	

July 9	CHARLES MINGUS/HAMPTON HAWES/DANNIE		
New York City	RICHMOND		
	Hampton Hawes (p); Charles Mingus (b); Dannie Richmond (d)		
JB889	**I can't get started**	(10) Jubilee JLP1054	
JB890	**Hamp's new blues**	(10)	–
JB891	**Yesterdays**	(10)	–
JB892	**Dizzy moods**	(10)	–
JB893	**Back home blues**	(10)	–
JB894	**Summertime**	(10)	–
JB895	**Laura**	(10)	–

July 10	JIMMY KNEPPER QUINTET		
New York City	Jimmy Knepper (tb); Joe Maini (as); Bill Triglia (p); Charles Mingus (b); Dannie Richmond (d)		
	Latter day saint	Debut (D) DL101	
	Cunningbird	–	
	Jumpin' the blues	–	
	The masher	–	

July 18	CHARLES MINGUS JAZZ WORKSHOP		
New York City	As for March 12 except Bill Triglia (p) replaces Legge; Clarence Shaw (tp); Frankie Dunlop (perc-3); Ysabel Morel (castanets-3) added		
H4JB5030	**Boston tea party**-(?)	unissued	
H4JB5224	**Dizzy moods**-2	(34) RCA-Victor LPM2533**,LSP2533**	
H4JB5225	**Tijuana table dance (Ysabel's table dance)**-1,3	(34) –**	–**
H4JB5227	**Los mariachis**-1	(34) –**	–**
July 20	Dunlop and Morel out		
Great River,	**Dizzy moods**-2	VOA	
Long Island	**Tijuana table dance**-1	–	
July 21	Charles Mingus (solo b)		
Great River,	**Woody'n you**	–	
Long Island	**Haitian fight song**	–	

Same concert	BLOSSOM DEARIE TRIO	
	Blossom Dearie (p,vcl); Charles Mingus (b); Roy Eldridge (d)	
	unknown titles	VOA
	Note: The above VOA recordings of the first Great South Bay Festival are thought to have been confiscated by the A.F.M.	

August 6	CHARLES MINGUS JAZZ WORKSHOP	
New York City	As for July 20	
H4JB5228	**Flamingo**-1	(34) RCA-Victor

267

		LPM2533**,LSP2533**
H4JB5230	**Tijuana gift shop**-1	(34) RCA-Victor,
		LPM2533**, LSP2533**

Note: Lonnie Elder (narr), not heard on the issued material, took part in these RCA-Victor sessions but it is not known on which tracks

August	Bill Evans (p) replaces Triglia	
New York City	**East coasting (East coast ghost)**-2	(35) Bethlehem 3041,
		BCP6019, BCPS6019
B6466/7	**5 lst street blues Pts 1 and 2**-2	(35) Bethlehem 11041,
		BCP6019, BCPS6019
	Memories of you-2	(35) BCP6019, BCPS6019
	West coast ghost-2	(35) – –
	Celia-1	(35) – –
	Conversation-2	(35) – –
October	Bob Hammer-3, Horace Parlan-4 (p) replace Evans; Melvin	
New York City	Stewart (narr-5) added	
	Scenes in the city-2,3,5	Bethlehem 3041, BCP6026,
		BCPS6026
	New York sketchbook (i.e. **Tourist**	
	in Manhattan)-2,3,4	BCP6026, BCPS6026
	Duke's choice-2,4	– –
	Slippers-2,4,6	– –
	6-Shaw out	
Same period	Bill Hardman (tp) replace Shaw	
New York City	**Nouroog**-2,4	– –

1958:
March 18
New York City

LANGSTON HUGHES WITH THE HORACE PARLAN QUINTET

Jimmy Knepper (tb); Shafi Hadi (ts); Horace Parlan (p); Charles Mingus (b); Kenny Dennis (d); Langston Hughes (narr)

Consider me	MGM E3697
The stranger/Midnight stroll/	
Backstage/Dream montage:	
Weird nightmare/Double G	
train/Wednesday night prayer	
meeting	–
Jump, Monk-1	–
1-Hughes out	–

c. Spring
New York City

CHARLES MINGUS JAZZ WORKSHOP

Jimmy Knepper (tb); Shafi Hadi (ts); Horace Parlan, Phineas Newborn (p); Charles Mingus (b); Dannie Richmond (d); unknown tp, fl, as

Nostalgia in Times Square	Soundtrack*
unknown titles	–*

Note: Remaining music for soundtrack of 'Shadows' by Shafi Hadi (solo ts)

1959:
January 16
Nonagon Art

John Handy (as); Booker Ervin (ts); Richard Wyands (p); Charles Mingus (b); Dannie Richmond (d)

Gallery,	**Nostalgia in Times Square**	(36) United Artists
New York City		UAL4036, UAS5036
	I can't get started-1	(36) UAL4036, UAS5036
	No private income blues	(36) – –
	Alice's wonderland	(36) – –
	Take the 'A' train	unissued
	Jelly Roll jellies	–
	Billie's bounce	–
	Wednesday night prayer meeting	–
	1-Ervin out	

February 4
New York City Jimmy Knepper, Willie Dennis (tb); Jackie McLean (as); Pepper Adams (bars) added; Mal Waldron-1, Horace Parlan-2 (p) replace Wyands

3346	**E's flat, Ah's flat too**-1	(37) Atlantic 1305**, SD1305**
3347	**My Jelly Roll soul**-2	(37) 1305, SD1305
3348	**Tensions**-2	(37) – –
3349	**Moanin'**-2	(37) –** –**
3350	**Cryin' blues**-2	(31a,37) –** –**
3351	**Wednesday night prayer meeting**-2	(31a,37) –** –**
4732/3	**Wednesday night prayer meeting Pts. 1 and 2**-2 (edited from **3351**)	Atlantic 45-5006

May 5
New York City Jimmy Knepper (tb); John Handy (as-1,cl-2) ; Booker Ervin, Shafi Hadi (ts); Horace Parlan (p); Charles Mingus (b-3,p-4); Dannie Richmond (d)

CO63154	**Better git it in your soul**-1,3	(38) Columbia CL1370, CS8171
CO63155	**Bird calls**-1,3,5	(38) CL1370, CS8171
	Bird calls-1,3,5 (as last, unedited)	(39) Columbia JG35717
CO63156	**Fables of Faubus**-1,3	(38) Columbia CL1370, CS8171
CO63157	**Pussy cat dues**-2,3	(38) CL1370, CS8171
	Pussy cat dues-2,3 (as last, unedited)	(39) Columbia JG35717
CO63159	**Jelly Roll**-1,3	(38) Columbia CL1370**, CS8171**
	Jelly Roll-1,3 (as last, unedited)	(39) Columbia JG35717
	Pedal point blues-1,3,4	(39) –
	GG train (i.e. **Double G train**)-1,3	(39) –
	Girl of my dreams-1,3,6	(39) –
	5-Knepper out; 6-Hadi out	
	Note: **Girl of my dreams** may be from the next session	

May 12
New York City Willie Dennis (tb) replaces Knepper

CO63337	**Open letter to Duke**-1,3	(38) Columbia CL1370** CS8171**
	Open letter to Duke-1,3 (as last, unedited)	(39) Columbia JG35717
CO63338	**Boogie stop shuffle**-1,3	(38) Columbia CL1370** CS8171**
	Boogie stop shuffle-1,3 (as last, unedited)	(39) Columbia JG35717
CO63341	**Self-portrait in three colors**-1,3	(38) Columbia CL1370, CS8171
CO63342	**Goodbye pork pie hat**-3,7	(38) CL1370, CS8171

269

July 4
Freebody Park
Newport, R.I.

Richard Williams (tp); Leo Wright (as-1,fl-2); Booker Ervin (ts); Roland Hanna (p); Charles Mingus (b); Dannie Richmond (d)

Shuffle stop boogie-1 (i.e. **Boogie
    stop shuffle**)   VOA
Box seats at Newport-1   –
Diane (i.e. **Alice's wonderland**)-1,2   –
Gunslinging Bird-1   –

November 1
New York City

Richard Williams (tp); Jimmy Knepper (tb); Jerome Richardson (fl, bars); John Handy (as); Booker Ervin, Benny Golson (ts); Teddy Charles (vib); Roland Hanna-1, Nico Bunink-2 (p); Charles Mingus (b); Dannie Richmond (d, tymp); Honey Gordon (vcl-3)

CO63881   **Gunslinging Bird**-1   (38) Columbia CL1440**, CS8236**

              Gunslinging Bird-1 (as last,
                 unedited)   (39) Columbia JG35717

CO63882   **Song with Orange**-1   (38) Columbia CL1440**, CS8236**

              Song with Orange-1 (as last,
                 unedited)   (39) Columbia JG35717

CO63884   **Diane**-1   (38) Columbia CL1440, CS8236

CO63885   **Farwell's, Mill Valley (Far Wells,
               Mill Valley)**-1   (38) CL1440, CS8236

CO63886   **New now know how**-2,4   (38) –**   –**
              New now, know how-2,4 (as last
                 unedited)   (39) Columbia JG35717

              Strollin' (i.e. **Nostalgia in Times
                 Square**)-2,3,4   (39)   –
              4-Charles out

Note: Both fl and bars heard simultaneously on **CO63885**

November 13
New York City

Don Ellis (tp); Jimmy Knepper (tb); John Handy (as); Booker Ervin (tb); Roland Hanna (p); Maurice Brown, Seymour Barab (cello-1); Charles Mingus (b); Dannie Richmond (d)

CO63888   **Slop**-1   (38) Columbia CL1440**, CS8236**

              Slop-1 (as last, unedited)   (39) Columbia JG35717

CO63889   **Put me in that dungeon**-1   (38) Columbia CL1440, CS8236

CO63890   **Mood indigo**   (38) CL1440, CS8236

CO63891   **Things ain't what they used to be**   (38) –**   –**
              Things ain't what they used to be
                 (as last, unedited)   (39) Columbia JG35717

1960:
May 24
New York City

Hobart Dotson, Clark Terry, Marcus Belgrave, Richard Williams, Ted Curson (tp); Eddie Bert, Jimmy Knepper, Charles Greenlee, Slide Hampton (tb); Don Butterfield (tu); Bob DiDomenica (fl); Harry Schuman (oboe); Eric Dolphy (as,fl,bcl); John LaPorta (as,cl); Bill Barron, Joe Farrell (ts); Yusef Lateef (ts,fl); Danny Bank (bars); Roland Hanna (p); Charles McCracken (cello); Charles Mingus (b); Dannie Richmond (d); Sticks Evans, George Scott, Max Roach

		(perc-1); Gunther Schuller (cond-1)	
	20093	**Half-mast inhibition**-1	(40) Mercury MG20627
✓	20094	**Mingus fingus no. 2**	(40) –
	20095	**Bemoanable lady**	(40) –
		Yusef Isef too	unissued
		Portrait	–

May 25
New York City
Ted Curson (tp); Jimmy Knepper (tb); Eric Dolphy (as,fl, cl,bcl); Booker Ervin, Joe Farrell (ts); Yusef Lateef (ts,fl); Paul Bley-1, Roland Hanna-2 (p); Charles Mingus (b); Dannie Richmond (d); Lorraine Cousins (vcl-3)

	20100	**Weird nightmare**-1,3	(40) Mercury MG20627
✓	20101	**Prayer for passive resistance**-2	(40) –
✓	20102	**Eclipse**-1,3	(40) –
	20103	**Do nothin' till you hear from me/**	
		I let a song go out of my heart-2	(40) –
	20104	**Take the 'A' train/Exactly**	
		like you-1	(40) –

July 13
Pinede Gould,
Antibes
Ted Curson (tp); Eric Dolphy (as-1,bcl-2); Booker Ervin (ts); Charles Mingus (b,p-3); Dannie Richmond (d)

	5260(37622)	**Cry for freedom (Prayer for**	
		passive resistance)-1	(41) Atlantic SD2-3001
✓	5261(37626)	**Better git it in your soul**-1,3	(41)Byg(J) YX7009*, –
	5262(37621)	**Wednesday night prayer meeting**	
		-1,3	(41) – –
	5263(37625)	**Ummh (Folk forms I) (Folk forms**	
		no, 2)-1	(41) – –
	5264(37623)	**What love**-2	(41) –
	5265(37624)	**I'll remember April**-1,4	(41) –
		4-Bud Powell (p) added	

October 20
New York City
Ervin out

What love-2	(42) Candid CJM8005, CJS9005
All the things you could be by now	
if Sigmund Freud's wife was	
your mother-1	(42) CJM8005, CJS9005
Folk forms no. 1-1	(42) Candid 45-601*, CJM8005, CJS9005
Stormy weather-1	(43) Candid CJM8021, CJS9021
Original Faubus fables-1,5	(42) Candid 45-601*, CJM8005,CJS9005

Same session
Lonnie Hillyer (tp); Jimmy Knepper, Britt Woodman (tb); Charles McPherson (as); Booker Ervin (ts); Nico Bunink-6, Paul Bley-7 (p) added

MDM-1,2,6	(43) Candid CJM8021, CJS9021

November 11
New York City

Vassarlean (i.e. **Weird**	
nightmare)-2,6	(44) Candid CJM8019, CJS9019
Lock 'em up-1,7,8	(43) Candid CJM8021, CJS9021

5-Mingus and Richmond vcl on this track
8-Knepper and Woodman out

Same session	**JAZZ ARTISTS GUILD**	
	Roy Eldridge (tp); Jimmy Knepper (tb-1); Eric Dolphy (as-1);	
	Tommy Flanagan (p); Charles Mingus (b); Jo Jones (d)	
	Mysterious blues-1	(44a) Candid CJM8022, CJS9022
	Wrap your troubles in dreams	(44a) CJM8022, CJS9022
	Me and you	(44a) – –
	R & R-1	(44) Candid CJM8019, CJS9019

1961:
early July
London

'ALL NIGHT LONG'
Tubby Hayes (vib); Ray Dempsey (g); Charles Mingus (b); Allan Ganley (d)

Noodlin' Fontana TFL5179,STFL591
Dave Brubeck (p); Charles Mingus (b)

Non-sectarian blues Columbia C30522
Harry Beckett (tp); Harold McNair (as); Charles Mingus (b,p); Jackie Dougan (d)

Peggy's blue skylight Soundtrack*
Note: Mingus plays b and p by overdubbing

October 21
Broadcast,
Birdland,
New York City

CHARLES MINGUS JAZZ WORKSHOP
Jimmy Knepper (tb); Yusef Lateef (ts); Roland Kirk (ts,strich, manzello); Charles Mingus (p); Doug Watkins (b); Dannie Richmond (d); Pee Wee Marquette (mc)

unknown title (Improvisation) (12) Alto 714
Ecclusiastics (Ecclesiastes) (12) –
Hog callin' blues Airshot*
Note: The first item bears no relationship to **Blue Cee**

November 6
New York City

Booker Ervin (ts) replaces Lateef

5756	**Devil woman**-1	(31a,45) Atlantic 1377, SD1377
5757	**Ecclusiastics**	(45) – –
5758	**'Old' blues for Walt's Torin**	Atlantic 1416, SD1416
5759	**Peggy's blue skylight**	– –
5760	**Hog callin' blues**	(45) Atlantic 1377, SD1377
5761	**Oh Lord, don't let them drop that atomic bomb on me**-1	(45) – –
5762	**Passions of a man**-2	(31a,45) – –
5763	**Wham bam thank you ma'am**	(31a,45) – –
5764	**untitled original**	unissued
5765	**Invisible lady**	Atlantic 1416, SD1416
5766	**Eat that chicken**-1	(45) Atlantic 1377, SD1377
5767	**Nuts**	unissued
5768	**untitled original**	–

1-Mingus vcl; 2-Mingus (narr) overdubbed on this track

1962:
March 24
Broadcast,

Richard Williams (tp); Charles McPherson (as); Booker Ervin (ts); Toshiko Akiyoshi (p); Charles Mingus (b); Dannie

Birdland,	Richmond (d); Symphony Sid (mc)	
New York City	**Take the 'A' train**	Session Disc 118
	Fables of Faubus (Mr Faubus)	–
	Eat that chicken (theme)	–*
March 31	**Monk, funk or vice versa (Monk)**	(12) Alto 714
Broadcast,	**Oh Lord, don't let them drop**	
Birdland,	**that atomic bomb on me**	Airshot
New York City	**Eat that chicken**	–
May 5	Henry Grimes, Herman Wright (b) added; Mingus plays b and	
Broadcast,	p alternately	
Birdland,	**Eat that chicken**	Airshot
New York City	**Reets and I**-1	–
	Monk, funk or vice versa	–
	Eat that chicken (theme)	– *
May 12	Wright and Richmond out	
Broadcast,	**Peggy's blue skylight**	(46) J For Jazz JFJ802
Birdland,	**Tijuana table dance**	–
New York City	**Eat that chicken** (theme)	–

1-Akiyoshi, Grimes, Wright and Richmond only

September 17	DUKE ELLINGTON	
New York City	Duke Ellington (p); Charles Mingus (b); Max Roach (d)	
	Money jungle	(47) United Artists
		UAJ14017,UAJS15017
	La fleurette africaine (Le fleurs	
	africain)	(47) – –
	Very special	(47) – –
	Warm valley	(47) – –
	Wig wise	(47) – –
	Caravan	(47) – –
	Solitude	(47) – –
	Blue Monk	unissued
	Slow blues	–
	Backward country blues	–

October 12	CHARLES MINGUS
Town Hall,	Ernie Royal, Snooky Young, Clark Terry, Richard Williams,
New York City	Lonnie Hillyer, Ed Armour, Rolf Ericson (tp); Britt
	Woodman, Quentin Jackson, Willie Dennis, Eddie Bert,
	Jimmy Cleveland (tb); Don Butterfield (tu); Charles
	McPherson, Charlie Mariano (as); Buddy Collette (as,ts,fl);
	Eric Dolphy (as,fl,bcl); Booker Ervin, Zoot Sims (ts); Dick
	Hafer (ts,fl,cl,oboe); Pepper Adams (bars); Jerome
	Richardson (bars,ss,fl); Teddy Charles (vib); Toshiko
	Akiyoshi, Jaki Byard (p); Les Spann, unknown other (g);
	Charles Mingus (b,narr-1); Milt Hinton (b); Dannie Richmond
	(d,tymp); Melba Liston-2, Bob Hammer-3 (arr)

Osmosis (two takes)	unissued
Epitaph 'Part I'	(48) United Artists
	UAJ14024,UAJS15024
Epitaph 'Part II'	(48) – –
Peggy's blue skylight-2	unissued
Freedom 'Part I'-1	(48) United Artists
	UAJ14024,UAJS15024
Freedom 'Part II' (Clark in the	
dark)	(48) –

	Portrait	unissued
	Duke's choice (Don't come back)-3	(48) United Artists UAJ14024* *, UAJS15024**
	Please don't come back from the moon	unissued
	My search	(48) United Artists UAJ14024,UAJ S 15024
	In a mellotone (Finale)	(48) – –

Note: The two parts of **Epitaph** and of **Freedom**, although performed separately, were originally intended to be edited together. Jimmy Knepper did not take part in this concert.

October 19
Broadcast,
Birdland,
New York City

Ed Armour (tp); Don Butterfield (tu); Charles McPherson (as); Pepper Adams (bars); Jaki Byard (p); Charles Mingus (b); Dannie Richmond (d)

	My search (The search)	Session Disc 118
	Monk, funk or vice versa (King-fish)	–
	Please don't come back from the moon (Moonboy)	–
	Eat that chicken (theme)	–*

October 26
Broadcast,
Birdland,
New York City

	Monk, funk or vice versa (Monk Bunk and vice versa)	Ozone 19
	O.P.O.P.	–
	My search (The search)	–
	Eat that chicken	Airshot

1963:

January 20
New York City

Richard Williams, Rolf Ericson (tp); Quentin Jackson (tb); Don Butterfield (tu); Charlie Mariano (as); Dick Hafer (ts,fl,oboe); Jerome Richardson (bars,ss,fl); Jaki Byard (p); Jay Berliner (g); Charles Mingus (b,p-1); Dannie Richmond (d); Bob Hammer (arr-2)

11300	**Celia**-2	(49) Impulse A54,AS54
11301	**Track A – Solo dancer**	(49) Impulse A35**,AS35**
11302	**Track B – Duet solo dancers**	(49) –** –**
11303(?)	**I X love** (i.e. **Duke's choice**)-2	(49) Impulse A54,AS54
11304	**Track C – Group dancers**-1	(49) Impulse A35**,AS35**
11317	**Mode D – Trio and group dancers**	(49) –** –**
11318	**Mode E – Single solos and group dance**	(49) –** –**
11319	**Mode F – Group and solo dance**	(49) –** –**

Note: Additional solos by Mariano overdubbed on last four tracks; for details of editing, see Appendix C

July 30
New York City

Charles Mingus (solo p)

90096	**Myself when I am real**	(50) Impulse A60,AS60
90097	**I can't get started**	(50) – –
90098	**Body and soul**	(50) – –
90099	**Roland Kirk's message** (i.e. **'Old' blues for Walt's Torin**)	(50) – –
90100	**Memories of you**	(50) – –
90101	**She's just Miss Popular Hybrid**	(50) – –
90102	**Song with orange** (mistitled	

September
New York City

PEPPER ADAMS

Thad Jones (tp, arr-1); Bennie Powell (tb); Charles McPherson (as); Zoot Sims (ts); Pepper Adams (bars); Hank Jones (p); Bob Cranshaw (b); Dannie Richmond (d); Teddy Charles (arr-2); Charles Mingus (dir)

Better git it in your soul-1	Workshop Jazz 219
Portrait	–
Haitian fight song	–

Powell, McPherson and Sims out; Paul Chambers (b) replaces Cranshaw

Fables of Faubus-1	Workshop Jazz 219
Black light	–
Song with orange-2	–
Carolyn	–
Reincarnation	–
Strollin' Honies	–

September 20
New York City

CHARLES MINGUS

As for January 20 except Eddie Preston (tp); Britt Woodman (tb); Eric Dolphy (as,fl,bcl); Booker Ervin (ts); Walter Perkins (d) replace Ericson, Jackson, Mariano, Berliner and Richmond

11756	**Hora decubitus** (i.e. **E's flat,**	(49)	Impulse A54**,AS54**
	Ah's flat too)		
11757	**Theme for Lester Young** (i.e.		
	Goodbye pork pie hat)	(49)	–	–
11758	**II B.S.** (i.e. **Haitian fight song**)	(49)	–**	–**
11759	**Freedom**-3		Impulse A99,AS99
11760(?)	**Better get hit in yo' soul**	(49)	Impulse A54**, AS54**
11761	**Take the 'A' train**		unissued
11762	**Mood indigo**	(49)	Impulse A54,AS54

3-Mingus (narr) on this track

Note: **Better get hit**, previously attributed to January 20 and to mat.no. **11303**, features Booker Ervin who is not present on that session; whereas **I X Love**, claimed as being mat.no. **11760**, features Charlie Mariano

1964:

April 4
Town Hall,
New York City

Johnny Coles (tp); Eric Dolphy (as-1,fl-2,bcl-3); Clifford Jordan (ts); Jaki Byard (p); Charles Mingus (b); Dannie Richmond (d)

So long Eric-1	(51) Charles Mingus
	JWS005
Praying with Eric (i.e.	
Meditations)-2,3	(51) –
Sophisticated lady-4	unissued

April 16
Bremen

Meditations-2,3	(52) Unique Jazz UJ23
A.T.F.W.Y.O.U.U.S.A.-5	(52,52a) –
Sophisticated lady-6	(52,52a) –
Hope so Eric (i.e. **So long Eric**)-1	(52a) Ingo 10

April 17 *Salle Wagram,* *Paris*	**So long Eric**-1 **Sophisticated lady**-6 **Orange was the color of her dress**-3 **Fables of Faubus**-3 **Parkeriana**-1 **Meditations**-2,3 **Peggy's blue skylight**-1	(53) America AM003/4/5 unissued – – – – –
April 19(a.m.) *Theatre des* *Champs Elysees,* *Paris*	Coles out **So long Eric (Goodbye pork pie hat)**-1 **Orange was the color of her dress**-3 **Parkeriana**-1 **Meditations for integration** (i.e. **Meditations**)-2,3 **Fables of Faubus**-3 **I can't get started**-2,7 **Sophisticated lady**-6	 (53) America AM003/4/5 (53) – (53) – (53) – (53) – (53) unissued (53) America AM003/4/5
April 26 *Town Hall,* *Wuppertal*	**Fables of Faubus**-3 **I can't get started (Starting)**-2,7 **Peggy's blue skylight (Charlemagne)**-1 **Sophisticted lady**-6 **Orange was the color of her dress.**-3 **A.T.F.W.Y.O.U.U.S.A.**-5	(54) Enja 3049ST (54) – (55) Enja 3077ST (55) – (55) – (55) –
April 28 *Mozartsaal,* *Stuttgart*	**A.T.F.W.Y.O.U.U.S.A.**-5 **Sophisticated lady**-6 **Peggy's blue skylight**-1 **Orange was the color of her dress**-3 **Fables of Faubus**-3 **So long Eric**-1 **Meditations**-2,3 **These foolish things**-2,7	(56) Unique Jazz UJ009 (56) – (57) Unique Jazz UJ007/8* (57) – (56) Unique Jazz UJ009 (57) Unique Jazz UJ007/8 (57) – (57) –

4-Mingus only; 5-Byard only; 6-Byard and Mingus only; 7-Dolphy and Mingus only

Note: **So long Eric** on America AM003/4/5 consists of the first part of the April 17 performance and the second part of the April 19 performance

June 2,3 *Jazz Workshop,* *San Francisco*	Clifford Jordan (ts); Jane Getz (p); Charles Mingus (b); Dannie Richmond (d) **Meditations for a pair of wire cutters** (i.e. **Meditations**) **New Fables** (i.e. **Fables of Faubus**)-1	 Fantasy 6017, 86017 – –

1-John Handy (as) added

September 20 *County* *Fairgrounds,* *Monterey*	Lonnie Hillyer (tp); Charles McPherson (as); Jaki Byard (p); Charles Mingus (b); Dannie Richmond (d); Jimmy Lyons (mc) **Duke Ellington medley: I got it bad/ In a sentimental mood/ All too soon/Mood indigo/ Sophisticated lady Take the 'A' train**-1	 (58) Charles Mingus JWS001/2 (58) –

Orange was the color of her dress	(58)	–
Meditations on integration (i.e. **Meditations**)-2	(58)	–

1-John Handy (ts) added
2-Bobby Bryant, Melvin Moore (tp); Lou Blackburn (tb); Red Callender (tu); Buddy Collette (as,fl,picc); John Handy (ts); Jack Nimitz (bars,cl) added

1965:

May 13
Tyrone Guthrie
Theater,
Minneapolis

As for September 20, 1964	(51) Charles Mingus
So long Eric	JWS009
Medley: She's funny that way/ Embraceable you/ I can't get started/Ghost of a chance/ Old portrait/Cocktails for two	(51) –

September 10
TV recording,
Village Gate,
New York City

Hobart Dotson, Lonnie Hillyer (tp); Jimmy Owens (tp,flh); Julius Watkins (fr-h); Howard Johnson (tu); Charles McPherson (as); Charles Mingus (b,p,narr-1); Dannie Richmond (d)

The arts of Tatum and Freddie Webster (Majonet)	Ozone 19
Don't let it happen here-1	–

September 25
Royce Hall,
University of
California at
Los Angeles

Meditation on inner peace	Charles Mingus JWS0013/4
Once there was a holding corporation called Old America (false starts)	–*
Ode to Bird and Dizzy-2	–
They trespass the land of the sacred Sioux	–
The arts of Tatum and Freddie Webster	–
Twelfth street rag (Muskrat ramble)-2	–
Don't be afraid, the clown's afraid too	–
Don't let it happen here-1	–
Once there was a holding corporation called Old America	–
I can't get started-3	Unissued

2-Hillyer, McPherson, Mingus and Richmond only; 3-Mingus only
Note: Mingus does not participate in the Cecil Taylor Quartet recording on Ozone 19, emanating from the same TV programme

1966:

November
Lennie's-on-the-
Turnpike,
Peabody, Mass.

Lonnie Hillyer (tp); Charles McPherson (as); John Gilmore (ts); Walter Bishop (p); Charles Mingus (b); Dannie Richmond (d)

All the things you are-1	Soundtrack *
Peggy's blue skylight-2	– *
Take the 'A' train	– *
Secret love-3	– *
Portrait-4	– *

November 21	Charles Mingus (p,vcl)		
Mingus's loft,	**unknown title**		– *
New York City	1-Bishop out; 2-Gilmore and Bishop out; 3-Bishop, Mingus and Richmond only; 4-Gilmore out		

Note: The soundtrack of the film 'Mingus' also includes excerpts from the 1960 recording of **Half mast inhibition**, the 1962 Town Hall **Freedom,** and the 1965 UCLA **Don't let it happen here**

1970:

October	Eddie Preston (tp); Charles McPherson (as); Bobby Jones (ts,		
Concert,	cl-1); Jaki Byard (p); Charles Mingus (b); Dannie Richmond (d)		
Rotterdam	**Orange was the color of her**		
	dress	(59) Joker(J) UPS2072	
	The man who never sleeps	(59)	–
	O.P.O.P.	(59)	–
prob. October 31	**Pithecanthropus erectus**	(60) America 30AM6109	
Paris	**Peggy's blue skylight**	(60)	–
	Love is a dangerous necessity	(60)	– *
	Reincarnation of a lovebird	(60) America 30AM6110	
	I left my heart in San Francisco	(60)	–
	Blue bird	(60)	–
November 5	**History**-1	Beppo BEP508	
Philharmonie,	**O.P.O.P.**	–	
Berlin	**Reincarnation of a lovebird**	–	
	The man who never sleeps	–	
Same period	**O.P.O.P. (Pithecanthropus**		
unknown concert,	**erectus)**	(61) Europa Jazz EJ1002	
Europe	Note: The last item is claimed as a 1959 recording featuring Richard Williams (tp); Jimmy Knepper (tb); etc.		

1971:

January 14	Eddie Preston (tp); Bobby Jones (ts); Charles Mingus (b)		
Tokyo	WITH TOSHIYUKI MIYAMA AND HIS NEW HERD: big band including Shigeo Suzuki, Hiroshi Takamu (as); Masahiko Sato (p); Yoshisaburo Toyozumi (d); Jaki Byard (arr)		
	The man who never sleeps	Columbia (J) NCB7008	
	O.P.O.P.	–	
	Portrait	–	
September 23	Big band including (on one or more of these sessions) Snooky		
New York City	Young, Jimmy Nottingham, Lonnie Hillyer, Joe Wilder (tp); Julius Watkins (fr-h); Charles McPherson, Jerry Dodgion (as); Bobby Jones (ts,arr-1); James Moody (ts); Roland Hanna (p); Charles Mingus (b); Sy Johnson (arr-2)		
	are some jive ass slippers (i.e.		
	Once there was a holding		
	corporation called Old		
	America)-2	(62) Columbia KC31039	
	The I of Hurricane Sue-2	(62)	–
September 30			
New York City	**Hobo ho**-1	(62)	–
October 1			
New York City	**Don't be afraid, the clown's**		
	afraid too-2	(62)	–

278

November 18	Big band including Jimmy Knepper (tb); Charles McPherson
New York City	(as); Charles McCracken (cello); Charles Mingus (b,p-1,narr-2); Ron Carter, Richard Davis, Milt Hinton, two others (b); Dannie Richmond (d); Jaki Byard (arr-3); Alan Raph (cond)

                 The chill of death-2   (62) Columbia KC31039

                 Adagio ma non troppo (i.e. **Myself**

                    when I am real)-1,3   (62)   –

Note: There is considerable overdubbing on all tracks of KC31039

1972:

February 4	CHARLES MINGUS AND FRIENDS
Avery Fisher	Eddie Preston, Lonnie Hillyer, Jon Faddis, Lloyd Michels (tp);
Hall,	Eddie Bert (btb); Sharon Moe, Richard Berg (fr-h); Bob
New York City	Stewart (tu); Charles McPherson, Lee Konitz, Richie Perri (as); George Dorsey, Gene Ammons (ts); Bobby Jones (ts,cl); Gerry Mulligan, Howard Johnson (bars); John Foster (p); Charles Mingus, Milt Hinton (b); Joe Chambers (d); Honey Gordon (vcl-1); Sy Johnson (arr); Teo Macero (cond); Bill Cosby (mc,vcl-2)

CO112563	**Honeysuckle rose**	Columbia KG31614
CO112564	**Jump, Monk**	–
CO112565	**E.S.P.** (i.e. **Extrasensory**	
	perception)	–
CO112566	**Ecclusiastics**	–
CO112567	**Eclipse**-1	–
CO112568	**Us is two**	–
CO112570	**Mingus blues**	–
CO112571	**Little Royal suite**	–
CO112574	**E's flat, Ah's flat too**-2,3	–
CO113019	**Ool-ya-koo**-2,4	–
	Strollin'-1	unissued
	unknown titles	–

3-James Moody (fl); Randy Weston (p); Dizzy Gillespie (vcl) added; 4-Dizzy Gillespie (vcl) added

July 6	NEWPORT IN NEW YORK JAM SESSION
Radio City	Cat Anderson, Jimmy Owens (tp); Charles McPherson (as);
Music Hall,	Buddy Tate (ts); Roland Hanna (p); Milt Buckner (org);
New York City	Charles Mingus (b); Alan Dawson (d)

25534	**Jumpin' at the Woodside**	Cobblestone CST9025-2
25535	**Lo-slo-bluze**	–

August 14,15	CHARLES MINGUS
Ronnie Scott's	Jon Faddis (tp); Charles McPherson (as); Bobby Jones (ts,cl);
London	John Foster (p); Charles Mingus (b); Roy Brooks (d,musical saw)

                 unknown titles   CBS(E) unissued

October 20	Joe Gardner (tp); Hamiet Bluiett (bars) replace Faddis,
Jazz Jamboree,	McPherson and Jones
Warsaw	**Celia** Muza XL0929*
November 5	**Fables of Faubus** Airshot
Philharmonie,	**Celia** (63) Unique Jazz UJ20
Berlin	**Perdido**-1 (63) –
	Blues for Roy's saw-1 Airshot

Peggy's blue skylight-1
1-Cat Anderson (tp) added

1973:
December 29,30,31 Ron Hampton (tp,tamb); George Adams (ts,fl); Don Pullen
New York City (p,org-1); Charles Mingus (b); Dannie Richmond (d)

28318	**Canon**	(31a,64)	Atlantic SD1653
28319	**Opus 4**	(64)	−
28320	**Moves**-2	(64)	−
28321	**Wee**	(64)	−
28322	**Flowers for a lady**	(64)	−
28323	**The newcomer**	(64)	−
28324	**Opus 3**	(64)	−
28325	**The call**	unissued	
28326	**Big Alice**-1	−	

2-Honey Gordon, Doug Hammond (vcl)

1974:
January 19
Carnegie Hall,
New York City Hamiet Bluiett (bars) replaces Hampton

29417	**Peggy's blue skylight**-3	unissued	
29418	**Celia**-3	−	
29419	**Fables of Faubus**-3	−	
29420	**Big Alice**-3	−	
29421	**Perdido**-4	(65)	Atlantic SD1667
29422	**C jam blues**-4	(65)	−
29423	**C jam blues ending**-4	unissued	

3-Jon Faddis (tp) added
4-Jon Faddis (tp); Charles McPherson (as); John Handy (as,ts);
Roland Kirk (ts,strich) added

December 27 Jack Walrath (tp); George Adams (ts,vcl-1); Don Pullen (p);
New York City Charles Mingus (b); Dannie Richmond (d)

31056	**Sue's changes**	(31a,66)	Atlantic SD1677
31058	**Duke Ellington's sound of love**	(31a,66)	−

December 28
New York City

31055	**Remember Rockefeller at Attica**	(66)	−
31057	**Devil blues**-1	(66)	−
31063	**For Harry Carney**	(66)	Atlantic SD1678

December 30
New York City

31059	**Free Cell Block F, 'tis Nazi U.S.A.**	(31a,66)	−
31060	**Orange was the color of her dress**	(66)	−
31061	**Black bats and poles**	(66)	−
31062	**Duke Ellington's sound of love**-2	(66)	−

2-Marcus Belgrave (tp); Jackie Paris (vcl); Sy Johnson (arr) added
Note: Titles of **31055** and **31059** (and recording dates?) may be reversed

1975:
early 1975
New York City Charles Mingus (narr – from interview with Ilhan Mimaroglu)

37244	**Mingus on Mingus**	(31a) Atlantic SD3-600

Note: Excerpts from the above issued as **Coin in the pocket**

	(Rap) and **Lucky (Rap)** on Elektra SE505	
April 22	Charles Mingus (p,vcl,narr); Susan Graham Mingus (vcl,narr);	
Mingus's apartment,	unknown others (vcl,narr)	
New York City	**Happy Birthday 1975 (Rap)**	(66a) Elektra SE505
	Funeral (Rap)	(66a) –

1976:

March 31, April 1	Jack Walrath (tp); Dino Piana (tb); Quarto Maltoni (as);	
Rome	George Adams (ts,fl); Anastasio del Bono (oboe,eng-h);	
	Roberto Laneri (bcl); Pasquale Sabatelli (bassoon); Danny	
	Mixon (p,org); Charles Mingus (b); Dannie Richmond (d)	
34957	**Music for 'Todo modo'**	(67) Atlantic SD8801
April	Charles Mingus (solo p)	
Jazz and Heritage	**Themes from a movie**	(67a) Flying Fish FF099
Festival,		
New Orleans		

1977:

March 9	Jack Walrath (tp); Ricky Ford (ts); George Coleman (ts,as);	
New York City	Bob Neloms (p); Larry Coryell-1, Philippe Catherine-2, John	
	Scofield-3 (g); Charles Mingus, George Mraz (b); Dannie	
	Richmond (d); Paul Jeffrey (arr-4)	
33950	**Better git hit in your soul**-1,2,4	(31a,68) Atlantic SD1700
33951	**Goodbye pork pie hat**-1,2,4	(31a,68) –
33952	**Noddin' ya head blues**-1,2,4	(68) –
Same period		
New York City	Jimmy Rowles (p,vcl) replaces Mraz	
33953	**Three or four shades of blues**-1,3	(68) –
	Sonny Fortune (as); Ron Carter (b) replace Rowles	
33954	**Nobody knows**-2,3,4	(68) –
March 10	Jack Walrath (tp, perc); Jimmy Knepper (tb,btb); Mauricio	
New York City	Smith (fl,picc,as,ss); Ricky Ford (ts,perc); Paul Jeffrey	
	(ts,oboe); Gary Anderson (bcl); Gene Scholtes (bassoon); Bob	
	Neloms (p); Charles Mingus (b,perc,vcl); Dannie Richmond	
	(d,vcl); Candido Camero, Daniel Gonzales, Ray Mantilla,	
	Alfredo Ramirez, Bradley Cunningham (perc)	
34956	**Cumbia and jazz fusion**	(67) Atlantic SD8801
March 29		
New York City	unknown personnel	
36289	**Slow waltz/Wedding march**	Atlantic unissued
c. July	Jack Walrath (tp); Ricky Ford (ts); Bob Neloms (p); Charles	
unknown concert	Mingus (b); Dannie Richmond (d)	
Europe	**Remember Rockefeller at Attica**	
	(Rockefeller and Attica)	Burning Desire
		MBDRM010
	Sue's changes (Swing ghost)-1	–*
	Cumbia and jazz fusion (Freedom	
	in riffs)	–*
	Koko (Cherokeekoko)	–
	Danny's beat-2	–
	Noddin' ya head blues (Secular	
	lullaby)	–
	So long Eric (Development of	
	a free rising II)	–

1-Walrath and Ford not heard in this excerpt
2-Richmond (d,vcl) only on this track

281

November 6 New York City	LIONEL HAMPTON Jack Walrath, Woody Shaw (tp); Ricky Ford (ts); Paul Jeffrey (ts,arr); Gerry Mulligan (bars); Lionel Hampton (vib); Bob Neloms (p); Charles Mingus (b); Dannie Richmond (d) **Just for laughs Pts. 1 and 2** (i.e.		
	Remember Rockefeller at Attica)(69)	Who's Who 21005
	Peggy's blue skylight (69)	–
	Slop (69)	–
	Caroline Keikki Mingus (69)	–
	Fables of Faubus (69)	–
	Duke Ellington's sound of love (69)	–
	Farewell Farwell (Farewell farewell) (69)	–
	So long Eric (69a)	Who's Who 21014
	It might as well be spring	Gateway GSLP10113

December 20 New York City **34666**	CHARLES MINGUS Unknown personnel **Way down blues**	Atlantic unissued

1978:

January 18 New York City	Randy Brecker, Mike Davis (tp); Jack Walrath (tp,arr); Jimmy Knepper, Slide Hampton (tb); Ken Hitchcock (ss,as); Lee Konitz, Charles McPherson, Akira Omori (as); George Coleman (ts,as); Mike Brecker, Daniel Block, Ricky Ford (ts); Pepper Adams, Ronnie Cuber, Craig Purpura (bars); Ken Wener (el-p); Bob Neloms (p); Larry Coryell, Ted Dunbar, Danny Toan, Jack Wilkins (g); Eddie Gomez, George Mraz (b); Joe Chambers, Dannie Richmond (d); Ray Mantilla (perc); Paul Jeffrey (cond); Charles Mingus (dir)	
36884	**Something like a bird**	(70) Atlantic SD8805
January 19 New York City	Konitz, McPherson, Werner and Toan out; Steve Gadd (d); Sammy Figueroa (perc) added	
36249	**Three worlds of drums**	(71) Atlantic SD8803
January 23 New York City	Keith O'Quinn (tb); John Tank (ts) replace Hampton and Coleman; Lee Konitz, Yoshiaki Malta (as) added; Gadd, Figueroa and Mantilla out	
36250	**Devil woman**	(71) Atlantic SD8803
36251	**Wednesday night prayer meeting**	(71) –
36252	**Carolyn 'Keki' Mingus**	(71) –
36885	**Farewell Farwell**-1	(70) Atlantic SD8805
	1-R. and M. Brecker out	

early 1978 New York City	Charles Mingus, Joni Mitchell (vcl) **I's a muggin' (Rap)**	(66a) Elektra SE505

Acknowledgements: As well as previous Mingus discographers Roy Wilbraham and Michel Ruppli, I should like to express my thanks for their assistance to Hugh Attwooll (CBS), Johs Bergh, Jim Björck, Mark Gardner, Graham Griffiths (Mole Jazz), Jim Fishel (Columbia), Lee Jeske, David Meeker (BFI), Tony Middleton (Dobells), Roger Rowland, Tony Russell, Horst Salewski, Chris Sheridan and J.R. Taylor (Smithsonian Institution).

B.P.

Index to Discography

(33)   Atlantic(F) 40030 (*The Clown*)
(33a) Columbia PC37012 (*Jazz Composition*)
(34)   RCA-Victor(F) FXLI 7295 (*Tijuana Moods*)
(35)   Affinity AFF86 (*East Coasting*)
(36)   United Artists(J) LAX3124 (*Jazz Portraits*)
(37)   Atlantic (F) 50232 (*Blues And Roots*)
(38)   Columbia CG30628 (*Better Git It In Your Soul* – includes original versions of *Mingus Ah Um* and *Mingus Dynasty*)
(39)   Columbia JG35717 (*Nostalgia In Times Square*)
(40)   Emarcy EXPR1015 (*Pre-Bird*)
(41)   Atlantic SD2-3001 (*Mingus At Antibes*)
(42)   Barnaby BR5012 (*Mingus Presents Mingus*)
(43)   Jazz Man JAZ5002 (*Mingus*)
(44)   Candid(J) SMJ6188 (*The Jazz Life*)
(44a) Candid(J) SMJ6187 (*Newport Rebels*)
(45)   Atlantic(F) 40387 (*Oh Yeah!*)
(46)   J for Jazz JFJ802 (*Broadcasts*)
(47)   Blue Note (F) BNF25113 (Duke Ellington *Money Jungle*)
(48)   Blue Note (E) BNS40034 (*Town Hall Concert*)
(49)   Jasmine JAS36 (*Mingus, Mingus, Mingus, Mingus, Mingus*)
(49a) Jasmine JAS13 (*Black Saint and the Sinner Lady*)
(50)   Jasmine JAS49 (*Mingus Plays Piano*)
(51)   Prestige P24092 (*Portrait* – includes *Town Hall Concert* and *My Favourite Quintet*)
(52)   Unique Jazz UJ23 (*Mingus Sextet Live In Europe*)
(52a) Ingo 10 (*Charles Mingus Orchestra with Eric Dolphy Vol.1*)
(53)   Prestige P34001 (*The Great Concert of Charles Mingus*)
(54)   Enja 3049ST (*Live In Europe Vol.1*)
(55)   Enja 3077ST (*Live In Europe Vol.2*)
(56)   Unique Jazz UJ009 (*Mingus In Stuttgart*)
(57)   Unique Jazz UJ007/8 (*Mingus In Stuttgart*)
(58)   Prestige P24100 (*Mingus At Monterey*)
(59)   Passport 11.108 (*Statements*)
(60)   Prestige P24028 (*Reincarnation Of A Lovebird*)
(61)   Europa Jazz EJ1002 (*Sarah Vaughan/Maynard Ferguson/Charlie Mingus/ Dizzy Gillespie*)
(62)   Columbia KC31039 (*Let My Children Hear Music*)
(63)   Unique Jazz UJ20 (*Mingus Quintet Meets Cat Anderson*)
(64)   Atlantic SD1653 (*Mingus Moves*)
(65)   Atlantic SD1667 (*Mingus At Carnegie Hall*)
(66)   Atlantic(F) 60108 (*Changes One And Two*)
(66a) Elektra(E) K53091 (*Mingus*)
(67)   Atlantic(F) 50486 (*Cumbia And Jazz Fusion*)
(67a) Sonet(E) SNTF812 (*New Orleans Jazz And Heritage Festival*)
(68)   Atlantic(F) 50390 (*Three Or Four Shades Of Blues*)
(69)   Philips (Du) 9123.603 (*Lionel Hampton Presents The Music Of Charles Mingus*)
(69a) Philips(Du) 9123.612 (*Giants Of Jazz Vol.2*)
(70)   Atlantic SD8805 (*Something Like A Bird*)
(71)   Atlantic(F) 50571 (*Three Worlds of Drums*)

References

NB   Unreferenced quotations are from the author's own interviews.

1 – *Bass-ically Speaking pages 1-23*

1   *Black, Brown and White*, Vogue LDM 30037
2   *Pops Foster: the Autobiography of a New Orleans Jazzman*, University of California Press, 1971, p.65
3   Interview with Mike Dean, BBC-TV, August 1972
4   Notes to Atlantic 1260 (also in Ray Horricks *et al., These Jazzmen of Our Time,* Gollancz, 1960; and Nat Hentoff, *The Jazz Life,* Peter Davies, 1962)
5   Quoted by Nat Hentoff, notes to Bethlehem BCP 6026
6   Pops Foster, op.cit., p.20
7   Interview with Vernon Gibbs and Sharif Abdul Salaam (Ed Michael), WKCR-FM, December 1971
8   Interview with Stanley Dance, *Jazz,* November/December 1963
9   Interview with Mike Dean, op.cit.
10   Quoted by Nat Hentoff, *The Jazz Life,* op.cit., p.161
11   Interview with Mike Dean, op.cit.
12   Quoted by Nat Hentoff, notes to Bethlehem BCP 6026
13   Interview with Ira Gitler, *Down Beat,* 21 July 1960
14   Ibid.
15   Notes to Impulse AS 35
16   Interview with Ira Gitler, op.cit.
17   Charles Mingus, *Beneath the Underdog*, Alfred A. Knopf, 1971, p.92
18   Notes to Columbia KC31039
19   Interview with Mike Dean, op.cit.
20   Quoted by Nat Hentoff, notes to Impulse AS 60

21 Notes to Columbia KC 31039
22 Ibid.
23 Columbia KC 31039, copyright Jazz Workshop Inc. Used by permission
24 Interview with Ira Gitler, op.cit.
25 Interview with Russell Davies (September 1980) for BBC Radio (unpublished)
26 *Jazz Monthly,* January 1966
27 Interview with Paul Bullock and David Hoxie, *Jazz Heritage Foundation*, Vol. III No. 1, January 1982
28 Interview with John Shaw, *Jazz and Blues,* September 1972
29 Quoted by Nat Hentoff, notes to Bethlehem BCP 6026
30 Interview with John Goodman (1971), *Playboy*, November 1979
31 Atlantic SD 3-600
32 Quoted by Nat Hentoff, *The Jazz Life,* op.cit., p.164
33 Interview with John Litweiler, *Down Beat*, 27 February 1975
34 *Down Beat*, 1 September 1942
35 Interview with John Litweiler, op.cit.
36 Ibid.
37 *Metronome,* April 1943
38 Interview with Ira Gitler, op.cit.
39 Interview with Vernon Gibbs and Sharif Abdul Salaam (Ed Michael) op.cit.
40 *Music Dial,* December 1944/January 1945

2 – *West Coast Ghost pages 24-44*

1 Notes to Savoy SJL 2215
2 Charles Mingus Enterprises JWS 001/2
3 Atlantic SD 3-600 (also in edited form on Joni Mitchell, *Mingus*, Elektra SE 505)
4 Apollo 396
5 Interview with Mike Dean, BBC-TV, August 1972
6 Notes to Impulse AS 35
7 Interview and correspondence with Ray Horricks, *Jazz Monthly,* July 1959
8 Ibid.
9 Interview with Arnold Jay Smith, *Down Beat,* 12 January 1978
10 Quoted by Nat Hentoff, notes to Bethlehem BCP 6026 (also in Ray Horricks *et al., These Jazzmen of Our Time*, Gollancz, 1960; and Nat Hentoff, *The Jazz Life,* Peter Davies, 1962)
11 Interview with Stanley Dance, *Jazz,* November/December 1963
12 Interview with Russell Davies (September 1980) for BBC Radio (unpublished)
13 Quoted by Nat Hentoff, ops. cit.
14 Interview with Mike Dean, op.cit.
15 *Mingus*, directed by Tom Reichman, 1968

16 Interview with W. Dressen, *Jazz Podium*, June 1964 (re-translated from the German by Anne-Marie Priestley)
17 Interview with Russell Davies, op.cit.
18 Interview with John Litweiler, *Down Beat*, 27 February 1975
19 Interview with Vernon Gibbs and Sharif Abdul Salaam (Ed Michael), WKCR-FM, December 1971
20 Ibid.
21 Interview with John Litweiler, op.cit.
22 Interview with Mike Dean, op.cit.
23 Interview with Gerard Rouy, *Jazz Magazine*, January 1978 (re-translated from the French by Brian Priestley)
24 Letter to Ralph J. Gleason, *Down Beat*, 1 June 1951
25 Quoted by Ralph J. Gleason, *Down Beat*, 14 January 1949
26 Jimmy Lyons, *Dizzy, Duke, The Count and Me,* California Living Books, 1978, p.40
27 *Down Beat*, 1 June 1951
28 *Down Beat*, 25 March 1949
29 Notes to Impulse AS 60
30 Quoted by Whitney Balliett, *New Yorker*, 18 June 1979 (also in Whitney Balliett, *Night Creature*, Oxford University Press, 1981)
31 Quoted by Patricia Willard, notes to Savoy SJL 2215
32 *Down Beat*, 3 October 1956 (also in slightly different form on United Artists UAS 14024 and Impulse AS 99), copyright Jazz Workshop Inc. Used by permission
33 Quoted by John S. Wilson, *New York Times*, 12 June 1981
34 Quoted by Nat Hentoff, *The Jazz Life*, Peter Davies, 1962, p.60
35 Quoted by John S. Wilson, op.cit.
36 *Down Beat*, 9 March 1951
37 *Down Beat*, 19 October 1951
38 Quoted by A.B. Spellman, *Black Music: Four Lives*, Pantheon Books, 1966, p.214

3 – Bird Calls pages 45-70

1 WNYC-FM, 26 May 1979
2 Interview with Russell Davies (September 1980) for BBC Radio (unpublished)
3 Interview with Vernon Gibbs and Sharif Abdul Salaam (Ed Michael), WKCR-FM, December 1971
4 *Down Beat*, 18 June 1952
5 Interview with Mike Dean, BBC-TV, August 1972
6 Notes to Columbia KC 31039
7 Quoted by Mingus, notes to Charles Mingus Enterprises JWS 009
8 Interview with Nat Hentoff, *Down Beat,* 8 April 1953
9 Quoted by Nat Hentoff, *Village Voice*, 5 & 12 March 1979
10 Quoted by Robert Reisner, *The Jazz Titans,* Doubleday, 1960, p.56

11 Quoted by Alun Morgan, *Jazz and Blues*, April 1973
12 Interview with Brian Case, *Melody Maker*, 14 March 1981
13 Quoted by Nat Hentoff, *Down Beat*, 6 May 1953
14 Notes to Debut DEB 124
15 Interview with Al Fraser, *Dizzy: To Be or Not to Bop*, Doubleday, 1979, p.374
16 *Coda*, March 1968
17 Interview with Vernon Gibbs and Sharif Abdul Salaam (Ed Michael), op.cit.
18 Interview with Mike Hennessey, *Down Beat*, 13 May 1971
19 Interview with Russell Davies, op.cit.
20 Interview with Phil Schaap, WKCR-FM, 24 February & 13 March 1981
21 Interview with Zan Stewart, *Down Beat*, June 1981
22 Quoted by Nat Hentoff, notes to Bethlehem BCP 6026 (also in Ray Horricks *et al., These Jazzmen of Our Time*, Gollancz, 1960; and Nat Hentoff, *The Jazz Life*, Peter Davies, 1962)
23 Interview with John Goodman (1971), *Playboy*, November 1979
24 Notes to Columbia KC 31039
25 Interview with Mitch Seidel, *Down Beat*, January 1982
26 *Metronome*, March 1954
27 *Metronome*, July 1954
28 Letter to Bill Coss, notes to DEB 127
29 Quoted by Rafi Zabor, *Musician Player and Listener*, 15 December 1977
30 Interview with Arnold Jay Smith, *Down Beat*, 12 January 1978
31 Notes to Savoy MG 14021
32 Interview with Bob Blumenthal, *Down Beat*, April 1981
33 *Down Beat*, 12 January 1955
34 Quoted by Nat Hentoff,*Village Voice*, 5 & 12 March 1979
35 Ibid.
36 Notes to Charles Mingus Enterprises JWS 009, copyright Jazz Workshop Inc. Used by permission
37 Interview with Vernon Gibbs and Sharif Abdul Salaam (Ed Michael), op.cit.
38 Lecture-demonstration, Kingston Polytechnic, 1972
39 Anon. (possibly Eddie Bert), quoted by Burt Goldblatt, *Newport Jazz Festival*, Dial Press, 1977, p.23
40 Notes to Debut DEB 120
41 Ibid.
42 Interview with Charles Fox, BBC Radio, 3 February 1982
43 Interview with Nat Hentoff, *Down Beat*, 2 November 1955
44 *Down Beat*, 30 November 1955
45 Notes to Debut DEB 123
46 *Down Beat*, 11 January 1956
47 Ibid.
48 *Jazz News*, 19 & 26 July 1961

49   Quoted by Nat Hentoff, *Down Beat,* 11 January 1956
50   Interview with Ira Gitler, *Down Beat,* 21 July 1960
51   Notes to Atlantic 1237
52   Interview with Max Horrowitz, *Metronome,* July 1957
53   Interview with Stanley Dance, *Jazz,* November/December 1963
54   Quoted by A.B. Spellman, *Black Music: Four Lives,* Pantheon Books, 1966, p.216
55   Interview with Jasper Hampton (unpublished)

4 – *Fifty-First Street Blues pages 71-96*

1   Martin Williams, *The Jazz Tradition,* Oxford University Press, 1970, p.21
2   Quoted by J.C. Thomas, *Chasin' the Trane,* Elm Tree Books, 1976, p.62
3   Notes to Bethlehem BCP 6019
4   Quoted by Nat Hentoff, *Down Beat,* 8 August 1956
5   Quoted by Jack Maher, *Metronome,* September 1956
6   Interview with Ira Gitler, *Down Beat,* 21 July 1960
7   *Down Beat,* 3 October 1956
8   Notes to Impulse AS 35
9   Notes to RCA-Victor LSP 2533
10   Quoted by Sy Johnson, notes to Columbia JG 35717
11   Quoted by Nat Hentoff, notes to Atlantic 1260
12   Interview with Arnold Jay Smith, *Down Beat,* 12 January 1978
13   Atlantic 1260, copyright Jazz Workshop Inc. Used by permission
14   Interview with Russell Davies (September 1980), BBC Radio, 2 August 1981
15   Notes to Atlantic SD 1416
16   Interview with Stanley Dance, *Jazz*, November/December 1963
17   Interview with John Litweiler, *Down Beat*, 27 February 1975
18   *Jazz Monthly*, June 1967 (also in Max Harrison, *A Jazz Retrospect*, David & Charles, 1976)
19   *Metronome*, August 1957
20   *New Yorker,* 3 August 1957 (also in Whitney Balliett, *The Sound of Surprise,* Dutton, 1959)
21   Quoted by Nat Hentoff, op.cit.
22   Interview with Russell Davies, op.cit.
23   Interview with Brian Case, *Melody Maker,* 22 March 1980
24   Interview with Arnold Jay Smith, op.cit.
25   Notes to Atlantic SD 1305
26   Notes to ABC-Paramount ABC 149
27   Notes to Verve VSPS 36
28   Interview with Don DeMichael, *Down Beat,* 30 January 1964
29   Interview with Paul-Henri Boinaud, *Jazz Magazine,* May 1960 (translated from the French by Brian Priestley)

30   Interview with Arnold Jay Smith, op.cit.
31   Ibid.
32   Dorothy Kilgallen, *Dorothy Kilgallen Column*, 7 March 1958
33   Quoted by Whitney Balliett, *New Yorker*, 18 June 1979 (also in
      Whitney Balliett, *Night Creature*, Oxford University Press, 1981)
34   Quoted by Nat Hentoff, *The Jazz Life*, Peter Davies, 1962, p.60
35   Interview with Nat Hentoff, *Down Beat*, 6 May 1953
36   Quoted by Nat Hentoff, *Village Voice*, 5 & 12 March 1979
37   Interview with Nat Hentoff, BBC Radio, 2 November 1964
38   *Jazz News*, 19 & 26 July 1961
39   *Mingus*, directed by Thomas Reichman, 1968
40   Interview with Vernon Gibbs and Sharif Abdul Salaam (Ed Michael),
      WKCR-FM, December 1971
41   Interview with Stanley Dance, op.cit.
42   *New Yorker*, 16 August 1958 (also in Whitney Balliett, *The Sound of
      Surprise*, Dutton 1959)
43   Notes to Candid CJS 9021
44   Notes to Columbia JG 35717

5 – *All The Things You Could Be By Now pages 97-121*

  1   Notes to Impulse AS 35
  2   Interview with Bret Primack, *Down Beat*, 7 December 1978
  3   Quoted by Diane Dorr-Dorynek in Dom Cerulli *et al.*, *The Jazz Word*,
       Ballantine, 1960 pp.15–18
  4   *New Yorker*, 24 January 1959 (also in Whitney Balliett, *The Sound of
       Surprise*, Dutton, 1959)
  5   Quoted by Nat Hentoff, notes to Bethlehem BCP 6026
  6   Interview with Brian Case, *Melody Maker*, 25 October 1980
  7   Notes to Atlantic SD 1305
  8   Interview with Pierre Lattès, *Jazz Hot*, March 1965 (re-translated from
       the French by Brian Priestley)
  9   Interview with Ira Gitler, *Down Beat*, 21 July 1960
 10   Ibid.
 11   Charles Mingus, *Beneath the Underdog*, Alfred A. Knopf, 1971, p.3
 12   Interview with Russell Davies (September 1980), BBC Radio, 2
       August 1981
 13   Anon. (possibly John Hammond), quoted by Gene Lees, *Down Beat*,
       18 August 1960
 14   Quoted by Nat Hentoff, notes to Atlantic SD 1678
 15   Notes to Columbia CS 8171
 16   Notes to Columbia CS 8236
 17   Ibid.
 18   *Jazz Monthly*, November 1966
 19   Interview with Russell Davies, op.cit.
 20   *Down Beat*, 25 May 1961

21 Interview with Lee Jeske, *Down Beat,* August 1981
22 Interview with Pierre Lattès, *Jazz Hot*, July/August 1966 (re-translated from the French by Brian Priestley)
23 Quoted in *Jazz News,* 2 January 1963
24 Interview with Leonard Feather, *Down Beat,* 26 May 1960
25 Interview with Pierre Lattès, op.cit.
26 Interview with Paul-Henri Boinaud, *Jazz Magazine*, May 1960 (translated from the French by Brian Priestley)
27 Quoted by Whitney Balliett, *Dinosaurs in the Morning,* Lippincott, 1962, p.71 (part only in *New Yorker*, 20 February 1960)
28 Interview with LeRoi Jones, *Down Beat,* 30 August 1962
29 Interview with Russell Davies (September 1980), for BBC Radio (unpublished)
30 *Down Beat,* 31 March 1960
31 Interview with Russell Davies (September 1980), BBC Radio, 2 August 1981
32 Interview with Gary Giddins and Robert Rusch, *Cadence,* July 1976
33 *Jazz Magazine,* September 1960 (translated from the French by Brian Priestley)
34 *Jazz Hot*, September 1960 (translated from the French by Brian Priestley)
35 *Jazz News*, 19 & 26 July 1961
36 *Jazz*, November/December 1963
37 Quoted by Martin Williams, *Jazz Review,* June 1960.
38 Interview with John Goodman (1971), *Playboy*, November 1979
39 *Down Beat*, 18 August 1960
40 Quoted by Burt Goldblatt, *Newport Jazz Festival,* Dial Press, 1977, p.72
41 Ibid., p.80
42 Interview with Stanley Dance, *Jazz,* November/December 1963
43 Quoted by Gene Lees, *Down Beat,* 18 August 1960
44 Ibid.
45 Quoted by Nat Hentoff, *Village Voice,* 5 & 12 March 1979
46 Quoted by Burt Goldblatt, op.cit.
47 *New Yorker,* 16 July 1960 (also in Whitney Balliett, *Dinosaurs in the Morning,* Lippincott, 1962)
48 Quoted by Nat Hentoff, notes to Candid CJS 9022 (also in Nat Hentoff, *The Jazz Life,* Peter Davies, 1962)
49 Quoted by François Postif, *Jazz Hot,* December 1960 (also in part on Candid CJS 9005)
50 Interview with Russell Davies (September 1980) for BBC Radio (unpublished)
51 Candid CJS 9005, copyright Jazz Workshop Inc. Used by permission
52 *Down Beat*, 2 February 1962

6 – *Money Jungle pages 122-141*

1   Quoted by Dan Morgenstern, *Metronome,* June 1961
2   *Jazz News,* 19 & 26 July 1961
3   Quoted in *Jazz News,* 2 January 1963
4   *Jazz News*, 19 & 26 July 1961
5   Interview with Robert Levin, *Down Beat,* 12 April 1962
6   Interview with Don DeMichael, *Down Beat,* 23 May 1963
7   Notes to Impulse AS 35
8   *Down Beat*, 16 August 1962
9   *Down Beat,* 1 March 1962
10   Quoted in *Down Beat*, 21 December 1961
11   Notes to RCA-Victor LSP 2533
12   Interview with Jasper Hampton (unpublished)
13   Quoted by Mike Zwerin, *International Herald Tribune,* 5 February 1980
14   Interview with Steve Allen, BBC Radio, 9 October 1966
15   *Jazz Journal*, October 1962
16   *Down Beat*, 25 October 1962
17   Quoted by Dan Morgenstern, *Jazz,* November 1962
18   Interview with Stanley Dance, *Jazz,* November/December 1963
19   Interview with John Litweiler, *Down Beat,* 27 February 1975
20   *Jazz Monthly,* February 1969 (also in Max Harrison, *A Jazz Retrospect,* David & Charles, 1976)
21   Duke Ellington, *Music Is My Mistress,* Doubleday, 1973, p.243
22   Quoted by Stanley Dance, *The World of Duke Ellington,* Scribner's, 1970, p.267
23   Interview with Paul Bullock and David Hoxie, *Jazz Heritage Foundation,* Vol. III No.1. January 1982
24   *Down Beat*, 6 December 1962
25   *Down Beat,* 17 January 1963
26   *Jazz,* January 1963
27   Quoted by John S. Wilson, *New York Times,* 13 October 1962
28   *Down Beat*, 17 January 1963
29   *Jazz,* November/December 1963
30   *Down Beat,* 14 March 1963
31   Quoted by Alan Levin, *New York Post,* 17 March 1963

7 – *Black Saint pages 142-171*

1   Notes to Impulse AS 35
2   Notes to Prestige P 24092
3   *Jazz Hot*, January 1963 (translated from the French by Brian Priestley)
4   Quoted by Edmund Pollock, notes to Impulse AS35
5   *Jazz,* October 1964
6   Notes to Impulse AS 35

7   *Jazz Monthly,* November 1965
8   Interview with W. Dressen, *Jazz Podium,* June 1964 (re-translated from the German by Anne-Marie Priestley)
9   *Jazz Monthly,* November 1965
10 Interview with Steve Allen, BBC Radio, 9 October 1966
11 Interview with Vernon Gibbs and Sharif Abdul Salaam (Ed Michael), WKCR-FM, December 1971
12 *Jazz,* October 1964
13 Interview with Stanley Dance, *Jazz,* November/December 1963
14 Interview with Lee Jeske, *Down Beat,* August 1981
15 Quoted by Nat Hentoff, notes to Bethlehem BCP 6026
16 Interview with Stanley Dance, op.cit.
17 Interview with Bill Whitworth, *New York Herald Tribune,* 1 November 1964
18 Interview with Stanley Dance, op.cit.
19 Quoted by Jaki Byard, notes to Prestige P 24092
20 Impulse AS 60
21 Notes to Columbia KC 31039
22 Charles Mingus, *Beneath the Underdog,* Alfred A. Knopf, 1971, p.329
23 *Jazz Monthly,* November 1965
24 *Jazz,* October 1964
25 *Jazz,* April 1965
26 Interview with Bill Whitworth, op.cit.
27 Enclosure with Fantasy JWS 001/2
28 Interview with Stanley Dance, op.cit.
29 *Jazz,* October 1964
30 *New York Herald Tribune,* 1 November 1964
31 Interview with Vernon Gibbs and Sharif Abdul Salaam (Ed Michael), op.cit.
32 Notes to Columbia KC 31039
33 Charles Mingus Enterprises JWS 005
34 Interview with Russell Davies (September 1980) for BBC Radio (unpublished)
35 Ibid.
36 Notes to Prestige P 24092
37 Interview with Mike Hennessey, *Down Beat,* 13 May 1971
38 *Mingus,* directed by Tom Reichman, 1968
39 Interview with W. Dressen, op.cit.
40 *Jazz Podium,* February 1979
41 Interview with John Litweiler, *Down Beat,* 27 February 1975
42 *Musician Player and Listener,* 15 December 1977
43 Interview with Russell Davies (September 1980), BBC Radio, 2 August 1981
44 *Jazz Podium,* February 1979
45 *Jazz Monthly,* February 1965

46   Interview with Bill Whitworth, op.cit.
47   Interview with Ray Coleman, *Melody Maker,* 20 June 1964
48   *Jazz Monthly,* April 1965
49   Interview with Russell Davies, op.cit. (unpublished)
50   Interview with Ray Coleman, op.cit.
51   Interview with Russell Davies, op.cit. (unpublished)
52   *Jazz Monthly,* April 1965
53   Interview with Nat Hentoff, BBC Radio, 2 November 1964
54   Interview with Mike Dean, BBC-TV, August 1972
55   Interview with Bill Whitworth, op.cit.
56   Notes to Charles Mingus Enterprises JWS 001/2
57   Notes to Prestige P24092
58   Quoted in Humphrey Proctor-Gregg (ed.), *Beecham Remembered,* Duckworth, 1976, p.46
59   Notes to Charles Mingus Enterprises JWS 001/2
60   *Coda,* April–May 1965
61   Interview with Russell Davis (September 1980), BBC Radio, 2 August 1981
62   Interview with Dan Morgenstern, *Down Beat,* 21 October 1965
63   Charles Mingus Enterprises JWS 0013/4
64   Quoted by Jimmy Lyons, *Dizzy, Duke, The Count and Me,* California Living Books, 1978, p.40
65   Charles Mingus Enterprises JWS 0013/4, copyright Jazz Workshop Inc. Used by permission
66   *Down Beat,* 20 October 1966
67   *Down Beat,* 19 May 1966
68   Notes to Charles Mingus Enterprises JWS 005
69   Interview with Russell Davies (September 1980) BBC Radio, 2 August 1981
70   *Down Beat,* 3 October 1968
71   *Down Beat,* 12 January 1967

8 – *Put Me In That Dungeon pages 172-193*

1   Interview with Russell Davies (September 1980) for BBC Radio (unpublished)
2   *Mingus,* directed by Tom Reichman, 1968
3   Enclosure with Fantasy JWS 001/2
4   *Mingus,* op.cit.
5   Interview with Nat Hentoff, *New York Times,* 30 January 1972 (also in Nat Hentoff, *Jazz Is,* Random House, 1976)
6   *Down Beat,* 23 February 1967
7   Interview with Mike Hennessey, *Down Beat,* 13 May 1971
8   *Jazz Hot,* June 1967
9   *Down Beat,* 5 October 1967
10   Interview with Nat Hentoff, BBC Radio, 2 November 1964

11   *Coda*, April–May 1965

12   Interview with Nat Hentoff, *New York Times*, ops.cit.

13   Ibid.

14   Quoted in letter from Discurio Ltd to Roger Rowland, 21 June 1968

15   Enclosure with Fantasy JWS 001/2

16   *Down Beat*, 21 August 1969

17   Nat Hentoff, *New York Times*, ops.cit.

18   *Down Beat*, 27 November 1969

19   Quoted by Richard Williams, *Melody Maker*, 12 August 1972

20   Quoted by Nat Hentoff, *Village Voice*, 5 & 12 March 1979

21   *Coda*, op.cit.

22   Interview with John Litweiler, *Down Beat*, 27 February 1975

23   Letters to Roger Rowland, 12 July '1967' [1970], 8 September 1970 and undated

24   Interview with Dan Morgenstern, *Down Beat*, 30 March & 11 May 1972

25   Interview with Nat Hentoff, *New York Times*, op.cit.

26   Interview with Dan Morgenstern, op.cit.

27   Interview with Russell Davies, op.cit.

28   Interview with Valerie Wilmer, *Melody Maker*, 21 November 1970

29   Interview with Mike Hennessey, op.cit.

30   Interview with Valerie Wilmer, op.cit.

31   Quoted by Sy Johnson, notes to Columbia JG 35717

32   *New York Times*, 1971

33   Interview with Vernon Gibbs and Sharif Abdul Salaam (Ed Michael), WKCR-FM, December 1971

34   Notes to Columbia KC 31039

35   Ibid.

36   Interview with Vernon Gibbs and Sharif Abdul Salaam (Ed Michael), op.cit.

37   Interview with Russell Davies, op.cit.

38   Ibid.

39   Interview with Richard Williams, op.cit.

40   Interview with Mike Dean, BBC-TV, August 1972

41   Ibid.

42   *Jazz Nu* '1-2-1978' [1979] (translated from the Dutch by Joan Cruikshank)

9 – *Myself When I Am Real pages 194-215*

1   *Down Beat*, 10 May 1973

2   *Jazz and Blues*, July 1973

3   Interview with Lee Jeske, *Down Beat*, November 1979

4   Atlantic SD 3-600

5   Interview with Nat Hentoff, *New York Times*, 30 January 1972 (also in Nat Hentoff *Jazz Is*, Random House, 1976)

6   Interview with Vernon Gibbs and Sharif Abdul Salaam (Ed Michael),
     WKCR-FM, December 1971
7   Interview with Mike Hennessey, *Down Beat*, 13 May 1971
8   Interview with W. Dressen, *Jazz Podium*, June 1964 (re-translated
     from the German by Anne-Marie Priestley)
9   Interview with Bret Primack, *Down Beat*, 7 December 1978
10   Interview with Giacomo Pelliciotti, *Jazz Magazine*, May/June 1975
     (re-translated from the French by Brian Priestley)
11   *Coda*, July 1974
12   Interview with John Litweiler, *Down Beat*, 27 February 1975
13   Interview with Laurent Goddet, *Jazz Hot*, October 1976 (re-translated
     from the French by Brian Priestley)
14   Interview with Chip Stern,*Down Beat*, 7 September 1978
15   Interview with Neil Tesser, *Melody Maker*, 25 January 1975
16   *Down Beat*, 27 March 1975
17   Atlantic SD 1678, copyright Jazz Workshop Inc. Used by permission
18   Atlantic SD 3-600
19   Interview, Danmarks Radio, August 1976
20   Interview with Russell Davies (September 1980) for BBC Radio
     (unpublished)
21   Interview with Phil Schaap, WKCR-FM, 19 February 1980
22   Interview with John Litweiler, op.cit.
23   *Jazz Magazine*, December 1975 (translated from the French by Brian
     Priestley)
24   *HiFi*, January 1976 (translated from the German by Anne-Marie
     Priestley)
25   Quoted by Mike Zwerin, *International Herald Tribune*, 5 February
     1980
26   Interview with Maurice Cullaz, *Jazz Hot*, October 1976 (re-translated
     from the French by Brian Priestley)
27   Burt Goldblatt, *Newport Jazz Festival*, Dial Press, 1977, p.253
28   Quoted by Arnold Jay Smith, *Down Beat*, 27 January 1977
29   *Down Beat*, 21 April 1977
30   Interview with Bret Primack, *Down Beat*, 2 November 1978
31   Gary Giddins, *Riding on a Blue Note*, Oxford University Press, 1981
32   Interview with John Litweiler, op.cit.
33   *Down Beat*, 6 October 1977
34   Interview with Russell Davies, op.cit.
35   Quoted by Lee Jeske, notes to Soul Note SN 1004
36   Interview with Arnold Jay Smith, *Down Beat*, 23 March 1978
37   Interview with Arnold Jay Smith, *Down Beat*, 12 January 1978
38   *Musician Player and Listener*, 15 December 1977

10 – *Epitaph pages 216-226*

1 Interview with Russell Davies (September 1980) for BBC Radio (unpublished)
2 Interview with Neil Tesser, *Melody Maker*, 25 January 1975
3 *Down Beat*, 21 June 1979
4 Interview with Herb Nolan, *Down Beat*, 11 October 1973
5 Interview with Michael Cuscuna, WYNC-FM, 26 May 1979
6 Interview with Leonard Feather, *Down Beat*, 6 September 1979
7 Ibid.
8 Quoted in *Down Beat*, 7 September 1978
9 Quoted by Mike Zwerin, *International Herald Tribune*, 5 February 1980
10 Interview with Maurice Cullaz, *Jazz Hot*, October 1976 (re-translated from the French by Brian Priestley)
11 Quoted in *Down Beat*, 5 October 1978
12 Letter to Roger Rowland, 15 October 1978
13 Quoted by John S. Wilson, *New York Times*, 1 June 1979
14 Quoted by Nat Hentoff, *Village Voice*, 5 & 12 March 1979
15 Notes to Gatemouth 1002
16 Quoted by Nat Hentoff, op.cit.

Index

influence on others, 26, 54, 214, 220;
subdivision of beat, 25, 63; time playing
(4/4), 25, 54, 211, 213; tone, 10–11, 63; use
of bow (arco), 35, 43, 58, 102, 149, 167,
209, 212; use of right hand, 54, 63–4
Beatles, The (group), 135, 147, 160
Bebop, xi, 28, 30, 36, 40, 51, 53, 77, 84–5, 100,
107, 123, 203, 211, 218; seen as rigid
system, 47, 55–6, 70, 201
Bechet, Sidney (ss, cl), 36, 52
Beckett, Harry (tp), 127–8, 190
Bedspread (Collette), 30
Beecham, Sir Thomas (cond), 163
Beethoven, Ludwig van (comp), 9, 198, 217
Belgrave, Marcus (tp), 196
Bellevue Hospital, New York, 95–7, 115, 118,
120, 173
Bemoanable Lady (Mingus), 35
Beneath the Underdog (Mingus), xi, 2, 5, 8–9,
21–2, 28–9, 31, 40–1, 46, 72, 76, 88, 98,
102, 106, 123, 125, 131, 135, 148, 150, 152,
162, 168, 180–1, 185
Benedetti, Dean (as), 28
Benjamin, Joe (b), 195
Benton, Walter (ts), 116
Bernstein, Artie (b), 33
Berry, Chuck (vcl, g), 92
Bert, Eddie (tb), 56, 66–8
Bethlehem Records, 86, 89, 94
Better Git It in Your Soul (Mingus), 87, 102,
105, 113, 116, 151, 210
Big Alice and John Henry (Pullen), 201
Bigard, Barney (cl, ts), 18–19, 99
Bird at St. Nick's (album), 81
Bird Calls (Mingus), 102
Birdland, Miami Beach, 55
Birdland, New York, 44–5, 49, 55, 60, 76–7,
81, 104, 130, 134, 142–3, 148, 164–5
Bird on 52nd Street (album), 81
Bishop, Walter (p), 169–70
Black, Brown and Beige (Ellington), 140, 146,
204
Black Muslims, 148, 162
Blacks, attitudes to, 2–3, 9, 19–20, 34, 44, 47,
74, 86–7, 89, 92, 115, 119, 126–7, 132, 141,
148, 153, 157, 169, 171, 184, 193, 195; *see
also* 'Nigger'
Black Saint and the Sinner Lady, The
(Mingus), 14, 144–8, 150–1, 155, 166, 187–
8
Blackwell, Ed (d), 116
Blakey, Art (d), 54, 60, 74, 100, 123, 208
Blanton, Jimmy (b), 16, 21, 25, 42, 51, 54
Bley, Paul (p), 55, 108
Blue Cee (Mingus), 78–9, 84, 211
Blues (chord-sequences), *see* Compositional
style
Blues (style), 16, 26, 28, 48, 63, 77, 100–1, 113,
117, 131, 161, 188–9, 191, 196
Blues and Roots (album), 40, 100–2, 112, 122
Blues for the Jungle (film), 170
Bluiett, Hamiet (bars), 194–6, 201–3
Bo Diddley (vcl, g), 201
Body and Soul (Green), 24–5, 35, 39, 43, 58,
67, 167
Boogie Stop Shuffle (Mingus), 103
Booker, Benny (b), 24

Boppin' n' Boston (Mingus), 41
Box Seats at Newport (Mingus), 106
Bradley, Oscar (d), 29
Brant Inn Boogie (Hampton), 37
Braxton, Anthony (saxes, comp), 214
Broekman, David (cond), 82
Brooks, Dudley (p, arr), 21
Brooks, Roy (d), 190–1, 194–6, 200
Broonzy, Big Bill (vcl, g), 2, 131
Brown, Cameron (b), 225
Brown, Charles (vcl, p), 42
Brown, Clifford (tp), 57, 68
Brown, Garnett (tb), 151
Brown, Gatemouth (vcl, g, vln), 204
Brown, Lawrence (tb), 7, 11, 27
Brown, Ray (b), 35, 43, 54, 149, 195
Brubeck, Dave (p), 40, 46, 106, 119, 126–7,
133
Buckner, Teddy (tp), 6
Bunink, Nico (p), 107–8, 116, 178
Butterfield, Don (tu), 56, 136, 142–3
Byard, Jaki (p, arr), 80, 110, 140, 143–5, 149,
151, 155–9, 161, 163, 165–6, 182–6, 199,
203, 208

Café Bohemia, New York, 64–6, 68–9, 71–4,
81–3, 86, 91
Callender, Red (b, tu), 10–11, 16–17, 20, 24–5,
34, 38, 41–2, 163, 181
Callender, Reverend Eugene, 149
Calloway, Cab (vcl), 34
Candid Records, 116–17, 119–20, 130, 147,
181–2
Canon (Mingus), 200
Carney, Harry (bars), 75, 145, 203
Caro, Herb (ts, bars), 38
Carolyn (Mingus), 151
Carolyn 'Keiki' Mingus (Mingus), 214, 218
Carr, Lady Will (p), 27
Carter, President Jimmy, 221
Carter, Ron (b), 68
Caruso, Enrico (vcl), 52
Catherine, Philip (g), 210, 215
Catlett, Sid (d), 18–19
Celia (Mingus), 86, 145, 201, 205
Cello, Mingus's use of, 7–8, 10, 14, 31, 39, 105,
186
Chair in the Sky, A (Mingus), 220, 226
Chambers, Joe (d), 189
Chambers, Paul (b), 54–5
Changes (album), 203, 206
Charles, Ray (vcl, p), 88, 131, 203
Charles, Teddy (vib, comp), 56–7, 61, 64–5,
81, 106, 111, 116, 151, 181
Chazz! (album), 66
Chazz-Mar Inc., 47
Chazzanova (Mingus), 55, 72, 85
Chelsea Bridge (Strayhorn), 27, 60, 68
Cherokee (Noble), 74, 201
Cherry, Don (tp), 116, 118
Chill of Death, The (Mingus), 12, 14, 32, 35,
79, 82, 186
Christian, Charlie (g), 51
Cirillo, Wally (p, comp), 57–8, 60
C Jam Blues (Ellington), 201
Clarinet Lament (Ellington), 99
Clarke, Stanley (b), 214–15

301

302

303

305